"中国·宁波"政府门户网站系列成果

ningbo.gov.cn
中国·宁波

宁波地方文化读本

THE CULTURE OF NINGBO：A READER

主　编　屠国元

副主编　朱佳栋　南佐民

翻　译　邵益珍　陈文安

浙江大学出版社
ZHEJIANG UNIVERSITY PRESS

序

朱忠祥

　　宁波是中国东海之滨的港口城市。它既是古老的,七千年前的河姆渡文化书写了中华文明的灿烂篇章;又是年轻的,三十多年来的改革开放塑造了宁波活力四射的奋进形象。在这块古老而又年轻的土地上,出现过发达的农业、繁荣的商业、精致的手工业,积淀了厚实的地方文化,涌现出一批独具特色的名胜、名品,产生了一批对中国历史有影响的名人,真可谓物产丰富,人杰地灵。作为国家历史文化名城,即使放诸世界,我们也可以骄傲地说,宁波以其优越的地理位置、深厚的历史底蕴和蓬勃的发展活力,完全可以与世界上同类城市比肩而立、携手共进。

　　然而,令人遗憾的是,世人对宁波的了解还很不够,除了对宁波有一所古老的藏书楼——天一阁,有一个深水大港——北仑港,有一群举世闻名的商界精英——"宁波帮"有所知道外,对宁波的历史文化和地方风俗,普遍知之甚少,有的甚至根本不知。即使在宁波本地,也很难说得上有多少人对自己城市的文化家底有完整的了解。据报载,一项大学生暑期实践调查发现,七成市民不熟悉宁波历史。这无疑是一件十分遗憾的事情。有鉴于此,宁波市人民政府办公厅电子政务办公室在建设政府网站时,将宁波历史文化和地方风俗列为重要内容,开辟专栏加以介绍,并依托宁波大学外语学院,将相关内容翻译成英、日、德、法、韩等多国文字,向世界进行宣传,以期让世界了解宁波,让宁波走向世界。历经十年努力,集腋成裘,渐成规模,形成了一本内容丰富的《宁波地方文化读本》。这是很有意义的。

　　让世界了解宁波,让宁波走向世界,我们不但需要有广泛的经济合作,也需要有广泛的文化交流;不但需要举办各类经济贸易活动,也需要举办各类文化艺术活动;不但需要有政府层面的交流,也需要有民间的交往;不但需要有"2016东亚文化之都"这样的大型活动,也需要有润物细无声的日常生活浸润。《宁波地方文化读本》就是一个很好的载体。它虽非权威的学术著作,其体系的完整性、结构的合理性和内容的权威性也不无可以改进之处,但因其面向世界的定位,而有了特别的意义。对来到宁波创业的新宁波人来说,也是一把了解宁波的钥匙。对本地人来说,也不失为一本可资浏览的读物。尤其是对走出宁波、走向世界的年轻人来说,带上一本《宁波地方文化读本》,就像带上了家乡的山水、家乡的味道,有空时翻翻,既可一解乡愁,也可增进对家乡热爱,更可以据此向国外友人介绍宁波，一举而数得，则功莫大矣。

　　宁波自古就是一个开放的城市，"诚信、务实、开放、创新"的宁波精神来自于宁波历史悠久的农耕文明和商业文化，同时也吸收了唐宋以来对外交往带来的外来文化和近代发展起来的工业文明。宁波的名胜，既有自然风光之美，更有人文精神之美，体现了天人合一、物我共存的中华传统；宁波的名品，既蕴含了地方风土人情，更沉淀了精益求精、追求卓越的工匠精神；宁波的名人，或以思想见长，或以艺术取胜，或以经商致富，或以科教兴国，无不打上了宁波人爱国敬业、经世致用的地方文化烙印。这是一座文化的宝藏，这是一处精神的宝库，挖掘之，提炼之，消化之，吸收之，可以增强我们的文化自信，增添我们的创造动力和创新活力。

　　历史是一条奔流不息的长河。作为 21 世纪海上丝绸之路的节点城市，宁波迎来了新一轮发展。我们相信，乘着国际化的东风，宁波经济发展和社会进步将会有一个新的飞跃，一个充满生机活力的现代化国际港口城市将崛起在世界的东方。

　　是为序。

2016 年 7 月 14 日

目　　录

一、基本情况

历史沿革

宁波的历史,可以说始终与大海和城市连在一起。早在 7000 多年前,宁波人的祖先就以木桨和"干栏式"构筑,建立了背山面海、具有海洋特征的河姆渡部落。宁波城市这块地域,在 2000 多年前称为"贸",这是因为沿海一带常有海外之人持货来贸易,以后便在贸易的"贸"字旁加"邑",取名为"鄮"。1000 多年来,历经唐、宋、元、明、清各个朝代,宁波都是对海外各国开展贸易的重要城市,与世界上许多国家及其人民建立了深厚的友谊。进一步对外开放以来,宁波作为迈向现代化的港城,已与世界上 100 多个国家和地区开展了经济贸易和友好交往。宁波发展的历史与世界紧密相关。

(一)历史建制

7000 年文明史

宁波的历史,可以上溯到 7000 多年之前。

出城区西行约 20 公里处,便是余姚河姆渡村。该村位于姚江之滨,背靠四明山,面朝宁绍平原,风景秀丽。1973 年发现的我国最古老的新石器时代遗址之一的"河姆渡文化遗址"就坐落在这里。

"河姆渡文化遗址"现存面积 40000 平方米。通过几次发掘,出土了石器、骨器、木器、陶器等 7000 余件文物以及大量稻谷和果实。据考证,这个遗址距今已有 7000 多年历史。大量的遗址和文物证明,宁波是世界上水稻种植的最早发源地之一,像长江流域与黄河流域一样,都是中华民族灿烂文化的摇篮;它们还证明 7000 多年前,宁波人已在这块土地上繁衍生息,艰苦创业,用勤劳的双手书写灿烂的历史。

宁波的历史,至少可以上溯到公元前 2000 多年的夏代。据志书记载:"夏时有堇子国,以赤堇山为名,后加邑为鄞。"宁波古时候"鄞"的名称就是这样来的。春秋时,宁波这块地方为越国领地;春秋后期,越国被楚国所灭,成了楚国的辖地。

公元前 222 年,秦始皇平定楚国后,设置会稽郡,宁波现在这块区域,原属于会稽郡下的鄞、鄮、句章三个县。这三个县的治所，虽都不在今日的宁波市城区，但都以市区余姚江、奉化江、甬江"三江"作为分界线。鄞州在三江南侧，包括现在的奉化市东南和鄞州的西南部分，它的县治设在现在的奉化白杜。鄮县在东边，地处今之宁波市江东区以及东乡地区，治所在今鄞州宝幢的鄮山同谷。句章位于三江西北，包括今之江北区、慈溪、余姚一带，县治在城山，即今江北区乍山城山渡附近。

自两汉到南北朝，宁波的建制没有大的变化。到了隋朝，三县合并，称句章县。唐高祖武德四年(621年)，置越州总督府，统辖越、嵊、姚、鄞等11个州，句章、鄞、鄮三县地属鄞州，设州治于今宁波市区之三江口。武德八年(625年)，废鄞州和句章县，恢复鄮县的名称，鄮县县治迁至小溪，就是现在的鄞州鄞江桥。唐太宗贞观元年(627年)，分全国为10道，鄮县属江南道。

宁波简称"甬"

宁波简称"甬"，早在周朝就开始了。因为宁波的主要水道是甬江；甬江则因发源于甬山而得名。甬山位于鄞州、奉化交界处，"甬"字是个象形字，是"大钟"的意思，甬山峰峦形似覆钟，故名。这样，山下的江就成为甬江，这一带就称作甬地了。

明州以山为名

宁波古时候有"明州"之称，是因为宁波这块地域有四明山而得名。唐玄宗开元二十六年(738年)，分县为慈溪、奉化、翁山(今定海县)、鄮县4个县，别立明州以统之。明州、鄮县的州治和县治仍在小溪，慈溪县治在今江北区慈城镇，奉化县治在今大桥镇西，翁山县治初在项河之滨筑城，后徙鳌山之麓为镇。

唐玄宗天宝元年(742年)，改明州为余姚郡。唐肃宗乾元元年(758年)，复改为明州。唐代宗广德二年(764年)，象山县划归明州，明州由4县扩为5县。唐宪宗元和年间，分鄮县东侧至甬江海口地区另设望海镇。唐穆宗长庆元年(821年)，明州治从小溪迁到三江口。五代时，称明州为明州望海军，明州望海军下辖有鄞县、慈溪、奉化、翁山、望海5县。宋太祖建隆元年(960年)，改明州望海军为明州奉国军，下辖鄞县、奉化、慈溪、定海、象山、昌国6县。南宋光宗绍熙五年(1194年)，升明州奉国军为庆元府，仍领上述6县。元世祖至元十三年(1276年)，改庆元府为庆元路。朱元璋吴元年，改庆元路为明州府。

宁波名称的由来

宁波名称的由来要追溯到明洪武十四年，也就是1381年的时候。鄞县有个读书人叫单仲友，家住在宁波万寿寺西边，很有才气，他应召到南京献诗，受到明太祖朱元璋的赏识。单仲友便乘机向明太祖奏道："本府明州府，明与国号相同，臣以为不妥。请万岁改之。"朱元璋觉得有道理,便说:"卿所奏有理,你们那里有个定海,海定则波宁,就改明州府为宁波府吧。"就这样,宁波的名称,600余年来一直沿用至今。

清朝时仍沿袭宁波府建制,康熙二十六年于舟山置定海县,原定海县改称镇海县。

民国时,宁波府改为鄞县。

1949年5月25日宁波解放,把鄞县城区划出,设立宁波市,为省辖市。同时设置浙江省第二行政公署,后改为宁波专区,统辖鄞县、余姚、慈溪、镇海、奉化、定海、象山7个县。1952年,台州专区的宁海县划归宁波专区。1962年定海县从宁波专区划出,设置舟山专区。1958年撤销镇海县、鄞县,并入宁波市;1961年、1963年,鄞县、镇海县先后恢复县建制,从宁波市划归宁波专区。1978年镇海县复划入宁波市。1983年7月,经国务院批准实行市管县体制,撤销宁波地区行政公署,将其所辖鄞县、余姚、慈溪、奉化、象山、宁海6个县划归宁波市管辖。1984年4月,国务院决定宁波市为我国进一步对外开放的14个沿海港口城市之一。宁波市海曙区与镇明区合并,称为海曙区;江东区、江北区适当扩大;后又撤销镇海县,改置北仑区、镇海区,成为市辖区。1985年7月,经国务院批准,余姚撤县设市;1988年10月,慈溪、奉化两县也相继撤县设市(都为县级市)。2002年,鄞县撤县设区(鄞州区),成为市辖区。

(二)城廓建造

宁波城廓的建造,可以上溯到东晋时期。晋安帝隆安四年(400年),晋将刘牢之为防孙恩起义军而筑。当时,沿三江口只造土墙一道,三面依江屯兵防守。这就是宁波城廓的雏形。据《乾道图经》载:"西城外有城基,上生竹,俗称篠墙"。"篠墙"被后人讹称为"筱墙",现在宁波西门外有筱墙弄,就是它的故址。

唐穆宗长庆元年(821年),明州刺史韩察把明州州治自小溪迁至三江口,建造了一座内城,称为"子城",周围420丈,作为刺史衙署。现在位于中山路的"鼓楼",就是子城的南城门。

唐末,黄晟任明州刺史后,见明州地处险要,但无城廓可据,民众散居,常受盗寇骚扰。于是就征集百姓,依据明州地形,挑土运石,造起一座城池,曰罗城。周围18里,巍峨壮观。黄晟的墓碑云:"此郡先无罗城,民苦野居。晟筑金汤壮其海峤,绝外寇窥觊之患,保一州生聚之安。"

宁波城池,直至1928年才拆除城基。

（三）通商口岸

宁波地处东海之滨，长江三角洲的东南角，背山面海，地势平坦，土地肥沃，是我国历史上最早的造船和航运事业发源地之一，也是我国历史上对外贸易的重要口岸。

宁波航运和港口，可以追溯到7000年前的河姆渡新石器时期。在河姆渡遗址中，出土有木桨6支和陶舟模型1只，鱼遗骨若干，证明宁波在7000年前已能制造船只。据《周书》记载："周成王时（公元前1024—1005年）于越献舟。"《竹书纪年》也说，战国时，即公元前312年，越王派人至魏国献舟。有关专家认为，当时所献之舟，系属贡物，又要经过漫长海程，才能到达周、魏的政治中心，因此，是构造较为完备的大海舟。

宁波古时候称"鄞"，是因为当地居民常与海外人民聚货于此进行贸易，且日益繁荣，故以"贸"加"邑"为"鄞"，称"鄞县"。正如《鄞县舆地志》所载："邑中以其海中货产，方山下贸易，因名鄞县。"秦始皇三十七年（公元前210年），据晋《陆士龙集》载："始皇南巡，登稽岳，刻文于石。身在鄞县三十余日。"秦始皇住在鄞县干什么呢？据地方志记载："秦始皇东行郡县，登会稽山，刻石纪功。徐市（即徐福）上书言，海中有方丈、蓬莱、瀛洲，仙人所居，请得斋戒，与童男女求之。于是遣市发童男女数千人入海求仙。"徐福出海的地方，就在今宁波慈溪达蓬山。由此可见当时宁波造船和航海事业的发达。汉朝、三国时，宁波已是重要的军港。正如《史记·东越列传》载："东越王余善反，遣将军杨仆将兵讨之。仆遣将军韩说出句章浮海，求夷洲及亶洲。"《三国志·孙权传》载："吴大帝黄龙二年（公元前230年）春，遣将军卫温、诸葛直将甲士万人，浮海求夷洲及亶洲。"

唐朝时，宁波的海外贸易已相当发达，"海外杂国，贾舶交至"。宁波所产的越窑青瓷以及丝织品等物产远销海外，与日本、高丽以及东南亚20多个国家和地区有着频繁的贸易交往，并与扬州、广州一起成为全国三大对外贸易港口。

到了宋代，宁波于淳化元年（990年）设立了专门处理对海外各国商贾事务和税收的机构"市舶司"，是当时全国3个市舶司之一（另两个是广州、杭州）。同时，宁波也是全国三大对外贸易口岸之一（另两处是泉州和广州），特别是南宋时期，宁波背靠京都临安（今杭州），对外贸易的地位就显得更加重要了。

元朝时，宁波仍是我国的一个主要海运和外贸口岸。当时，全国在宁波（当时称庆元）、泉州、上海、澉浦都设有市舶司。

到了明朝的中前期，宁波在对外贸易中仍居于重要地位，设有市舶提举司、提举库、海仓管、税课司、嘉宾馆等机构。到了后期，特别是明嘉靖二年（1523年），宁波发生了日使争贡事件，宁波惨遭洗劫，以后又屡遭倭寇骚扰，烧、杀、抢劫。于是朝廷下令停止市舶，撤销了宁波市舶司，出海通商遭到禁止。

清代初期,康熙二十四年(1685 年),宁波设立海关行署,开展对外贸易。到了清乾隆二十三年(1757 年),清政府采取闭关自守政策,实行"海禁"。清政府在鸦片战争失败后,即 1842 年 8 月 29 日,被迫签订了丧权辱国的《南京条约》,宁波被辟为"五口通商"口岸之一(另四个为广州、厦门、福州、上海),各国列强纷纷来宁波设立领事馆,派驻使者,控制海关,垄断对外贸易。这种状况一直延续到新中国成立。

二、名胜古迹

（一）国家级文保单位

河姆渡文化遗址

河姆渡文化遗址位于姚江之滨，背靠四明山，面临宁绍平原，东距宁波市区约25公里，西距余姚市区22公里，北距萧甬铁路约4公里，是国家级重点文物保护单位，距今已有7000多年的历史，是我国最古老的新石器时代遗址之一。该遗址现存面积40000平方米，出土石、骨、木、陶、玉器7000余件，陶片不下50万件，还有大批动植物遗存，大面积的木结构干栏式建筑遗迹和20座墓葬，都是极为罕见的珍贵历史文物。它们证明7000多年前，宁波人的祖先已在这山水环抱的平原安家落户、劳动生息，并创造了辉煌的原始文化。河姆渡遗址中发掘了大量稻谷遗物，刚出土时呈金黄颜色，外形完好，是一种人工栽培的籼稻，以及大批用动物肩胛骨制成的骨耜。它们证明宁波先民早在7000年前已种植水稻，并用骨耜翻耕土地，从而改变了"新石器时代有粳无籼"的论断，把我国种植水稻的时间推前了2000多年，还证明宁波是世界上种植水稻最早的发源地之一。

河姆渡遗址中发掘出大批骨刀、木刀和矛、棒、匕、箭头等工具及动物遗骨，反映了当时狩猎、捕捞和饲养业已经发展到了一定的程度。还发现用动物肢骨做成的骨哨，至今仍能奏出完整的七个音阶。

河姆渡遗址中还出土了陶制和石制的纺织工具，有骨匕、骨针、纺轮、木刀等，证明宁波先民的原始纺织工艺已达到相当水平，符合科学原理。

河姆渡遗址中还发掘了带榫卯的木结构建筑遗址，是一幢面宽23米、进深7米的干栏式长屋。屋架中的柱、梁、枋、檩等构件大都用榫卯相接，构件上还有雕刻装饰。证明7000年前的河姆渡已建造原始大屋。

此外，遗址中还出土了大量夹炭黑陶、涂有天然漆的木碗、木筒、工艺饰品、象牙雕刻、儿童玩具等。河姆渡遗址的发现，证明长江流域和黄河流域一样，都是中华民族灿烂文明的发祥地。

河姆渡遗址经过两次发掘，出土的数千件珍贵文物，除一部分藏于浙江省自然博物馆

外,其余展出于遗址旁新建的由江泽民同志题写馆名的"河姆渡遗址博物馆"中。

上林湖越窑遗址

上林湖越窑遗址位于慈溪市最高山峰栲栳山,四面环山,湖面狭长,湖四周木勺湾、茭白湾、横塘山、吴石岭、大庙岭、鳖裙山、黄鳝山、马溪滩、林湖村、荷花心、燕子窝、皮刀山、竹园山、狗颈山、后施吞、施家斗、周家吞、大埠头、吴家溪、黄婆吞等地古窑址密布,仅环湖一带就已发现从汉代至宋代的古窑址90余处,地表暴露的碎瓷片、残窑床等遗物的覆盖面积达9万多平方米。据考证,上林湖越窑青瓷始烧于东汉,鼎盛于五代,一直延续到宋代,历千年不衰,是我国最早烧制青瓷器的产地之一。品种多达千余种,大多是茶具、餐具等日用器皿和各种工艺、陈设用瓷,色泽鲜艳,釉彩莹润,造型和图案丰富多彩,飞禽走兽、花草山水,栩栩如生。

尤其是唐、五代时,产品更加丰富多彩,有玉璧底碗、圈足碗、荷花碗、莲口碗、荷叶纹盘、葵口盘、方盘、盘口壶、喇叭口壶、瓜棱壶、罐、粉盒、油盒、盏托、水注等,灰白细腻、质地坚实,釉面晶莹、玲珑剔透。至此,上林湖青瓷质量已居全国各大名窑之首。于是,朝廷便在上林湖设置"贡窑",专门烧制向朝廷进贡的"秘色瓷"。"秘色瓷"精美绝伦,具有很高的欣赏和收藏价值。

唐朝的调音律官还给青瓷注入不同量的水,以箸击之,可以奏出不同的曲调,把它当作乐器使用。后人形容这种青瓷"青如天,明如镜,薄如纸,声如磬","片瓦值千金",唐代诗人陆龟蒙在诗中有"九秋风露越窑开,夺得千峰翠色来"的赞美。由于青瓷精美,故自晚唐开始就一直成为明州(即今宁波)港对外贸易的重要商品,远销 10 多个国家和地区,并形成了从明州经温州、泉州、广州,再绕马来西亚半岛,越印度洋,直抵波斯湾以至地中海沿岸各国的古代"陶瓷之路",为促进中外文化交流和贸易往来作出过重大贡献。

上林湖越窑遗址处青山环抱之中,湖水终年不竭,风景秀丽,是国家级重点文物保护单位。

保国寺

在宁波城区西北 15 公里的灵山上,有一座我国江南现存最古老的木结构建筑——保国寺。保国寺背靠鄮峰,右有狮子岩,左有马鞍山,寺在周围诸山环抱之中,因有"寺藏山腹不知门"之说。明代御史颜琼曾题款:"东来第一山"。灵山又名骠骑山,相传东汉光武帝时,骠骑将军张意之子、中书郎张齐芳弃官后,隐居于此,后舍宅为寺,名"灵山寺",也名"骠骑将军庙"。因寺建于山麓,游人未到山门,是看不到梵宫的。唐代会昌年间,寺宇毁坏,至唐广明元年(880 年)重建,并由唐僖宗李儇题寺名"保国寺"。现存的保国寺大雄宝殿建于北宋真宗大中祥符六年(1013 年),由德贤和尚重建,距今 1000 多年,故有"祥符千载永留名"之说。

保国寺作为国家级重点文物保护单位,具有独特的建筑风格。从灵山脚下登数百石级,过叠锦台,循"之"字形石径拾级而上,即可见飞檐耸脊、庄重秀丽的天王殿。天王殿后有荷花池一方,名为"一碧涵空",荷花池后即为驰名遐迩的北宋古建筑大雄宝殿。大雄宝殿气势雄伟,全部结构皆用斗拱之间的巧妙衔接和精确的榫卯技术,不用一钉便将建筑物的各个构件牢固地结合在一起,承托了整个殿堂屋顶的重量。保国寺大殿天花板上分别列有3个图形美丽的镂空藻井。因梁架被天花板和藻井所挡,下面不易看到,故有"无梁殿"之说。殿堂进深大于面阔,呈纵长方形,这在同时代的佛殿建筑中是少见的。内柱用较小木头组列而成瓜轮形大柱,小材大用,敲之有声,美观实用。这座风格特殊的木结构建筑,还有"虫不蛀、鸟不栖、鼠不入"之奇。对此,有人认为可能是大殿的建筑材料为一种带刺激性香味的黄桧木,令鸟雀和昆虫远避。但也有人不赞同这个说法。究竟是何原因,至今仍是一谜。

保国寺周围胜景环列,寺南狮岩峰上建有"多姣亭",寺北象鼻峰上有"望海亭",登亭远眺,秀山碧野尽收眼底,有"见大海混茫无际,海中诸岛皆在指顾间"之妙。

天一阁

天一阁坐落在宁波城西月湖之畔,是我国现存最古老的藏书楼,为全国重点文物保护单位,素有"南国书城"盛誉。它建于明嘉靖四十年至四十五年(1561—1566年),至今已有450多年历史。创建人范钦,号东明,鄞县人,嘉靖十一年进士,官至兵部右侍郎,因不满严嵩父子,告老还乡。他把宦游一生搜集到的数万卷奇书带回故里,以读书自娱。临终,他立下遗训:"代不分书,书不出阁。"清初著名史学家全祖望曾作诗赞曰:"历年二百书无恙,天下储藏独此家。"

天一阁原有藏书7万余卷,分经、史、子、集编藏,多数系宋、明的木刻和手抄本,有的是稀有的珍本和孤本。但由于历代屡遭劫难,使藏书散失较多,宁波解放时仅存1.3万卷。在解放大军南下时,周总理曾亲自嘱咐:要保护好宁波天一阁。新中国成立后,天一阁被列为全国重点文物保护单位。1962年10月,郭沫若到天一阁视察,题诗曰:"明州天一富藏书,福地琅环信不虚。历劫仅存五分一,至今犹有万卷余。林泉雅洁多奇石,楼阁清癯类硕儒,地六成之逢解放,人民珍惜胜明珠。"天一阁管理部门想方设法搜集散失在各地的原藏书,还陆续增添了由藏书家捐献及征集购得的珍贵古籍。目前,天一阁藏书已达30余万卷,其中珍版善本逾8万卷,大都是明代刻本和抄本,是研究我国古代历史、人物、风俗、民情以及天文、地理、地质、水文、医药、矿产等珍贵的历史资料。

天一阁原名"东明草堂",整个建筑由范钦亲自精心设计。范钦受《龙虎山天一池记》碑帖中"天一生水,地六成之"这句话的启发,改名为"天一阁",取"以水制火"之义。天一阁不但以其藏书之丰闻名于世,还以其书楼设计之奇特和园林构筑之秀美誉满全国。

为了防霉防潮,书楼构筑背北朝南,楼上为一统间,是珍藏古籍的地方,叫"宝书楼",干燥明亮;楼下并排六间,格局整齐,式样古朴;阁前凿有水池用以防火,名曰"天一池",有一半亭翼然其上,古树翠竹掩映,奇石垒山,有九狮一象似在嬉戏,发人异思遐想,百看不厌。藏书楼后为一花园,秀草、香花、修竹环植其间。在天一阁后面的"尊经阁"四周青砖平砌的高墙中,嵌有大小80余方石碑,这就是名闻遐迩的"明州碑林"。其中有珍贵的宋碑《赵隐居墓志铭》、绍兴丙子《施城碑》、楼钥《耕织图诗》等7方;元碑16方,以及明碑、清碑,成为研究各朝历史的颇有价值的文物。如今,已修葺一新的天一阁东园,水池映秀草,绿树掩小楼,古朴雅致,耐人寻味。园后的秦家祠堂,精雕细刻的古建筑,金碧辉煌,与整个天一阁建筑群珠联璧合,相得益彰。

白云庄

白云庄位于宁波市城西管江岸,是明末清初著名思想家、文学家、史学家黄宗羲讲学的地方,被著名史学家全祖望名为"甬上证人书院"。黄宗羲,字太冲,世称梨洲先生,余姚黄竹浦人。他是清初浙东史学派的代表人物,与顾炎武、王夫之并称为明末清初"三大思想家"。他通过"甬上证人书院"培育了浙东学派的多名杰出人才。白云庄原为明末户部主事万泰的庄园,后因其子万斯选著有文集《白云集》,死后葬于此,因名白云庄。白云庄作为黄宗羲讲学之地方,甬上文人曾荟集于此,盛极一时。

白云庄主体建筑坐西朝东,前后二进,均系砖木结构的平屋,古朴庄丽。南侧为万氏故居,"浙东学派"另一主要人物万斯同曾在这里居住过。西北侧为万邦孚和万斯选之墓。万邦孚系万泰之父,曾任左军都督府金事。万斯选系万泰第五子,是同辈人员中的领袖人物,黄宗羲亲自为他撰写墓志铭。

白云庄作为浙东史学的象征,在海内外有很大影响,是省级重点文物保护单位。庄内有"甬上证人书院"现场陈列及黄宗羲生平介绍。

庆安会馆

庆安会馆又称北号会馆,位于市区江东木行路,处于奉化江、甬江、余姚江三江会合处的"三江口"东岸。沿岸原是古代海运码头。是省级重点文物保护单位。该会馆始建于清道光三十年(1850 年)。庆安会馆原先是甬埠北洋舶商的一个行业联络场所。由于舶商笃信"天后神",会馆实际上也就成了祀神的宫殿,故亦称"甬东天后宫"。现馆内尚保存有学者董沛撰的《甬东天后宫碑帖》石刻。庆安会馆是宁波港口城市的标志性建筑,见证了宁波古代、近现代繁荣的海外交通和对外文化交流,是海上丝绸之路文化的重要遗存。与此同时,作为我国沿海规模较大的航运行业会馆,庆安会馆见证了历史上浙东地区航运业的发展。咸丰三年(1853 年),浙江漕粮始行海运,庆安会馆(包括其南侧的安澜会馆)成为浙江清代漕粮及南北贸易河海联运的主要管理和服务设施,南北号舶商在浙江漕粮海运中发挥重要作用。由此,庆安会馆成为大运河(宁波段)河海联运独特运输方式的实物例证,是大运河(宁波段)文化的核心遗产。2014 年 6 月,位列大运河 27 个申遗城市之一的宁波跻身世界文化遗产城市行列,而庆安会馆作为大运河(宁波段)"二段一点"的核心组成部分,也正式成为宁波市首个世界文化遗产点。

庆安会馆建筑以宁波传统的朱金木雕、砖雕和石雕为建筑装饰,富丽堂皇,可说是建筑上的一个小宝库。现存建筑为中轴线上的官门、正殿和后殿,总占地 3900 平方米。

庆安会馆建筑中成就最高的当算石雕艺术。主体建筑大厅,高十多米;明间一对蟠龙柱和次间一对凤凰牡丹石柱,高四米多。龙柱用整块青石料雕刻而成。蟠龙柱的两条盘龙,张牙舞爪,栩栩如生。与蟠龙柱相对应的凤凰柱,亦采用镂空刻法,精妙绝伦。此外,两边墙壁上多嵌有浅浮雕石刻,内容为"西湖十景"和清代雕刻艺术的重要史料,也是宁波港早年开辟海外通商的一个历史见证。

钱业会馆

钱业会馆为省级重点文物保护单位,位于市区东门口不远处的战船街10号。清同治年间,钱业同业组织形式称钱业会商处,在江厦一带滨江庙设有公所,曾毁于兵火,后于1862年由钱庄业筹资重建。至民国十二年(1923年),因原有公所"湫隘不足治事",乃购置建船厂跟(今战船街)"平津会"房屋及基地一方,兴建新会馆,即现在的钱业会馆,于1926年竣工。它是昔日宁波金融业聚会、交易的场所。会馆占地1500余平方米,是由前后二进亭台楼阁、园林组成的中西式砖木结构建筑,其建筑风格别具特色:前进廊舍环绕,两旁有石刻碑记,中有戏台;后进议事厅,是旧时宁波金融业最高决策地。厅前亭园花草,清静幽雅,是全国唯一保存完整的钱庄业的历史文化建筑。新中国成立后,被列为省级重点文物保护单位。会馆内环境幽雅,水陆交通方便。

会馆坐北朝南,前后三进楼房,包括戏台、亭阁等组成中西合璧的砖木结构建筑。内尚存记述金融业发展概况及建馆始末的石碑3通。钱业会馆是宁波当年钱庄业辉煌的标志。宁波钱庄业始于清初,据《鄞县通志》记载,甬上金融向以钱庄为枢纽,其盛时,资金在6万元以上的大同行有36家,万元以上的小同行有30余家,几百元以上的兑换庄有4000多家,其势力凌驾于沪(贷放达3000万元)。民国20年(1931年)全县钱庄业已发展到160家,资金总额计3866万元,而且首创了不用现金支付的"过账制"。金融业的兴旺是经济发达、繁荣的标志,当时曾有"走遍天下不及宁波江厦"的说法,足以说明当时宁波经济的昌盛与宁波人的骄傲。

老外滩

宁波老外滩坐落于宁波市三江口北岸的江北区,于1844年开埠,地处宁波市中心,位于甬江、奉化江和余姚江的三江汇流之地,唐宋以来就是最繁华的港口之一,曾是"五口通商"中最早的对外开埠区,比上海外滩还早20年。它是目前国内仅存的几个具有百年历史的外滩之一。宁波老外滩于1992年后开发,已经成为长三角大景观之一。

宁波在唐代即为中国四大港口之一,鉴真东渡的起始点就在宁波,在南宋时期为中国三大港口之一,并设立市舶司专门负责管理对外贸易。虽然清政府一直采取闭关自守的对外政策,但宁波与日本、南洋各地一直保持着藕断丝连的贸易往来。清初中国缺铜,政府铸铜钱和民间制铜器多通过宁波从日本进口铜及银等;而日本也从宁波进口江南的丝绸、棉布、瓷器等。在清代实行全面闭关之时,宁波是唯一保留了对外贸易的特殊港口。这种特殊的港口地位从1644年到1684年,时间长达约40年。

鸦片战争后,1842年清政府签订了《南京条约》,宁波成为五口通商口岸之一。1844年正式开埠。各国商人蜂拥至宁波,英、法等国采用夺取主权、建立据点、霸占海关、控制海口、垄断航运、推行洋化等一系列手段,把宁波港扭曲成半殖民地性质的港口。不久,江北岸便发展成为英、法、美三国侨民居留区域。它是中国最早的"租界"之一,历史上也称为"外滩",其开埠历史比上海外滩还要早上20年,是目前中国最古老的外滩之一,后来上海口岸崛起,宁波口岸的地位才被逐渐削弱。1927年,中国政府收回了江北岸外国人居留地的行政管理权。江北外滩在岁月的洗礼中完整地记录下了近代宁波的历史变化,体现西方工业文明的器物与各类设施集中在这里出现,如宽敞的马路、整洁的街面以及电灯、自鸣钟、脚踏车、洋房、教堂、医院、银行等,在客观上也推动了宁波城市的近代化进程,成为浙江省唯一现存能反映港口文化的外滩。

从最近一次文物普查情况来看,宁波外滩的54处文物建筑中至少有31处与宁波商帮有关。这些19世纪末至20世纪初的建筑物,反映了丰富多彩的西式和中西结合的建筑风格。从建筑功能看,既有办公和宗教活动场所,又有金融、贸易建筑和豪华住宅。为此,外滩历史文化保护区作为宁波近代历史的标志性地段,被《宁波市城市总体规划》确定为6片历史文化保护区之一。这一历史文化保护区的保护范围为:东滨甬江,南接新江桥,西界人民路,北至轮船码头。在目前开发改造范围内,巡捕房、宏昌源号、朱宅和严氏山庄四幢建筑被列为市级文保建筑。

沿着江边,外国领事馆、天主教堂、银行、轮船码头一字排开,几乎记录了宁波开埠的整段历史。目前保存下来的文物建筑有:原英国领事馆、巡捕房、侵华日军水上司令部、浙海关、天主教堂、江北耶稣圣教堂、宁波邮政局、通商银行等;还有一些民房,如老"宏昌源号"、商人私宅"严氏山庄"、"朱宅"等,这些建筑具有浓郁的欧陆风格,代表了英、法、德、荷

等多国建筑风格。与中国传统民居形成鲜明对比。

慈城古县城

慈城——江南第一古县城、江南古乡文献之邑、中国历史文化名镇。唐开元二十六年（738年）设慈溪县城于此，故名慈城，是目前江南地区保存最为完整的千年古县城。城内历史遗迹丰厚，"慈城古建筑群"是全国重点文物保护单位。慈城地形地势风貌独特，城池环境钟灵毓秀，规整的"双棋盘格局"被专家赞为"中国传统县城的典型代表"。

慈城地处东海之滨，姚江之畔，为全国环境优美乡镇。《史记》载，"周元王三年（公元前473年），越王勾践城勾余"。这是慈城最早的古名，后改称"句章"。至唐开元二十六年设慈溪县，因县城建此取名慈城。经过2400多年的历史沉淀，慈城拥有极其深厚的文化底蕴，尤以古县衙、孔庙、校士馆、清道观、城隍庙、甲第世家、符卿第等古建筑为标志；城内遍布官宦宅第、祠堂牌坊、学宫书院和粉墙绮窗留存，文物古迹众多，历史遗迹丰厚，在约5平方公里的区域内拥有国家、省、市、区四级重点文物保护单位33家。2006年，"慈城古建筑群"被列入全国重点文物保护单位。慈城还是一块人杰地灵的沃土，历代文化学者、名人层出不穷。自唐宋至明清，慈城一带出进士519人，素有"鼎甲相望，进士辈出，举人比肩，秀才盈城"之誉；到了近现代，又涌现出周信芳、秦润卿、应昌期、谈家桢、冯骥才等一大批名人名家。

慈城古县城的文化价值，不仅在于悠久的人文历史，而且表现在钟灵毓秀的独特风貌。全城山水相映成趣，其中五磊山、太宗山等山脉丘陵构成"九龙戏珠、四灵围合"的朴素形态，姚江、城河等江河湖溪造就"四水归堂"的水系格局；城区穿隆起顶，街衢坤龟成形，生态环境秀丽清幽，凝聚了古人追求"天人合一、人杰地灵"居住环境的美好愿望。

它山堰

它山堰位于鄞州西鄞江桥它山旁,是我国古代著名的水利工程之一,国家级重点文物保护单位。2015年10月13日,成为宁波市首个世界灌溉工程遗产。

它山堰历史悠久,至今已有1150多年的历史。唐太和七年(833年),琅琊人王元暐任鄮县(今宁波)县令。他是一位关心民间疾苦的地方官,见鄞江之水由四明山各路溪水自西而来,一泻入海,无所积蓄,以致旱时禾苗枯死,涝时咸潮涌入将庄稼淹死,不是枯死就是淹死,百姓饱受鄞江之苦。为此,他经实地考察,组织民众兴建了这一排灌工程,因位于它山,故名"它山堰"。

它山堰全长134.4米,堰脊阔4.8米,高10米,左右各36石级。据传,堰身共用数千根大木打桩,木桩之上覆盖大石板。为防止堰身移动,又在堰下用逾抱大梅木枕卧江沙之中,南北两端伸入山岩,故虽经洪流冲击而岿然不动。大梅木,原产于鄞州大梅山上,被三国时吴主孙权给砍了,锯为三段。一段运去做了点将台,一段运往绍兴做了禹王祠的大梁,一段做了它山堰大梁,历千年而不朽。

它山堰筑于水道咽喉处,发挥了江溪分流、阻咸蓄淡、引水泄洪和灌溉农田的作用。河水少时,溪水七成入河,三成入江;河水大时,则三成入河,七成入江。并引鄞江水自南门入宁波城,汇储而成月湖和日湖(日湖已填),给城内民众带来极大好处,并使鄞西平原160平方公里农田得到灌溉,终使鄞江之水由害变利。它山堰历经千载仍巍然屹立,至今仍发挥着巨大作用。前人有"十里犹闻震地雷,海神惊惧勒潮回"的赞叹。

　　宁波人民为纪念王元暐筑堰功绩,于它山堰旁边建庙,刻石立碑,以表彰这位为民造福的地方官。

　　它山堰处青山秀水之间,风光秀丽,景色宜人。每当雨后,远山逶迤,吞云吐雾,泄洪的观音瀑如银蛇飞舞,气吞山河,蔚为奇观。

镇海口海防遗址

　　镇海地处我国海岸线中段、甬江的入海口,北上齐鲁,南下闽粤,溯甬江可达苏杭,自古商贾云集、樯帆如林。在招宝山半山亭所镌刻的"百舸争流通异域,一山招宝耀中州"柱联,即是当时海运盛况的生动写照。镇海历来又是兵家必争之地,素有"海天雄镇""两浙咽喉"之称。

　　在这片英雄的土地上,一代又一代爱国志士用自己的血肉,凝聚成不畏强暴、抵御外侮、自强不息的民族精神,为后人留下了一部生动形象的爱国主义教材——镇海口海防遗址。

　　据史书记载,镇海自东晋以来历经大小战事46次。自明中叶以来,镇海先后经历了抗击倭寇和抗英、抗法、抗日等抵御外侮的战争,留下许多先辈可歌可泣的英雄事迹和珍贵丰富的海防遗迹。在镇海口南北两岸不到2平方公里的范围内分布着各个时期的海防遗迹30多处,并已分别被命名为全国百家爱国主义教育示范基地、全国青少年教育基地、省爱国主义教育基地、省国防教育基地和省妇女爱国主义教育基地。1996年11月被国务院公布为全国重点文物保护单位。

　　在镇海口北面,现存的主要海防遗迹有浙江军民抗倭的重要遗迹威远城、月城、安远炮台、烽难、明清碑刻,以及后海塘遗址等。其中,后海塘遗址城塘合一,既能挡住海潮冲击,又能抵御外敌入侵。城塘是用大块条石构筑而成的夹层塘,气势宏伟,蜿蜒数千米。在镇海口南面,现存的主要海防遗迹有金鸡山顶涂望台、靖远炮台、宏远炮台、戚家山营垒等。如此集中的海防遗迹,在全国都是罕见的。它们既是我们的先辈用血肉之躯铸成的历史丰碑,同时也记录了外国侵略者的累累罪行。此外,在现存的海防遗址中,还有各个历史时期军政首脑题词碑记、民族英雄殉难处、侵略军登陆处,以及历次战争留下的各种兵器、各类古籍史料等文物。

奉化溪口

　　奉化溪口为浙江宁波奉化市所辖建制镇、国家重点风景名胜区。溪口镇为蒋介石的出生地及蒋氏父子的故里,民国时期一度成为国民党军政指挥中心。现为首批全国特色景观旅游名镇。溪口风景名胜区由溪口镇、雪窦山、亭下湖三个景区组成,以剡水、古刹、蒋氏故里和幽谷飞瀑名闻遐迩。溪口风景名胜区为首批国家5A级旅游区,东靠武岭,南濒剡溪,北临雪窦山,水绕山环,景色秀丽。景区总观赏面积140平方公里,主要景点蒋氏故居丰镐房,为全国重点文物保护单位。

　　据清乾隆《奉化县志》记载,宋仁宗时,监察御史樊良忠因与王安石不合,弃官归里,隐居溪口沙堤村。至宋景德五年(1006年)溪口建村。据宋宝庆年间统计,人口已近八千。南宋丞相魏杞奉孝宗命出使金国,不辱使命,成为一时重臣,淳熙十一年(1184年)去世。

他是安徽寿县人,却选择溪口飞凤山安葬,可见宋时溪口在当时已颇有名气。

溪口位于宁波市区的西南方向,奉化市西北方向,距宁波市区22公里,沿宁奉公路南行至江口右转弯再行8公里即可到达。溪口以剡溪之水而得名。剡溪源头,主流出于剡界岭,由新昌入奉化境,称"剡源"。沿溪风光优美,剡源九曲为古代旅游胜地。九曲公棠以下称"剡溪",由西向东流过全镇,至东端,有武岭头与溪南山阻隔成口,"溪口"之名由此而来。又以武岭横亘镇东,以山名命地,故也称"武岭"。这里山水如画,风景秀美,骚人墨客,寻幽探胜,古代即已形成"溪口十景",即奎阁凌霄、武潴浪暖、平沙芳草、碧潭观鱼、松林晓莺、溪船夜棹、锦溪秋月、雪峰晚照、屏山雪霁、南园早梅。特别是西北的雪窦山,名胜古迹众多,为浙东著名旅游胜地,汉代即有人以"海上蓬莱,陆上天台"来赞美她。

溪口虽小,却曾经是中国政治的一个风暴眼。蒋介石、蒋经国皆出生于此,大权在握后还经常回来,并在此策划了许多历史事件。张学良于"西安事变"后,也曾被软禁于此,其亲手栽下的五棵楠树仍生机勃勃。中国历史在这留下了深重的痕迹。

蒋氏的出生地、故居别墅、祖墓宗祠、家庵等遗迹错落有致地分布在溪口镇武岭街旁,其中的"玉泰盐铺""小洋房"和"丰镐房"是全国重点文物保护单位。

雪窦山宋时被称为"天下禅宗十刹之一",是佛教界公认的"未来佛"弥勒佛的道场。

正是由于这些独特的人文景观、自然风光和佛教文化,构成了溪口独特的旅游资源。

(二)文化遗迹

鼓楼

鼓楼是宁波市唯一的古城楼遗址,坐落在宁波市中心公园路。唐长庆元年(821年),明州(今宁波)刺史韩察将州治从小溪迁到宁波三江口,以现今的中山公园至鼓楼这一带为中心,建立官署,筑起城墙,历史上称为"子城",鼓楼即是子城的南城门。以后曾改称望海军门、奉国军楼、奉国楼神祠等。元初被毁,后重建时命名为"明远楼"。元末方国珍起兵攻打宁波,明远楼又遭大火焚烧。明万历年间重修时,取"云霞出海曙,梅柳渡江春"中"海曙"二字,改名为"海曙楼"。海曙楼在清代时曾经多次修建,至清咸丰五年(1855年)重建此楼时,因当时楼上置有更鼓,故俗称"鼓楼"。清以后,在三层楼中间建筑水泥钢骨正方形瞭望台及警钟台,并置标准钟一座,四面皆见,即现在鼓楼之风貌。

鼓楼在南宋时曾被宋高宗封为"奉国军楼神祠"。据《鄞县志》载,当时鼓楼内供有唐天宝年间为抗击安禄山叛军、坚守睢阳而殉难的张巡、许远等五位将军神像。宋高宗赵构因被金兵追逐,到鼓楼上躲避而脱险,以为是五位将军保驾之功,便下诏:"封五大将军肖像天楼以祀之,称为奉国军楼神祠。"

鼓楼系三层木结构建筑,雄伟古朴。墙壁为砖砌成,下部用大型条石作基础,高8米,中间有南北向顶门洞,宽6米。登海曙楼,诸景历历,是宁波市中心一大形胜。

老城隍庙

老城隍庙位于市中心县学街东端,全称"宁波府城隍庙",也称郡庙。建于五代后梁贞明二年(916年),地点在"子城西南五十步",即今鼓楼东南侧。宋嘉定九年(1216年),程覃奏请朝廷,赐庙额曰"灵祐"。由于香火特别旺盛,屡遭火毁。明洪武四年(1371年)又一次遭火焚时,郡府张琪便将城隍庙徙到"握兰坊帝师殿故址",也就是县学街现老城隍庙这个地方重建。当时的规模不是很大,到了明正统二年(1437年),知府郑珞重修殿宇廊庑,增筑轩楹于正殿之南,使之更加气派。清光绪十年(1884年),城隍庙再次重建,这次的规模比以往几次都大,有头门、二门、戏台、大殿和后大殿四进。从二门到主体建筑大殿之间,两侧建有配楼,戏台的藻井均用斗拱雕花贴金盘旋而上,精巧绝伦。庙门前为跨街拱月宫墙,正前面为照墙,树立旗杆;庙前并列三双扇大门,门前配一对石狮子。整个建筑群显得雄伟古朴,飞檐耸脊,精雕细刻,富丽堂皇。

老城隍庙在旧时候,塑有城隍神像以及牛头马面、地狱众相,楹联上写有"天知,地知,尔知,我知,何谓无知;善报,恶报,迟报,速报,终须有报"。神秘恐怖,惊心动魄。城隍庙终日香烟缭绕,顶礼膜拜的善男信女络绎不绝;还有求签诗、放焰口、卖关牒,在庙宇内外测字、看相、批命纸、唱文书、说武书、讲善书、变戏文等,三教九流、五花八门,都荟萃于此。至于饮食摊贩,更是内外林立,荤素面食,馄饨包子,随意小酌,水果糕点,应有尽有。每逢正月灯头戏或节日酬神戏时,各戏台同时演出各色好戏,其时张灯结彩,特别热闹。去城隍庙的,除了拜菩萨外,更多的是去赶热闹、买点小吃的,因而城隍庙总是熙熙攘攘,盛况不衰。

清顺治二年(1645年)六月,正值明朝垂亡,清兵大举南下之时,民族英雄钱肃乐、张苍水、董志宁等为抗击清兵入浙,曾在老城隍庙内聚集数千人起义。民国十六年(1927年)时,老城隍庙的神像被捣毁,成为没有菩萨的城隍庙;抗战胜利后,又重塑菩萨神像。

1983年,城隍庙大事修缮,面貌一新;1995年,城隍庙大规模扩建,新商城继承了老城隍庙古朴典雅、雄厚壮观的明清建筑风格,总建筑面积2万平方米。在新老建筑之间,还建有一条长108米、宽6米的步行街,沿街设有数十家特色店铺,使城隍庙成为集大型商场、特色小店、美食城为一体的著名游览场所。

月湖

　　月湖位于宁波城区西南隅,古称"西湖",从宁波火车南站步行数百步即至。该湖呈狭长形,面积为 0.2 平方公里。月湖形状曲折多姿,圆处像满月,曲处似眉月。古时候在北湖东边不远,尚有一湖称"日湖"。这是析明州之"明"字,而名日、月两湖。日湖湮没而月湖独存。月湖是唐太宗贞观十年(636 年)由鄞县县令王君照开凿的。北宋哲宗元祐八年(1093 年)明州太守刘淑大举浚湖,环植松柳,填各处积土分成十洲。南宋绍兴年间(1131—1162 年)太守刘珵又布楼阁亭榭,集四时花卉,建成十洲胜景:东三洲是"菊花洲""月岛"和"竹屿",西三洲是"芙蓉洲""雪汀"和"烟屿",中四洲是"芳草洲""柳汀""花屿"和"竹洲"。宋嘉祐和明万历年间又筑三堤七桥:筑偃月堤于湖北,广生堤于湖中,桃花堤于湖南。七桥,即花屿至烟屿间的湖心西桥,花屿至月岛间的湖心东桥,柳汀至烟屿间的幢幢西桥,柳汀至菊花洲间的幢幢东桥,雪汀至芙蓉洲间的虹桥,芙蓉洲至月湖北滨间的袭绣桥,菊花洲至月湖北滨间的四明桥。现部分已拆除改筑马路。

　　月湖是历史上文人荟萃之地。据传,唐代著名诗人贺知章辞官归隐后曾在月湖住过,他自称"四明狂客",才气横溢,很得人望,现湖滨柳汀尚有"贺秘监祠"。宋代王安石任鄞县县令时,在湖西修筑"西亭",世称"荆公读书台"(现已圮)。南宋时,两朝宰相史浩曾在竹洲设"真隐馆",宋孝宗亲笔为他写了"四明洞天"相赠。当时的一些著名学者都曾在此讲学。以后,清代著名史学家全祖望又在此设"竹洲三先生书院"。明州文风之盛,历数百年不衰。

宁波之有月湖,如杭州之有西湖,自唐宋以来,是宁波的繁华之地。据地方志记载:"其四时之景色不同,而仕女游赏,特盛于春夏,飞盖成荫,画船漾影,无虚日也。"

新中国建立后,月湖几经疏浚,环湖遍植树木花草,新建亭榭楼阁,使月湖益添妩媚。徜徉湖滨,荡舟湖心,如临画境中。

天封塔

天封塔位于宁波市区大沙泥街,宁波城隍庙附近。创建于唐武后"天册万岁"和"万岁登封"(695—696年)年间,故名"天封"。据传说,当时的宁波城形如一条船,浮动于奉化江、余姚江之间,屡遭水淹。后来在城中央建起了这座塔,如同船上立起了一支桅杆,才绝了浪巅水漫之苦。天封塔塔高54.5米,呈六角形,七层明七层暗,外加地下四层,故有"天封塔十八格"的民谣。据文献记载,天封塔在建造时,采用泥沙层层堆积,把砖石运送上去,直至塔顶,塔建成后再把泥沙运走。由于附近的泥沙堆积甚多,所以,天封塔附近的两条马路至今仍称"大沙泥街"和"小沙泥街",可见工程之艰难、浩大。当年,登上塔顶远眺,可见云烟苍茫,四野尽集眼底,三条江如同三条蛟龙,于城东汇合,蜿蜒经招宝山入海。古人有诗写道:"天地苍茫渤海浮,潮声百里接城头。浮屠绝顶青霄伴,俯见飞云似水流。"

天封塔,作为古时候宁波的象征,久负盛名。据传,古人建造此塔的另一用途是把塔作烽火台使用。天封塔与宁波东乡小白岭上的镇蟒塔,同是唐塔,两塔遥遥相对,如发现有外敌入侵,就燃烽烟为号,以此召集四方驻军;太平时则塔顶悬挂明灯,指示水陆要道。由于天封塔维系着一郡之安危,人们便把它视为镇郡之宝塔。正因如此,也曾使宝塔遭受无妄之灾。传说,南宋建炎三年(1129年)十二月,南下金兵追捕康王打了败仗,临走时下了一道焚城令,天封塔也被焚烧几尽。宋高僧正觉,八方募捐,才于宋绍兴十四年(1144年)修复天封塔。重修的天封塔,比以前更为壮观。

天封塔作为千年古塔,历经风霜雨雪,又多次遭受兵火之灾,屡毁屡建屡修。新中国成立后,人民政府对天封塔虽采取许多保护措施,但由于塔身不断倾斜,便决定拆建。1982年在清理塔基时,意外地发现在天封塔地宫内珍藏着150多件文物,其中,有制作于1144年的银质天封塔地宫殿,并在银殿上刻有南宋绍兴十四年题记,以及银质香炉、元版《大乘妙法莲华经》、古纸币、石匣、佛像等,为重新建造天封塔,恢复南宋绍兴年间江南歇山顶殿堂建筑提供了实物模型。

天封塔作为古代宁波最高建筑物,早负盛名,为历代名人雅士游览必登之地,由此也留下了许多题咏的诗文。明朝诗人李堂《咏天封塔》诗写道:"瑶空露玉簪,试脚下危尖。日近光摇幌,岚清翠入檐。天风凉飒飒,花雨晚纤纤。笑指云霄逼,星辰手可拈。"重建后的天封塔,系仿宋塔式样在原地重建。风姿绰约的天封塔,为今日宁波增添了新的风采。

咸通塔

咸通塔即天宁寺塔,是省级重点文物保护单位,坐落在市区中山西路庄家巷口。

咸通塔古朴庄重,但塔身矮小,形似乌龟,故又俗称"乌龟塔"。此塔是浙江省现存年代最久,且唯一的一座唐代砖塔。亦称天宁寺塔。天宁寺,原名国宁寺,始建于唐大中五年(851年),规模宏大。后寺名数易,至民国初年改为天宁寺。天宁寺前原建有左右两塔,可惜左塔已在清光绪年间圮废,右塔即为咸通塔;因其塔砖右侧有真书"咸通四年造此砖记"的铭文,故名。解放初,天宁寺被拆,众多寺院古迹荡然无存,仅留古塔。咸通塔为砖结构,平面呈正方形,底层每边长3.2米,占地面积10余平方米。外塔顶部已无塔刹,全塔高约12米;塔内空呈方形,穹隆顶;塔体基本正直,无明显倾斜趋势,但剥蚀风化较严重。该塔共五层,底层略高并开有壶门,以上塔身逐层收缩变小;每层四壁均设有供奉佛像的龛,四周用砖砌叠涩檐,出挑密度0.7米左右。塔身古朴庄重,没有柱、枋和斗拱,每层覆以层层密叠的腰檐,具有唐代密檐式砖塔的明显特征,是我国长江以南现存唯一的原体保持最完整的唐代密檐式方形砖塔。

咸通塔对研究江南古城明州(即宁波)的环境坐标、唐代的砖结构建筑技术、制砖技术,以及宗教的历史和唐代寺观的规模等具有重要的价值。它也典型地体现了江南唐塔凝重、含蓄的特点与风格。它实际上是唐代明州人理性精神和美学追求的一种象征。

1981年12月,咸通塔被列为市级重点文物保护单位。1989年12月12日,被公布为省级重点文物保护单位。咸通塔经维修后,重显昔日风采。

梁山伯庙

梁山伯庙亦称梁圣君庙,坐落在鄞州西乡高桥附近,离市区约10公里。宁波有句谚语:"若要夫妻同到老,梁山伯庙到一到。"每逢农历三月初一和八月十七,双双对对前去瞻仰者络绎不绝。

梁山伯和祝英台是我国家喻户晓的民间传说人物。据说,全国有梁、祝墓七处之多,而梁山伯庙仅宁波一处。据《义忠王庙记》载:"神讳处仁,字山伯,姓梁氏,会稽人也。东晋穆帝永和壬子三月一日生……"晚唐张读的《宣室志》上说:"英台,上虞祝氏女,伪为男装游学,与会稽梁山伯者同肄业。山伯字处仁。祝先归,二年,山伯访之,方知其女子,怅然如有所失。告其父母求聘,而祝已字马氏子矣。山伯后为鄮令,病死,葬鄮城西。祝适马氏,舟过墓所,风涛不能进。问知有山伯墓,祝登号痛,地忽自裂陷,祝氏遂并埋焉。晋丞相谢安奏表其墓曰'义妇冢'。"梁山伯死后被封为"义忠王",据说是因为梁山伯的鬼魂帮助官军平寇有功而被封。以上记载说明，不仅梁山伯和祝英台，就连马氏也实有其人。

到了北宋末年，明州职官李茂城写了一篇记文，记述了梁山伯是三月一日生，祝英台名贞，马氏为鄮城廊头人；祝氏出嫁是在晋孝武宁康元年(373年)八月十六日，合葬地在鄮西清道源九陇墟，等等。李茂城在梁祝死后七百多年写的这篇记文，比《宣室志》更加具体了，进一步反映出人们强烈地反对封建礼教和追求自由美好生活的愿望。

梁山伯庙，正殿直匾曰"义忠神王庙"，内塑梁山伯坐像，峨冠博带。祝英台凤冠霞帔坐右侧，左右两厢书僮和丫环各担书籍、食盒。后殿为梁祝寝宫，有精工雕镂的古式木床及罗帐锦被之类，一应俱全。殿后为梁祝坟墓，石碑书"梁山伯之墓"。

郑氏十七房

郑氏十七房位于镇海澥浦镇的择山之阳，是全国最大的明清建筑群。"十七房"之名的由来，大体有两种说法，一种认为十七房即一个族中的十七门望族，是十七个房派的总称；另一种认为十七房是明朝时澥浦郑氏一位叫郑十七公的第六代后裔所建，因而得名。不管十七房因何得名，其精妙的宅构建筑和深厚的历史底蕴无不透露出鲜明的明清时代特色。

十七房建筑群离海不远，择山上城堡高于山巅约30多米，周长200余米，辟有东西城门二座，均以条石砌成，固若金汤。扼高远眺可视海上动静，沿驿道下山直入宅群，从择山上俯视，整个十七房宅群是在棋盘方阵间建造，宅群四周有濠河相连，户户皆通水，门门均临江。有清水绕屋而过。几百年前郑氏为子孙设计的这种"家家有水埠，户户有小桥"的格局，具有交通之便，以及防盗、防火及调节气温之功效。

现存的十七房建筑,光是大祖房、小九房、陆房、三房堂前、新房、立房、恒房、后新屋、正室等就有4万多平方米。从表面上看,幢幢建筑连为一体,走廊、厅门、大小天井都家家相通,但实际上却有差异。幢幢建筑的门楼之上有的以植物花卉作案,有的则以虫鸟动物作图。植物有草花之分,动物有勇悍之别。官小的宅第以草饰,官高一些便以花为缀,更高的以虫鸟,甚至以走兽壮之。屋檐、屋斗、墙角、门楼、垛墙之上的砖雕均以此为据,不越雷池半步。

马头墙是明清两代建筑中的显著特点,全国大凡马头墙的尖角皆为灰泥搪塞。而十七房的马头墙尖角则以各种动物虫鸟作装饰,并有三节、四节、五节之分。据说马头墙节数是祖上官封等级的标志。

十七房的建筑风格颇能体现中国封建社会都城以宫廷为主体的规划思想。一条自西向东的百米中轴线为全宅骨干,所有重要建筑均沿中轴线结合。十七房以"幢"组成庭院,并且院院相通,显示了规模大、气势壮的特点。在局部建筑中,采用了斗拱、曲轩、雕梁画栋的装饰。这种仿宫殿、宗庙的建筑方式显示了十七房的显赫门第。现存的牌坊、匾额、石鼓、旗杆甚多,如"父子登科""父子及第"等至今仍可散见于十七房屋间。此外,还有数以百计的以百果镂刻的窗饰,花格镶嵌的门,"八卦图"的石板等,散于各处。

郑氏十七房犹如一块未经雕琢的璞玉,正渐渐放射出夺目的光彩。

前童古镇

前童镇,始建于南宋绍定六年(1233年),地处浙江省宁海县西南,面积68平方公里,人口2.6万,是一个历史悠久,文化积淀深厚,地理环境独特的江南古镇,先后被命名为浙江省历史文化名镇和浙江省旅游城镇。

前童镇位于浙江省宁海西南。街径卵石铺就,屋基也大多为卵石垒成。街巷异常狭小,建筑异常密集,村落按"回"字九宫八卦式布局。童姓祖先按照八卦原理,把白溪水引进村庄,潺潺溪水挨户环流,人人可在溪水中洗菜净衣,家家连流水小桥,户户通卵石坦途。青藤白墙黑瓦,石头镂花窗户,雕梁画栋门楼,苍凉中显现出昔日曾经的繁华。

前童拥有完整的古建筑群,灿烂的人文景观和优美的自然风光等旅游资源,已基本形成了以传统建筑风貌和民间生活为特色的历史文化保护区,保护开发了各具特色的传统民居区、梁皇山风景区、石泄龙吟景区和福泉山景区四大旅游景点,吸引着越来越多的国内外游客前来观光。

前童以民居布局奇特,明清古建筑群保存完善以及人才辈出而闻名遐迩,始建于宋末而盛于明清,至2005年仍保存有1300多间各式古建民居。"家家有雕梁,户户有活水",为江南集镇独特之奇观。八卦水系,哗哗鸣唱,幽幽潜行,流遍家家户户,不是水乡,胜似水乡。前童镇西北与东南边境群山环列,西北边境之梁皇山主峰海拔768.2米。中部为平洋。主要溪流有白溪和梁皇溪。白溪由西面岔路镇进入境内,流经前童村前,然后东出竹林村。梁皇溪源出梁皇山东南麓,经前童村后,迂回至竹林村后,汇于白溪。梁皇山南麓有建于唐武德年间(618—626年)之梁皇寺(崇福寺)。明代地理学家、旅游家徐霞客曾过梁皇山。前童南岙山麓有明初儒士童伯礼营建之石镜精舍,方孝孺曾在此讲学。塔山、鹿山峙立东西两侧,景色秀丽。孝女湖、庙湖、致思厅、学士桥、南宫庙等古迹,今尚存。明初方孝孺所设计之童氏宗祠建筑,仍大致完好。明洪武年间所建的宗祠,引起省内外建筑专家的高度重视。鹿山有革命烈士墓及碑亭。

前童历代人才辈出。在科举时代,前童有功名者200余人;近代史上也有不少名人,如25岁任浙江临时都督的童保暄。整个前童镇有村古、民朴、泉神、山秀的特色。竹林村浙江樟树王、南岙方孝孺手植柏等名木古树弥足珍贵,神奇的连头药泉令人惊叹,巧夺天工的工艺珍品选进了北京故宫和人民大会堂。梁皇山为徐霞客写游记的首站,风光秀丽的鹿山、塔山、石镜山吸引着四方游人。境内东北福泉山与附近连头山为该县旅游胜地,福泉山之巅有福泉寺,连头山上有永福寺。有王槐秋领导的浙东游击队"铁流"纪念馆。2007年6月,前童镇荣膺全国历史文化名镇。

石浦古镇

　　石浦是有 600 余年历史的渔港古城,素有"浙洋中路重镇"之称,位于长三角经济中心区的南翼,浙江中部沿海,宁波市象山县南部的石浦港畔,依山面港,陆地总面积 119.5 平方公里,沿海岛礁 176 个。古城沿山而筑,依山临海,人称"城在港上,山在城中"。它一头连着渔港,一头深藏在山间谷地,城墙随山势起伏而筑,城门就形而构,居高控港。现为中国历史文化名镇,全国六大中心渔港之一。

　　石浦历史悠久,始建年代无参考,因先民聚落于大金山麓峡谷中,三面环山,以"溪流入海处山岩直逼海中"而得名石浦。石浦在唐代以前为鄞县属地;《汉书·地理志》已有内容涉及先民在此耕海牧渔,生息繁衍。唐神龙二年(706 年)象山立县,石浦即为所属村落。

　　宋改东门寨,属归仁乡后门保;元设东门巡检司;明属归仁乡三都。明洪武二年(1369年)置石浦巡司,隶东门寨巡检司。明洪武二十年(1387 年),徙昌国卫于东门山,石浦巡司迁往青山头,调昌国之前、后二所于石浦,筑城。"城东南面海,西北依山,高二丈,广六丈,周六百零七丈,辟西、南、北三门",为浙东抗倭右翼,故有"浙洋重镇"之称。

　　明末清初,石浦将军张名振以石浦为基地,建立抗清大本营;后张苍水也以此为抗清基地,直至被捕。清顺治十八年(1661 年),清廷为扼杀抗清力量,强令沿海居民内迁,石浦所城毁,现尚残存城垣 700 余米。康熙二十三年(1684 年)修复,属归仁乡二十一都。

　　康熙三十三年(1694 年)城重修,置昌石营,千总防守。雍正年间(1723—1735 年)驻昌石水师营。道光五年(1826年)设宁波府海防同知署。宣统二年(1910年)石浦隶昌石镇。民国元年(1912年),昌石镇、奠南乡划归南田县,县治迁至石浦,翌年秋仍归象山县。民国21年(1932年),石浦分建东来、南熏、西成、北平4小镇,民国23年合为东来、金山2镇,翌年再合为石浦镇。

1941年4月,日军侵占石浦,沦陷近5年。1949年7月,石浦解放,为石浦区区署驻地。1953年浙江省批准为县属建制镇,后曾改称人民公社,1961年复称镇。1973年石浦港被国家计委列为全国四大群众渔港之一。1984年,番头乡并入。1991年被命名为浙江省历史文化名镇。1992年,石浦撤区扩镇,金星、东门、檀头山3乡并入。1993年被列为二类开放口岸。2002年,昌国镇并入石浦。

2005年被命名为中国历史文化名镇。2009年12月,被宁波市委、市政府批准成为宁波市首批卫星城市建设试点镇。2010年12月,又被省委、省政府批准成为浙江省首批小城市培育试点镇。

(三)名寺古刹

五磊寺

五磊寺位于慈溪市密家垯象王山南麓。旧名灵山禅院,唐文德年间,令頵禅师筹建。据《五磊寺志》载,吴赤乌间,有西域梵僧那罗延结庐于此。宋大中祥符初赐五磊普济院额。明永历间定为五磊禅寺。清咸丰三年(1853年)大殿毁于火,后几经重修。

五磊寺建筑规模宏大。据寺志载,原有千华阁、法藏阁、净香阁、冰香阁、归光阁等。周围群峰秀出,风光秀丽,气象万千。古人诗曰:"万山山下云如海,一望空天上有亭;何必数椽容我足,自然长啸任人听。"

五磊寺名胜古迹较多,寺门前有一水池,取名"真明池"。碧水从东面的象眼冢汩汩流出,注入真明池后又经小渠流到月亮湖,常年不枯竭。据说这也是那罗延亲率众弟子日夜开凿成的,其间曾与山中妖魔斗法,死伤多人,故又名"万工池"。池水清冽甜爽,能助人祛病驱邪。池旁有赤松五棵,作为五磊寺的香木,为后世传人所栽。离寺不远的山坡上,有参天古树数株,有些树龄难以估计,需几人才能合抱。寺内以樟树居多,枝繁叶茂,四季常青,与五磊寺的金黄建筑交相辉映。到了唐僖宗文德元年(888年),五磊寺的规模得到了极大的扩展。

1995年,五磊寺在政府支持下进行大规模重建。重建后的大雄宝殿面宽7间,进深6间,建筑面积490平方米,共耗修建经费150万元,除部分为善信乐助外,大部为寺院积累。寺院现有殿堂楼阁及各类客舍230间,建筑面积8000平方米,寺院围墙内房基及庭院面积43亩,另有余地10亩,竹林30亩,柴山94亩。常住僧众11名,挂单僧人20余名,在各部门服务职工14人。石湫头下院有楼房10间(上下),平房17间。建筑占地面积3亩,分三条轴线布置。中轴线上有山门、万工池、大雄宝殿、方丈殿,东轴线上有钟楼、迦蓝殿等,西轴线上有鼓楼、观音殿、三圣殿等。

五磊寺被佛教视为灵山。民国时,弘一法师曾在此创律学研究会,现已部分修复并重新开放。每年清明前后,游客如云。

阿育王寺

阿育王寺位于宁波东 16 公里的太白山麓华顶峰下的育王岭下,在中国佛教史上占有显著的地位。阿育王寺始建于晋武帝太康三年(282 年),至今已有 1700 多年历史。它远近闻名,不仅因为山光秀丽,殿宇巍峨,更由于它有一座举世瞩目的舍利宝塔。相传公元前 3 世纪,在天竺国(印度)建立印度历史上第一个统一国家的阿育王,曾造了 8.4 万座宝塔,把释迦牟尼的真身舍利藏于塔中,并把宝塔分别深藏在世界各地的"八吉祥六殊胜地"。到了西晋太康三年(282 年),僧人慧达在病中梦受梵僧指授,遍寻舍利宝塔。一天走到宁波太白山麓,忽听地下有钟声殷殷,当即诚心祷告,经过三日三夜,果然有一座宝塔从地下涌出,光明腾耀,眩人心目。东晋义熙元年(405 年),为保护这一佛国珍品,始建安置舍利的塔亭,并筑禅堂一所。至梁普通三年(522 年),才兴建殿堂楼阁,梁武帝因东天竺赐释迦牟尼舍利之谊,即以印度国王的名字,赐寺额为"阿育王寺"。

阿育王寺建筑规模宏大,主要以山门、鱼乐池、天王殿、大雄宝殿、舍利殿、法堂和藏经楼为中轴线,右侧有云水堂、郑峰草堂、拾翠楼、祖师殿、承恩堂、方丈殿、宸奎阁、寮房等,左侧有松光斋、钟楼、舍利殿、先觉堂、禅堂、大悲阁等,共拥有殿、堂、楼、阁、轩共 660 多间,建筑面积 1.17 万平方米。其中供奉舍利塔的舍利殿,是寺内最庄严场所,系 1909 年按北京皇宫样式建造,用黄色琉璃瓦盖顶,整个建筑金碧辉煌,鹤立于全寺建筑群中。这座国内独一无二的"舍利塔",塔身青色,高一尺四寸,宽七寸,五层四角,四面窗孔,每层雕有菩萨神像,塔内顶悬宝磬,极小的一颗舍利珠(佛顶骨)就在磬中,游客须细心窥视才可见到。因光线照射角度缘故,看到的色彩不一。传说如能看到红色,就能交好运,蓝色次之,黑色最糟。六渡重洋到日本传经的高僧鉴真,第三次遇险时曾在阿育王寺住过,并鉴

赏过舍利。历代帝王、高僧和文人墨客在此留下了不少手迹、碑刻,殿上有宋高宗书写的"佛顶光明之塔"和宋孝宗写的"妙胜之殿"匾额。月台两侧壁上有唐代万齐融撰文、范的重写的"大唐阿育王常住田碑",殿壁回廊还有宋代张九成、苏东坡和明清以来董其昌、梅调鼎、章炳麟等名人书写的碑、匾、楹联和铭志近百件。

阿育王寺风景优美。寺东侧和西侧建有上塔和下塔,附近还有佛迹亭、极目亭、仙书岩、妙喜泉和七佛潭等胜迹。

阿育王寺在日本、东南亚一些国家影响很大,历史上有很多交往。古代有位日本使者曾赋诗赞道:"偶来揽胜鄮峰境,山路行行雪作堆。风搅空林饥虎啸,云埋老树断猿哀,抬头东塔又西塔,移步前台更后台。正是如来真境界,腊天香散一枝梅。"

天童寺

天童寺是国家级重点文物保护单位和著名风景旅游胜地,位于鄞州太白山麓,离市区30余公里。该寺有"东南佛国"之称,为佛教禅宗五大名刹之一。相传,西晋永康元年(300年)时,有个叫义兴的法师云游到此,结茅开山,建造精舍,日夜诵经,一片虔诚,感动了玉帝,便命太白金星化作童子,从天而降,为他服侍供奉。待精舍建成,太白金星才腾云而归。太白山、天童寺即由此得名。唐开元二十年(732年),僧人法璇在山麓始建寺。唐肃宗至德二年(757年),僧人宗弼择地另建新寺,即今天童寺现址。北宋时曾改名为景德禅寺。明太祖朱元璋册封天下名刹时,改为现称。现存建筑系清代重建,1979年又全面整修。

天童寺傍山而筑,层层递升,建筑宏伟,有天王殿、大雄宝殿、罗汉堂、千佛阁、藏经阁、御书楼、回光楼、返明楼、钟楼、方丈殿、法堂、禅堂、戒堂等20多幢古建筑。原有殿、堂、楼、阁、局、轩等999间,因几经毁建,现存730余间,占地面积5.8万平方米,其规模之宏大,为国内罕见。殿内有7米多高的释迦牟尼佛和四大金刚;寺内有唐柏,有清顺治、康熙、雍正皇帝御书的敕命、诏书、玉玺、碑刻等众多文物古迹。殿堂建筑,玲珑剔透,飞檐耸脊,画栋雕梁,蔚为壮观。寺前有"万工池",山门口有"琵琶石",寺西有"玲珑岩",寺东有"古天童"和义兴和尚墓。天童寺周围群山环抱,古木参天,景色特佳。

天童寺已有1600多年历史,鼎盛时期,住过数千僧人,现在遗存的"千僧锅"是350多年前明崇祯年间铸造的。天童寺系日本曹洞宗祖庭,在日本拥有信徒800万。被尊为"画圣"的日本著名画家雪舟,于15世纪中曾在天童寺创作了不少作品。1980年秋,日本曹洞宗管长、大本山永平寺住持比丘秦慧玉率众朝礼天童寺祖庭时,特树"日本道元禅师得法灵通碑"。

天童寺四周有茂密树林,占地5000亩,1981年已辟为天童森林公园之一,植被保存完好,树种繁多,满山皆绿,处处滴翠,是一个天然的避暑、游乐场所。

雪窦寺

雪窦寺,全称雪窦资圣禅寺,是天下禅宗十刹之一,也是大慈弥勒菩萨道场,与普陀观音、五台文殊、峨眉普贤、九华地藏四道场共称佛教五大名山。它位于奉化市溪口镇西北8公里雪窦山之巅,青峰环拱,其中最为奇特的有九峰,气势峥嵘,各展形姿,有"九龙抢珠"之称。雪窦寺历史悠久。晋时有尼结庐山顶,名瀑布院。唐会昌元年(841年)移建今址,改名瀑布观音院。唐景福元年(892年)大规模扩建,建筑面积达6000平方米,寺田90公顷。宋代时,几朝皇帝曾对雪窦寺下过四十多道敕谕。宋咸平三年(999年),宋真宗赵恒御赐"资圣寺"额,故称雪窦寺圣寺。景佑四年(1037年),宋仁宗梦游雪窦山,遂称"应梦名山"。南宋理宗曾御书"应梦名山"四字,勒石建亭。明代时被称为"天下禅宗十刹之一"。古诗云:"青山面面削芙蓉,尺尺犹疑千万峰。野草逢春都是药,碧潭和雨半藏龙。池开锦镜晴波阔,路入珠林暖翠重。试采新茶寻涧水,一双元鹤下高松。"

雪窦寺历经兴衰,寺宇屡毁屡建。最后一次毁于20世纪60年代初。但宋理宗御赐玉印、龙袍、龙钵以及5760册"钦赐龙藏"经书仍保存完好。雪窦寺最近一次重建是1985年,由雪窦寺方丈光德和尚负责筹建。新建的大雄宝殿、弥勒殿等建筑先后落成,整个建筑群飞檐翘角,金碧辉煌,气象万千。

雪窦寺香火鼎盛,高僧辈出,在佛教界享有很高地位。宋代高僧永明延寿禅师在雪窦寺说法并撰写了佛学名著《宗镜录》一百卷,名播海外。宋代高僧重显也曾驻于此寺,即雪窦禅师。民国初期,中国佛教整理委员会主任委员太虚大师应蒋介石之请,任雪窦寺方丈。太虚大师曾去许多国家考察佛教,著有《太虚大师全书》。他圆寂于上海玉佛寺,骨灰在雪窦寺起塔。

雪窦寺作为弥勒道场,其规模制度与别的寺院不同。弥勒菩萨正冠庄严地端坐在大雄宝殿之中。弥勒菩萨是佛国中的未来佛,在五代后梁时显身于奉化岳林寺,自名"契此",俗称布袋和尚。因系奉化长汀人,又号"长汀子"。他常以杖荷一布袋,凡供身之具,尽贮袋中。他生性诙谐,袒胸露腹,笑颜常开,讨人欢喜,人也称他为"欢喜和尚"。当地流传他种种神秘莫测的言行。他圆寂后几年,人们在福建遇到了他,他念动偈言道:"弥勒真弥勒,化身千百亿。时时示世人,世人自不识。"人们才知他是弥勒菩萨的化身。从此,各寺院都按布袋和尚生前形象塑弥勒像,安放于天王殿。雪窦寺弥勒殿于1994年上半年举行盛大的弥勒菩萨开光大典。弥勒殿内千尊弥勒佛像栩栩如生,香火兴旺。

七塔禅寺

七塔禅寺位于浙江省宁波市江东区,南至百丈路,西靠箕漕街,北接箕漕街38弄,东近彩虹北路,历史上即为浙东佛教四大丛林(即天童寺、阿育王寺、七塔寺、观宗寺)之一。1983年,被国务院批准为全国首批重点开放寺院。寺院殿堂结构典雅,古朴庄严,为典型的禅宗伽蓝七堂建制,主要建筑有:七佛塔、山门牌楼、天王殿、圆通宝殿、三圣殿、法堂暨藏经楼、玉佛阁、祖堂、钟楼、鼓楼、东西厢房、综合楼等。玉佛阁上供玉佛一尊,庭前有假山玲珑,秀竹婆娑。

一般寺院的大雄宝殿塑的都是释迦牟尼佛,唯七塔寺塑的却是千手观音像,故时人称之为"南海普陀"或"小普陀"。寺内现有唐咸通十二年造的栖心寺心镜禅师舍利塔一座,北宋和南宋时铸的大铜钟两座,明代古木槎一座,以及嵌于大雄宝殿壁上的湘刻五百罗汉像等珍贵文物。

七塔禅寺始建于唐大中十二年(858年),距今已有1150多年历史。据寺志记载,寺初名东津禅院,当时有江西分宁宰任景舍宅为寺,并礼请天童寺退居方丈心镜禅师居之,是为本寺开山始祖。860年(唐咸通元年)浙东起兵事,四明亦遭荼毒。一日有巨魁率兵入寺,手执刀枪,耀人心目,寺众骇散,唯心镜禅师于殿中瞑目禅定,神色不变,众兵惊异,作礼而退。翌年,郡守奏闻朝廷,盛称师德,诏改东津禅院为栖心寺。宋大中祥符元年(1008年),真宗敕改栖心寺额为崇寿寺。明洪武十九年(1386年),朱元璋手下将领信国公汤和将普陀山居民遣徙内地,为御倭作坚壁清野计,焚宝陀寺(即普济寺前身)殿舍三百余间,迎观音圣像于宁波府崇寿寺供奉。明洪武二十年(1387年),诏改寺额为补陀寺。

从此遂成观音道场,素有"小普陀"之誉,七塔寺与普陀山历史渊源非浅,职此故也。清康熙二十一年(1682年)建大悲殿,因寺前建有七浮屠,故俗称"七塔寺"。寺经洪杨之役,佛殿、山门及钟楼并遭兵火,付之一炬。

七塔禅寺自创建以来,屡经兴废,特别是十年动乱之际,更遭严重破坏,七塔道场名存实亡。1980年落实宗教政策,成立七塔寺修复小组,由宁波市佛协会长月西大和尚任组长。在政府领导重视和四众弟子支持之下,月西大和尚经过10余年苦心经营,终于将寺院殿堂一一修复,使寺貌焕然一新,重现往日庄严恢宏气象,成为市区内唯一一所大型寺院。

三、宁波名人

(一)历史名人

虞世南

永兴文懿公虞世南(558—638年),字伯施,汉族,越州余姚(今浙江省慈溪市观海卫镇鸣鹤场)人。南北朝至隋唐时著名书法家、文学家、诗人、政治家,凌烟阁二十四功臣之一。陈朝太子中庶子虞荔之子,隋朝内史侍郎虞世基之弟。

虞世南生性沉静寡欲,意志坚定努力学习。在陈朝时,曾任建安王法曹参军。入隋后,官秘书郎、起居舍人。隋亡后,被窦建德任命为黄门侍郎。李世民灭窦建德后,引虞世南为秦王府参军、记室参军、弘文馆学士,与房玄龄共掌文翰,为"十八学士"之一。唐太宗贞观年间,历任著作郎、秘书少监、秘书监等职,先后封永兴县子、永兴县公,故世称"虞永兴、虞秘监"。他虽容貌怯懦、弱不胜衣,但性情刚烈,直言敢谏,深得太宗敬重。贞观十二年(638年)卒,年81岁,获赠礼部尚书,谥号文懿,配享昭陵。贞观十七年(643年),绘像凌烟阁。

唐太宗称他德行、忠直、博学、文词、书翰为五绝。善书法,与欧阳询、褚遂良、薛稷合称"初唐四大家"。日本学界称欧阳询、褚遂良、虞世南为"初唐三大家"。其所编的《北堂书钞》被誉为唐代四大类书之一,是中国现存最早的类书之一。原有诗文集30卷,但已散失不全。民国张寿镛辑成《虞秘监集》4卷,收入《四明丛书》。

王应麟

王应麟(1223—1296年),南宋官员、经史学者。字伯厚,号深宁居士,又号厚斋。庆元府鄞县(今浙江省宁波市鄞州区)人,祖籍河南开封。宋理宗淳祐元年进士,宝祐四年复中博学宏词科。先为太常寺主簿、台州通判,召为秘节监、权中书舍人,后知徽州、迁礼部

尚书兼给事中。其为人正直敢言,因冒犯权臣丁大全、贾似
道而遭罢斥,后辞官回乡,专意著述二十年。

王应麟学宗朱熹,早年致力于典章制度研究,对经史百
家、天文地理等都有涉猎;他长于考证,编撰大型类书《玉海》
200卷,分天文、地理、官制、食货等21门,引证完整,特别于
宋代史事,辑录尤详。其中《玉海·艺文类》,保存了丰富的
目录学参考资料,包括宋代国史艺文志、实录、会要,崇文院
内三馆秘阁的各种官修目录,汉、隋、唐诸史艺文、经籍志和
唐宋时代著名私人藏书目录,以及十七史、十三经注疏及前
四史中的诸家注解、唐宋两代重要类书中所有与文化典籍有
关的历史文献。在编排方法上,按主题编类。王重民评其为
"反映着向主题目录过渡的新趋向"。《玉海》对于考证宋代

宋代王应麟书法

文化学术源流有重要价值。王应麟另有考订性札记《困学纪闻》一书,综罗文献,贯串古
今,最为后世推重。宋理宗御书"汲古传忠"赐其父,遂名"汲古堂"。凡著述20余种、600
余卷。清代学者全祖望称其"四明累世之文献莫与伦也"。一生著作,有《困学纪闻》、《小
学绀珠》、《通鉴地理考及通释》、《玉海》、《诗地理考》、《通鉴答问》、《汉书艺文志考证》、《深
宁集》、《玉堂类稿》、《掖垣类稿》、《诗稿》等,但是知名度最高的,是他所编著的家喻户晓的
《三字经》。

方孝孺

方孝孺(1357—1402年),宁海人,字希直,一字希古,号
逊志,明代学者、文学家、散文家、思想家。因其故里旧属缑
城里,故称"缑城先生";又因在汉中府任教授时,蜀献王赐名
其读书处为"正学",亦称"正学先生"。后因拒绝为发动"靖
难之役"的燕王朱棣草拟即位诏书,牵连其亲友学生870余
人全部遇害,成为中国历史上唯一一个被"诛十族"的人。直
至万历年间,明神宗朱翊钧才为其"平反"。后南明弘光帝朱
由崧追谥"文正"。

方孝孺的政论、史论、散文、诗歌俱佳,绝大部分收集在
《逊志斋集》中。其文学作品,如《蚊对》、《指喻》、《越巫》、《鼻
对》、《吴士》、《越车》等,颇有特色。"主题鲜明,议论大胆"是
方孝孺文学作品的重要特色之一。如他写的《越巫》一文,通
过一个以"治鬼术"骗人的越巫,最后被人装鬼反其道吓死的

方孝孺

故事,辛辣地嘲讽了社会上巫祝欺人为生的可恶与可悲。他还善于以"寓热于冷、以形传神"的手法抒发愤世嫉俗之情。如《吴士》一文即属此类,文中借张士诚的形象讽刺那些偏听偏信、轻于用人的当权者,又借与吴士交游的"钱塘无赖"的群体形象,揭露了浮夸之风的社会基础。"选材严、开掘深"也是他文学作品的特色。《指喻》可视为范例,其是一篇议论性散文,由叙事和论理两部分组成,前一部分叙事,后一部分阐发所叙之事中蕴含的道理,借"喻"立说,两者紧密结合,相得益彰。还有一个特点是善于借喻,运用对比寓言等写作技巧。最具代表性的属《鼻对》和《蚊对》,《蚊对》是一篇探讨生活哲理的伦理散文,即事论理,从被蚊虫叮咬这一具体的日常生活琐事,升华到人生重大的哲理原则。方孝孺还撰有《周礼考次》《大易枝辞》《武王戒书注》《宋史要言》《帝王基命录》《文统》等。

王阳明

王守仁(1472—1529年),汉族,幼名云,字伯安,别号阳明。浙江绍兴府余姚县(今属宁波余姚)人,因曾筑室于会稽山阳明洞,自号阳明子,学者称之为阳明先生,亦称王阳明。明代著名的思想家、文学家、哲学家和军事家,陆王心学之集大成者,非但精通儒家、佛家、道家,而且能够统军征战,是中国历史上罕见的全能大儒。封"先儒",奉祀孔庙东庑第58位。弘治十二年(1499年)进士,历任刑部主事、贵州龙场驿丞、庐陵知县、右佥都御史、南

赣巡抚、两广总督等职,晚年官至南京兵部尚书、都察院左都御史。因平定"宸濠之乱"军功而被封为新建伯,隆庆年间追赠新建侯。谥文成,故后人又称王文成公。

王守仁(心学集大成者)与孔子(儒学创始人)、孟子(儒学集大成者)、朱熹(理学集大成者)并称为孔、孟、朱、王。其学术思想传至中国、日本、朝鲜半岛以及东南亚,立德、立言于一身,成就冠绝有明一代。弟子极众,世称姚江学派。其文章博大昌达,行墨间有俊爽之气。著有《王文成公全书》。他以诸葛亮自喻,决心要作一番事业,刻苦学习,学业大进,骑、射、兵法,日趋精通。

正德十二年(1517 年),江西南部以及江西、福建、广东交界的山区爆发民变。山民自建军队,方圆近千里。地方官员无可奈何,遂上奏明廷。兵部举荐时任右佥都御史的王守仁巡抚江西,镇压民变。正德十三年(1518 年)正月,王守仁平定池仲容(池大鬓)部,奏请设立和平县,并兴修县学。三月,王守仁抵达江西莅任。他迅速调集三省兵力,镇压了信丰等地的民变。七月,王守仁念战争破坏巨大,上奏朝廷请求允准招安。明廷遂委以地方军政大权,准其便宜行事。十月,王守仁率兵攻破实力最强的江西崇义县左溪蓝天凤、谢志山军寨,并会师于左溪。王守仁并亲自前往劝降。十一月,王守仁遣使招安,并攻破蓝天凤部。就是在这烽火连天的两年里,他掌握了一样神秘的工具——知行合一。王守仁一生最大的军事功绩,是平定南昌的宁王朱宸濠之乱。

政治上他主张明"赏罚"以提高统治效力,行德治礼教以预防"犯罪"。强调执法要"情法交申",区别对待。他反对"贪功妄杀,玉石不分",要求重视"纲纪",整肃执法之吏,杜绝"法外之诛"。他认为"法之不行,自上犯之"。王守仁是我国宋明时期主观唯心主义集大成者。

日本近代的著名军事家东乡平八郎,曾为王阳明学说所折服,特意佩一方印章,上面篆刻"一生俯首拜阳明"。由于明末的朱舜水远渡日本,把阳明学传到了日本,现在日本的水户市还存有朱舜水的雕像。阳明学在日本,成为日本在明治维新中传统思想抵制全盘西化的基础,所以现在的日本,传统保留得比中国好很多。

黄宗羲

黄宗羲(1610—1695 年),浙江绍兴府余姚县人。字太冲,一字德冰,号南雷,别号梨洲老人、梨洲山人、蓝水渔人、鱼澄洞主、双瀑院长、古藏室史臣等,学者称梨洲先生。明末清初经学家、史学家、思想家、地理学家、天文历算学家、教育家。"东林七君子"黄尊素长子。与顾炎武、王夫之并称"明末清初三大思想家";与弟黄宗炎、黄宗会号称"浙东三黄";与顾炎武、方以智、王夫之、朱舜水并称为"明末清初五大家";与陕西李颙、直隶容城孙奇逢并称"海内三大鸿儒"。

黄宗羲提出"天下为主,君为客"的民主思想。他说,"天下之治乱,不在一姓之兴亡,

而在万民之忧乐",主张以"天下之法"取代皇帝的"一家之法",从而限制君权,保证人民的基本权利。黄宗羲的政治主张抨击了封建君主专制制度,有极其重要的意义,对以后反专制斗争起到了积极的推动作用。

黄宗羲为学领域极广,成就宏富,于经史百家及天文、算术、乐律、释道无不涉猎,而于史学造诣尤深。清廷撰修《明史》,"史局大议必咨之"。他身历明清更迭之际,认为"国可灭,史不可灭"。他论史注重史法,强调征实可信。在哲学上,认为气为本,无气则无理,理为气之理,但又认为"心即气","盈天地皆心也"。在政治上,他从"民本"的立场深刻批判封建君主专制,提出"君为天下之大害,不如无君",主张废除君主"一家之法",建立万民的"天下之法"。他还提出以学校为议政机构的设想。他精于历法、地理、数学以及版本目录之学,并将其所得运用于治史实践、辨析史事真伪、订正史籍得失,多有卓见,影响及于整个清代。

黄宗羲一生著述大致依史学、经学、地理、律历、数学、诗文杂著为类,多至50余种、300多卷,其中最为重要的有《明儒学案》、《宋元学案》、《明夷待访录》、《孟子师说》、《葬制或问》、《破邪论》、《思旧录》、《易学象数论》、《明文海》、《行朝录》、《今水经》、《大统历推法》、《四明山志》等。黄宗羲生前曾自己整理编定《南雷文案》,又删订为《南雷文定》、《文约》。黄宗羲的启蒙思想完全没有外来思想的影响,空前绝后,被称为"中国思想启蒙之父"。

张苍水

张煌言(1620—1664年),字玄著,号苍水,鄞县(今浙江宁波)人,南明儒将、诗人,著名抗清英雄。崇祯时举人,官至南明兵部尚书。1645年(清顺治元年、明弘光元年)南京失守后,与钱肃乐等起兵抗清。后奉鲁王,联络十三家农民军,并与郑成功配合,亲率部队连下安徽二十余城,坚持抗清斗争近二十年。

康熙三年(1664年),随着永历帝、监国鲁王、郑成功等人相继死去,张煌言见大势已去,于南田的悬嶴岛解散义军,隐居不出。是年被俘,后遭杀害,就义前,赋《绝命诗》一首。谥号忠烈。

张煌言一生仅活了45岁,其诗文著述甚丰,后人收集整理名《张苍水集》。但此文集在清朝一直被列为禁书,故仅有传抄稿本。直至1901年时,始有国学大师章炳麟将其排印(二卷本),附《北征录》一卷问世。1909年,又有国学保存会的排印本十二卷、补遗一卷、附录八卷出版。别有《四明丛书》本九卷、附录八卷传世。1959年,由中华书局对文集的诗文重加整理、校勘后,将《张苍水集》分为四编,包括《冰槎集》、《奇零草》、《采薇吟》及《北征录》;又附录一卷,载有年谱、传略、序跋等。

张煌言诗文多是在战斗生涯里写成,其诗质朴悲壮,充分表现出忧国忧民的爱国热情。张煌言与岳飞、于谦并称"西湖三杰"。《瀺州行》、《闽南行》、《岛居八首》、《冬怀八首》等诗抒情言志,表现艰苦卓绝的战斗生活。尤其是《甲辰八月辞故里》二首及《放歌》、《绝命诗》,写于就义之前,饱含血泪,是传世之作。

清国史馆为其立传,《明史》有传。乾隆四十一年(1776 年)追谥忠烈,入祀忠义祠,收入《钦定胜朝殉节诸臣录》。

朱舜水

朱之瑜(1600—1682 年),浙江余姚人,明末贡生,明清之际的学者和教育家。字楚屿,又作鲁屿,号舜水。因在明末和南明曾二次奉诏特征,未就,人称征君。其学特点是提倡"实理实学、学以致用",认为"学问之道,贵在实行,圣贤之学,俱在践履"。他的思想在日本有一定的影响。朱舜水和黄宗羲、王夫之、顾炎武、方以智一起,被称为"明末清初五大家";与王阳明、黄梨洲、严子陵并称为余姚四先贤。

1644 年清军入关后,长驱南下。为匡复社稷,朱舜水这位年轻的隐士投入到风险极大的抗清复明斗争中,与浙东抗清义师首领王翊相佐,以舟山为抗清根据地。1651 年农历八月十四,王翊不屈而死,朱舜水闻知后于八月十五设祭,终身废中秋赏月。他参加了郑成功、张煌言的北伐,往返于两军,亲历战阵。1657 年,暂居越南的朱舜水想回国支持郑成功抗清。恰逢越南国王征召识字者做文官,有人举荐了朱舜水,朱舜水回国受阻,被带进了越南王宫。在异国国王面前,朱舜水誓死不肯跪拜。越南国王大怒,扬言要杀他。朱舜水却说,"今日我为遵守明朝礼节而死,死而无憾。我死后,如可收尸,请题'明征君朱某之墓'。"此举赢得了越南国王的尊重,终于放他回国。1659 年,清兵攻克舟山,朱舜水见大势已去,复明无望,怀抱孤愤,前往日本。在日本,他常面向故乡泣血,背朝北方切齿。他自号"舜水","舜水者敝邑之水名也",以示不忘故国故土之情。就这样,他开始了二十余年的寓日讲学生涯。流亡海外的朱舜水受到了日本文化界的敬重。他在东洋讲学二十余载,培育了无数精英,被尊为"日本的孔夫子"。

朱舜水在日本不仅高扬儒学、标示道德、还传去了中国的服饰、建筑、饮食等方面的技艺。现在诸多领域的人士在从事学术研究时,都能从朱舜水那里获得书面借鉴。他坚守中国的传统文化,要求前来探望的孙儿必须是中华炎黄子孙形象。1682 年 4 月 17 日,朱舜水客死于日本江户,首相德川光国用厚礼将他葬于日本茨城县常陆太田市的瑞龙山德川诸侯家族墓地。作为唯一的族外人士,朱舜水的墓地被安排在山地的中央位置,墓碑由德川光国亲笔用隶书体题写"明征君子朱子墓"。日本学者谥他为"文恭先生",取古言"德道博闻曰文,执事坚固曰恭"之意。

全祖望

全祖望(1705—1755 年),鄞州(今浙江宁波)人。字绍衣,号谢山,小名补,自署鲒埼亭长,学者称谢山先生。清代浙东学派的重要代表人物,著名藏书家、历史学家、文献学家,博学才俊。乾隆元年(1736 年),荐举博学鸿词,同年中进士,选翰林院庶吉士。因不附权贵,于次年辞官归里,不复出仕,专心致力于学术,相继讲学,足迹遍布大江南北;曾主讲于浙江蕺山书院,从者云集。他一生大部分时间用于文献的收集及整理,是这一时期文献学的代表人物。

在学术上,全祖望推崇黄宗羲,自称为梨洲私淑弟子,又受万斯同影响,专研宋和南明史事,留意乡邦文献,尤好搜罗古典文献及金石旧拓,曾编成《天一阁碑目》。其著作颇丰,撰有《鲒埼亭集》38 卷及《外编》50 卷,《诗集》10 卷,还有《汉书地理志稽疑》、辑补《宋元学案》、《古今通史年表》、《经书问答》、《句余土音》等,又七校《水经注》,三笺南宋王应麟《困学纪闻》,续选《甬上耆旧诗》,为我国文化宝库增添了许多珍贵遗产。

全祖望卒年 51 岁,葬在六世祖全少微墓之西南。墓呈横长方形,墓碑上刻"谢山全太史墓"。

全祖望秉笔直书、文采斐然,他以卓越的成就奠定了他在中国史学史上的崇高地位,是继司马迁之后最有文采的传记史家。其人生虽仕途坎坷,但人品却冰清玉洁,以耿直清正的品格和汪洋恣肆的才情,构成了德才皆备的人格,成为浙东人民敬仰的先贤。

蒋介石

蒋介石(1887—1975 年)是近代中国著名政治人物及军事家,名中正,字介石,幼名瑞元,谱名周泰,学名志清。祖籍江苏宜兴,生于浙江奉化。历任黄埔军校校长、国民革命军总司令、国民政府主席、行政院院长、国民政府军事委员会委员长、特级上将、中国国民党总裁、第二次世界大战同盟国中国战区最高统帅、"中华民国总统"等职。

蒋中正受孙中山赏识而崛起于民国政坛,在孙中山去世后长期领导中国国民党达半世纪;其于国民政府时代一直居于军政核心,领导中国度过对日抗战与二次大战,曾任"中华民国总统"长达 27 年,但其政治手腕与独裁统治亦遭受批评。其从政生涯横跨北伐、训政、国共内战、对日抗战、"行宪"、败退台湾及东西方冷战,在中国近代史上有重要地位。

1908 年赴日本并加入同盟会,1924 年担任黄埔军校校长。1926 年先后制造"中山舰事件""整理党务案""4.12 事件",打击共产党和革命势力。后任国民政府军事委员会主席、国民革命军总司令。1928 年任南京国民政府主席,继续进行新军阀混战。1931 年"9·18"事变后,任军事委员会委员长,推行"攘外必先安内"政策,围剿红军革命根据地。1936 年"西安事变"后,被迫接受抗日主张,实行第二次国共合作。抗日战争期间,任国防最高委员会委员长、同盟国中国战区最高统帅。"皖南事变"后,掀起第三次反共高潮。蒋介石领导 200 多万国民革命军坚持八年抗战,虽然有其过失之处,但仍不失为民族的领袖。1943 年参加美、英、中三国领导人参加的开罗会议。抗日战争胜利后,与中共代表团在重庆进行和平谈判,旋即于 1946 年撕毁《停战协定》《政协决议》,命令进攻解放区;单独召开"制宪国民大会",通过"宪法"。1948 年擅自召开第一届国民大会,当选"中华民国总统"。1949 年,蒋介石父子败退台湾,但之后一直反对台独,反对美国分裂、"托管"台湾。

纵观中国近现代史,如果没有蒋介石,当时中国的台湾、东北被日本占领,中国将被各地军阀分割成多个小国家,当时中国唯一可以控制各地军阀、中央军、黄埔系、准嫡系和嫡系的强权人物,除蒋介石外没有第二人,所以公允地说,蒋介石的存在起到了维护中国领土完整的重要作用。

(二)宁波帮

王宽诚

王宽诚(1907—1986 年),宁波鄞县人。1937 年到上海开设维大洋行。抗日战争胜利后,先后在伦敦、纽约等地成立分公司。1947 年迁居香港,设立维大洋行(香港)有限公

司,随后创立幸福企业有限公司等数十家有限公司,经营金
融财务、地产建筑、国内外贸易等业务。中华人民共和国建
立后,历任中国民主建国会中央委员,中华全国工商联第五
届常委、执行委员,中国国际信托投资公司董事,香港中华总
商会荣誉会长。他拥护"一国两制",为中华人民共和国香港
特别行政区基本法咨询委员会执行委员会副主任。他是第
四、五届全国人大代表,第二、三、四届全国政协委员,第五届
全国政协常委。

王宽诚曾为支持抗美援朝捐献一架飞机和一些其他
物资。

王宽诚关心内地及香港教育事业和社会福利事业,几十
年来,他先后捐款支持香港及内地 20 余所学校或社团,包括
香港培华教育基金会、中国残疾人福利基金会、宋庆龄基金会、中国癌症研究基金会等
单位。

他的捐资办教育之举开了现代"宁波帮"捐赠的先河。1963 年捐资 100 万元人民币
创建宁波东恩中学、小学。1980 年与俞佐宸一起倡议成立甬港联谊会,任香港甬港联谊
会会长,后任名誉会长。1984 年捐资兴建东恩中学宽诚实验楼,设宽诚奖学金;捐百万元
助建浙江树人大学;又资助上海工商学院、广东暨南大学等。1985 年又出资 1 亿美元成
立"王宽诚教育基金会",并在家乡宁波特别设立了"王宽诚育才奖",为国家培养人才。

1986 年 8 月,在他去世前的几个月,王宽诚还不顾 80 岁高龄和旅途劳顿,带领港澳
委员 20 余人前往新疆、陕西、甘肃等地考察,并提出发展西北地区的许多有益建议。

王宽诚先生对事业兢兢业业、艰苦奋斗;对朋友、对同事宽厚真诚,乐于施善,慷慨助
人;对自己节俭朴素,从不宽懈。在国际国内赢得了崇高的信誉。他为发展家乡的物质文
明及精神文明作出了意义深远的贡献。2000 年,浙江省人民政府授予其"爱乡楷模"荣誉
称号。

董浩云

董浩云(1912—1982 年),浙江舟山人,中国东方海外货柜航运公司的创办人,被誉为
"现代郑和",是"世界七大船王"之一。

董浩云 1911 年出生,1927 年 10 月中学毕业后考入航运业训练班,1928 年到天津航
运公司当职员,后逐步升任为常务董事,开始了经营航运业的生涯。

1931 年 11 月底,董浩云奉派与友人顾联青一同乘火车经南京来到天津。12 月初到
职后,董浩云担任天津航业公司秘书,从此开始了他与海洋紧密相连的传奇人生。董浩云

在天津航业公司一干就是 6 年。在这 6 年中,他积极倡导"自船、自货、自运"的经营理念,并在 1933 年通过山西太原绥靖公署主任阎锡山的帮助,冲破英国航商的重重干扰,打破了外商长期垄断中国航运的格局,将同蒲路材料运输交与国人承运,北宁路当局随之附和,国人的航运从此打入华北运输业的咽喉要道,为中国远洋航运的发展奠定了坚实的基础。

1934 年 6 月 3 日,董浩云升任天津航业公司船务部主任,先后任天津轮船业同业公会执委、常务执委。同年 3 月至 12 月,公司经理王更三多次赴上海执行公务,此间,公司所有文书往来均由董浩云草拟和批阅,经理职务也由他全权代理。他以自己的聪明才智和努力钻研的敬业精神,赢得了公司高级管理层的高度信任,赢得了航业界同仁的广泛认同。

1935 年,他利用外交手段,与天津英工部局、港务局多次周旋,经过数月的口舌之战,最终将"九号码头"收归天津航业公司名下。同年 10 月 21 日,公司迁址至该址办公。从此,天津航业公司有了自己的码头,结束了租借洋人码头、长期受外国人无端刁难的历史。

1935 年底至 1936 年初,渤海湾大沽口内外的一场空前的冰难,造成 140 余艘中外大小船只被重冰围困达 20 余日,各船断水、绝粮,船上人、货岌岌可危。董浩云挺身而出,在多次赶往现场视察冰情后,一面与海河工程局、港务局和航业公会多方积极协调,制订营救方案,一面派公司"天行"号破冰船前往救助,更亲自乘坐飞机两次投放食物、饮用水、燃煤和各种必需品,为船员和旅客提供了生存保障。

1938 年初,董浩云调往上海。在津 6 年积累的经验,为他日后成为世界船王打下了坚实的基础。董浩云凭着"勇于竞争,大胆创业"的精神,几经努力,开创了中国、亚洲和世界航运史上的多项"第一",因而享有"现代郑和"的美誉。在鼎盛时期,他拥有各种船只 149 艘,总吨位达 1100 万吨,是世界"风流船王"奥纳西斯的近一倍;虽不及"世界船王"包玉刚的环球集团多,但其船舶的种类之多、单船吨位之大、机械设备之新,均超过环球集团。

包玉刚

包玉刚(1918—1991 年),名起然,浙江宁波人。香港环球航运集团原主席,宁波旅港同乡会及香港甬港联谊会名誉主席,中华人民共和国香港特别行政区基本法起草委员会副主任委员。他是世界上拥有 10 亿美元以上资产的 12 位华人富豪之一。他创立的"环

球航运集团"是香港十大财团之一。他是世人公推的华人世界船王,1978 年,包玉刚的海上王国达到了顶峰,稳坐世界十大船王的第一把交椅。他是第一个进入英资汇丰银行的华人董事,1976 年,他被英国女王封为爵士。他热情支持祖国建设,除捐献巨资为家乡兴建兆龙学校、中兴中学、宁波大学外,还建造北京兆龙饭店、上海交通大学包兆龙图书馆、包玉刚图书馆,设立包兆龙、包玉刚留学生奖学金等。

稳扎稳打的方式让包玉刚区别于其他的船主,坐上了世界船王的宝座,称王于海上。他刻苦钻研、勤奋不已,有极强的事业心和责任心。1981 年,包玉刚拥有船舶 2100 多万吨,从而使香港仅次于美国,成为世界航运中心之一。这些发展是与他对航运事业的贡献分不开的。由于他在国际船运业的地位,他受到各国首脑和大企业家的关注和赞赏。除了英国女王伊丽莎白封他为爵士外,比利时国王、巴拿马总统、巴西总统、日本天皇都曾授予他高级勋章。这是世界上任何大企业家都未曾获得过的殊荣。英国前首相希思曾特地邀请他到别墅赴宴,详细询问他的经营方法。1981 年,美国总统里根举行就职典礼时,特邀包玉刚作为贵宾参加。他的电话可直通白宫,随时可与美国总统对话。

尽管这样,他却是一个朴实无华的人,一个勤俭节约的人,他从来不允许自己和亲属的生活过分奢侈。1991 年 9 月 23 日,包玉刚因病在家中去世,享年 73 岁。他的去世在全球范围内引起了轰动,也标志着一个时代的结束。

邵逸夫

邵逸夫(1907—2014 年),原名邵仁楞,生于浙江宁波镇海。香港电视广播有限公司荣誉主席,邵氏兄弟电影公司的创办人之一。香港苏浙同乡会、宁波旅港同乡会永远名誉会长,中华人民共和国香港特别行政区筹备委员会委员。

1958 年,邵逸夫在香港成立邵氏兄弟电影公司,拍摄过逾千部华语电影。他旗下的电视广播有限公司(无线电视)主导着香港的电视行业。

1977 年,邵逸夫获英国女王伊丽莎白二世册封为下级勋位爵士,成为香港娱乐业获"爵士"头衔的第一人。1990 年,中国政府将中国发现的 2899 号小行星命名为"邵逸夫星"。1991 年,美国旧金山市(三藩市)将每年的 9 月 8 日定为"邵逸夫日"。2002 年,创立有东方诺贝尔奖之称的邵逸夫奖,每年选出世界上在数学、生命科学与医学及天文学卓有成就的科学家进行奖励。2011 年正式退休,邵逸夫也是全球最长寿、任期时间最长的上市公司董事长。2014 年 1 月 7 日,邵逸夫逝世,享寿 107 岁。

邵逸夫并非香港最有钱的人,但却是香港富豪中屈指可数的大慈善家,他在香港的影响力源自他的影视王国,而他在内地的口碑则主要是因为他的慈善捐赠。1973年,邵逸夫设立了邵氏基金会。据统计,自1985年以来,邵逸夫通过邵氏基金与教育部合作,连年向内地教育捐赠巨款建设教育教学设施,截至2012年,赠款金额近47.5亿港元。邵逸夫历年捐助社会公益、慈善事务超过100多亿港元,兴建了6000多个教育和医疗项目。尤其是对教育事业和科技事业,邵逸夫捐赠的项目遍布神州大地,全中国多家高等院校均有以邵逸夫命名的"逸夫楼"。香港多所大专院校的建设也曾得到邵逸夫捐助,如香港中文大学的逸夫书院、香港大学的邵逸夫楼、香港城市大学的邵逸夫图书馆等。

卢绪章

卢绪章(1911—1995年),浙江省鄞县(今宁波市鄞州区)人,中国金融工作者、政府官员;曾任中国进出口公司经理,被认为是中国对外贸易事业开拓者和奠基人之一。卢绪章14岁时便前往上海,先在上海源通轮船公司当练习生,业余就读于上海总商会商业补习夜校,并积极参加社会活动。1933年大学毕业后,卢绪章在上海合伙创办广大华行,主营进出口业务,并以此作为中共秘密工作机构;1940年出任广大华行总经理,随后积极扩展广大华行业务,在重庆、贵阳、成都、昆明等地设立分行,并先后组建民生保险公司、民孚企业股份有限公司等企业。卢绪章于1937年加入中国共产党,1940年赴重庆,成为周恩来的得力助手;1945年回到上海。

1949年5月上海解放后,卢绪章参加了上海市军管会工作,出任上海市财经接管委员会贸易处副处长、华东军政委员会贸易部副部长等职;不久调至天津,出任中国进出口公司经理,后公司迁至北京。1952年9月,卢绪章调任外贸部局长、部长助理、副部长等职。"文革"期间遭受迫害,受尽折磨。打倒"四人帮"后,回北京任外贸部顾问。1977年8月,卢绪章调任国务院侨办党组成员、华侨旅行社社长;次年转任新成立的国家旅游总局第一任局长、党组书记,成为我国旅游事业的开拓者。1981年2月,卢绪章调任国家进出口委员会和外国投资委员会副主任;同年8月,又奉调回外贸部任常务副部长、党组副书记。1982年3月,卢绪章退居二线,改任对外经济贸易部顾问。卢绪章是新中国外贸事业的开拓者和奠基人之一,为中国外经贸事业的发展作出了重大贡献。

卢绪章曾先后两次到香港,会见了包玉刚、邵逸夫等宁波籍人士,向他们介绍了家乡的情况,并邀请他们回家乡考察。由于卢绪章的积极推动和一些著名"宁波帮"人士的带动,5万多名在海外的"宁波帮"人士陆续回宁波访问、探亲、旅游,为家乡宁波的建设贡献了自己的力量,他们或捐赠巨资兴办教育、卫生等福利事业,或投资建厂办实业。1988年10月,由他和其他著名的宁波籍人士发起,宁波经济促进协会正式成立,他亲自担任首任会长。

(三)艺术家

周信芳

周信芳(1895—1975年),浙江慈城人。出身艺人家庭,是我国卓越的京剧表演艺术家,京剧麒派艺术创始人,艺名麒麟童。

周信芳的基本功精湛,他声音宽响,沙而不嘶,晚年转具苍醇之音色,拔高时反觉圆润,低音更见出浑厚特色。他的唱腔以苍凉遒劲为特色,朴而不直,顿挫有力,往往有极富曲折跌宕之处,尤其注意抒发人物感情,高拨子、汉调等唱腔有独特的韵味。念白有较重的浙江方音,苍劲、爆满,讲究喷口,富于力度,口风犀利老辣且音乐性强,善用语气词,有时接近于口语,生活气息浓厚,无论表达风趣、庄重、愤恨、哀伤的情绪,语气都极为自然生动。表演中运用水袖、身段、步法,结合眼神和面部表情,都能吻合剧情及人物的特定处境

于思想,显示了他提炼生活、再现生活的深厚功力。一些特殊技法的运用更有浓墨重彩的效果,如靠旗、髯口、甩发、帽翅种种功夫,纯熟自如。他的代表作品有《徐策跑城》、《乌龙院》、《萧何月下追韩信》、《四进士》、《扫松下书》、《斩经堂》、《清风亭》、《坐楼杀惜》、《义责王魁》、《打严嵩》等。

周信芳勇于创造,在继承的基础上多了大量的改革创新,除对传统剧目作去芜存菁的整理改动之外,无论唱、念、做、打与剧目、唱词、服装、扮相等均有适合自己风格而与众不同的设计,如对现代剧艺术中新的表演手段的吸收,以夸张的手段用外部形象与动作塑造人物,造成强烈的艺术感染力。

潘天寿

潘天寿(1897—1971年),浙江宁海人。早年名天授,字大颐,自署阿寿、雷婆头峰寿者、心阿兰若主持、寿者。现代画家、教育家,擅画花鸟、山水,兼善指画,亦能书法、诗词、篆刻。1915年考入浙江省立第一师范学校,受教于经亨颐、李叔同等人。其写意花鸟初学吴昌硕,后取法石涛、八大山人,布局奇险,用笔劲挺洗练,境界雄奇壮阔。曾任中国美术家协会副主席、浙江美术学院院长等职。为第一、二、三届全国人大代表,中国文联委员;1958年被聘为苏联艺术科学院名誉院士。著有《中国绘画史》、《听天阁画谈随笔》等。

1924年,任上海美专教授,着手编著《中国绘画史》,1926年7月出版发行。应邀担任杭州国立艺术院中国画主任教授,兼书画研究会指导教师。自此一直定居杭州。同时兼任上海美专、新华艺专等校授课教师。1932年,出版二集《白社画集》,参加"新华艺专教授近作展览"。1933年,作品参加徐悲鸿在法国巴黎主持的"中国近代绘画展览";编写《中国书法史》初稿。1936年,所编《中国绘画史》经修改后再版,列入"大学丛书"。8月,作《梦游黄山》。1937年4月1日,潘天寿作品《墨猫》、《行书立轴》在南京美术陈列馆举办的"第二届全国美术展览会"展出;同年,《江洲夜泊图》在"中国画会第六届展览会"展出。1943年,编写《中国画院考》;整理历年诗作,编为《听天阁诗存》付梓;作《秋酣》、《行书画论手卷》。

新中国成立后,1950年,任中央美术学院华东分院"民族美术研究室"主任,与吴茀之等一起大量收购、鉴定民间藏画,分类造册,装裱修整,充实院系收藏,为教学提供了充分的直观教材。1962年4月,在《东海》杂志1962年10月号上发表《谈黄宾虹山水画的成就》;为缅甸驻华大使馆作《雨霁》。1963年元旦,"潘天寿画展"由上海美协、中国画院主办,在上海美术馆展出。

潘天寿精于写意花鸟和山水,偶作人物,尤善画鹰、八哥、蔬果及松、梅等。落笔大胆,点染细心;墨彩纵横交错,构图清新苍秀,气势磅礴,趣韵无穷;画面灵动,引人入胜。潘天寿绘画题材包括鹰、荷、松、四君子、山水、人物等,每作必有奇局,结构险中求平衡,形态精简而意远。

沙孟海

沙孟海(1900—1992年),鄞县沙村人。原名文若,字孟海,号石荒、沙村、决明。出生于名医书香之家,幼承庭训,早习篆刻,曾就读于慈溪锦堂学校,毕业于浙东第四师范学校。1922 年,沙孟海到上海担任家庭教师期间,有幸接触令他十分仰慕的康有为、吴昌硕等大师,对以后沙孟海的书法和篆刻产生了深远的影响。1925 年他任教商务印书馆图文函授社,其间,从冯君木、陈屺怀学古文学,学艺大进。章太炎主办的《华国月刊》,多次刊载他的金石文字。曾任浙江省文物管理委员会常务委员、浙江省博物馆名誉馆长、中国书法家协会副主席、浙江省书法家协会主席、西泠印社社长、西泠书画院院长、浙江考古学会名誉会长等职。其书法远宗汉魏,近取宋明,于钟繇、王羲之、欧阳询、颜真卿、苏轼、黄庭坚诸家,用力最勤,且能化古融今,形成自己的独特书风。兼擅篆、隶、行、草、楷诸书,所作榜书大字,雄浑刚健,气势磅礴。沙孟海学问渊博,于语言文字、文史、考古、书法、篆刻等均深有研究。

　　30 岁以前,沙孟海先生临写的碑帖有《集王圣教序》、《郑文公碑》、《张猛龙》等。这一阶段,可称为但求平正阶段。进入中年以后,随着学养的日渐丰厚和阅历的渐次拓展,沙孟海先生多用功地关注字的"体势"和章法的"气势"当然,原有精耕细作的楷书不是全然放弃,偶作楷书。这一时期沙先生的作品可谓是"既知平正,务追险绝"时期,横跨时间近四十年,大致可分为前后两个阶段。进入 20 世纪 80 年代以后,随着"新时期"文艺事业的复苏,沙孟海迎来了他书法艺术蓬勃向上的春天,进入了鼎盛时期。他精神勃发,满怀激情地投入到书法艺术创作之中。这一时期,他的创作进入一个鼎盛时期,"既能险绝,复归平正"。这个时期的作品,行草书和擘窠大字占据了的主导地位,使人们看到了有希望的当代书坛。

　　书法风格由秀逸儒雅到浑厚华滋,最终归于古拙朴茂,一如草木之由春之绚丽多姿到夏之煊赫灿烂而入于深秋的豪迈深远,最终归于冬之空旷无际。沙孟海的字斜画紧结,不主故常;用笔的侧锋取势,迅捷爽利,锋棱跃然;线条的浑厚朴拙,于纵横之间任其自然,令人羡叹不已。

邵荃麟

　　邵荃麟(1906—1971 年),浙江慈溪人。原名邵骏远,曾用名邵逸民、邵亦民,笔名荃、力夫、契若。中国文艺理论家、现代文学评论家、作家。曾任中国作家协会副主席、主席、党组书记。早年就读于上海复旦大学经济系,参加学生爱国运动。1926 年加入中国共产主义青年团,同年加入中国共产党。曾参加 1927 年上海工人第三次武装起义。1934 年任反帝反战大同盟宣传部长;同年被捕入狱。后经中共党组织营救出狱,从事革命文艺创作和翻译工作。出版有短篇小说集《英雄》及剧本集《喜酒》等;翻译过陀思妥耶夫斯基的长篇小说《被侮辱与被损害的》。重要论文有《论主观问题》等,显示了他对文艺现状和理论现状的独到而深刻的见解。

邵荃麟于1936年前后开始文学写作和翻译,早期作品有《糖》、《车站前》等。抗日战争爆发后,他参与中国共产党浙江省委文化领导小组工作,任中共东南文委书记;主编《东南战线》。1941年"皖南事变"后,转移到桂林工作,任中国共产党的文化工作组组长,主编《文化杂志》,创办《青年文艺》,积极扶持文艺新作,对青年作者做了大量的辅导工作。创作集有:短篇小说集《英雄》(1942)、《宿店》(1946),独幕剧集《喜酒》(1942)等,受到文学界的重视。抗战胜利后,先到武汉开展收复区文艺界统一战线工作,随后经上海去香港,担任中国共产党香港工作委员会文委委员、南方局文委书记等职务。主编《大众文艺丛刊》,并为《群众》(香港版)、《正报》、《华商报》等报刊撰写政论及文艺论文,宣传党的文艺方针政策,介绍解放区的文艺成就。由他执笔的《对于当前文艺运动的意见》、《论主观问题》,对当时国民党统治区文艺运动的发展产生过较大影响。这一时期,还译有《游击队员范思加》(1941)、《被侮辱与被损害的》(1943)、《意外的惊愕》(1943)、《阴影与曙光》(1946)等。

新中国成立后,邵荃麟曾任政务院文教委员会副秘书长、文教委员会党委委员、中共中央宣传部副秘书长等职务。1953年,任中国文学工作者协会(后改为中国作家协会)党组书记;同年被选为中国文学工作者协会副主席,主编《人民文学》。邵荃麟曾当选为一、二、三届全国人民代表大会代表。1962年7月,他在大连主持召开了"农村题材短篇小说创作座谈会",强调"现实主义深化",提倡人物形象多样化,除正反两类人物形象外,还应该写中间状态的人物。这对于克服农村题材小说创作的浮浅单调现象起了积极作用,但后来却因此受到公开批判,在"文化大革命"中遭到残酷迫害,于1971年6月含冤病死狱中。

1979年9月21日,为邵荃麟举行了追悼会,宣布恢复名誉,平反昭雪。1981年4月,人民文学出版社编辑出版了《邵荃麟评论选集》。

巴人

王任叔(1901—1972年),宁波奉化连山乡大堰村(今奉化市大堰镇)人。名运镗,字任叔,号愚庵,笔名巴人等。著有长篇小说《莽秀才造反记》,散文《邻人们》、《任生及其周围的一群》,专著《文学初步》,短篇小说集《监狱》、《在没落中》、《破屋》,文学剧本《费娜小姐》、《杨达这个人》,中篇小说《阿贵流浪记》、《证章》。

　　1941年3月奉命去香港,7月赴新加坡,执教南洋华侨师范,与胡愈之、郁达夫等领导文化界开展反法西斯斗争;12月,太平洋战争爆发,任星(新加坡)华战时工作团宣传部长。次年2月与雷德容等漂泊到印度尼西亚苏门答腊,辗转先达、棉兰等地。1943年,遭侵印尼日军通缉,隐居原始丛林中泗拉巴耶小村,以刀耕火种自活。1945年8月日本投降后,参加苏岛华侨民主同盟,主编《前进周刊》、印尼文《民主日报》,写成大型话剧《五祖庙》。1947年7月被荷兰军队逮捕,经组织营救获释,10月到香港。1948年8月奉命去河北省平山县,任中共中央统战部第三室综合研究组组长等职。翌年出席全国第一次文学艺术工作者代表大会、政治协商会议第一次全体会议。1950年任中华人民共和国驻印度尼西亚特命全权大使。1952年1月卸任回国,任外交部党组成员、政策研究委员会委员。1954年《文学论稿》问世;同年4月调任人民文学出版社副社长、总编辑,1957年任社长兼党委书记。

　　1959年康生点名批评巴人,指巴人和蒋介石是同乡,且巴人曾在国民党任职,从而导致巴人作为文学界的代表人物,与史学界的尚钺、经济学界的孙冶方一起受到严厉批判,撤销党内外一切职务。在被剥夺文学创作权利后,他转向史学研究,于1966年初完成160万字史学专著《印度尼西亚历史》的初稿。"文化大革命"中,巴人遭到批斗、隔离审查,1966年被抄家,受尽折磨。1968年开始,有大字报诬指巴人是郁达夫被害事件中"向日本人告密的叛徒",使得巴人遭到更严重的迫害,于1970年3月被遣返家乡,安置在村西头的两间旧茅屋里。严重的摧残使得他精神崩溃,1972年7月25日病逝,葬大堰村后山。

陈逸飞

　　陈逸飞(1946—2005年),生于宁波,著名油画家、文化实业家、导演。

　　1965年,陈逸飞毕业于上海美术专科学校(现上海大学美术学院),进入上海画院油画雕塑创作室,曾任油画组负责人。他于20世纪六七十年代创作了《黄河颂》、《占领总统府》、《踱步》和《周庄》等知名的优秀油画作品。

　　1980年,陈逸飞怀揣38美元赴美国留学。1984年获艺术硕士学位,后在纽约从事油画创作,专注于中国题材油画的研究与创作,水乡风景、音乐人物、古典仕女,还有西藏,都是他画笔下的主要题材,并在华盛顿、纽约、东京等地举办个人画展。他的作品多次参加香港和国内的油画精品拍卖会,屡创华人油画作品拍卖新纪录,其作品被中国美术馆、中国人民革命博物馆和国内外收藏家广泛收藏。1985年,美国石油大王哈默博士访华时,曾将陈逸飞的作品《家乡的回忆——双桥》作为礼物送给邓小平。

陈逸飞,无疑是20世纪中国油画百年史上值得记载的重要人物。夸张一些说,陈逸飞的成就和成功是一个神话。近年在亚洲艺术界、在中国社会掀起大波乃至狂飙的,是陈逸飞及其画作在艺术市场接二连三创下的新高:1991年,《浔阳遗韵》在香港佳士得以137.5万元港币成交,首创中国油画作品过百万元的纪录;1994年,西藏题材的《山地风》,在中国嘉德国际拍卖会上,以286万元人民币高价拍出,创华人油画作品最高拍卖价。

陈逸飞以"大美术"的理念,在电影、服饰、环境设计等诸多方面都取得了创造性成就,成为文化名流,是闻名海内外的华人艺术家。

2005年4月10日,由于长年辛勤工作,因胃出血在上海华山医院去世,英年早逝。

(四)院士

童第周

童第周(1902—1979年),鄞县(今宁波市鄞州区)塘溪镇人,是享誉海内外的卓越的生物学家、教育家、中共党员,曾担任过中国科学院副院长、动物研究所所长。1927年毕业于复旦大学哲学系,1927—1930年任国立第四中山大学(南京大学前身)自然科学院生物系助教,后长期在山东大学任教。1951年任山东大学副校长。他是卓越的实验胚胎学家,中国实验胚胎学的主要奠基人,20世纪生物科学研究的杰出领导者。1978年,在全国科学大会上,被授予全国科学技术先进工作者称号。

千百年来,人类渴望破解生物繁衍生息的遗传奥秘,历尽沧桑,艰辛探索。20世纪,世界科技领域在生命科学上取得了空前的辉煌。2000年,中、美、英等国科学家同时宣布,人类基因图工程全部完成。但早在 20 世纪 60 年代初，原中国科学院副院长、第五届全国政协副主席童第周就将人类对生物进化和细胞遗传与变异研究推进到了世界前列，开创了人类按照需要而人工培育新物种的历史先河，被誉为世界克隆第一人，在 20 世纪 90 年代即被列入世界 100 位最优秀的科学家之一。

贝时璋

贝时璋(1903—2009 年)，镇海县(今宁波市镇海区)人，实验生物学家，细胞生物学家，教育家。中国细胞学、胚胎学的创始人之一，中国生物物理学的奠基人。曾任浙江大学生物系主任、理学院院长。

贝时璋早年从事无脊椎动物实验胚胎学和细胞学的研究，对细胞数恒定动物与再生的关系作了深入的研究；20 世纪 30 年代初发现了中间性丰年虫，并观察到其雌雄生殖细胞的相互转化现象；70 年代提出了细胞重建学说。重视交叉学科，致力于中国生物物理学的发展，先后组织开拓了放射生物学、宇宙生物学、仿生学、生物工程技术、生物控制论等分支领域和相关技术，并培养出一批生物物理学骨干人才。贝时璋是民国时期第一届"中央研究院"院士和新中国成立后第一届中国科学院院士，曾任中国科学院生物物理研究所荣誉所长。他也是最后一位去世的第一届中央研究院院士。

由于贝时璋在科学上的突出成就，1948 年当选为"中央研究院"院士后，同年被邀任荷兰国际胚胎学研究所研究员，1949 年被选为荷兰国际胚胎学研究所委员，1955 年被聘为中国科学院生物学部委员。他曾多次以科学家或科学组织者身份出访苏联、英国、瑞典、加拿大、美国、法国、意大利、奥地利、捷克、匈牙利、尼泊尔、巴基斯坦、越南等国，尤其是 1972 年在中美关系解冻后，他率领中国科学家代表团，作为友好使者访问了美国。

贝时璋在近 70 年的科研及教学生涯中，为中国的科学事业作出了重大的贡献。

谈家桢

谈家桢(1909—2008 年)，浙江宁波人，国际著名遗传学家，中国现代遗传学奠基人之一，杰出的科学家和教育家。他为我国遗传学研究培养了大批优秀人才。曾任浙江大学理学院院长、复旦大学副校长。新中国成立后，他在复旦大学建立了中国第一个遗传学专业，创建了第一个遗传学研究所，组建了第一个生命科学学院，并担任中国特大型综合性辞典《大辞海》的副主编。

1978 年以来,先后发起和担任中国遗传学会副会长、会长和名誉会长,遗传学报主编,中国环境诱变剂学会理事长和中国生物工程学会会长。他在国际上享有崇高荣誉,曾任第八届国际遗传学大会常务理事,第十五届、十六届、十七届国际遗传学大会副会长,1996 年又当选为第十八届国际遗传学大会会长。自 1978 年以来,他先后当选为日本和英国遗传学会名誉会员,被美国罗斯福夫人肿瘤研究所聘为高级研究员,获美国加州理工学院杰出校友奖,德国康斯登茨大学功勋奖,美国加州政府荣誉公民称号,被联合国工业发展组织国际遗传工程和生物技术中心聘为科学顾问,被国际遗传学报、国际生物学与哲学杂志和美国《科学家》报等聘为顾问编辑。1984 年、1985 年分别被加拿大约克大学、美国马里兰大学授予荣誉科学博士。1995 年获求是科学基金会杰出科学家奖。1999 年,获国际正式批准,中科院紫金天文台发现的、国际编号为 3542 号的小行星命名为"谈家桢星"。

谈家桢 1980 年当选为中科院院士,1985 年当选为美国国家科学院外籍院士和第三世界科学院院士,1987 年当选为意大利国家科学院外籍院士,1999 年当选为纽约科学院名誉终身院士。

陈中伟

陈中伟(1929—2004 年),浙江宁波人,骨科与显微外科专家专家。1954 年毕业于上海第二医学院医疗系。毕业后在上海市第六人民医院工作,曾任该院骨科主任、副院长。复旦大学医学院中山医院外科教研室主任,骨科教授,博士生导师,中国科学院院士,第三世界科学院院士,中华医学会常务理事,国际显微重建外科学会创始会员,国际外科学会会员。12 个国际著名医学中心客座教授。

1963 年,陈中伟首创世界首例断手臂再植成功;1974 年,在北美手外科年会作"断肢再植"创始者报告;1978 年又获断指再植成功。国际上称他为"再植之父",在国际上首创了"断手再植和断指再植"等六项新技术。1996 年,他与上海交通大学合作,又首创"再造手指控制的电子假手"。由于他在断肢再植与显微外科领域的突出贡献,1963 年获中央卫生部记大功一次,1981 年获国务院颁发国家科学大会奖,1994 年被求是基金会和国务院授予杰出科学家奖,1999 年获国际显微重建外科学会颁发的"千年奖"。专著有《显微外科》、《创伤骨科与断肢再植》等 10 种,发表各种论文 130 篇,其中 33 篇发表在国外医学杂志上。

李庆逵

李庆逵(1912—2001 年),浙江宁波人,著名土壤学家、农业化学家。九三学社社员。中国科学院学部委员(院士),中国土壤植物营养化学的奠基人之一。

李庆逵主要从事土壤—植物营养和施肥的基本性质、发生分类及利用研究。1937 年发表的《土壤分析法》和1953 年以后多次再版的《土壤分析法》,在我国土壤分析工作中发挥了重要作用。20 世纪 50 年代初,我国迫切需要发展生产,他接受国家任务,带领科技人员参加橡胶科研考察,提出选择北回归线以南种植的土壤学依据,通过对橡胶树生长气候、土壤条件和有效施肥的研究,将栽培线推广到北纬 18—24 度,为世界上热带北缘种植橡胶树提供了样板。1981 年,我国干胶产量达 12.5 万吨,居世界第六位。这项成果于 1982 年获国家发明一等奖。20 世纪 70 年代初,他提出碳酸氢铵深施技术,为氮肥的合理施用和提高氮素利用率做出了贡献。1978 年,获全国科技大会奖。

他系统地研究了中国土壤中磷、钾元素的状况和磷、钾肥施用效应,并主持编制了中国第一幅土壤磷素分布图,为中国磷钾化学肥料的发展和施用提供了依据。其中,有关磷矿粉的有效条件和合理施肥技术,生产上进行了大面积推广,最高年份推广面积达 1000多万吨,取得了显著的社会效益和经济效益。他所主编的《中国磷矿的农业利用》专著对中国磷矿资源的合理利用、发展磷肥品种的技术和合理施用磷肥都有参考价值。1990年,获国家科技进步三等奖。在多年研究红壤的基础上,他主编了《中国红壤》一书,对中国红壤的生成发育、基本特性、开发利用和改良措施进行了系统论述,积累了完整资料,在生产上发挥了积极作用。1987 年,获国家自然科学三等奖。

1959—1980 年间,李庆逵三次当选为江苏省劳动模范。他曾担任《中国科学》、《科学通报》、《土壤学报》、《土壤学进展》、《农业现代化研究》等全国性刊物编委和国际《肥料研究》杂志编委。他先后主编了《中国红壤》、《中国土壤》、《中国磷矿农业利用》、《中国水稻土》等专著,刊出论文 90 余篇。享受国务院政府特殊津贴。

李庆逵一直关心爱国统一战线事业。1953 年,他加入了九三学社,数十年来积极参加九三学社的工作,为九三学社的建设和发展作出了重要贡献。在担任人大代表期间,密切联系人大代表和人民群众,以高度的责任心,依法履行职责,积极参与地方性法规的制定工作,宣传我国的民主与法制,并深入实际,视察调研,了解民情,广泛倾听群众的意见,提出了许多很好的意见和建议,为推进依法治省、推进教科文卫事业的发展,作出了积极的贡献。

翁文波

翁文波(1912—1994 年),鄞县(今宁波市鄞州区)西乡石塘人。1934 年清华大学物理系毕业,两年后又赴英国伦敦帝国学院攻读地球物理学,1939 年获博士学位。正值抗战时期,他毅然转道法国、越南回国,投身中国石油地球物理勘探研究,培养了一批人才,取得了一系列成果。

新中国成立后,翁文波不但创立了我国的地球物理勘探、地球化学理论,而且积极参加我国石油天然气的勘探实践,为我国的石油工业,以及石油工业的人才培养,作出了突出的贡献。特别是 20 世纪 50 年代末、60 年代初,为发现大庆油田作出重大贡献,获得"石油工业杰出科学家"称号。1966 年,邢台发生地震后,他受周恩来总理重托,开始致力于天然地震的预测研究,后来又将其扩展到洪涝、干旱等灾害远期预测,在预测理论和实践上取得了重大突破,独创了自己的信息预测科学基础。据统计,他先后作过 252 次各类天灾的预测,实际发生的有 211 次,占总次数的 83.73%,标志着我国预测科学已处于世界前沿,被人们誉为"天灾预测宗师"。

翁文波曾任中国石油天然气总公司石油勘探开发科学研究所总工程师、中国地球物理学会理事长和名誉理事长、中国石油学会副理事长、中国地震学会名誉理事、中国科学技术协会委员、国家天灾预测专业委员会主任等职。他的著作有《中国石油资源》、《预测论基础》等多部。1980 年,翁文波当选为中国科学院学部委员。他是第三届全国人大代表,第五、六、七届全国政协委员。

四、文化习俗

（一）宁波戏曲

甬剧

宁波甬剧是用宁波地区方言演唱的戏曲剧种,属于花鼓滩簧声腔。它最早在宁波及附近地区演唱,当时称"串客"。始于清乾隆末期(1790—1795 年),1880 年"串客班"到上海演出后又称"宁波滩簧",1924 年"宁波滩簧"在上海遭禁演后称"四明之戏",1938 年上演时装大戏后又称"改良甬剧",直到 1950 年,这一剧种才正式定名为"甬剧"。

甬剧音乐曲调丰富,共计约有 90 种。主要有从农村田头山歌、对山歌演化而来的"基本调",从宁波乱弹班中带来的"月调""三五七""快二簧""慢二簧"及四明南词和一些地方小调。甬剧基本调(也称老调)主要用于塑造人物,表现人物较复杂的思想表情,叙述故事情节;小调则用来作为情节和片段之间的穿插。

1949 年之前,在上海、宁波等地有较多的甬剧表演团体,当时著名的甬剧艺人有贺显民、徐凤仙、金翠香、金玉兰、黄君卿等。新中国成立后,上海成立堇风甬剧团,宁波成立宁波市甬剧团。上海堇风甬剧团以改编整理传统剧目为主,如《半把剪刀》《天要落雨娘要嫁》《双玉蝉》《借妻》等。宁波市甬剧团以编演反映现代生活为主,如《两兄弟》《亮眼哥》《红岩》等,同时也整理了如《田螺姑娘》等一批传统戏。

甬剧适宜于演清装戏、20 世纪 30 年代西装旗袍戏,特别擅长于演现代戏,因此受到党和各级政府的重视和广大观众的欢迎。新中国成立后,宁波、上海两地甬剧团演出的区域主要集中在宁波、上海、舟山等地。其中上海堇风甬剧团曾在 1962 年晋京演出,宁波市甬剧团在 1990 年和 1995 年两次赴京演出,均产生过较大影响。目前甬剧专业表演团体仅存宁波市甬剧团一家。2008 年 6 月 14 日,甬剧被列入第二批国家级非物质文化遗产代表保护名录。

宁波甬剧团于 2000 年后并入宁波艺术剧院,为宁波艺术剧院甬剧团,由著名甬剧演员王锦文担任团长。新创作剧目《典妻》《秋海棠》《贵妇还乡》等戏在业内获得不同凡响的效果。王锦文获第七届上海白玉兰奖和第二十届中国戏剧梅花奖。

宁海平调

宁海平调,是中国古老的地方戏曲剧种之一。起源于明末,盛行于清朝,已有三四百年历史,主要流行于宁海、象山、三门一带。系属浙江高腔之支派,因以宁海方言演唱,且唱腔"平缓",故称为"宁海平调"。"耍牙"是平调中的绝艺,堪与川剧"变脸"相媲美,粗犷中不失细腻,野性中凸显灵动。传统剧目有100多种,其中以《前十八》、《后十八》最为著名。

它的唱腔具有声调高亢而婉约,一唱众帮,锣鼓助节,不托管弦的特点;其帮腔有混帮、清帮、全句帮、片断帮、一字帮等多种形式;其语音,除小丑用苏白外,基本用宁海方言、故县人又称之为"本地班"。主要流行于宁海、象山、黄岩、温岭、临海、仙居、天台、奉化等地,也到宁波、舟山、杭嘉湖以及上海一带作过短期演出。

自晚清起,不少艺人来自宁波的甬昆班(既唱昆曲又唱调腔的班社),它是明末清初浙东流行的一支调腔。清中叶后,受昆曲影响,自成一家。"平调"这一称谓,显然受调腔、昆曲、曲牌的影响,又受县域的地理环境和独特的邑人个性诸因素而产生。

宁海平调在辛亥革命后一度盛行,1932年起趋向衰落,至民国后期,几已湮没。1956年,三门县有关部门把流散在宁海的十余名平调艺人组织起来,成立半专业性的演出队。该队于1957年赴杭州演出传统剧目《金莲斩蛟》(《小金钱》的一折),受到好评。1960年初,正式成立宁海县平调剧团,并着手发掘、整理一批传统剧目和现代戏。1966 年后剧团解散,1978 年恢复建制。1982 年,宁海县成立平调整理研究小组,系统地对这一剧种进行艺术改革和剧目整理。1999 年 10 月,参加文化部在湖南长沙举办的"映山红"全国戏曲会演,荣获表演、导演等 11 项大奖。2004 年 7 月,宁海平调《银瓶仙露》又应邀赴杭州参加中国第七届艺术节展演,受到了好评。如今在先进文化前进方向的指引下,国家非常重视非物质文化遗产的保护,2006 年 5 月 20 日,宁海平调经国务院批准列入第一批国家级非物质文化遗产名录。

姚剧

姚剧原名"余姚滩簧",是主要流行于浙江余姚、慈溪、上虞的一种汉族地方戏曲剧种。1950 年后定名为姚剧。姚剧是在当地汉族民间歌舞曲艺"马灯""旱船""采茶篮""崔冬冬"等的基础上发展起来的,因此在余姚一带,姚剧又被称作"灯戏""灯班"。

姚滩的唱腔淳朴优美,节奏明快,由基本调和小调两部分构成。基本调常用的是"平四"和"紧板"。曲体为"起、平、落"形式,平腔只用清板演唱,男女同调异腔,转换自然,女调的"平四"下韵,常衬有"嗳嗳唷"的衬音,清亮委婉,富有特色。"平四"一般用于叙述性唱词,较抒情,可以表达不同的感情;"紧板"多用于剧情紧张、气氛热烈的场面。另一类是小调,共有 40 余首,或为江南民歌,或为明清俚曲,常用的有《夜夜游》《小扳艄》《紫竹调》《对花十送》《五更调》等,音色醇厚,节奏轻快,雅俗共赏,并富有乡土气息。

　　姚滩艺人多数是农民与手工业者,如漆匠、篾匠、泥水匠、棕棚匠等,闲季组班。姚滩道具也十分简单,一块手帕,一把扇子便可粉墨登场。正因为其十分简便,人数又少,所以很适合在农村演出。但是,由于当时对这一剧种的偏见和滩簧班在演出过程中常夹杂一些不很文明的念白,滩簧班是不准在祠堂内或神庙内演出的,只能在野外倒置几只稻桶,上面铺些木板作为演出场地。

　　新中国成立后,部分艺人对姚滩的内容和演出形式进行了改革,如排演现代剧目,实行男女合演,等等。在党和政府的关心下,于1954年成立了姚剧团。余姚和慈溪西北地区、上虞东部一带,广大农村中的业余姚剧团也如雨后春笋蓬勃发展,据不完全统计,在20世纪五六十年代,业余姚剧团曾有150多个,足见这一地方剧种生命力之强和群众基础之深。2008年6月14日,姚剧被列入第二批国家级非物质文化遗产名录(传统戏剧类)。

(二)宁波曲艺

四明南词

　　四明南词曾称"宁波文书",也叫"四明文书",是浙江省汉族地方曲艺的一种,用宁波方言说唱的弹词。四明南词迄今已有三百余年历史,主要流传于浙东一带。原为文人的业余演唱,清末出现专业艺人。早期为按生、旦、净、末等分角色演唱,后发展为一人自弹三弦演唱,一人打扬琴伴奏,也有二三人加用琵琶、二胡等伴奏的。唱词为七字句。传统书目均为长篇,有《珍珠塔》《玉蜻蜓》《双剪发》等三十余部。四明南词系宋代的陶真、明代的弹词衍变而成的浙江曲种,流传至宁波城区和郊县。清末至民国初期为鼎盛期,20世纪40年代开始衰落。现已濒临失传。

总的来说,四明南词可概括为一个"文"字。它的唱词典雅,当是经过文人再创作而成。有些言情的内容,也写得辞藻雅丽含蓄,曲调优雅,深受士大夫们喜爱,故多在寿诞、喜庆堂会上演唱。它分双档、三、五、七、十一和十三不等,唱、奏、念、白、表相间,灵活多变。主要乐器有箫、笙、扬琴、二胡、琵琶、小三弦等。演奏时演员根据乐器特色,围绕主旋律,自由发挥,音乐清丽优雅,委婉动听。

1958年,原宁波曲艺团曾建立四明南词演出队,后因"文革"而夭折。20世纪80年代有著名老艺人作展览性演出。2000年,曾由宁波市群众艺术馆组织经过改革的开篇形式演出(为业余组合,演唱形式已改变)。四明南词的唱词讲究平仄格律,曲调有"上中下韵"之分,"赋调""词调"为基本曲调,其唱腔对甬剧和宁波走书有较大的影响。

2008年6月14日,四明南词被列入第二批国家级非物质文化遗产代表保护名录。

宁波评话

宁波评话,在宁波民间称为武书,以示与"四明文书(南词)"区别。宁波评话是浙江宁波的汉族说唱艺术形式。除正式专业评话艺人之外,也有南词和走书艺人中兼讲评话的,艺人中称为"单拍"。相传宁波评话在宋、元时期已很活跃,当时民舍(书棚)里"讲史""小说"十分普遍。主要流行于市区各茶楼(书场)及鄞县、慈溪等县城。

说书时,艺人仅凭一块惊木、一把折扇、一张嘴,不配音乐、不伴奏,一个人分口饰演几个至十余个角色,要把生旦净末丑,三教九流,书中人物的形态、个性、口吻描述得神态毕现,惟妙惟肖。说书的"单凭一张嘴,要靠真功夫",手中的一把折扇,既可比作刀枪,又可拟做笔纸;一块醒木既要用作静场,又可作衬托书中情节气氛之用。传统书目有《水浒》、《三国》、《岳飞传》等。

宁波评话主要演唱场所是城区集镇的茶楼和书场,流行面遍及浙东沿海各县(市)、区。清道光年间,宁波城区有评话艺人演唱的茶楼就达数十处。民国时期仍很兴旺,著名的评话艺人有张霭林、闻才章等人。尤以张霭林、张一册、张少策祖孙三人讲的《水浒》,经过几代人的改进、充实,内容丰富,与众不同,有独到之处,在江浙一带颇享盛誉。

宁波走书

宁波走书原称"莲花文书",又称"犁铧文书",是浙江宁波的汉族地方戏曲之一,以宁波方言演唱,1956年定名宁波走书。形成于清光绪年间(1875—1908年)的余姚农村,大约在清末流传入宁波城区,继又向镇海、舟山地区拓展。20世纪五六十年代演唱区域甚广,除宁波、舟山地区外,还演唱于台州地区的临海、天台、黄岩和杭州等地,至90年代初开始衰落。

据艺人传,宁波走书最早从上虞流入。当时,曾有佃工在农作中你唱我和,自我娱乐,借以消除疲劳。后由唱小曲发展到唱有故事情节的片段,当时伴奏只用一副竹板和一只毛竹根头敲打节拍,曲调也十分简单。光绪年间,这种演唱形式已流行于余姚农村。后余姚有农闲时从事曲艺演唱的农民、小贩和手工业者成立"杭余社",交流演唱经验,研究曲艺书目。其中有位许生传老先生,吸收绍兴莲花落的曲调,率先采用月琴伴奏,自弹自唱,很受群众欢迎。在其影响下,许多艺人也都采用各种乐器伴奏,并从四明南词、宁波滩簧、地方小调中引进不少曲调,加以改造应用。同时,书目方面也有发展,出现了《四香缘》、《玉连环》等一些长篇,演唱活动范围逐渐扩大到宁、舟、台地区。宁波走书表演开始为一人自拉自唱的"坐唱",后出现简单伴奏的形式,演员坐于桌后,乐队坐于桌子两旁。演员因于桌后表演,动作幅度较小,故称"里走书"。再后,演员与乐队相对各坐一旁,演员在台上有较大空间作表演圈,称为"外走书"。其时鄞西谢宝初的表演,城里段德生的唱腔,慈北毛全福的武功,各有千秋,名噪一时,在群众中很有影响。

因其表演者在说唱时走动表演,与坐唱的"四明南词"不同,故称"走书"。走书演员能"一人唱出一台戏",唱词多用生动形象的群众词汇,通俗易懂。伴奏人员可多可少,曲调丰富,既善抒情,又长于叙事。传统书目有《百鹤图》《黄金印》等。

2008 年 6 月 14 日,宁波走书被列入第二批国家级非物质文化遗产代表保护名录。

蛟川走书

蛟川走书是浙江宁波最具乡土气息、风格独具的汉族曲艺曲种,发源于清光绪(1875—1908 年)年间的镇海,主要流行于镇海、舟山、鄞州等地。追溯渊源,据蛟川走书老艺人口传,约光绪年间,一个住在镇海县城小南门名叫谢阿树(又名谢元鸿)的蛟川走书艺人,因所住小南门拱形城墙上刻着"蛟川"二字,遂以此为名,称"蛟川走书"。艺人们都认为他是"蛟川走书"的创始人。谢阿树的师承关系,已无案可稽。

早期蛟川走书仅一人演唱,没有乐器伴奏,也无后场和唱,艺人只用两只酒盅,一根竹筷,有节奏地敲打,自唱自和。抗日战争前夕,逐渐演变成以一唱一和的形式,在庙宇、祠堂或晒场地用木板搭成一个小平台,演唱者开始用静木、纸扇、手帕等作小道具,伴奏也改用竹板、竹鼓打出有板有眼的节奏,并在落调时用清口唱和"哎哎哩啊……"的基本调。

抗战胜利前夕,开始使用二胡、扬琴等乐器进行伴奏。新中国成立后,发展到多档形式,有时还增加琵琶、三弦、箫、笛等多种乐器伴奏。其和音跌宕悠扬,表演生动,曲调有30余种。

蛟川走书的传统书目有《东汉》、《西汉》等。2006年6月,被列入宁波市首批非物质文化遗产代表保护名录。

小热昏

小热昏是广泛流行于江浙沪一带的汉族吴语曲艺谐谑形式,又名"小锣书",俗称"卖梨膏糖的",是一种植根于民间的马路说唱艺术。始于清末民初,20世纪20年代传入平湖。"小热昏"本意是一个人因发高烧热昏了头而胡言乱语,以该词汇命名的曲艺则是"满嘴荒唐话"的说唱艺术。由于"小热昏"的演唱内容大多取材于社会新闻,最了解劳苦大众的疾苦,艺人要为百姓代言,以泄露胸中之闷,以讽刺的手法揭露社会的阴暗面,所以深受大众喜欢。但为了避免被当时的反动当局所迫害,故把这一说唱内容和形式化成"贾雨村言”,"满嘴荒唐话"的说唱艺术。

小热昏用地道的杭州方言演唱,一般以小锣或三巧板伴奏,常用曲调有"锣先锋""三巧赋""东乡调"以及"五更""四季""十叹"等流行小调。

小热昏的演出时间没有限制,东边唱了一二小时,见群众不散,继续唱下去。如果人群稀少,就换到西边再开始演唱。演唱也没有固定场所,一般在闹市街头或船埠、车站、菜场附近,以及农村中庙会、集市之中。演唱前选择一块空地,用白粉洒划一个表演圈,打竹板、敲锣鼓,吸引听众,等人群聚集,便开始演唱。

小热昏由于言语发噱,唱句通俗,很受群众欢迎。名艺人有陈长生(艺名小得利),后有陈国安、徐和其、俞笑飞等。20世纪50年代后,小热昏艺人多半成为滑稽评弹演员,与今天活跃在上海舞台的"轻松艺术"——独脚戏、滑稽戏颇有渊源。

"杭州小热昏"是浙江省首批民族民间艺术保护曲种。2006年5月20日,"杭州小热昏"经国务院批准列入首批国家级非物质文化遗产名录。

唱新闻

唱新闻,又称"新闻",是浙东地区流行的一个汉族地方曲艺剧种,主要流行于北仑、奉化和象山等地。演唱者皆为盲女瞽男。唱新闻的历史悠久,距今约有百余年历史。再往上,则可以追溯至南宋时期盲人的唱"朝报"(官方新闻),后来逐渐演变为唱社会新闻。

20世纪50年代,镇海区从事唱新闻的艺人约有四五十人,多为盲人。其中,较为著名的说唱艺人有严梅方、顾阿火等人。新闻的内容多是当地街头巷尾流传的古今故事和流行小调,用乡音俚语进行演唱。艺人在演唱时,右手挟一根鼓杆及打锣木片,左手提一面小锣,两膝膝盖上按着一只小鼓,边唱边用鼓槌或锣片有节奏地叩打鼓壳或小锣。艺人往往走街串巷,选择谷场、庭院、码头、航船等处,或一人演唱,或二人对唱,曲调达几十种。

1949年之前,唱新闻是很低贱的职业,盲艺人要走街串巷、连村越户去演唱。其演唱形式有:唱门头,即沿门唱几个小曲,类似乞讨;逻便场,在民众天井、明堂之中,唱一段或一场,兜几个钱;唱航船,这在水网地带较为流行,在日夜航船里卖唱;唱灯头,逢到庙会、集市进行演唱;唱场子,这是能唱大书、相对水平较高的民间艺人,进书场演唱,但为数不多。

唱新闻多是一人进行演唱,也有两人对唱的。其伴奏的乐器有鼓、小锣,也有用竹板敲打的。新闻书目可分两类:一种是小书目,也叫开场书,如《光棍调》《打养生》《游码头》等,也有用小调唱社会新闻的。另一种是大书目,也叫当家书,有《三县并审》《拆鸳鸯》《钉鞋记》等。

2006年,唱新闻被列入首批宁波市非物质文化遗产代表保护名录。2011年,被列入第三批国家级非物质文化遗产名录。

（三）节令民俗

春节

农历正月初一为春节，也是农历新年，是民间最重要的节日。宁波习俗，这一天要清晨起床，大人小孩都换上新衣，带新帽，穿新鞋，表示"辞旧迎新"，然后由男子开门，在院子里燃放三个炮仗，称为"开门炮"，放得越高，声音越大，表示新的一年越吉利。然后在厅堂里具香烛、果饵，挂祖宗像，祭拜天地和祖先。有家祠的还要到祠堂去祭祖。家人相见时，小辈向长辈拜年，称为拜岁，平辈或亲朋邻里相见互相拱手，并互祝"恭喜恭喜"或"新年发财"。早餐，合家吃猪油汤团，表示甜甜蜜蜜，团团圆圆，有的地方还喝红枣汤和桂圆汤，表示早日红火、富贵团圆。早餐后，给长辈敬用青果、金柑泡的茶，称为元宝茶。这一天，不出门拜客，在家庭中也不汲水、不扫地、不动刀剪、不点灯，晚饭后就上床睡觉，称为太平夜。正月初二开始，亲戚朋友之间相互走访拜年或互相请吃饭欢聚，馈赠酒、蛋糕、滋补品等礼物。家中则用高脚盆摆上瓜子、花生、糖果、水果等以招待来客。

春节最热闹的是观看或参与各种文化娱乐活动。在农村，如打正月锣鼓、舞龙舞狮、跑马灯、放各种花炮；在城市，街头、公园有各种杂耍表演和供应应时糕点、商品，戏院、电影院都上演新剧目、放映新影片，并加演日场，有的戏院还在开演前加演《跳加官》《迎财神》等小戏，祝贺节日。一些马灯班子也临时组织起来，挨家挨户跑马灯，唱马灯调，换取

主人一些实物或赏金。还有一些无业游民,头上扎彩,手持扎有彩带的扫把,每到一户,就往里作扫地状,称为"佯扫地",边扫边唱,唱词中都是一些吉利话,由此博得主人的好感,可以得到年糕和若干金钱的酬赏。

正月初五以后,商店开业,职员上班,春节就算过去了。

元宵节

元宵节是中国的传统节日,早在2000多年前的秦朝就有了。据资料与民俗传说,正月十五在西汉已经受到重视,汉武帝正月上辛夜在甘泉宫祭祀"太一"的活动,(太一:主宰宇宙一切的神),被后人视作正月十五祭祀天神的先声。

元宵,原意为"上元节的晚上",因正月十五"上元节"主要活动是晚上的吃汤圆赏月,后来节日名称演化为"元宵节"。元宵之夜,大街小巷张灯结彩,人们赏灯,猜灯谜,吃元宵,将从除夕开始延续的庆祝活动推向又一个高潮,成为世代相沿的习俗。元宵在早期节庆形成过程之时,只称正月十五日、正月半或月望,隋以后称元夕或元夜。唐初受了道教的影响,又称上元,唐末才偶称元宵。但自宋以后也称灯夕。到了清朝,就另称灯节。

传说元宵节是汉文帝时为纪念"平吕"而设。汉高祖刘邦死后,吕后之子刘盈登基为汉惠帝。惠帝生性懦弱,优柔寡断,大权渐渐落在吕后手中。汉惠帝病死后,吕后独揽朝政,把刘氏天下变成了吕氏天下,朝中老臣、刘氏宗室深感愤慨,但都惧怕吕后残暴而敢怒不敢言。

吕后病死后,诸吕惶惶不安,害怕遭到伤害和排挤。于是,在上将军吕禄家中秘密集合,共谋作乱之事,以便彻底夺取刘氏江山。此事传至刘氏宗室齐王刘襄耳中,刘襄为保刘氏江山,决定起兵讨伐诸吕,随后与开国老臣周勃、陈平取得联系,设计翦除了吕禄,"诸吕之乱"终于被彻底平定。平乱之后,众臣拥立刘邦的第二个儿子刘恒登基,称汉文帝。

文帝深感太平盛世来之不易,便把平息"诸吕之乱"的正月十五定为与民同乐日,京城里家家张灯结彩,以示庆祝。从此,正月十五便成了一个普天同庆的民间节日——"闹元宵"。

元宵节的节期与节俗活动,是随历史的发展而延长、扩展的。就节期长短而言,汉代才一天,到唐代已为三天,宋代则长达五天。明代更是自初八点灯,一直到正月十七的夜里才落灯,是中国历史上最长的灯节,白昼为市,热闹非凡,夜间燃灯,蔚为壮观。特别是那精巧、多彩的灯火,更使其成为春节期间娱乐活动的高潮。至清代,又增加了舞龙、舞狮、跑旱船、踩高跷、扭秧歌等"百戏"内容,只是节期缩短为四到五天。

清明

农历三月初为清明节,按照习俗,家家户户都要准备青团、黑饭和各种菜肴为亲人扫墓,以示纪念。扫墓时要在墓前焚香上供,跪拜叩头,并燃放鞭炮,给坟头培土。一些富有人家还要以鼓乐前导,祭仪十分隆重。寓居外地的死者亲属,也必于清明前返乡,参与祭祀。清明节又正是严冬已过、春回大地的季节,人们又往往在这一天郊游踏青。因此在去郊外扫墓时,常常是举家出动,祭扫完毕后,即以所带供品在坟头或就近草地上野餐,儿童还折柳枝插于头上,即俗谚所说"清明戴杨柳,下世有娘舅"。回来时还要折几枝野杜鹃,俗称"柴白浆花",回家插在案头上。不到郊外扫墓的男女老幼,也往往在此日结伴去城区名胜处游乐,如月湖一带,清明之日,红男绿女,熙熙攘攘,终日不绝。

中国汉族传统的清明节大约始于周代,距今已有两千五百多年的历史。受汉族文化的影响,中国的满族、赫哲族、壮族、鄂伦春族、侗族、土家族、苗族、瑶族、黎族、水族、京族、羌族等 24 个少数民族,也都有过清明节的习俗。扫墓祭祖、踏青郊游也是基本主题。

清明最早只是一种节气的名称,其变成纪念祖先的节日与寒食节有关。晋文公把寒食节的后一天定为清明节。在山西大部分地区,是在清明节前一天过寒食节;榆社县等地是在清明节前两天过寒食节;垣曲县还讲究清明节前一天为寒食节,前二天为小寒食。

还有一种传说,清明节始于古代帝王将相"墓祭"之礼,后来民间亦相仿效,于此日祭祖扫墓,历代沿袭而成为中华民族一种固定的风俗。

2006年5月20日,清明节被国务院批准列入第一批国家级非物质文化遗产名录

立夏

立夏是二十四节气中的第七个节气,更是阳历辰月的结束以及巳月的起始;时间点在公历5月5—6日之间,太阳到达黄经45度时。立夏在农历上的日期并不固定,为每年四月初一前后,此因农历是阴阳历。"斗指东南,维为立夏,万物至此皆长大,故名立夏也。"

在天文学上,立夏表示即将告别春天,是夏天的开始。人们习惯上都把立夏当作是温度明显升高,炎暑将临,雷雨增多,农作物进入旺季生长的一个重要节气。

立夏在公元前239年就已经确立了,预示着季节的转换,为一年四季之夏季开始的日子。

实际上,若按气候学的标准,日平均气温稳定升达22℃以上为夏季开始,"立夏"前后,我国只有福州到南岭一线以南地区是真正的"绿树浓阴夏日长,楼台倒影入池塘"的夏季,而东北和西北的部分地区这时则刚刚进入春季,全国大部分地区平均气温在18~20℃上下,正是"百般红紫斗芳菲"的仲春和暮春季节。进入了五月,很多地方槐花也正开。立夏时节,万物繁茂。

宁波习俗,立夏家家户户以红茶煮蛋,称为茶叶蛋或立夏蛋,并以倭豆、糯米煮饭、乌笋(脚骨笋)、君踏(软菜)为菜,说是吃了皮肤光滑、脚骨轻健,含有强身祛病之意。在立夏

节最有趣的是拄蛋和称人。作家长的在立夏之前,先用五色丝绒结成蛋套,放入茶叶蛋,让孩子们挂在胸前。孩子们则手持茶叶蛋,以一头相互挤压,蛋壳保持不碎者为胜,称为"拄蛋"。有的蛋壳坚硬者,可接连拄碎别人好几个蛋,以此为乐。有些成人觉得有趣,也常常参与这种游戏。立夏还要称人,旧时用一只大箩筐,人蹲在里面,由两人用一杆大秤逐个称出重量。这一习俗目前在农村仍保持,城区则因电子秤、磅秤的普遍使用,已逐步改变了。

端午

农历五月初五为端午节,也称端阳节。这天家家户户都用箬壳包糯米煮成粽子,一般有白粽和豇豆粽两种,也有包肉粽和豆沙粽的。又因端午正值春夏之交,气候温暖潮湿,百虫滋生,疾病容易流行,宁波习俗中也有不少和祛病消灾有关,如挂菖蒲剑,插艾旗,并用艾叶、苍术、白芷等在正午焚烧,称为"熏蚊烟",以求辟邪驱虫。还要喝雄黄酒,用雄黄在孩童额上写"王"字或涂抹身上,防止病虫侵害。有的还佩避毒钱,其形如普通铜钱,正面铸有"五月初五"字样,反面则为蛇、蝎、蜈蚣、壁虎、蜘蛛等"五毒"图形,佩之可以诸毒不侵。此外,端午最有意思的是画端午老虎和做香袋。端午老虎是由大人自描或从店铺里购买一张上面画有一个胖乎乎的小孩骑在老虎背上的图,并让孩子涂上颜色,称为"描端午老虎",然后张贴在床壁上或门上,用以驱邪保平安。香袋是用五色丝线和各种绸缎零料制作,内储絮砂、香料、棉花等,制成后可以挂在床上,或儿童脖子上,成人也有系在腰带上的。香袋可按需要和爱好,自行设计制作,有球形、菱形、星型、六角形、鸡心形等几何图形,也有十二生肖等动物图形,或色彩斑斓,或憨态可掬,既是令人爱不释手的精美工艺

品,又可作为端午节的礼品赠送给亲戚朋友。

　　赛龙舟也是在端午节举行的一项季节性民间传统文艺活动,和吃粽子一样,都是为了纪念楚国爱国诗人屈原而流传下来的习俗。宁波的赛龙舟活动以往都在湖西河和各乡间的河道上进行。龙舟一般分为青、白、黄等色,船边绘出片片鳞甲,前后安装龙头、龙尾。划船赛手身穿与龙舟同色服饰,分坐船舷两旁。比赛时,舟首有锣鼓,由一人站立呼喊指挥,号令一响,锣鼓齐鸣,划船赛手随着锣鼓节奏奋力划桨,岸上观众呐喊助威,情景热烈壮观,以先抵达者为优胜,可获赏酒数坛,并当场开封喝酒,以示庆贺。

七夕

　　七夕节,又名乞巧节、七巧节或七姐诞,发源于中国,是华人地区以及部分受汉族文化影响的东亚国家传统节日。农历七月七日夜或七月六日夜,妇女在庭院向织女星乞求智巧,故称为“乞巧”。其起源于对自然的崇拜及妇女穿针乞巧,后被赋予了牛郎织女的传说使其成为象征爱情的节日。

　　在我国,农历七月初七的夜晚,天气温暖,草木飘香,这就是人们俗称的七夕节,也有人称之为“乞巧节”或“女儿节”,这是中国传统节日中最具浪漫色彩的一个节日,也是过去姑娘们最为重视的日子。在晴朗的夏秋之夜,天上繁星闪耀,一道白茫茫的银河横贯南北,在银河的东西两岸,各有一颗闪亮的星星,隔河相望,遥遥相对,那就是牵牛星和织女星。

　　七夕坐看牵牛织女星,是民间的习俗,相传在每年的这个夜晚,是天上织女与牛郎在鹊桥相会之时。织女是一个美丽聪明、心灵手巧的仙女,凡间的妇女便在这一天晚上向她乞求智慧和巧艺,也少不了向她求赐美满姻缘。传说在七夕的夜晚,抬头可以看到牛郎织女的银河相会,或在瓜果架下可偷听到两人在天上相会时的脉脉情话。女孩们在这个充

满浪漫气息的晚上,对着天空的朗朗明月,摆上时令瓜果,朝天祭拜,乞求天上的女神能赋予她们聪慧的心灵和灵巧的双手,让自己的针织女红技法娴熟,更乞求爱情婚姻的姻缘巧配。过去婚姻对于女性来说是决定一生幸福与否的终身大事,所以,世间无数的有情男女都会在这个晚上,夜深人静时刻,对着星空祈祷自己的姻缘美满。因此,七夕节又被称为"中国情人节"。

2006 年 5 月 20 日,七夕节被列入第一批国家非物质文化遗产名录。

中元节

中元节俗称鬼节、七月半,佛教称为盂兰盆节,是中国民间传统节日。时在农历七月十五日,也有在七月十四日的。这天,家家祭祀祖先,有些还要举行家宴,供奉时行礼如仪。酹酒三巡,表示祖先宴毕,合家再团坐,共进节日晚餐。断黑之后,携带炮竹、纸钱、香烛,找一块僻静的河畔或塘边平地,用石灰撒一圆圈,表示禁区。再在圈内泼些水饭,烧些纸钱,鸣放鞭炮,恭送祖先上路,回转"阴曹地府"。过去,民间在七月初七就要通过一定仪式接先人鬼魂回家,每日晨、午、昏,供 3 次茶饭,直到七月十五日送回为止。现在,逐渐剔除迷信色彩,只保留祭奠形式,作为对祖先的缅怀和纪念。

七月原是小秋,有若干农作物成熟,民间按例要祀祖,用新米等祭供,向祖先报告秋成。东汉时道教定下三元、三会、五腊日。三元是天、地、水神的诞辰,三会是道民到治所接受三位神仙的考校,五腊日的主要内容是祭祀先祖。其中七月七日为道德腊,又是中会日,即固定的道民到治所接受考校的日子,而七月十五日还是中元日。这样,七月十五日就演变成为一个重要的祭祖日期。

中秋节

中秋节又称月夕、秋节、仲秋节、八月节、八月会、追月节、玩月节、拜月节、女儿节或团圆节,是流行于中国众多民族与东亚诸国中的传统文化节日,时在农历八月十五;因其恰值三秋之半,故名。也有些地方将中秋节定在八月十六。

中秋节始于唐朝初年,盛行于宋朝,至明清时,已与元旦齐名而成为中国的主要节日之一。受中华文化的影响,中秋节也是东亚和东南亚一些国家尤其是当地的华人华侨的传统节日。2006 年 5 月 20 日,经国务院批准列入第一批国家级非物质文化遗产名录。自 2008 年起,中秋节被列为国家法定节假日。

中秋节是中国三大灯节之一,过节要玩灯。但中秋没有像元宵节那样的大型灯会,玩灯主要是在家庭、儿童之间进行。

各地都以农历八月十五为中秋佳节,但甬俗则以八月十六为中秋。这一习俗的改变,志书上记载有两种说法,一说元末方国珍因他自己生日是八月十六,就以这一天作为中秋节;一说南宋越王史浩的母亲生日是八月十六,他为了给母亲做寿同时又过中秋佳节,就把节日推后了一天。这天月光皎洁,史浩兴高采烈地大宴宾客,向老母亲拜寿。自此以后,宁波人就在每年八月十六过中秋佳节,举行各种活动,吃月饼、赏月,各戏院则演《嫦娥奔月》等应时戏。

重阳

重阳节,又称重九节、晒秋节、"踏秋",汉族传统节日。庆祝重阳节,一般会包括出游赏秋、登高远眺、观赏菊花、遍插茱萸、吃重阳糕、饮菊花酒等活动。

每年的农历九月初九日,也是中国传统四大祭祖的节日。重阳节,早在战国时期就已经形成,到了唐代被正式定为民间的节日,此后历朝历代沿袭至今。重阳与三月初三日"踏春"皆是家族倾室而出,重阳这天所有亲人都要一起登高"避灾"。

重阳节已有两千多年的历史。重阳节的起源,最早可以推到春秋战国时期。战国时代,重阳已受到人们重视,但只是在宫廷中进行的活动。汉代,过重阳节的习俗渐渐流行。相传汉高祖刘邦的妃子戚夫人遭到吕后的谋害,其生前一位侍女贾氏被逐出宫,嫁与贫民为妻。贾氏便把重阳的活动带到了民间。贾氏对人说:在皇宫中,每年九月初九,都要佩茱萸、食蓬饵、饮菊花酒,以求长寿。从此重阳的风俗便在民间传开了。魏晋时期有了赏菊、饮酒的习俗。唐朝时,重阳节才被定为正式节日。从此以后,宫廷、民间一起庆祝重阳节,并且在节日期间进行各种各样的活动。宋代,重阳节更为热闹,《东京梦华录》曾记载了北宋时重阳节的盛况。《武林旧事》也记载南宋宫廷"于八日作重九排当",以待翌日隆重游乐一番。明代,皇宫中宦官宫妃从初一时就开始一起吃花糕庆祝。九日重阳,皇帝还要亲自到万岁山登高览胜,以畅秋志。清代,明代的风俗依旧盛行。

20世纪80年代起,中国一些地方把夏历九月初九日定为老人节,倡导全社会树立尊老、敬老、爱老、助老的风气。1989年,中国政府将农历九月初九定为"老人节""敬老节"。2012年12月28日,中国全国人大常委会表决通过新修改的《老年人权益保障法》,明确每年农历九月初九为老年节。

冬至

冬至,是中国农历中一个重要的节气,也是中华民族的一个传统节日,俗称"冬节""长至节""亚岁"等。早在两千五百多年前的春秋时代,中国就已经用土圭观测太阳,测定出了冬至,它是二十四节气中最早制订出的一个,时间在每年的公历 12 月 21 日至 23 日之间。

冬至这天,太阳直射地面的位置到达一年的最南端,几乎直射南回归线(南纬 23°26'）。这一天北半球得到的阳光最少,比南半球少了 50％。北半球的白昼达到最短,且越往北白昼越短。冬至过后,夜空星象完全换成冬季星空,而且从这一天开始"进九"。而此时南半球正值酷热的盛夏。

与中国北方冬至主要吃饺子的习惯不同,宁波人过冬至的习俗主要是吃"浆板汤果",或"浆板圆子",即用糯米粉搓成小圆子,并加浆板(酒酿)和番薯一起煮吃。圆子意为团圆,浆板意为涨息,番薯意为翻头,都含有吉利之意。冬至还要做羹饭祭祖。有祠堂的,还要到祠堂去祭拜,挂祖宗像,备各种祭品,大户人家还要请戏班子到祠堂演戏,称为冬至戏,往往从下午演到晚上,十分热闹。祠堂还要准备好芝麻饼,分发给每个人,称为"吉饼"。冬至是一年中夜间最长的日子,甬人有"困困冬至夜"的习俗,这天晚上都较早睡觉,希冀做一个好梦,求得合家平安。

(四)民间习俗

二月放鹞子

农历二月,正是春回大地、风和日丽的季节。甬谚有"正月嗑瓜子,二月放鹞子"的说法,放鹞子成为青少年最喜爱的一项户外活动。鹞子,即风筝,以竹为骨,以纸作面,可以制成各种式样的纸鹞。甬人制作的最简单的纸鹞,一是布兰鹞,用细竹扎成"王"字形,糊上薄纸,再用纸做成四条长尾,缚上线,即可放飞;二是瓦片鹞,用竹扎成瓦片状,下面挂一根草绳即可。这两种鹞子制作简易,费用省,效果好,是最常见的。除此之外,还有做成老鹰、鸽子、蜈蚣等动物形状,并加上彩绘。有的纸鹞还扎上橡皮筋或系上小响铃,放飞时受风力影响,会发出悦耳的声音。至今二月放鹞子的习俗仍然存在,只是自己动手制作的少了,都从店铺里买现成的,缺少了以往的那一份情趣。

当年的余姚鹞子以工艺精细见长,并屡屡在国内外获金奖,远近驰名。鹞子以竹篾为架,鹞骨多用细竹签扎成,要刮得光溜溜,然后绑扎骨架。绑扎时要把握中心,左右大小一致,上下轻重均匀,质轻纸透。以薄纸为翼,薄似蝉翼。再涂以各色颜料。鹞子形状,有雄鹰、蝴蝶、蜜蜂、燕子、仙鹤、凤凰、蜻蜓、鸳鸯、喜鹊、巨龙、蝙蝠等。宁波民间鹞子的图案寓意吉祥喜庆,有"福寿双全""龙凤呈祥""百蝶闹春""鲤鱼跳龙门""麻姑献寿""百鸟朝凤""连年有鱼"等。有些鹞子为丝绸面料,韧如筋,可折叠。

新鹞制就,纵之于旷野陇亩间,则风吹碧落,或俯或仰,仿佛真物穿行于云间。观鹞者欢呼雀跃,放飞者童心怡然。宁波老话:"鹞子放嘞高,回去吃年糕。鹞子放嘞低,回去出眼泪。鹞子放嘞远,回去吃汤团。鹞子翻跟斗,塞进灶屋洞。"

若将风筝系之以铃,则清音悠扬,倍添情趣。宁波老话讲:"鹞孟篁篁响,天日日日长","鹞孟",指鹞子上用纸或竹片做的发声器;"篁篁",拟声词;"天日",白天。全句意思是,在放鹞子的阴历三月,白昼一天比一天长了。入夜,人们系小灯于鹞之牵线,串串小灯,燦若明星,人称"神灯"。

过去,有的人在鹞子放上蓝天后,特意剪断牵线,任凭清风将其送往天涯海角,据说,这样能祛病消灾,给自己带来好运。

三月三踏沙滩

在象山石浦、昌国一带，民间有这样一个习俗，即每年农历三月初三，人们都要到昌国东门外沙滩去走一走，玩一会，或拾海螺烧食。这一习俗的由来是源于一个传说。

古时候，在昌国东沙角岩头村里，住着一只很大的乌龟精，经常兴风作浪，淹没稻田，冲倒房屋，卷走人畜，害得这一带老百姓民不聊生。当时在昌国卫城里住着九条龙，眼见乌龟精残害百姓，十分愤怒，决心要除去这个祸害。

一天，乌龟精又兴妖作怪，掀起海浪，直往村庄里卷来，受害的百姓顿时慌作一团，哭声振天。哭声惊动了九条龙，知道又是乌龟精在作祟，便"呼"的一声飞到沙滩头，指责乌龟精道："你这一孽畜一再残害百姓，我要捉你去见玉帝治罪。"乌龟精不服，双方就在沙滩上狠命地争斗起来，一打打了九九八十一天，双方都斗得筋疲力尽，乌龟精伏在沙滩上只会喘气，九条龙也只会躺在沙滩上蠕动，只有最小一条小龙见乌龟已无力动弹，就挣扎着飞到乌龟背上，把其紧紧按住。乌龟精无力再兴风作浪，海水渐渐退了，乌龟精却因为被小龙压住，越挣扎就陷得越深，最后陷到沙滩底下去了，而压在乌龟精上面的小龙，却变成了一条长长的沙堤。

后人为了纪念九条龙，就在每年九条龙和乌龟精打斗的日子——三月初三，带着供品，成群结队来到沙滩凭吊。年复一年，就成了当地的一种习俗了。

赛会

赛会亦称行会、迎会。宁波习俗,过去城乡各地每年都要举行几次迎神赛会活动,以神的诞日作为活动日期,在城区就有四月半会、九月半会和十月朝会等。

规模最为盛大的四月半会,也叫都神会,因为迎的是五都之神。宁波都神殿在大沙泥街,正殿内供有青黄赤白黑五个瘟神像,称为五路都元帅。每年四月十一至十三连续三天,抬着都神在城区游行。迎神活动由东南西北中五社组织,各行业出资,彼此争奇斗胜,极为奢华。行会时,由三丈高的五彩大旗为前导,其后为九联灯、十八联灯和廿四联灯,有制作精致的纱船,船首和船尾坐着艄公和船娘,有装扮成各种戏曲人物的大小抬阁,有形似亭子的鼓亭,挂着大小锣、钹、铃等响器,还有几十人组成的十番细乐,边走边吹奏。还有金猊、玉象、彩马、高跷、铳手等,吹吹打打,热闹非凡,沿途观众人山人海,途为之塞。游行经过的府县衙门,都要设香案迎神。由于围观者过多,常发生事故。清同治八年(1869年),因观看赛会人数过多,新江桥(浮桥)断为两截,淹死300多人;光绪年间,又因赛会在大教场引起兵民械斗,以后遭到官府禁止,才停止举行。

九月半会,亦称社火,迎协佑候神,十月初一称十月朝会,虽然也都是迎神赛会,但仪仗比较简单,较之四月半会就逊色多了。

在各乡间,也有迎神赛会的习俗,但规模大小不一。比较著名的有:鄞西的高桥会,姜山的礼拜会,东南乡的稻花会等。每次赛会都是三到四天,沿街挂灯结彩,祠堂庙宇内演戏祭神和抬着神像游行。各县(市)的迎神赛会活动也十分普遍。如三北(姚北、慈北、镇

北)沿海地区二月十九迎观音赛会最为壮观,从南到北涉及 16 个社庙,各式执事、仪仗、扛头繁多,观者如堵,万人空巷。有民谣这样描述赛会盛况:"二月十九芦城庙,礼拜社头真热闹,年轻妇女兴致高,胭脂花粉打扮俏,东约姑娘西约嫂,又借罗衫又借袄,庙前庙后都赶到,一世为人难得瞧。"余姚城区及姚南三月廿八迎东岳神赛会,其盛况不亚于三北。迎会期间,各社庙演戏,沿江一带有 40 多只龙舟竞渡,晚上两岸聚观神灯,明代皇甫汸有两句诗"遥瞻三帝祠前火,散作人间不夜城",正是描述这一盛况的。

稻花会

旧俗,每年六月,在鄞西鄞江桥、鄞东邹溪、鄞南茅山、斗门桥和镇海等地,都要举行稻花会,农民们手举彩旗,敲锣打鼓,到田头巡游,吸引许多村民前去观看。其时正是新稻抽穗扬花的季节,所以叫稻花会。据说行过稻花会后,就会有一个好收成。

关于稻花会,还有这样一个传说:当时镇海长石一带,都是塘内滩地,土薄碱重,收成不好,农民都过着半年糠菜半年粮的生活,如遇大灾,田里颗粒无收,就只好挖树皮草根充饥。但天无绝人之路,一天,海面上驶来一队粮船,原来是福建一家米行老板,得知这里灾情严重,想乘机卖高价、赚大钱。领头的叫何行久,是账房先生。他上了岸,看到这里家家断绝炊烟,人人嗷嗷待哺,不觉动了恻隐之心,就吩咐伙计将几船大米全部施舍给了灾民,另有两船稻谷,也按户分赠,用作来年播种。当地村民得到救济,有了活路,就把这位何先生看做是救命恩人,感激不尽。但何行久却因此无法向东家交账,就滞留当地,迟迟没有回去。在此期间,他也经常到田头巡游,看到他分赠的稻谷生根发芽,抽穗扬花,收获有望,心里十分宽慰。但正当村里的人温饱有望的时候,何行久却为了无法向东家交账而苦恼万分,终于有一天他悄悄投河自尽了。在他的住处还留下这样一首遗诗:"几船粮食赠

灾民,再难回去复使命;幸喜如今稻花香,九泉之下目也瞑。"

当人们发现他的尸首和遗书时,都禁不住放声痛哭,对这位为了救活一大批灾民而自己最后献出生命的账房先生感念不已。为了纪念他,人们以最隆重的礼节将他安葬,后来又建起了一座"何仙庙",时常进行祭奠,还在每年新稻抽穗扬花的时候,举行盛大的"稻花会",表示对这位舍己救人的"何仙"永远的悼念。

"稻花会"的习俗就这样一直保留下来,直到20世纪50年代初期才逐步废止。

六月六

甬谚有"六月六,狗汏浴""六月六,晒红绿"的说法。民间在农历六月初六这天,烧水为孩子沐浴,说是夏天不会生痱子、疮毒;为猫、狗等动物洗澡,可防止生虱子。如果阳光充足,家家户户还要翻晒衣物图书,可以防蛀。"红绿"指的是五颜六色的衣服。寺庙里这一天也要请一些信佛的老婆婆帮助曝晒经书,并要念佛,称为念晒经佛;有些大户人家还会把藏在祠堂里的宗谱拿出来晾晒。象山石浦旧时还要在这一天行庙会,把城隍、戚老爷(戚继光)、周公公等神像抬到街上游行,并有乐队、彩龙,十分壮观,每户还要设香案迎神,附近村民则万人空巷出来观看。这一习俗在20世纪50年代已废止。

选择这一天,是因为此时恰逢长江中下游地区的梅雨季即将或者已经过去,经历了一个以"霉腐"为特色的时节,自然是要晒一晒,防止衣物、被褥损坏的。而"六月六,黄狗猫汏浴",看起来好像跟"晒"没啥关系,但其最终目的和"晒红绿"是一样的。在江南地区,梅雨季一过,就到了炎炎夏日,猫猫狗狗身上的毛很容易长寄生虫,所以要彻底地清洗一下。

跟过去人们给小孩起名,名字"越贱越好养"一样,"黄狗猫汏浴"的习俗也被演绎到孩子身上。大人们在六月初六这一天也要给自家的孩子洗澡,希望自家孩子像小猫小狗一样好养活,无病无灾。

"六月六,晒红绿"还有一个特别"高大上"的说法,叫"六月六,家家晒龙袍"。相传清乾隆皇帝巡行至扬州,突遇大雨,外衣被淋湿。皇帝很"傲娇",不愿借百姓的衣服换,只好等天晴将衣服晒干,这一天恰好是农历六月初六。百姓不如皇帝"高冷",自然要借"晒龙袍"的名头,沾沾贵气。

七月三十插地香

相传农历七月三十晚上为地藏王菩萨的生日,而在宁波,七月三十有插地香的习俗。宁波七月三十插地香风俗由来已久。传说地藏王平时的眼睛紧闭,惟到此夕人间遍插地香才开眼。民国张延章写的《鄞城十二个月竹枝词》中的七月,是专门描写宁波插地香情景的,曾被广泛地引用:"七月秋风海角凉,儿童竞插地藏香,连宵焰口青莲寺,万盏红灯放水乡。"

民间故事传说,专管人间万物的地藏王,见人刀耕火种,生活艰难,看在眼里,急在心头,便对牛魔王讲:"侬介大力气在这里吃吃困困没意思,下凡帮人耕田去吧。"牛魔王摇头讲:"耕田我倒勿怕,怕就怕老了没力气给人一刀杀了当菜。"地藏王讲:"勿会,我敢担保。"牛魔王推三阻四,横竖不答应。地藏王急红了脸讲:"耕田原是侬的本职,咋好怕死不去。若是人真的杀了你,算我没长眼睛,你就来挖掉我的眼珠。"说着,双手一推,牛魔王勿防,从天上跌下来一头栽倒地上,上爿牙齿都敲光了,只好老老实实替人耕田。

过了十多年,老牛耕不动田了,果然被人杀掉。牛魔王满肚皮怨恨,赶到天上找地藏王算账,一把挖出地藏王眼珠,顺手抛出南天门。地藏王的眼珠滴溜溜落到江南水田里,变成田螺。玉皇大帝见地藏王瞎了眼,不能管事,对牛魔王大发雷霆,把牛魔王痛骂一顿,罚其下凡做牛耕田,永远不准再回天廷。

地藏王仍旧很关心人间疾苦,看不见就用耳朵贴在地上听人们说啥话、做啥事。观世音见他可怜,发了慈悲,每年七月三十送地藏王甘露一瓶洗眼,让他开眼一天。人们为了报答地藏王,每到这天夜里,家家户户都要插地香纪念他。

庙会

庙会,又称"庙市"或"节场",是汉族民间旧时宗教及岁时风俗,一般在春节、元宵节等节日举行。也是我国集市贸易形式之一。其形成与发展和地庙的宗教活动有关,在寺庙的节日或规定的日期举行,多设在庙内及其附近,进行祭神、娱乐和购物等活动。庙会流行于全国广大地区,是中国民间广为流行的一种传统民俗活动,具有浓厚的汉族民俗风情和乡土气。民俗是一个国家或民族中被广大民众所创造、享用和传承的生活文化,庙会就是这种生活文化的一个有机组成部分,它的产生、存在和演变都与老百姓的生活息息相关。

旧时宁波各地的庙会著名的有:鄞西的高桥会、慈溪的泽山会、奉化的稻花会、姚西北的迎神赛会、宁海的胡公大帝生日会等,每逢此时,舞龙、舞狮、抬阁、高跷、民乐队等民间文艺队伍全部活动,游行队伍绵延数里,各种文艺表演目不暇接,常常出现万人空巷参加

集市、争看赛会的盛况。例如鄞江庙会是集祭祀、歌舞、文娱、商贸于一体的汉族传统民俗活动,现在是国家非物质文化遗产重点保护项目。在一年中有三个庙会,即"三月三""六月六""十月十"。其中以"十月十"场面最为盛大。

新中国成立后,庙会活动逐步减少,代之以群众性的大型文化艺术节、商品节等活动。

祭灶

腊月廿三"祭灶节",宁波民间把这一天也叫做"送灶节""辞灶节""小年""小年节""小年夜"等。按宁波旧俗,腊月廿三灶神临行前,家家早起,将应市祭灶果品罗列灶前,入夜焚香饯祖。"祭灶果"是祭拜灶君供品中的"重头戏",祭灶时分,备供灶糖、灶马及供灶马吃的草料,外加一盆熟黄豆和一杯清水。香烛元宝、焚香祷告毕,小孩分食祭灶果。

宁波乡俗"男不拜月,女不祭灶"。实际上往往是男性先祭,女性后拜,男女共同参与。祭灶节的供品,因贫富不一而丰俭由人。士绅世家可供 24 碗菜,有金针、木耳、腐筋、肉皮、花生、瓜子、灶糖灶饼、柑橘果子、荸荠、甘蔗、豆腐、红枣、蜜饯等。贫者仅供一节甘蔗尾也可。腊月廿三那天,等灶君双眼被烟气所迷茫,无法细细查看之际,主人会悄悄地在筷笼中加上一束新筷,好让灶君摸到后,感到这户人家"添丁"了,应该"添财"了。

送灶仪式过后,小孩子们就开始分食灶饼、灶糖、麻球了。祭灶之俗源于宁波古代先民对火的崇拜、对火神的祭祀。古人赖火取暖、照明、煮食,产生了崇拜火及原始祭祀活动,视火为神。随着砌石垒灶的出现,火神也就转化为灶神了。

宁波民间流行的《祭灶歌》歌谣:"又到腊月二十三,老灶爷爷要上天。剪好草,拌香料,壮马喂得咴咴叫。走大道,过小桥,一路顺风平安到。别忘人间糖瓜甜,玉皇面前添好言。多说好,不说坏,五谷杂粮多多带,大胖小子抱个来,家家敬仰人人爱。祭灶果,供小菜,除夕夜晚迎您来。多施恩,别作怪,老少早晚把您拜。"

宁波民间"小年夜"的节日观念犹存。"小年夜"有别于"大年夜",它是除夕、春节等一系列大节的前奏。其时过节的氛围逐渐浓厚,从这一天起应该就算是进入过年时段了。

农历二十五六搡年糕

所谓年糕就是取年年高的意思,所以宁波人到了过年的时候是要吃年糕的。宁波的年糕与别处又不同,称为水磨年糕,口感细滑有韧劲,不论是长时间煮和切成薄片炒都不会有含糊的口感,所以很多久居海外的宁波人常常怀念宁波水磨年糕,然别处买的都没有正宗的口感好。

现在叫上海白年糕的就是宁波水磨年糕。商业做法是:精选当年新米(糯性粳米,少量糯米)加水磨成米浆,蒸熟后机器挤压成条,口感糯、软、滑,很筋道。而在旧时,宁波人过年做年糕成是一件十分隆重的事情。孩子们是早已知道父亲将做年糕的米浸泡在水里了的,浸泡几日的米才能磨成细腻的米粉。做年糕不称,称为搡年糕。到了农历二十五六,家里的男人们便会将浸泡好了的米洗干净,用水磨磨成粉,蒸熟。接着便开始最重要的仪式:搡年糕。庭院里会摆上一个石头雕成的大臼,配一个木柄石制的捣捶。孩子们会欢快地围在一边,等待父兄们将蒸熟的粉放入臼内捶捣,这便叫"搡"。

搡年糕搡得越透,年糕就越有韧劲,半天后年糕粉团便有了,女人们就会把年糕揉成条状,按上红印。而孩子们是等不得到那时的,老早就向哥哥要了搡到一半的粉团捏在手里边玩边吃了。

守岁

宁波习俗,每年除夕都要守岁,家家灯光明亮,不时燃放爆竹,人人坐以待旦。

关于除夕守岁习俗,也有一个很有趣的传说。很早以前,宁波太白山上住着一个恶魔,常常喷水成河,淹没房舍农田;或唤来烈日,晒得土地寸草不生。只有家家户户每天做一桌好酒菜送给他吃,才能免灾,弄得民不聊生。

这样过了许多年,来了一位喜爱喝酒的名叫清水的法师,善于酿酒。他看到恶魔如此残害百姓,十分痛恨,就一心想制造一种烈酒,让恶魔喝了之后一年四季不醒来。于是他查找了各种酒书,搜集了十一种酿酒用的稻米和三十三斤辣蓼,花了整整三年多时间,终于制造出一种烈度很高的酒来。

正月初一那天,清水法师打开酒坛,顿时酒香扑鼻,直冲九霄,他和几个在场的徒儿还未喝上酒,就一个个醉倒在地,酣然大睡。恶魔在太白山上闻到了这股奇香,忍不住寻下山来,一眼见到放在佛桌上的美酒,馋得捧起坛来一饮而尽,顿时醉意朦胧,回到山上倒头便睡,还不住地叫"好酒,好酒……"。但是这种酒喝了只能昏睡三百六十四天,到除夕那天,恶魔还是要醒来害人。怎么办呢?

清水法师又想了一个办法,除夕那天,让家家户户都供上三牲、果馔和烈酒,并把毛竹锯成一段段分给百姓,到时用火燃烧,就会发出噼啪的爆裂声。这样一来,或者把恶魔吓走,或者让他吃了烈酒再睡三百六十四天,不再害人。果然,腊月三十那天,恶魔闻到酒食香味,正要扑下来享用,突然听到家家户户火光熊熊,噼啪之声大作,火星溅在恶魔身上,痛得它哇哇大叫,转身就逃,再也不敢来危害人类了。

清水法师见到恶魔已经逃走,太高兴了,竟于当天晚上与世长辞。百姓为了纪念他,也为了防止恶魔再来作祟,每年腊月三十晚上就在家里供上三牲、果馔和烈酒,燃放爆竹,坐以待旦。这一守岁习俗一直被保留下来。

五、工艺特产

（一）工艺名品

朱金木雕

宁波的朱金木雕，又名"漆金木雕"，是宁波传统的工艺品之一。它采用樟木、椴木、银杏木等优质木材做原料，有浮雕、透雕、圆雕等形式，运用了贴金饰彩，结合沙金、碾金、碾银、沥粉、描金、开金、撒云母、撒罗钿、铺绿、铺蓝等多种工艺手段，并涂以中国大漆，而成为朱金木雕。

宁波朱金木雕构图饱满，内容多是喜庆吉事、民间传说，画面充实，丰富多彩，形成宁波自己独特的地方风格。它的画面以"热闹"为主，取材于戏剧场面，所以又称京班体，造型古朴生动，刀法浑厚，金彩相间，绚烂富丽，具有极强的艺术性和实用性。

宁波朱金木雕历史悠久，自汉、唐、宋以来盛传不衰。庙宇、祠堂、居民建筑、花轿、木床等无不施雕上漆。宁波保国寺保存的朱金木雕千工床、万工轿，朱金辉煌，巧夺天工，集朱金木雕之精华。以万工轿为例，花轿采用木质镂花，朱漆铺地，金箔贴花，夹以镜片，玲珑剔透。万工轿结构前后对称，左右对称，制作精细而浩繁。仅顶部就分上下七层。万工轿上雕有 24 只凤凰、38 条龙、54 只仙鹤、174 只喜鹊、92 只狮子、22 只鹰、22 只螳螂、12 个小天使、124 处石榴百子、18 组梅鹊图、12 组松鼠偷葡萄群雕，以及大小 250 个人物，反映天宫赐福、麒麟送子、魁星点状、独占鳌头、八仙过海、昭君出塞、木兰从军、王羲之爱鹅、林和靖放鹤等吉祥主题及历史人物。轿四周还饰有宁波风格的刺绣帷，各色精致的小宫灯、小铃铛和工彩流苏。要八个人抬，在轿子抬行过程中，大小人物就左右摆动，和着小铃铛发出悦耳的响声。

朱金木雕这朵工艺之花，新中国成立以后开得更加绚丽。在许多重要建筑上广泛雕饰，用朱金木雕制成的屏风、箱柜、古代人物、佛像、狮子、灯彩等，还远销欧、美、亚、非许多国家和地区，受到人们的广泛欢迎。

其实，作为宁波传统工艺的朱金木雕，早在唐代就已从宁波东传日本。唐高僧鉴真在唐天宝二年(743 年)第二次东渡日本，船到明州(宁波)狼沟浦时遇到风暴，船遭击破，被

明州地方官员安置于阿育王寺,其时他曾研究和考察宁波工艺美术,东渡日本时带去的就有从事朱金木雕的工匠。鉴真于天宝十二年(753年)渡日成功,住奈良东大寺。此寺为日本奈良第一有名的寺院。鉴真于755年11月在该寺讲堂,运用朱金木雕工艺塑造二丈五尺千手观音像安置其中。756年6月,日本圣武帝遗物向大佛献纳,有佛百铺,卢舍那佛、观音一铺,纯金观音一躯作成。这些雕像工艺,有鉴真和他率领的明州、扬州雕塑师参与。东大寺的献物,也包括鉴真带去的工艺珍品在内。同时,由鉴真和他的弟子创建的日本唐招提寺内部,也多是用宁波式的朱金木雕作为装饰,其讲经大殿、舍利殿西北隅开山堂等的朱金木雕则与宁波阿育王寺相仿佛。

泥金彩漆

宁波的漆器工艺,有非常悠久的历史。在距今已有7000多年历史的余姚河姆渡遗址中,出土了一只涂有朱红漆的木碗,可见宁波这一工艺的古老。

中国是发现和使用天然漆最早的国家。《韩非子》中就有记载:"尧禅天下,虞舜受之,斩山木而财之,削锯修之际,流漆墨其上,输之于宫为食器,……禹作祭器,墨染其外,朱画其内……"在日本也有"漆之使用,始于中国太古"之说。据资料记载,宁波漆器在唐代已基本形成了自己的风格,并且对东邻日本有比较深刻的影响。

唐代时,宁波的漆器工艺已有相当水平,到明代更见兴盛。据《浙江通志》载:"大明宣德年间,宁波泥金彩漆、描金漆器名闻中外。"

宁波漆器工艺以中国生漆为主要原料。漆器以木胎为主,也有以竹片、竹编为胎。制作分为浮花、平花、沉花三大类。浮花,就是在用生漆漆过的工艺品漆膜上,堆塑各种山水、花鸟、人物、楼阁等图案,待堆塑坚硬如石后,贴金上彩;平花,就是在漆膜上上彩或绘图;沉花,则是在透明的漆膜下面绘制花纹。唐著名诗人白居易曾这样描述过中国漆器:"缀珠陷玉贴云母,五金七宝相玲珑。"

宁波漆器在唐代东传日本。唐高僧鉴真在东渡到达日本前,曾一度在宁波住过,搜集了许多宁波漆器,于东渡时带往日本。日本唐招提寺的有些佛像工艺就采用了宁波的漆器工艺。以后两国不断往来,交流技艺,互相影响。如日本的推光漆、坯沥漆、描金、嵌罗钿、贴云母等工艺,不论在选料、操作,甚至产品造型上都与宁波的传统漆器十分相似。日本正仓院至今仍收藏着不少隋唐时期的漆器。另外,宁波的夹苎漆器佛像、家具之类传入日本,也影响了日本的佛像和家具工艺,并逐步发展成为日本的民族工艺——莳绘。

宁波漆器工艺经过数千年的曲折发展,到新中国成立之后,进一步获得发扬光大,成为宁波重要的出口工艺品。产品有屏风、鼓凳、茶几、果盘以及电视橱、书橱、写字台等,雕塑生动逼真,富有立体感,布局优美,玲珑剔透,金银彩色,光耀悦目,受到各国人民的赞赏。

骨木镶嵌

宁波骨木镶嵌,是我国古老手工艺品中的佼佼者。它作为完整工艺品的出现,约在隋唐时期,已相当发达。到了清代乾隆、嘉庆、道光年间,宁波骨木镶嵌工艺以它独特的地方风格和精巧、高超的制作技艺而驰誉中外,与扬州罗钿嵌、广东象牙嵌并驾齐驱。宁波镶嵌制品一直被列为"贡品",现在北京颐和园的乐寿堂内就陈列有宁波制作的骨木镶嵌制品。

宁波骨木镶嵌在表现形式上,分为高嵌和平嵌。前者花纹凸起,后者花纹与木坯嵌平。主要采用象牙、螺钿、木片、铜片等锯成花纹,嵌入木坯后用雕刻刀划线而成。骨木镶嵌与建筑、家具相结合,既可作为高贵的装饰,又有实用价值。

宁波骨木镶嵌工艺,与朱金木雕、漆器工艺一样,在唐代时由高僧鉴真传入日本。日本所建唐招提寺内陈列的骨木镶嵌家具、器皿多系从明州带去的明州工艺品。寺内僧人所用的诸如"紫檀木棋盘""双陆盘"等器皿,也是明州工匠所制的宁波骨木镶嵌之作。镶

嵌的图案古雅，奏雕工致，手艺精绝。据日本真人元开所撰《唐大和上东征传》载，鉴真带往日本去的有绣像、画像、雕像、金铜像……骨木镶嵌佛具等制品。其造像和寺院建筑镂雕工艺，给日本的塑像与寺院的雕饰作了取法的式样。

宁波骨木镶嵌虽历史悠久，但流传到民国晚期，几乎濒临绝艺。新中国成立以后，工艺复苏，推陈出新，运用骨木镶嵌技艺制作了大批座椅、摇椅、茶桌、茶几、插屏、大橱、小橱以及屏风、挂屏等，工艺精绝，几同汉画，花草、人物栩栩如生，受到中外人士的赞叹。

金银彩绣

宁波金银刺绣，历史悠久，是宁波传统工艺品。长期以来，宁波民间有"家家织席，户户刺绣"的传统习惯。明清两代出现了不少民间刺绣艺人，绣品销路也日益增大。据《鄞县通志》记载，在 1932 年，宁波刺绣品销售量达 15000 多件，产品远销东南亚一些国家，与苏绣、湘绣、蜀绣竞相争辉，各具特色。

宁波金银刺绣有独特的地方风格。它构图概括，色泽鲜艳，多采用黑色、灰色、石青、酱红、赭黄、灰绿等柔和色彩。主要针法有斜针、扣针、胖针、抽丝、朝纱、夹丝、晒毛针、打子针等，再以金银线盘绣装饰。刺绣品的图案多取材于民间喜闻乐见的龙凤、如意、牡丹、百鸟等，使绣品显得典雅华贵，古色古香，朴实沉着，富有宁波民间地方风格。

宁波金银刺绣的原料，多选用各色真丝、人造丝交织的绸缎，用金银线绣在彩色平绣的图案周围；有的则将金银线紧密排列，垫满图案的空间，融盘金与色绣为一体，富有高雅的装饰韵味。

94

近年来,宁波刺绣按照"工艺品日用化、日用品工艺化"的要求,对产品进行不断创新,使产品既具有艺术欣赏价值,又是生活日用品,更是旅游纪念、馈赠亲友的佳品。1978年冬,赵朴初在考察宁波、参观艺人们的刺绣技艺时,极为赞赏,写下了"斟古酌今,裁云剪月,奇花异草,神笔妙针"四句赞词,高度概括了宁波刺绣所具有的特色。

艺人们在继承传统工艺的同时,吸收国外先进刺绣方法,使宁波刺绣更上层楼。1989年宁波刺绣大型屏风《百鹤朝阳》荣获中国工艺美术百花奖珍品奖,并为中国美术馆所收藏。

翻簧竹刻

翻簧竹刻,是用大毛竹劈去青皮,通过分层开剥,翻出竹簧,再经造型、彩绘、细刻、油漆等加工而成,是宁波传统的工艺品。

竹刻艺术在我国具有悠久历史。相传,明嘉靖、万历年间,有嘉定朱松林祖孙三代,抚宋元小景、名画刻之于竹,为时人所珍爱,得之者如获至宝,其刀法技艺多为后人所效仿。到了清代,因浙东一带盛产毛竹,就地取材极为方便,名手大家辈出,名扬四海,不少佳品还被选入内府。

宁波奉化是大毛竹的主要产地,翻簧竹刻已有100多年历史。新中国成立前,奉化城里曾开设过"挹素斋""贫民艺术所""竹器公司",制作过不少翻簧竹刻工艺珍品。宁波博物馆收藏有多种竹刻珍品,就是实证。

翻簧竹刻制作时,须选取口径大、竹节长的鲜毛竹,去青皮,取里层2毫米厚的竹簧,用水煮后压平,再用胶将其胶合在木板或竹片制成的半成品上,拼接时做到天衣无缝;刨

95

光成形后,再施雕刻或绘画装饰工艺。由于翻簧色彩自然洁净,嫩黄如同象牙,再经喷漆上蜡,更显得鲜艳悦目,可与玉雕、漆器媲美。

翻簧竹刻工艺品,宁波各地多有生产,但以奉化最为有名,生产有100多个品种,如镜箱、提篮、花瓶、台灯、棋盘、茶盒、动物玩具、大型屏风等,刻有人物、花鸟,形象逼真,栩栩如生。雕刻的作品,既有中国传统的白描特点,又有古朴苍劲的金石刻风格,融观赏与实用于一体,深受海内外人士的欢迎。

宁波丝织

宁波作为历史上全国三大对外贸易口岸之一和鸦片战争后"五口通商口岸"之一,在海内外最负盛名的是丝织品,其地位和名声,远远超过杭嘉湖地区。

丝织品原料是蚕丝,要养蚕就首先要种桑。宁波面海靠山,面海有大批冲积平原,靠山又有众多丘陵沙质地,加上气候湿润,适宜种桑养蚕。种桑的历史相当悠久。《尔雅》中称之为"女桑"。为什么会称作女桑呢?《搜神记》中载有这样一个故事:很久很久以前,有一人远行,家里仅留下一个女儿和一匹马。女儿想念父亲,就对马开玩笑说:"你要能替我把父亲接回来,我就嫁给你。"马听后,拽断缰绳跑了,跑到她父亲那里,父亲见到马,怀疑家里出了事,就乘马返回家里。马以后一见到女儿,就发怒蹦跳,父亲便特别奇怪,悄悄地问女儿,女儿就原原本本告诉父亲。父亲便把马射死,并将皮剥下来晒在院中。女儿走到晒马皮的地方,用脚踢着它说:"你是一匹马,却想娶人做妻子,自己找死,还要怎样?"话还没有说完,马皮竟一下蹦飞起来,将女儿卷走了。后来父亲在大树的树枝间,找到了女儿和裹在她身上的马皮,可是都已分别变成了蚕和茧,挂在树枝上。现今世人称蚕为"女儿",这种叫法是从古代流传下来的,因而也把这树叫做"桑树","桑"是取"丧"的谐音。

其实,宁波地区种桑养蚕的历史,可追溯到 7000 多年前的河姆渡时期,从河姆渡遗址中出土的象牙雕刻蚕纹盅形器,便是重要的实物见证。用蚕丝加工成为丝织品,在许多古籍上都有大量记载。《汉书·货殖志》载:"殷国之盛……冬,民既入,妇女同巷,相从夜织,女工一月得四十五日,必相从者,所以省燎火,同巧拙,合习俗也。"可见当时妇女夜织的规模已相当可观了。妇女们织布的原料是什么呢?据《后汉书·乐羊子妻传》载:"乐羊子远寻师学,一年来归,妻跪问其故,羊子曰,久行怀归,无他异也。妻乃引刀趋机而言曰:'此机生自蚕茧,成于机杼'……"可见 2000 多年前,妇女所织的是蚕丝。唐宋时期,仅宁波(当时称明州)西乡养蚕的有千家之多,每年产丝达万斤以上。明朝诗人赵谦在诗中写道:"吴蚕眠起正纷纭,桑柘斜曛十里云。白眼看它闲草木,只将红紫媚东君。"清学者沈對在《蚕词》中写道:"小姑居处最难夸,镇日养蚕不出家。会见提筐行陌上,鬓边好插野田花。"以上描述的是种桑和养蚕,接下来就是缫丝了。清宁波诗人潘朗在一首《缫丝》诗中写道:"春色斜残陌上桑,缫车上罢织布忙。功成双手空憔悴,半与小姑半与姑。"当时,宁波城中的纺织巷、织纱巷,绫户鳞次栉比,纺丝织纱之声自晨至晚不绝。织出的绫帛,最著名的要算吴绫、白附子、交棱绫、大花绫等,并作为贡绫。自唐至元各代地方志籍均有记载,宁波所产的各种贡绫,是一种主要用于夏季的衣料,轻飘精美,鲜艳夺目,穿着凉爽,受到朝中君臣的赞扬,认为质量之好,世上少有。明代、清代,宁波生产深青宁丝、白生丝、平罗纱、白绉纱、红线,青熟线及白丝、农丝、荒丝等五素丝纱。清学者全祖望有诗写道:"未若吴绫夸独绝,大花璀璨状五云。交织连环泯百结,濯以飞瀑之赤泉。蜀江新水不足捋,浃月四

十有五红。上为戴座补衮阙,女野先芒烛帝室……"到了清道光年间,宁波地区养蚕纺织尤以樟村、密岩一带最为密集。这一带十有九家农户以养蚕种贝为生,全年产丝五万多斤。万斯同在《鄞西竹枝词》中写道:"独喜林村蚕事修,一村妇女几时休。织成广幅生丝绢,不数嘉禾濮院绸。"以后随着科学技术的发展,丝织品生产逐步由手工向机械化生产发展。到1932年,宁波城区有织机近千台,年产塔夫绸、华丝葛等三、四万匹。

宁波的丝织品以及丝织技术,自古以来便闻名海内外,并成为对外贸易的重要商品。唐代时,宁波生产的丝绸,包括江苏一带产的丝绸销往日本后,被称为"唐绫",受到日本朝野的喜爱。正如日本学者藤原定家在《明月记》中所说:"近年来,无论上下各色人等,均喜穿'唐绫',于是命都城织工仿织'唐绫'。"这种'唐绫'的纺织技术很快在由宁波至日本的港口——博多港盛行起来,成为日本古代丝绸业的中心,并把这种纺织法称之为"博多织",社会上也出现了"唐绫"的仿制品。宁波的丝织品除远销日本、高丽外,还输往印尼、柬埔寨、越南、伊朗等国家。

有悠久历史的宁波丝织品,由于日本人造丝的倾销和蚕茧产量的下降,到了民国后期,丝绸行业已日趋衰落。新中国成立后,各地纷纷创办丝绸织厂,生产又有发展,且各类丝织品的质量又有新的提高,受到人们的喜爱。

宁波瓷器

宁波瓷器历史悠久。宁波余姚瓷器的历史,至少可以追溯到2000多年前的越窑青瓷。

宁波是中国越窑青瓷的发源地。据有关专家考证,中国古陶器出现于8000多年之前,而出现瓷器则是在东周时期,当时称"原始青瓷"。到了东汉时期,开始生产青瓷。宁波古代属越地,故称越窑。越窑遗址位于慈溪市鸣鹤镇西栲栳山麓上林湖一带,包括白泽湖、杜湖、古上呑湖、古银锭湖在内,四周有古窑址120多处。烧制始于东汉,盛于唐、五代,延至宋代。东汉至隋代,烧制的瓷器比较古朴粗重。到了唐代,随着对外通商发达,商业繁荣,烧制的瓷器胎质细腻,如冰似玉,成为向朝廷进贡的贡品。徐寅《贡余秘色茶盏》一诗中写道:"捩翠融青瑞色新,陶成先得贡吾君。巧剜明月染春色,轻旋薄冰盛绿云。"赞颂贡窑青瓷高超的质地。上林湖烧制的进贡瓷器,具有胎质细腻、品种丰富的特点。唐诗人陆龟蒙在《秘色越器》一诗中也写道:"九秋风露越窑开,夺得千峰翠色来。好向中宵盛沆瀣,共稽中散斗遗杯。"到了五代十国时,钱越王贡奉中原的贡品青瓷,已发展到采用釉下彩绘工艺,金、银、铜镶边,分别称"金扣""银扣""铜扣",花纹装饰采用刻、划、镂、堆塑等手法,题材有珍禽、异兽、金鱼、花草、人物,技巧熟练,构图新颖,题材广泛。如蝴蝶飞舞、鸳鸯戏水、蛟龙出水,鸟翔花间等图案,无不引人入胜。

越窑以灿烂晶莹的釉色和丰富多彩的图案驰名于世。陆羽在《茶经》一书中称:"碗越

州上，鼎州次，婺州次，岳州次，寿州、洪州次之。或以邢州处越州上，殊不为然。盖邢瓷如银，越瓷类玉，邢不如越，一也；若邢瓷类雪，则越瓷类冰，邢不如越，二也；邢瓷白而茶色丹，越瓷青而茶色绿，邢不如越，三也。"从中可见越瓷之精美。

上林湖越窑青瓷进贡朝廷数量相当可观。有时一年就达 14 万件，除作贡品外，还大量远销国外。由于上林湖得海运之便，经明州港远销日本、高丽、越南、柬埔寨、马来西亚、菲律宾、印度以及东非、北非等 20 多个国家，是当时宁波主要对外贸易商品之一。现代印度、伊朗、埃及、日本等国古港口、古城堡遗址，均发现有上林湖产的越窑青瓷遗物，成为宁波作为"瓷器之路"起泊地最有力的实证。

越窑青瓷色如玉而不浮光，质如冰而不流俗，美名远扬。唐代诗人施肩吾有诗赞道："越碗初盛蜀茗新，薄烟轻处搅来匀。山僧问我将何比，欲道琼浆却畏嗔。"

余姚瓷器在越窑瓷器的基础上又开出了新花。它继承传统越窑瓷器技术，搞了数十个配方，试验成功了余姚细瓷和骨灰瓷。余姚细瓷具有"洁如玉，光如镜，声如磬"的特点，瓷质可同景德镇瓷器媲美。名式餐具，白如羊脂，光洁如玉，釉色晶莹，花样新颖；人物动物，栩栩如生。余姚瓷器中的骨灰瓷填补了浙江省空白，各类产品受到人们的赞赏。

宁波草席

草席是宁波鄞州的重要特产，尤以黄古林一带草席历史悠久，质量特优。

由于黄古林一带气候土壤适宜，所产席草色泽青白而带绿，粗细均匀而挺直，草壁薄而坚韧，草芯丰满而有弹性，拉力强而不易断，加上编织技术悠久而精湛，故织成的草席质地精良，挺括硬实，柔软光滑，收藏简便。不用时卷席成筒，不占地方；使用时，一经温水拭抹，不但更加光滑，且能透出一股沁人的幽香。草席一般是由白麻或绿麻为筋编织而成，

而以白麻筋草席为佳。

黄古林一带所产草席历史悠久。据《四明郡志》载,早在唐代,宁波草席已远销各地。距今已有 1000 多年历史。宁波作为全国三大对外贸易口岸,在宋元明各个朝代,宁波草席都作为特产销往海外。到了清代,宁波草席生产达到鼎盛时期,除内销外,还远销东南亚各国和欧洲、非洲等一些国家,成为重要的出口产品。1954 年,周恩来总理参加日内瓦会议时,还特地带了四十条宁波草席馈赠国际友人,备受欢迎。

宁波草席以质量好、品种齐、工艺考究而著称于世。历史上宁波草席还为抗击金兵入侵作出过重要贡献。这个故事发生在南宋时期。据《佛祖统记》、《宁波府志》记载,自从康王赵构建立南宋朝廷以后,由于偏安临安,根基薄弱,难以抵御强大的金兵,便于建炎三年(1129 年)放弃临安,跸驻明州。因明州背负大海,便准备艨艟,一旦受到金兵攻击,即扬帆出海。建炎四年正月,金兵以更大规模南犯。大队金兵渡钱塘,破绍兴,占余姚,直逼明州。赵构闻报,大惊失色,随即带领后妃、侍从,登上艨艟,直驶定海。当时,留守明州一带的御营前营统制张俊与副统制刘洪道守于城楼,遣兵掩击,杀伤金兵无数,首战大捷。金兵只得屯守余姚,请求大元帅兀术增援。兀术闻报大怒,便带领大队兵将再犯明州。张俊见兀术来势凶猛,准备于鄞县西乡高桥一带迎战金兵。他骑马实地勘察这一带地形,骑着、骑着,突然战马四蹄打滑,竟至四脚朝天,把张俊掀翻在席草地里,弄得浑身泥浆。张俊爬起身来一看,只见地上晾着几领草席,马蹄被草席打滑,顿时计上心来。他管不了擦洗泥浆,立即召集当地百姓,晓以抗击金兵之大义,动员百姓把家里草席悉数铺到过往大道。众百姓一听,都愿意为保卫乡土,奋勇参战,纷纷把草席铺于沿途路上。次日,宋军以大队埋伏于高桥下,而以小队在前路迎战金兵。战不几个回合,宋军便循着河边长有青草的小路撤退,金兀术以为可欺,挥动大队人马追杀过来。不料战马一踏上路上草席,便马蹄打滑,人仰马翻。在后面的骑兵不知前边情况,扬鞭催马而来,也被滑倒在地,自相践踏。此时,埋伏在桥下、田塍里的宋军和义兵一齐杀出,杀得金兵血流成河,杀得兀术魂飞魄散,赶紧败退。正如清代著名学者万斯同在《鄞西竹枝词》中写道:"高宗航海驻鄞邦,曾把高桥作战场。却恨元戎轻纵敌,复教兀术渡钱塘。"古时候,人们叫金兵为"鞑子",自从草席滑倒金兵、打了胜仗以后,宁波人就叫席子为"滑子"了。

宁波草席在国内外享有盛誉,全年总产量数百万条,除畅销全国各地外,还销往日本、东南亚等国家和地区。

(二)名点名菜

溪口千层饼

溪口千层饼,是宁波奉化溪口传统特产。它外形四方,内分 27 层,层次分明、金黄透绿、香酥松脆、甜中带咸、咸里带鲜、风味独特,食后令人口齿留香,百食不厌。

溪口制作千层饼已有 100 多年历史。据说,清光绪八年,即 1882 年,溪口王毛龙开设王永顺饼店,1886 年开始产脆酥饼。一次,其弟在制饼时加了些奉化特产苔菜粉,制成的饼清香扑鼻,风味独特,顾客盈门。自此以后,便用苔菜粉作为辅料制作酥饼,人称"毛龙千层饼"。100 多年来,师徒代代相传,加上制作精细,声名远扬,盛销不衰。

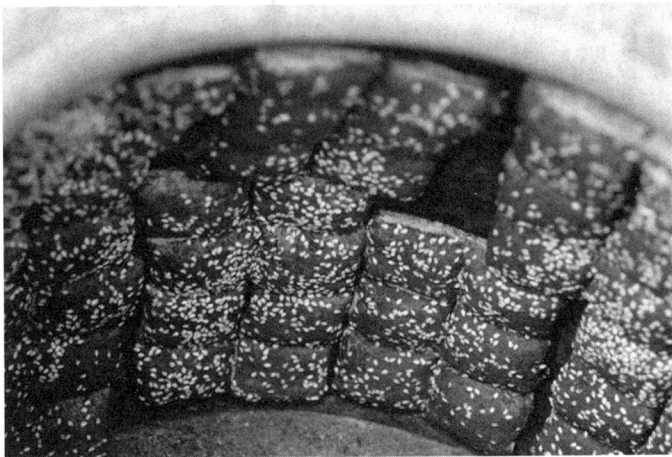

溪口千层饼制作,用料十分讲究。须选用上等面粉、精炼生油、脱壳芝麻、洁净焦糖,以及奉化特产优质冬苔粉等为原料,经过配料、蒸粉、制馅、造层、烙酥、包装等 12 道工序制成。制成的千层饼,在 1.5 厘米厚的小饼内并列 27 层隔层,故松脆酥润,油素充足,苔菜香浓,食后令人齿颊生津,老幼妇孺都爱吃。

溪口千层饼作为地方风味食品,成为中外游客品尝和馈赠亲友的旅游食品,特别是背井离乡在海外的游子,都要托回乡的亲友带一些回去,以慰思乡之念。千层饼除了畅销浙东地区外,还销往日本、东南亚国家和香港地区。

龙凤金团

龙凤金团,是浙东一带城乡妇孺皆知的传统名点,也是宁波十大名点之一。由于制作精良,入口甜糯,价廉物美,深受群众的喜爱。旧时,宁波有许多制作金团的糕团店,但以赵大有制作的龙凤金团最为有名,称"赵大有金团"。

龙凤金团作为宁波的传统食品,它的历史至少可以追溯到南宋时期。民间有这样一个传说:南宋康王赵构自建都临安后,因金兵强渡长江,杀奔江南,康王自知临安难守,便带领近臣、后妃一路逃难来到明州,被大队金兵冲散。他落荒而逃,正在急难之间,鄞县地方有一位村姑骗走了金兵,救了康王。当时康王饥饿难忍,便向村姑求食。村姑给了他一个有馅的糯米团子,康王吃了团子后告别而去。金兵退去以后,康王返回临安,为了报答村姑救命之恩,就封浙东女子出嫁时可使用半副銮驾,乘坐龙凤花轿。他吃过的糯米团子也被封为"龙凤金团"。

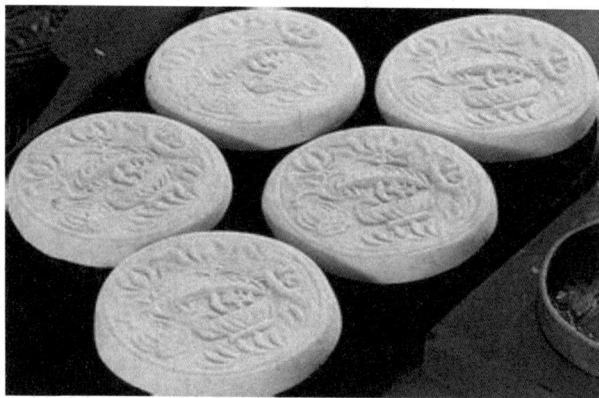

赵大有金团店最早系由一位姓赵的上虞人所开,他制作的金团特点是:用糯米四斤掺和粳米六斤,按天时冷热下缸浸水十至四小时不等,捞起用清水淋去酸汪味,然后磨成粉。馅子是用豇豆或黄豆,一斤半加糖二斤,炒得透而不焦,再加适量的橘饼、瓜子肉、橙丁、红绿丝、桂花等,使金团更加香甜。旧时,赵大有老板为了做出牌子,选料上等,制作精良、薄利多销,并做到童叟无欺,因而在宁波市民中有很高的声誉,生意也很兴隆。一些商人为了借牌子、抢生意,也在市里相继开设了许多赵大有糕团店。如开设在江东大戴家弄口的赵大有德记、开设在灵桥门口的赵大有园记、开设在西门口的赵大有莫记、开设在鼓楼前的赵大有信记、开设在开明街口的赵大有文记、开设在江北中马路的赵大有祥记、开设在仓桥头的赵大有富记和开设在江东后塘街的赵大有祥记分店等,都以制作糕点出名。

金团,不光味道好,还寓有团圆吉庆的意思。并按照用途不同,又生出许多有趣的名称,如种田时节有种田金团,割稻时节有割稻金团,做生意有五代金团,结婚时有龙凤金团,新生儿满月时则又有子孙金团等。

赵大有金团以龙凤金团最为著名。龙凤金团形圆似月,色黄似金,面印龙凤浮雕,显示吉祥、团圆。其特点是:皮薄馅多、口味甜糯、清香适口,令人百吃不厌。

慈城年糕

慈城年糕是浙江地区著名汉族小吃。它已有上千年生产历史,以选料讲究、精工制作著称。它是用优质晚粳米洗净后,用水浸泡3~7天,用水磨成粉,压去水分至不干不湿之恰到好处,粉碎后置蒸笼中猛火蒸透,或舂或轧,做成大小均匀的条状年糕。

年糕是一种老幼皆宜、贫富咸尝的食品,因而十分普及,也特别为人们所喜爱。传统上,每逢春节来临,宁波城乡居民备办的年货中最要紧的食品之一就是年糕,而宁波年糕以慈城产最为著名,因称慈城年糕。

年糕的读音,寓有"年年如意年年高"的意思,故宁波一带有"年糕年糕年年高,今年更比去年好"的民谚。人们还用年糕印版压成"五福""六宝""金钱""如意"等等形状,象征"吉祥如意""大吉大利";有的则做成"玉兔""白鹅"等小动物,构成真正意义上的内容与形式的完美结合。

关于慈城年糕的最早来历,还有一个有趣的传说。相传春秋末期,吴国大夫伍子胥在现今宁波慈城一带作战。他临死前对部下说:"如果国家有苦难,百姓断粮,你们到城墙下挖地三尺可得到粮食。"伍子胥死后,他的部下被越军包围,城中断粮,已饿死不少人。这时有人想起伍子胥的话,就去挖城墙,挖了三尺多深,果然挖到了许多可吃的"城砖",即年糕,结果打了胜仗。原来当年伍子胥在慈城督造城墙时,已做好屯粮防饥的准备。从此以后每逢过年,慈城家家户户都做年糕,以年糕汤为年夜饭,纪念伍子胥。

猪油汤团

宁波人在大年初一都有吃猪油汤团的传统习惯。汤团含有团圆、如意的意思。即使在海外的游子,他们"每逢佳节倍思亲",在新春佳节也忘不了要吃家乡的猪油汤团,盼望团圆,以慰思乡之念。

汤圆,原名元宵,原是指元宵节。旧时候,农历正月十五是元宵节,也叫元夜。

汤团以元宵命名,起源于隋朝。相传,隋炀帝在610年正月十五那一天晚上,在洛阳搭台歌舞,"与民同乐",并用实心的圆子、汤中撒糖,赐给臣下和歌姬作晚点食用。因这一天恰好是元宵夜,故名"元宵"。这种为人们喜爱的食品传至宁波,经过长期发展,逐步改进,才形成现在用水磨糯米粉嵌猪油馅的宁波汤团特有的风味。

传说八洞神仙吕洞宾在阳春三月变身一位卖汤团的老翁,在西湖边叫卖。许仙吃了吕洞宾的汤团,不小心将一颗汤团"的溜溜"滚落西湖,被白蛇吞吃了,白蛇成了仙,与许仙结为夫妇。又传说,宁波于"鸦片战争"后被辟为"五口通商"口岸之一,大批洋人涌进宁波,他们吃了宁波猪油汤团,在津津有味之余,对这滚圆雪白、软糯香甜的汤团发生了兴趣,产生了疑问,翻来覆去总是弄不懂,这汤团馅子是如何嵌进去的。

宁波汤团已有700多年历史。因系用水磨方法把糯米磨成浆制作,故又被叫做"吊浆汤团"。制作方法是:用上百斤糯米,水浸三天后磨成浆,盛入布袋吊起,沥至不干不黏时取用。这样做成的汤团,皮薄而滑,白如羊脂,油光发亮,糯而不黏。汤团馅须选用优质肉猪板油,去筋除皮;把黑芝麻炒捣成粉,加绵白糖,三料反复揉捏均匀,搓成玻璃弹子似的小球,嵌入糯米皮子内。这种馅子香甜油烫,油而不腻,独具特色。汤团做成后,入汤煮沸至上浮,加入少许冷水、再煮沸,即可捞起食用。旧时,汤团一般只能在春节期间吃到,平时民间很少制作。宁波有一首儿歌这样唱道:"拜岁拜嘴巴,坐落瓜子茶,猪油汤团烫嘴巴。"

宁波汤团以"缸鸭狗"汤团店历史最久。"缸鸭狗"老板实名江阿狗。他原来在宁波开明街开店,就将人名叫做店名,在招牌上绘了一只缸、一只鸭子、一只狗作记,这个别出心裁的招牌,引起人们的广泛兴趣和传播;同时他因制作精细,价廉物美,各界人士都喜欢吃他做的汤团,生意越做越大,使得远近闻名,日渐兴隆。旧时还流传着这样的顺口溜:"三点四点饿过头,猪油汤团'缸鸭狗'。吃了铜钿还勿够,脱落衣衫当押头。"

青塊麻糍

青塊和麻糍,都是宁波及周围地区清明节期间的时令点心。

青塊,又叫青团,系用糯米粉加少许开水拌和,掺入艾叶而成。艾是一种菊科植物,多年生草本,揉之有香气,可以入药。将蒸熟的糯米粉与艾叶反复揉搓至粉团光滑、软硬适中、色泽均匀后,搓成长条,摘成一个个块子,嵌入豆沙、黄豆、芝麻等不同馅子搓成球状,即成青塊。将做好的青塊放入蒸笼蒸数分钟,蒸熟之后涂些麻油即可食用。青塊色泽翠绿、软糯清香、甜润可口,是清明节时用来祭祖和作点心的必备食品。

麻糍,系用糯米饭和艾青放在石臼或碾机中捣烂,放在铺有松树花粉的木板上,然后压成半寸厚,上面再撒上松花,切成方形或菱形而成。麻糍内青外黄,烘煎随意,蒸熟而食,蘸以白糖,甜糯可口,香味俱佳。麻糍主要用于祭祖和扫墓后,充足点心,平时则不易吃到。

关于麻糍,还有这样一个传说:很古很古以前的人们,都有 10 节尾巴,黄了 9 节,人就要死了。有人看到自己 9 节尾巴黄了,知道快要死了,就在山里挖个洞,自己爬进去等死。没死前,他就用麻糍做成麻糍被,上面撒上松花,带进洞里、盖在身上,肚子饿了就咬上一口。不料,麻糍被他吃了一条又一条,一直活到一百多岁。大家见他命长,知道是吃了麻糍的缘故,就分着吃老人没吃完的麻糍。以后,每次上坟,也都分着吃麻糍,就相沿成俗了。

冰糖甲鱼

宁波菜肴,以冰糖甲鱼最为著名。冰糖甲鱼的制作特点,是以甲鱼为主要原料,加以冰糖等佐料,以小火焖烧至甲鱼肉和裙边软糯,随即改用旺火收汁。冰糖甲鱼色泽黄亮,绵糯润口,滋味鲜美,并由于烹制时用芡汁热油裹紧甲鱼,能保持较长时间的热度。

冰糖甲鱼的别称为"独占鳌头",则是由甬江状元楼首创的,是宁波十大名菜之一。

相传在 100 多年前,在宁波江北岸临江有一家小酒铺,掌柜以烧冰糖甲鱼著称。他烧的这道菜,清香、绵糯,咸甜兼有,滋味可口,有独到功夫。一天,外地来了两位举人,正欲赴京赶考。途经宁波,相约到这家酒楼饮酒,观赏江景。伙计见是书生,便问:"相公欲尝何菜?"两位举人都是富家子弟,便说:"凡是名菜,俱都上桌品尝便是。"于是,伙计陆续送上各道名菜。两位举人见最后端上来的冰糖甲鱼,鳌头上翘,晶莹透亮,清香扑鼻,便夹起品尝,一到嘴里,顿觉绵糯香甜,滋味非同凡响。两位举人赞不绝口,便问掌柜:"此菜何名?"掌柜见两位随身都带有赶考的行头,便灵机一动,暗送彩头,道:"相公,此乃'独占鳌头'是也!"举人听了,连呼"妙哉!"尽欢而去。

事有凑巧,待到秋季揭榜,其中一位举人果然中了状元。他衣锦还乡,春风得意,特地重登甬江这座小酒楼,指名要吃"独占鳌头",说是吃了此菜,身健神旺,金榜高中,乃此菜之功也。掌柜闻说，便又精心制作一道"冰糖甲鱼"，让状元公品尝，并捧上文房四宝，展开宣纸，恭请他为酒楼题名。状元老爷正在兴头，也不推却，端起笔来，写了"状元楼"三个大字。

从此以后，状元楼名噪浙东。状元楼名菜冰糖甲鱼，也名扬海外。后来上海也开起了两家状元楼，一名"甬江状元楼"，一名"四明状元楼"，并都以善烹冰糖甲鱼著名。

雪菜大黄鱼

雪菜大黄鱼，又称大汤黄鱼，是富有宁波地方特色的名菜。

雪菜大黄鱼选料和制作都十分讲究。选取新鲜大黄鱼，洗净后在背部两面肉厚处用刀略划几个口子，用本地种植的雪里蕻腌制的咸菜切成末，冬笋切成薄片，备用。然后，将大黄鱼用油煎至两面稍黄，烹入黄酒，加盖焖片刻后，加水、加姜，放入咸菜、笋片以及食盐、味精，用猛火烧沸后，再用小火烧数分钟，待汤汁呈乳白色时，撒些葱末，即可装碗，把汤汁倒入碗内即可。

大黄鱼肉嫩、味鲜、少骨，自古有"琐碎金鳞软玉膏"之誉。雪里蕻咸菜质地脆嫩，鲜美可口，有一种特殊的鲜香味。以这两种为主料烧制的雪菜大黄鱼，具有鱼肉嫩、菜香浓、清口鲜洁、营养丰富的海特点，备受食客青睐。

（三）土特产

奉化蚶子

蚶子，又名泥蚶、芽蚶、血蚶，宁波沿海各地都有生产，但以产于奉化的蚶子品质最佳，称奉蚶,是宁波著名的海特产。

蚶子属瓣鳃纲蚶科贝类动物。外壳两瓣,白色坚硬,上有瓦垄状放射肋18～21条,体小壳薄,肉肥血多,营养丰富,味道鲜美,是宴席上不可多得的美味佳肴。

奉化蚶子具有悠久养殖历史。唐元和四年(809年),奉化蚶子因品质特优,被列为"贡品",每年送一石五斗至京师长安。宁波至长安相距数千公里,沿途传送路役数以万计。到了唐元和十五年(820年),越州刺史兼浙东观察使元稹见民众疾苦,便上书穆宗,说是蚶役"人不胜其疲"。唐长庆三年(823年),朝廷下旨免除"蚶役",奉化各地民众闻此消息,欢声雷动"道路歌舞之"。

奉化一带蚶子人工养殖,大致开始于元代,主要养殖区在鲒埼、莼湖一带。元至元《四明续志》载:"有芽蚶,壳棱细布,肉肥,多出鲒埼,冬月有之。亦采苗种之海涂,谓之蚶田。"因这一带地处象山港底部狮子口,温度和盐度适宜,滩涂以泥沙质、水质肥、饵料充足,适合泥蚶生长。所产蚶子颗粒大,肉肥满,血鲜艳,无泥气,味鲜爽。古人有《蚶》诗写道:"荤荤瓦垄子,纷产东海涂。剡川尤著名,风味良不粗。在昔元和间,往往充天厨。赖有贤长官,奏罢免贡输。"

到了明代,奉化蚶子养殖已具一定规模。明嘉靖《奉化县志》载:"明洪武二十四年(1391年)蚶田四亩二分五厘,蚶涂一顷三十六亩。"泥蚶喜欢栖息在潮流畅、风浪小、有淡水注入的内湾及河口附近的软泥滩涂,主要以滤食硅藻类为主,经两年的养殖,便达到食用规格。泥蚶养殖方法一般采用筑塘蓄水法养殖。蚶苗多来自山东文登、荣城、乳山一带,少量采自乐清、玉环。冬季放养,并以小寒到大寒期间采捕为最肥。

宁海青蟹

青蟹,学名锯缘青蟹,又称黄甲蟹,亦称蝤蛑,甲壳纲,蝤蛑科,栖息于泥涂,喜穴居于有淡水流出的地方。宁波出产的青蟹,具有个大、体肥、肉鲜、壳青的特点,是宁波著名的海特产。

青蟹甲壳呈椭圆形,体扁平、无毛,头胸部发达,双螯强有力,后足形如棹。青蟹一年四季都有产,但以每年农历八月初三到廿三这段期间最肥,此时青蟹壳坚如盾,脚爪圆壮,只只都是双层皮,民间有"八月蝤蛑抵只鸡"之说。著名诗人苏东坡在《蝤蛑》一诗中曾写有"半壳含黄宜点酒,两螯斫雪劝加餐"之句。

青蟹生性凶猛,攻击性特强。相传,过去宁波江滨建有蝤蛑庙,说是有渔人捕获一只巨大蝤蛑,力不能胜,为巨螯钳而至死,后人立庙以记其事。又有一说是蝤蛑能与虎斗,故又有"八月蝤蛑健如虎"之说。古人有《煮蟹》诗写道:"釜中爬部索,釜底益薪火。笑尔久横行,今宵受奇祸。"

宁波沿海人民捕捉青蟹历史悠久。据《象山县志》记载:"胡家峙渔民二十,本籍船三艘,捕蝤蛑运销上海、宁波。青蟹每年夏季到浅滩产卵,冬季则穴居冬眠。按照青蟹生存习性,捕捉的方法很多。可以网捕;可在海涂上找蟹洞抓捕,亦可在涂面营造蟹穴捕捉。冬季时,青蟹穴居冬眠,可掘洞捕捉。但野生青蟹产量有限,现在宁波沿海已开始人工养殖青蟹,并已发展到数千亩。

青蟹肉黄丰满,味道鲜美,营养丰富,个体最大可达一公斤。它既是人们夏秋季节佐酒、待客之佳肴,又是妇女"坐月子"吃的滋补佳品和治疗小孩"夜尿症"的良药。

西店牡蛎

牡蛎,即蛎黄,系软体动物、瓣鳃纲、异柱目、牡蛎科、牡蛎属,有褶牡蛎(又称金钱蛎)和近江牡蛎(又称草鞋蛎)两种。牡蛎附岩而生,相连如房,每潮来,诸房皆开,有小虫入,则合之以充饥。牡蛎是一种贝壳类海产品,在山珍海味中属"下八珍"之一。

牡蛎分野生和人工养殖。野生者,大如拇指,用铁片拨开缝隙,挑取蛎肉,蛎肉较小;人工养殖的牡蛎,则以块石点播,经春打滩、夏采苗、秋移植,历二年精心管理,石上已长得重重叠叠,即可以收获。养殖以褶牡蛎为主。

宁海西店是浙江省最大的牡蛎基地。宁海西店养殖牡蛎已有700余年历史。据《宁海县志》载:"铁江之中有两屿,曰石孔双山,县北三十八里,两岛矗立,状如印,内一岛平夷,古神庙在焉。宋进士冯唐英避乱隐此,见岩边牡蛎盛生,教居民聚石养之。"并有"牡蛎出铁江尤佳"的赞语。自此,牡蛎成为这一带著名海产品。县志中提及的"铁江",位于象山港底部狮子口内,港口水色清晰,风平浪静,滩涂宽阔平缓,有凫溪等大小20多条溪河淡水注入港内,土质肥沃,是贝类养殖的优良场所,沿港群众世代养殖牡蛎。铁江一带所产蛎肉,肥壮鲜嫩,蛎肉青玉色,质量特佳。

蛎肉是一种营养价值很高的海珍品、肉味鲜美,素有"海牛奶"之称。蛎肉生食和熟食皆宜,可炒蛋,可煮面。"牡蛎炒蛋"是宁波一道风味名菜。冬春是食牡蛎季节,尤其春节期间,是佐酒待客的佳肴。

牡蛎还可用于医药。据《本草纲目》载,牡蛎有止虚弱、解丹毒、止渴等药用价值;牡蛎壳经煅后,有收敛功能。

长街蛏子

蛏子,学名缢蛏,属软体动物,系瓣鳃纲,真瓣鳃目、竹蛏科。贝壳脆而薄,呈长扁方形,自壳顶到腹缘有一道斜行的凹沟,故名缢蛏。宁波沿海一带多滩涂,对养殖蛏子有得天独厚的优势,是宁波大宗海特产品。宁海长街一带濒临三门湾,常年有大量淡水注入,海水咸淡适宜,饵料丰富,涂质以泥沙为主,因而蛏子生长快、个体大,肉嫩而肥,色白味

鲜,故得名长街蛏子。蛏子是城乡居民非常喜食的一种美味。

蛏子适宜生长于海水盐度低的河口附近和内湾软泥海涂中。养殖蛏子要选择风平浪静、潮流畅通,常有淡水注入的港湾或平坦的滩涂,地质以泥质或泥略带沙为宜。在开春清明前后播苗,等到第二年五月以后,蛏子长到每公斤 100 只左右时即可起捕。蛏子按养殖时间长短,又分为一年蛏、二年蛏、三年蛏。

蛏肉不仅味道鲜美、营养丰富,而且还有一定的医药作用。蛏肉甘、咸寒,用于产后虚寒、烦热痢疾,壳可用于医治胃病,咽喉肿痛。

蛏子食法很简单。从蛏田起捕的蛏子,洗净后,放养于含有少量盐分的清水中,待蛏子腹中泥沙吐净,然后用薄刀片轻轻剖开蛏子背面连接处,倒在沸水中,稍为停留,加入葱末,即可捞起食用。蛏子因其肉嫩味鲜、风味独特,为佐酒的佳肴。古人曾有诗赞道:"沙蜻四寸尾掉黄,风味由来压邵洋。麦碎花开三月半,美人种子市蛏秧。"

黄泥螺

泥螺,学名吐铁。《辞源》中载有泥螺条:"即吐铁,宁波出泥螺,状如蚕豆,可代充海错。"在"吐铁"条则载有:"软体动物,一名泥螺,俗称黄泥螺,状如蜗螺而壳薄,吐吞含沙,沙黑如铁,至桃花时味乃美,腌食之一。一作土铁。"泥螺为宁波著名特产。宁波著名学者全祖望有"年年梅雨后,万瓮入姑胥"之记述。

泥螺在宁波沿海均有产,每年桃花季节,泥螺肚内的"铁"吐尽,肉质鲜嫩而无泥筋,称"桃花泥螺",为上品,并以产于慈溪龙山一带为佳,俗称"龙山黄泥螺"。

龙山黄泥螺早在宋代就有采食的记载。据史料记载:三北黄泥螺以桃花盛开时所产的质量最佳。此时泥螺刚刚长发,体内无泥无菌,味道特别鲜美。中秋时节所产的"桂花

泥螺",虽然比不上桃花泥螺,但也粒大脂丰、味道鲜美。龙山所产黄泥螺之所以特别肥美,是因为慈溪沿海有大批低潮海涂,由钱塘江、曹娥江等河流泥沙及长江出口泥沙驾潮冲积而成,土壤肥沃,尤其龙山一带,条件更加优越,故所产泥螺质量特佳。明代学者张如兰在《吐铁歌》中写道:"土非土,铁非铁,肥如泽,鲜如屑。乍来自,宁波城,看时却似嘉鱼穴。盘中个个玛瑙乌,席前一一丹丘血。见尝者,饮者捏,举杯吃饭两相宜,腥腥不惜广长舌。"

相传,为中国创办民族航运事业作出过重要贡献的申江巨子虞洽卿,其家就在龙山脚下,山孤零零靠在海边,远远望去像只爬在泥涂上的大泥螺。虞洽卿小时候也在泥涂上拾过泥螺。当虞氏显赫时,乡人给他起了个"大泥螺"的外号,并用土语作歌道:"龙山阿德哥,绰号大泥螺,电话通宁波,火车通曹娥。"

泥螺大都经腌制后食用。新捕到的泥螺用海水洗净,放入容器内,加盐后快速搅拌,静置若干时候,待泥螺死亡后,去掉水分,再加盐,加酒若干,将容器口封住,经一星期后即可食用,异香扑鼻。只要不开封,久储不坏,味极鲜脆香美。古人有诗赞道:"次第春糟土冰储,舟移万瓮入姑胥。安期写罢神仙簏,酒墨都成蝌蚪书。"

新鲜泥螺可以放汤。煮前先用清水浸半天,待泥沙吐出后下锅略煮即熟,再加些酱油及葱花即可食用,肉粒变小而色褐,其味鲜不亚于牡蛎汤。

泥螺体表黏液及内脏中含有一种毒素,经腌熟后毒素可以消除。个别人吃了未经腌熟的泥螺,会产生面部浮肿、足趾僵硬的症状,宁波人称为"发泥螺胖",一般几天后症状会消失。所以食时最好用醋蘸食,既可杀菌,又能增加美味。

泥螺既营养丰富,又具一定医药作用,据《本草纲目拾遗》记载,泥螺有补肝肾、润肺、明目、生津之功效。民间还有以酒渍食,防治咽喉炎、肺结核。

象山梭子蟹

象山梭子蟹是宁波著名海特产。

梭子蟹,因头胸甲呈梭子形而得名,属于甲壳纲、十足目、梭子蟹科。有些地方俗称"白蟹"。梭子蟹甲壳的中央有三个突起,所以又称"三疣梭子蟹"。雄性脐尖而光滑,螯长大,壳面带青色;雌性脐圆有绒毛,壳面呈赭色,或有斑点。梭子蟹肉肥味美,有较高的营养价值和经济价值,且适宜于海水暂养增肥。由于梭子蟹生长迅速,养殖利润丰厚,已经成为中国沿海地区重要的养殖品种。梭子蟹在冬季徊游季节个体最为健壮,一般重250克左右,大的可达500克。

象山梭子蟹肉质细嫩、洁白、肉多,脂膏肥满,富含蛋白质,味鲜美。尤其是雌蟹,红膏满盖,口味极佳。

梭子蟹可鲜食,或蒸、或煎、或炒,或切为两半炖豆板瓣酱,或用蟹炒年糕、炒咸菜、煮豆腐,是沿海一带居民餐桌上的常菜。也可腌食,就是将新鲜梭子蟹投入盐卤中浸泡,数日后即可食用,俗称"新风炝蟹";或将新鲜梭子蟹捣糊加盐等调味料制成蟹酱。过去,渔民因梭子蟹产量高,常挑选膏满活蟹,将蟹黄剔入碗中,风吹日晒令其凝固,即成"蟹黄饼",风味特佳,但产量少,一般人难尝此味。还有将蟹卵漂洗、晒干做成"蟹籽",亦是海味品中之上品。

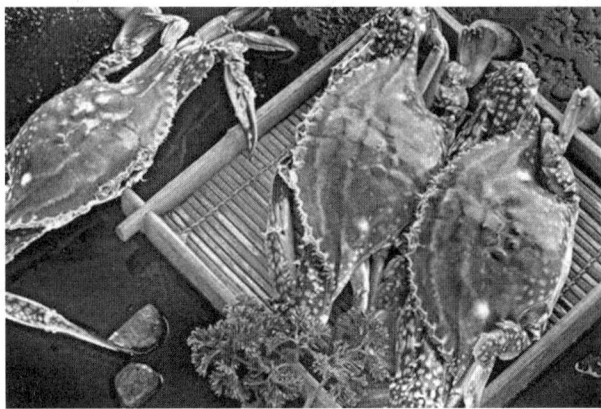

奉化水蜜桃

宁波靠山面海,物产丰富。但在众多水果珍品中,又以奉化水蜜桃独占鳌头,并以"琼浆玉露""瑶池珍品"的美称驰名遐迩。奉化水蜜桃有别于其他地方蜜桃的特点是:果大皮薄,色泽鲜艳,核紫肉厚,蜜汁丰富,甘美清香。

奉化水蜜桃的历史,最早可以追溯到两千年前。据《幽明录》记载:汉明帝永平五年,剡县刘晨、阮肇共入天台山,取谷皮,迷不得返,经十三日,粮食乏尽,饥馁殆死。后来在山上发现桃树,食桃充饥,才免于饿死。文中所载的"天台山",其实就是现在天台山、四明山的总称。

奉化水蜜桃的大规模栽种,则是在清晚期。其实,早在明清年间,奉化一带种的主要是红桃、白桃。到了清光绪年间,浙江东阳县有一位叫张崇银的园艺人,流落到奉化雪窦山三十六村,他见这一带山高雾多,天暖地肥,便从上海引进优良的"上海龙华水蜜桃"品种作母本,选取本地最优良的土桃作父本,嫁接繁殖,去劣留优,经过长期选择,终于培育出今日闻名海内外的奉化玉露水蜜桃。后经竞相引种,很快普及全县。品系也由原来单一品种逐步发展到平顶玉露、玉露蟠桃,以及黄桃、皱叶黄露等 40 多个品种。

奉化水蜜桃的栽种、采摘都十分讲究。先是育苗、选种、接枝。接活的桃种在第一年开花时,要将桃花打掉,以免造成先天不足,降低整株树的品质。第二年开花时,再将花打掉,只留极少几朵花,待果实成熟时作品尝之用,以便留优劣汰。第三年开始结的果实,便精心爱护。长在树上的每一颗桃子,都要用纸包起来,以防虫害和曝晒,使桃子成熟时色泽青白玉润,浓甜清口,不留红斑,芳香飘溢。

玉露桃是奉化水蜜桃中芳香、鲜味、甜度最好的水蜜桃,成熟时,桃皮呈半透明状,近核处略带红色,肉质细软,皮薄如蝉翼,甜汁饱满,芳香诱人,最宜鲜食。玉露桃以在树上长得熟透的为最佳。撕开薄薄的很有韧性的一层表皮,一口下去,满嘴琼浆玉液,令人欲舍不能。玉露桃一般分早、中、迟三种,从六月中旬上市,直至立秋前后还有应市。

水蜜桃不仅营养丰富,而且有一定保健功效。据《本草纲目》载,桃子有增进人体胆汁分泌,促进胃肠蠕动,治疗便秘等功效。

奉化芋艿头

"跑过三江六码头,吃过奉化芋艿头",浙江一带的人们常用这样一句话来表示自己到过很多地方,吃过很多山珍海味,并以吃过味道特别好的奉化芋艿头引为骄傲。

芋艿,一名"岷紫",天南星科宿根性植物,原产于东南亚,秦汉时传入我国,我国南方多有栽培。奉化芋艿头是奉化的传统特产,在海内外久享盛名,并以萧王庙镇一带所产品质最优。有个叫陈著的奉化人,在他的《收芋偶成》一诗中有"数窠岷紫破穷搜,珍重留为老齿馐"之句。

奉化芋艿头种植历史悠久。据有关史料记载,已有700多年历史。大量栽种的芋头,在饥荒时可以充当备用粮。1773年清乾隆时修的《奉化县志》称:"芋,种来自日本,取熟芋为粉作砖,积数十年不坏,和屑可以备荒。"相传,这个记载来自于这样一个传说:

奉化有个富绅,家有良田千亩,但独养儿子却是吃喝嫖赌,很不争气。富绅知道自己死后,儿子会把家产败光,而后必定饿死。他冥思苦想,终于想出了一个办法。某一年,他待芋艿头成熟时便大量收买,尔后把芋艿头蒸熟、捣烂,制成一块块砖头,并用这种砖头造了一间普通的平屋。十年后,富绅临死时叮嘱儿子,以后若是贫穷了,可以变卖家产,但切不可变卖这间平屋,这间平屋是可以吃的。老人死后,家产果然被劣子变卖一空,最后只好退居这间平屋。而这一年正闹饥荒,劣子在挨饿中忽然想起父亲临死时的话,便试着啃起了砖头,觉得味道很好,确可充饥。他自吃有余,还把它送给其他村民,保住了一村生灵。

奉化芋艿头品种很多,种在旱地的叫"旱芋艿",种在水田里的叫"水芋艿"。其品种有香广芋、乌脚鸡、黄粉箕、大芋艿、红芋艿等多种,并以红芋艿头独享盛名。

奉化芋芳头的种植,对土壤适应性很强。奉化萧王庙一带气候温和、土壤肥沃,并含有沙质,这里出产的芋芳头皮薄、形圆、头大、光滑,呈红褐色,芋肉粉,煮熟后清香可口,一般每只重约二、三斤,大的可达四、五斤。一般在八月上旬采掘上市,表皮晾干后久藏不坏。

奉化芋芳头食法甚多。可烘蒸、生烤、熟炒、白切、做糊烧汤;若烘蒸,清香扑鼻,味若板栗;若烧汤,滑似银耳。把芋芳头剖成数块、加上佐料,清炖鸭子,即"鸭子芋芳",别具风味,是溪口人每逢中秋佳节时家家户户必备的一道菜,也是招待宾客的一道佳肴。

奉化芋芳头美名远播。早在 20 世纪 30 年代就风行上海市场,被视为珍品。大江南北都有人到奉化溪口一带采购芋芳头,尤其是旅居在我国港澳台地区以及东南亚一带的游子,到溪口游览探亲时都要品尝一下奉化芋芳头的滋味,并带几颗回去,以慰思乡之念。

象山白鹅

象山大白鹅是宁波著名特产,其品种优良,是全国优良鹅种之一,以体型肥大、色泽光亮、脂肪分布均匀见长。象山大白鹅不仅具有很高的观赏价值,还因其个体硕大、肉味鲜美而闻名海内外;加工成"冻宁波鹅"出口,在港澳市场享有盛誉。现今每年饲养量近百万羽。

相传,象山大白鹅是一千多年前晋朝大书法家王羲之所传。王羲之曾做过右将军、会稽内史,有很多故事流传于世。后因与骠骑将军不和,辞去官职,回家隐居,以写字养鹅自娱。王羲之家乡六诏村(今属奉化市)风景秀丽,为剡溪九曲之第一曲。他选购各地品种优良的白鹅,精心饲养,因而鹅体硕大,色泽柔润,肉味鲜美,与众不同。

王羲之模仿鹅的各种姿态运笔写字。现在在天台山国清寺保存有王羲之书写的独笔"鹅"字碑;绍兴兰亭鹅池碑"鹅池"二字,则是王羲之父子合写的。王羲之写的字"飘若浮云,矫若惊龙",但他写字随写随撕,世人以得他一字为稀世珍宝。相传,国清寺方丈欲在寺内立碑,想请王羲之书碑而不能。他冥思苦想,终于想出了一个办法。他从各地选购了一群体型肥大、毛羽整洁的大鹅,经精心饲养后,把鹅笼到剡溪一曲,等待时机。一天,王羲之写罢字,漫步溪畔,忽见溪流中一群大白鹅,"白毛浮绿水,红掌拨清波"。他越看越爱,喜不自禁。只见溪边站着一位头戴竹笠的老汉,便上前说道:"请将鹅卖我,银价任你讨。"装扮成老汉的方丈和尚,佯装不肯,经王羲之再三请求,才说:"你若能为我写一个字,我便将这群鹅送你也无妨。"王羲之大喜,回家拿起大笔,惊龙翔凤般地在宣纸上一笔写成一个"鹅"字,和尚赶紧收起"鹅"字,珍重地放进黄色袱,回到寺院便把这个"鹅"字刻在碑上,成为流传千古的鹅字碑。王羲之则将和尚这群鹅精心饲养,成为象山大白鹅优良品种开端。后来鹅种在象山、奉化一带广为引养,名闻遐迩。

象山大白鹅适应性强,生长快,成年的公鹅体型高大雄伟,叫声宏亮,昂首挺胸,性喜水,善斗,一般重达15~16斤。母鹅性情温顺,腹部宽大下垂,鸣声低沉,一般重13~14斤,肉质肥嫩。每逢过年过节、婚嫁喜庆,人们都把它作为馈赠亲友的礼品。1842年以后,宁波成为五口通商口岸之一,象山大白鹅也随之远销海外。

慈溪杨梅

慈溪市位于杭州湾跨海大桥的南岸,素有"中国杨梅之乡"的称谓。杨梅是慈溪市特有的名产,人工栽培已有1300余年,野生杨梅更有7000余年历史。2000年,慈溪市被国家林业局命名为"中国名特优经济林杨梅之乡",现已通过杨梅原产地保护认证。慈溪杨梅以名闻遐迩的"荸荠种"和"早大种"杨梅为主,果大、核小、色佳,肉质细嫩、汁多味浓、香甜可口,其品质优势极为明显,鲜食、加工均可。慈溪杨梅通过各种网络远销到我国香港地区、新加坡、法国、日本等市场,成为海外游子的家乡珍果。宋代大文豪苏东坡曾赞道:"闽广荔枝、西凉葡萄,未若吴越杨梅。"

慈溪杨梅以横河镇梅园村杨梅最为有名。在梅园村,有大小数家杨梅旅游景点,每年六月,梅园山上的杨梅树上结满了一个个深红色、浅紫色或白色的杨梅,闪红烁紫。梅农们背着刀笠上山采摘,山上洋溢着山里人纯朴而又幸福的笑声。匡堰镇游源村是慈溪市已通过绿色认证的杨梅生产基地,也是指定的杨梅旅游接待中心之一。游源杨梅在慈溪市杨梅评比中多次获得金牌杨梅的称号。因游源村山地土壤中富含微量元素"硒",而使游源杨梅果实中的"硒"含量达到其他杨梅产区果实硒含量的四倍。

青山拂云,翠竹绕林,茶园倚于山岭,杨梅红满山头,可谓是回归大自然的好去处。每年六月中旬慈溪都举办"杨梅节",在杨梅节上会选出"杨梅仙子"。

邱隘咸菜

宁波土地肥沃,雨水充沛,利用秋冬季闲地种植雪里蕻鲜菜,具有悠久历史。由于水稻田肥沃,产量很高,可作为粮菜互补,增加收入。据《广群芳谱》载:"四明有菜,名雪里蕻,雪深诸菜冻损,此菜独青,雪里蕻之得名盖以此。味稍带辛辣,腌食绝佳。"古人有诗云:"种得园蔬味颇香,城南附近学宫墙。每逢雪里初抽蕻,不数秋菘与伏姜。"在冬春两季,选用新鲜雪里蕻菜,经过加工腌制而成雪里蕻咸菜,是宁波的传统特产。

雪里蕻咸菜,又叫咸齑,以鄞县东乡邱隘地区加工腌制的最为著名。当地种植和制作雪里蕻咸菜,已有数百年历史。以前家家户户都种菜腌制,备作长年菜肴。制作雪里蕻咸菜的方法是:选用冬季或春季新鲜雪里蕻菜,从田里割下后,晾 2 至 4 小时,散开放平,至外叶稍黄,削去老根,放入缸内腌制。腌制时一层菜撒一层盐,层层踏实,隔天再踏压一次,上铺竹片,用洁净的大石块压住,一般腌制一个月后即可食用。近年来大批量种植,成为当地农民致富的重要来源之一。当地农民除腌制咸菜出售外,还办起了精制雪菜厂,制成小包装咸菜,畅销全国各大城市及东南亚、香港等地。

雪里蕻咸菜色泽黄亮,有一种特殊的香味,具有香、嫩、脆、鲜、微酸特点,食之生津开胃。宁波地区流传有"三天不吃咸齑汤,脚骨酸汪汪"和"家有咸菜,不吃淡饭"的民谚。清朝诗人李邺嗣在《鄮东竹枝词》中称赞雪里蕻咸菜道:"翠绿新齑滴醋红,嗅来香气嚼来松。纵然金菜琅蔬好,不及吾乡雪里蕻。"

雪里蕻咸菜可以生吃、熟吃,亦可作为佐料,制作多种菜肴。尤以"咸菜大黄鱼""咸菜肉丝汤"最为有名。

余姚榨菜

　　榨菜,是宁波新发展起来的特产,盛产于余姚及慈溪一带,尤其是余姚。由于土质及气候等自然条件得天独厚,余姚所产的榨菜,鲜头块形圆匀,质地脆嫩肥厚,色泽鲜艳,空心率低,并具有生长快、产量高的优点。榨菜又称茎用芥菜,系十字花科,芥菜属,以其肥大的肉质茎经腌制压榨加工后而成为榨菜。加工成的榨菜,具有鲜、香、脆、嫩的特点,味道鲜美,营养丰富,深受群众的喜爱。

　　余姚、慈溪一带种植榨菜始于 20 世纪 60 年代,由萧山引种成功后大面积推广,栽培面积逐年扩大,产品销往全国各地,并出口日本、东南亚各国及港澳地区。

　　由鲜菜加工成榨菜须经过 18 道工序,其中关键性的工序有 10 道。鲜菜收获后,去叶、去根、剥去老筋、削去斑点,然后放入菜池,层层加盐后踏实,铺上干净的竹排后压以石块,经数十小时后出池上榨,然后再经腌制,经月余放置,鲜菜头在微生物酶的作用下,便形成榨菜的基本风味。再经过整形、分级、淘洗、压榨,拌入一定比例的多种香料,然后装坛、压实,并用水泥封口而成榨菜。

　　余姚榨菜含有多种营养成分,富含维生素、铁、磷等矿物质和蛋白质、氨基酸等。菜色香味独特、咸辣适度、味鲜爽口,是四季皆宜的佐餐佳品。

宁海白枇杷

　　宁海白枇杷产自宁波市宁海县东南的一市镇。一市镇地理位置优越,三面环山、南临三门湾,山青水绿,景色诱人,具有独特的小气候和土壤条件,所产枇杷果形圆润,果色清黄,果肉乳白,果味鲜嫩,果香芳醇,皮薄汁多,深受广大消费者喜爱。

　　宁海白枇杷是培育成功的枇杷新品种,抗逆性强,丰产,品质综合指标超过国内外同类产品。国内外的专家学者对该品种的形、色、味给予高度评价,称"白枇杷"是宁海一宝,是枇杷界的优秀品种,南方枇杷中的精品结晶。宁海白枇杷按无公害生产标准培育,自1997 年产出以来,曾多次在省、市、县农产品展销会、枇杷品尝会上获奖,是屈指可数的优质绿色果品。

尚田草莓

尚田草莓是浙江省宁波市奉化市尚田镇的特产。奉化尚田镇是中国草莓之乡,有"中国草莓第一镇""浙江草莓之乡"美誉,拥有万亩草莓基地,草莓个大味甜、色泽红艳、芳香醇厚、营养丰富,深受广大游客喜爱。近年来,尚田镇相继成立了草莓"购销中心""农民草莓协会""草莓研究所"等,引进和扶持了多家以加工草莓为主的农业龙头企业,有力地推进了种养加、产供销、贸工农相结合的现代化农业新格局。

尚田草莓在优越的地理环境条件下,通过绿色标准化栽培管理。根据国家农业部绿色食品质量监督检验测试中心测定,鲜草莓果实各项指标突出,各项产品质量和农药残留指标都符合国家绿色食品要求,属绿色水果之精品。尚田草莓还有一定的保健作用,对人们美容养颜、抗衰防癌、延年益寿等具有良好的功效。

三北豆酥糖

三北豆酥糖是浙江宁波慈溪余姚一带传统食品,与三北藕丝糖齐名,是浙江宁波汉族传统名点之一,名扬江浙地区和海外。宁波豆酥糖属于典型的宁式茶食,口感酥松,易溶化,无糖渣,不黏牙,有黄豆香味,营养丰富,老小皆宜。

三北豆酥糖创始于清代,有悠久的制作历史。相传在清代晚期,余姚陆埠镇上开有一家叫"乾丰"的南货茶食店,一位宁波师傅试制成功了豆酥糖。由于配料考究、加工精细,制作的豆酥糖香甜可口、松脆无渣,入口即化、不黏牙齿,且香味独特,食后令人口齿留香,回味无穷,一时顾客盈门,名噪浙东,方圆数百里慕名争购者,络绎不绝。从此以后,宁波豆酥糖一直是宁波"三北"的名点。

制作豆酥糖,选料要求极为严格。豆酥糖经多道工序精心制作后,再用纸包装得四方棱角分明,厚薄均匀。底封不用浆糊,免得豆酥糖发潮,这样就能长久保持豆酥糖香、甜、酥、松的品质。每逢年末,宁波地区农村大都做年糕以备春节期间享用。用火热年糕团嵌豆酥糖,又香又长又糯,是深受老幼喜爱的时令食品。新中国成立后,"三北豆酥糖"在传统特色的基础上,又有了新的提高。

(四)宁波老字号

"缸鸭狗"甜食店

"缸鸭狗"是宁波有名的百年老店,以小吃闻名。由宁波人江定发于1926年创建。江定发小名阿狗,人称"江阿狗",起初在城隍庙设摊卖酒酿圆子和红枣汤,积资后在开明街开店。他别出心裁地以"水缸、麻鸭、黄狗"图案作店号,故门庭若市,顾客络绎不绝。"缸鸭狗"以经营猪油汤团、酒酿蛋花圆子、八宝饭和百果圆子著称,甜点具有质糯、汤清、形美、味甜等特点。

20世纪初,因为家境贫寒,年纪尚小的江定发跟着大人出海做帮工。为了好养活,父母给他取了个小名叫"阿狗"。江阿狗长到18岁,被母亲应氏送到三北的顺和祥学做生意。江阿狗聪明勤快,眼头活络,掌柜一心留他在铺子里帮忙,但刚刚20岁出头的江阿狗,已经打定主意回家照顾母亲。应氏信奉男人"先成家后立业"的说法,已经给阿狗说好了一门亲事。阿狗私底下和媳妇何凤秀闲聊,"我们家孤儿寡母的,也没什么家底,你为何愿意嫁过来?"何凤秀的回答出乎阿狗意料,"我吃过咱妈送来的汤圆,又大又甜,觉得到了你家也苦不了。"

媳妇这一说,倒是让江阿狗茅塞顿开。街坊邻里都称赞母亲的汤圆包得好,为何不摆个卖汤圆的摊子?阿狗和母亲一说,应氏很是支持,于是一家三口关了老屋的门,带着之前攒下的一些银两,来到了宁波城隍庙摆起汤圆摊。开始只有汤圆,阿狗为人和善,客人要多加点白糖、桂花的,他一一照办。不过很快他就意识到,只卖汤圆是不行的,客人迟早会厌烦,于是又有了酒酿丸子、豆沙丸子,汤圆的各种馅料也是换着法子做,到他摊位吃甜点的客人络绎不绝。

四年下来,江阿狗的汤圆摊在城隍庙已小有名气,他用攒下的辛苦钱在开明街的泰和桥边租了间店面。有店就要招牌连店名都没一个,没读过书的江阿狗犯了愁。有不少熟客帮着出主意,但无非是一些寻常小吃店的名字,最后阿狗还是觉得用自己的名字"江阿狗",叫得响亮。他自己不会写几个字,就请来了当时宁波越剧团小有名气的舞美王云标先生,在招牌上画了一只缸、一只麻鸭和一只黄狗,中间嵌着"汤圆"两个小字。

一天,有个老秀才在店里吃了好几碗汤圆,最后却没钱付账,江阿狗也不计较。秀才说,看你这个店名是个画,大家不好传播,我给你写个店名。两人一商量,就用"缸鸭狗"作招牌,取"江阿狗"在宁波话里的谐音,通俗易懂,也和原来的画都对应上了。

"三更四更半夜头,要吃汤团'缸鸭狗'。一碗落肚勿肯走,两碗三碗上瘾头。一摸铜钿还勿够,脱落布衫当押头。"这段不少老宁波人耳熟能详的俗语,说的就是这家从城隍庙街口一家无名的露天小摊一步一步发展起来、众人争相品尝的百年老字号。

状元楼

状元楼,坐落在宁波市区东门口,原址在江北岸三江口畔。创建于清乾隆五十年

(1785年),以经营正宗甬帮菜扬名。

相传旧时有两客地举人赴京赶考路经甬城,上这家酒楼临窗对江小酌。酒酣耳热之际,跑堂送上一盘"冰糖甲鱼"。两人看到盘中青黄相映,油汁紧裹鱼块,入口绵糯,香甜酸咸诸味俱全,禁不住绝口称妙。问跑堂:此系何菜?跑堂看他俩一身读书人打扮,一副赶考行头,就随机应变,暗送吉利说:"此乃'独占鳌头'也!"两举人听了好不开心。事有凑巧,其中一举人果然金榜题名,中了状元。在衣锦还乡途中特地重登此楼,提笔挥毫,写了"状元楼"三字,让店家作招牌。从此以后,楼以菜扬名,菜为楼增色,生意更加兴隆,仕宦缙绅继踵。状元楼遂赢得了"浙东第一楼"的美誉。

1936年,状元楼移至日新街16号,为有三楼五开间门面,由28名员工合股经营,顾客多为工商、金融、军政各界人士。1946年,蒋经国曾两次携妻光顾就餐。该年又迁至新江桥南堍江厦街4号。1949年9月,店房遭国民党飞机轰炸倾坍。后由10名职工合资在江北岸新江桥旁开设"甬江状元楼",但经营惨淡。1956年实行公私合营,营业有所转机,但规模较小,至1959年又因木结构房屋超负荷倒坍而闭歇。在此后的20多年里,一些老宁波和海外游子一直期待着"何日重登状元楼,伴旧把盏话春秋"。

1985年10月,由宁波市政府和香港甬港联谊会牵头,宁波市饮食服务公司与港方合资在中山东路和义路口重建状元楼,定名"宁波状元楼股份有限公司"。共有经营场地1100平方米,古典宫廷式门楼,大堂宽敞整洁,包厢高雅舒适,使状元楼重振英姿,迎来了侨胞"重登状元楼,品尝家乡菜"的盛况。"船王"包玉刚曾在此设宴款待家乡父老。1992

年,状元楼股份有限公司改由市饮服公司(市东亚集团公司)独资经营,并兼并了毗邻的明州大旅社,再度投入巨资,扩建、装修,更名为"状元楼宾馆"。

1995 年,状元楼被国家授予"中华老字号"金匾。

升阳泰南货铺

升阳泰南货铺由宁波知府华少湖于清同治年间(1862—1874 年)创建,迄今已有 140 多年的历史。其店名寓意兴旺平安。以经营南北货、宁式糕点为主,所产豆酥糖、苔生片、万年青、香糕、水涤豆糕、胡桃茯苓糕、椒桃片等独具地方风味。与大同南货店、大有南货店、董生阳南货店合称甬上南北货"四大家"。

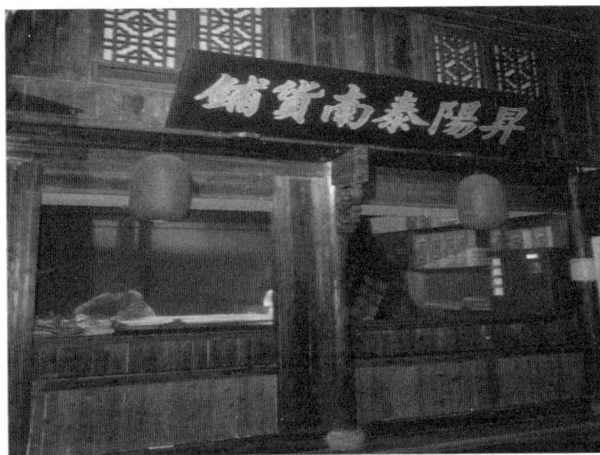

升阳泰南货铺在经营上采取前店后场形式,现做现卖,经营的商品以南北果品和宁式糕点而闻名,兼生产和销售酱制品、豆制品。各类宁式糕点中,油包、四面黄香糕、水绿豆糕、胡桃茯苓糕等传统产品更具地方风味。经营的南北果品都经筛选分类,按质论价,服务周到,称准量足,包装考究,声誉颇佳,在江、浙、京、津、沪等地和港、澳等地的宁波籍人士中享有盛誉。该店原由王瑞祥掌管,后于 1949 年停业。

1950 年,葛来潮在原址又以"升阳泰"招牌恢复营业。1956 年实行公私合营,1958 年改名为"鼓楼食品商店"。1987 年,在原址兴建了 6 层大楼,总面积 3500 平方米,定名"宁波升阳泰商场",有职工 200 余人。新商场继承老店的优良传统,保持老店经营特色,增添现代化设施,组建了宁波市首家大型自选商场,采用电脑收款系统。

1992 年,再次全面扩建装修后,总面积达 7000 平方米,商场营业大楼设中央空调,双向自动扶梯,经营范围在原有的糖果、烟酒、乳制品、腌腊制品、蜜饯和粮食制品基础上,新增冷冻食品、百货、家电交电、服装、钟表、儿童用品、各类皮具等大类商品或精品,并新开设了升阳泰西饼房,供应各式时新糕饼、西点,并开设了传统名特糕点专柜,不断开发具有地方传统特色的糕点食品,商誉日隆,经济效益和社会效益显著。

从2001年9月份起,更名为"升阳泰宁波特产商场",专营宁波特产食品和旅游纪念品。同年,被宁波市命名为宁波市"旅游定点接待单位",为了更好地营造原汁原味的传统经营风格,升阳泰再建升阳泰旅游食品厂,恢复宁波传统食品的现做现卖。如今升阳泰旅游食品厂的产品有宁式传统糕点系列、"泰"字宁式糕团系列、绿色植物农家系列、干海鲜系列、宁式月饼系列、蛋糕系列等近200种产品,其中宁式豆酥糖、相思糕等被评为宁波市旅游推荐商品,食品厂还被命名为"宁波市旅游商品定点生产企业"。与此同时,对传统文化的挖掘整理也让"升阳泰"焕发生机。"状元糕""平安糕""财神糕""吉祥糕"等带有好口彩糕点的推出,吸引了许多"老宁波"前来购买。

楼茂记酱园

楼茂记创建于清乾隆八年(1743年),系甬上传统老字号名店,起初叫"楼恒盛茂记酱园",迄今已有270多年的历史。楼茂记经营具有江南风味特色的各档花色酱菜,还有酱醋、酱油、香干、鲜麸、黄酒等产品,其中秘制的"楼茂记"香干因为色香味俱佳,清口细糯,名扬甬上,成为一大风味食品。

相传康熙年间,奉化楼岙(现为奉化楼隘)的一对楼氏小夫妻来宁波,在江东百丈街、灰街拐角处摆豆芽摊谋生。由于楼氏夫妻待人和善,又善经营,豆芽生意不久就红火起

来。为了扩大业务范围，夫妻俩又开设了豆腐水作工场，在原址自产自销豆腐、豆芽、素鸡、香干、鲜麸等。几年后，收益化作积累，积累又作投资，作坊的规模越来越大。乾隆八年，通过一个在京城做官的亲戚，夫妇俩领了准卖官盐的烙牌，开始卖盐造酱，"楼恒盛茂记酱园"隆重开张。后来在道光年间，楼茂记还在祖籍奉化开设过楼恒昌酱园。

楼茂记原是楼家的"子孙店"（子孙代代相传），沿袭多代。1956 年公私合营改造后，"楼恒盛茂记酱园"改名为"楼茂记"酱品商店。1988 年，由宁波江东蔬菜食品股份有限公司接手管理，十年后改制成立"宁波市楼茂记食品有限公司"。目前，楼茂记食品不但在宁波周边地区销售，其酱醋、腐乳等产品还远销我国香港、台湾地区，并长年出口到欧美、东南亚等地。据传店主系奉化楼姓夫妇，始在百丈街开设豆腐作坊，后定名"楼茂记"。

宁波有句老话说："勿吃楼茂记香干，生活做煞唔相干。"意思是最苦最累的活要做，但楼茂记香干必须要吃，否则就失去生活的意义。可见其影响之大。

大有南货店

大有南货店创设于清咸丰三年（1853 年），店主朱氏，为"谨""慎"两房所共有。店址在药行街、灵桥门附近，经营南北果品、茶食，尤以自制特色品种闻名。用料讲究，制作精细，色香味俱佳，所制酱油瓜子、大有香糕、大有蛋糕均为宁式名点，经营以质取胜，开设后不久即享有盛名。旧时门面蓝底金字，嵌字联曰："大名重宇宙，有美尽东南。"显示店家创业雄心，为甬上老字号名店之一。在大有开设之初，宁波南北货业中有大同、方怡和、董生阳、升阳泰四家。由于"大有"经营得法，便后来居上，把开设在"大有"对面的"大同"收购，所以有"大有兴，大同落"之说。

大有南货店能在同业竞争中取胜，主要是因为在经营管理上有独到之处。大有南货店传到"慎"房朱榕青时，对"大有"的经营管理作了一系列改革，营销手段都有自己的特

色。朱榕青亲自抓进货,坚持做到"货真价实"。干果供应要在店内拣选、分出档次,如供应兴化正三全桂圆每斤不多于96颗;供应胡桃当面敲开,发现次货立即掉换。在服务态度上,不管是上层人物还是普通人,同样热情亲切、敬重如宾,如旧时农民上城惠顾,赠给标有"大有"字号灯笼一盏,借作广告。有些乡下顾客上城不便,往往委托船老大代买,"大有"对这些船老大常以茶水点心甚至酒饭招待。1923年朱榕青去世后,其次子朱元升(瑜章)继承父业,除沿用上代的经营经验外,又作了一系列的创新改革。如认真物色、聘请各部门头脑,量材录用头柜店员、一般店员及拣货员;给员工的报酬略高于同行业,在年终还分红包,因此,员工爱店如家。值得一提的是朱元升对"三角包""斧头包"的包装改革,他不墨守成规,试用纸盒,并印上五彩图案、"大有"字号及地址,既大方美观,又解决了原包装比较松脆、不便携带的缺点,还起到了广告作用,深受顾客欢迎。

20世纪三四十年代,大有南货店屡遭祸难。1938年,九如里仓库被日机轰炸烧毁,损失惨重;在宁波沦陷期间,店堂又受药行街人和药店大火连累而遭烧毁,规模一落千丈。抗日战争胜利后,由于物价飞涨、币制贬值,种种打击之下,只能勉强维持。1949年9月,国民党飞机轰炸闹市区,店铺又遭到巨大损失。

1956年,实行公私合营。20世纪70年代,店堂不幸遭到火灾,资产损失殆尽,"大有"只剩下空牌子。1980年,国家重新投资,在原址重新开设大有南货店,商店继承发扬传统优良经营特色,并开拓创新,大力推行优质服务,因此多年来生意十分兴旺。可惜的是,因近十多年来城市改建,大有南货店不复存在。

赵大有糕团店

"赵大有"为宁式糕团著名品牌,肇始于清同治年间(1862—1874年),最早是上虞梁湖赵家村族人来甬开的年糕店,距今约一百四五十年。清宣统三年(1911年),宁波人赵培德在名师指点下于江东百丈街开设"赵大有糕团店",经营"喜庆""时令""常年"三类糕团,品种有龙凤金团、水晶油包、桂花糖年糕、青塸、雪团、松花蛋、水磨年糕、薄荷糕等,尤以龙凤金团和水晶油包最负盛名。

那时紧邻宁波余姚的上虞经济萧条,生活艰苦,做出来的糕点很少有人问津。为了生计,赵氏先祖邀同族人装运一船梁湖米来宁波谋生,在宁波江东租得单间店面,季节性地制作年糕,招牌取名"赵大有"。他们从农历十一月开业,试销两月,颇受宁波市民好评,因为梁湖米远比宁姚帮使用的晚粳米绵糯、有韧劲。加以梁湖帮师傅操作精细,以及凭借经过选择的优良石磨,制作出来的年糕特别细、滑、韧。赵大有还规定,"粉酸馅漏""花纹不著""松花脱皮"三不卖。

当时宁波糕团店林立,赵大有草创伊始,自知欲求发展,必须要有与同业竞争的勇气。那年自农历七月廿一开始,通宵生产,另有两家糕团店也不退让。赵大有初露锋芒,生意

鼎盛,顾客公认他的糕团质量胜过其他各店。不到三五年,百丈街上几家糕团店纷纷关门,唯有赵大有独存。

站稳脚跟后,赵氏族辈竞相来甬盘租店面,这样赵大有的基业便从江东扩展到城区,四乡人民旅外、同乡探亲往来,农村祭祖、进谱,以及祝寿、婚嫁、庆生等喜庆活动,都少不了赵大有糕点。连当年身为国民政府"大总统"的蒋介石也不能例外,每次回乡路过宁波,他都要特别吩咐部下买些赵大有糕点,以赠送亲朋好友。

改革开放以来,赵大有糕团店又取得长足进步,产品多次被宁波市消费者协会评为"消费者推荐商品"。2008 年,"赵大有"在"中华老字号精品博览会"上被消费者评为"最喜爱的中华老字号品牌"。现今的赵大有糕团已形成以糯米制品为代表的软糕及酥饼系列共 160 多个品种,产品不仅在省内外大卖场上柜,还远销我国港、澳、台地区。

寿全斋

寿全斋原名"寿全斋国药号",创建于清乾隆二十五年(1760 年),创始人为王立鳌、孙将壳。后孙氏退出,而由王氏独家经营,代代相传。原店址在最繁华的今中山东路 56 号。寿全斋以高档参茸补品、地道药材为经营特色,店名取"延年益寿,药品齐全"之意,当时还特地延请翰林杨亨泰书写了贴金匾额。

寿全斋中药以货真价实为宗旨,遵古法炮制为典律,采用紫铜锅、铁船、锡盘、瓷盅等古工具,精制各种膏、丹、散、丸、露、饮片,以及参茸补酒和其他药酒,如"十全大补膏""水眼药""鹅毛管眼药""小儿退烧膏",等等。其独特的制剂方法和严谨的经营风格可概括为四个字:"正""证""精""真",即:进料做到药源路正,储运做到质量和品种保证,加工做到道道精细精心,撮药做到味味认真。两百多年来,寿全斋在宁波民间和同业中享有盛誉,故虽历经波折,至今仍然是宁波人心目中的大药店。

新中国成立后,寿全斋历经公私合营、股份制改造等,现为民营公司。改革开放后,为适应现代医学进步、迎合现代市场需求,寿全斋老店新开,从以前的鼓楼老店(中山东路56号)重返药行街(天一店),受到市民的好评。

寿全斋药店经过两百多年的经营,创出了牌子,赢得了信誉,并形成了享誉海内外的寿全斋文化。每年冬至前的膏方节也是宁波寿全斋的一大特色。寿全斋作为一家百年老店,被浙江省定为"浙江名店"。1995年,寿全斋被贸易部授予"中华老字号"称号。

源康布店

源康布店,始建于清代晚期(1904年),为浙江宁波鄞州西乡人屠景山所开。先开设于日新街口,后因生意兴隆,迁至东门大街。源康布店主要经营黑白蓝粗布、呢绒、绸缎、麻织品等,价廉物美,花色齐全,染料上等,工艺考究。并自设染坊,店坊合一。当时乡人中流传着一句顺口溜:老板屠景山,资本三万三,开店三月三。

源康布店的百年历史,是一部克服困难不断发展的历史。1955年"源康"成为公私合营商店,营业扩大。1973年进行装修扩建,营业面积增加一倍。1980年恢复"源康布店"老字号,新辟二楼营业部,专营服装,业务进一步扩展。1987年改名为"源康纺织商场",分为8个营业部组,专营棉布、绸缎、呢绒、化纤、织品和服装。从1999年开始,中山路全面拆迁,源康第一次迁移至东渡路(崔衙街55号)营业,2004年又遇拆迁搬至狮子街207号,2012年搬迁到现址君子街营业至今。源康坚强地生存着,凭借着老字号的口碑,适时调整的经营特色,在调整中求发展。

源康布店在面料的名、特、优上为宁波市同行之冠,所经营的既有传统面料,又有新品

高档面料,一直受到新老顾客的青睐。源康的另一特色是花色齐全,纺织品除黑白蓝粗布扬名外,呢绒、绸缎、麻织品和各类棉布应有尽有。营业员售货实行"串柜"的办法,凡一位顾客要买多种纺织品,不论是棉布、呢绒、绸缎或鞋口、裤腰等其他配件,都由一名营业员接待、收款、发料,服务到底,使顾客倍感贴心。

1989年,源康布店被评为"省级先进企业"。2010年,源康布店获得"浙江省老字号"称号。

1. Overview of Ningbo

Ningbo has a history featuring seafaring and urban development. More than 7,000 years ago, primitive people in Ningbo formed the Hemudu Tribe with marine life features as the settlement was close to the East China Sea. They used oars and built ganlan-type farm houses with wood stem-columns. Some 2,000 years ago, Ningbo, known as the county of Mao, received many overseas merchants. That was why the place got the name of Mao (which literally means Trade). For over 1,000 years, Ningbo has been an important port city open to foreign trade, thus having cultured friendship with many peoples. In early 1980s, Ningbo started its transformation into a modernized port city, and established trade relationship with more than 100 countries and overseas regions. It has forged close ties with the rest of the world on the way of social and economic progress and advancement.

1.1 Jurisdiction System in History

Historic Background

7,000 years of civilization

Located along the bank of the Yaojiang (or the Yao River), 20 kilometers west of downtown Ningbo, is Hemudu Village of Yuyao, facing Ningbo Plain on one side and Mountains Siming on the other and enjoying a picturesque view. It is where Hemudu Site is situated, which is one of China's most ancient Neolithic sites unearthed in 1973.

Covering about 40,000 square meters, the Hemudu Culture Site has over 7,000 relics unearthed, including stone artifacts, bone artifacts, wood wares and pottery, as well as grains and fruits. Archaeological findings suggest the site has a history of over 7,000 years. All the cultural relics show that Ningbo was one of the first places in the world in rice cultivation, suggesting that like Yellow River Basin, Yangtze River Basin is another cradle of the splendid Chinese civilization. They also testify to the fact that Ningbo people, having lived and worked in the land for thousands of years, survived all hardships and created a history of splendor with their diligence and wisdom.

According to *Record of Ningbo*, back in the Xia Dynasty (2,000 B.C.), there was a Jinzi State after the name of Mountain Chijin, and later, it was designated as the Yin Country. That was how Yinzhou (now a district of Ningbo) got its name. In the Spring and Autumn Period (770 B.C. — 476 B.C.), Ningbo was part of the Yue State, but later the Yue State was disintegrated after a war staged by the Chu State. It thus became part of Chu's jurisdiction.

In 222 B.C., after Qinshi huang, the First Emperor of Qin (259 B.C—210 B.C.), conquered the Chu State, Kuaiji Prefecture was established. Yinzhou of Ningbo used to be part of the prefecture, together with Mao and Gouzhang. The three counties were not situated where the current downtown Ningbo is, nevertheless they were bordered by the Yuyao River, Fenghua River and Yong River respectively. The Yin County (now Yinzhou District), which was to the south of the three rivers, included the southeastern part of Fenghua and the southwestern part of Yin County today. The county seat was at Baidu of Fenghua. The Mao County, which was at the east, included today's Jiangdong District and Dongxiang Township, with county seat at Tonggu of Maoshan. The Gouzhang County was to the northwest of the three rivers, including today's Jiangbei, Cixi and Yuyao, with county seat at Chengshan.

From the Western Han and Eastern Han Dynasties, Ningbo's jurisdiction system remained unchanged. In 621 A.D., the court of the Sui Dynasty established the Governor's Palace of the Yue Prefecture in Ningbo, governing 11 counties and the above three counties were made part of the Yin County, with the county seat at Sanjiangkou (the Three-River Junction) of Ningbo. In 625 A.D.., Yinzhou and Gouzhang Counties were repealed while Mao County was restored and it moved to Xiaoxi, or what is known as Yinjiang Bridge of Yin County. In 627 A.D., the central government of the Tang Dynasty divided the territory into 10 Daos (prefectures), among which the Jiangnan Dao (South of the Yangtze River) was where Mao County was situated.

Ningbo, Abbreviated as Yong

Yong standing for Ningbo was a popular name in the Zhou Dynasty as the major waterway of Ningbo was the Yong River (Yongjiang River), which got its name from the Mountain Yong. Located at the junction of Yin County and Fenghua County, Mountain Yong takes on the shape of a bell. As such, the river down the mountain is called the Yong River (or Yongjiang River) and the area the Yong.

Mingzhou Named after Mountains Siming

Ningbo was known as Mingzhou in ancient times, which was named after Mountains Siming. In 738, Ningbo was divided into Cixi, Fenghua, Wengshan (Dinghai County today) and Mao County by the Tang government. The prefectural seat of Mingzhou and the county seat of Mao remained in Xiaoxi, while the county seat of Cixi was at Cicheng of today's Jiangbei District, that of Fenghua County was at western Daqiao Town, and that of Wengshan County moved from coastal Xuhe to the foot of Mountain Aoshan(literally Dragon-turtle Mountain).

Mingzhou was changed into Yuyao Prefecture by Emperor Xuanzong of the Tang in 742 A. D. In 758 A. D., the name was changed back to Mingzhou. In 764 A. D., Emperor Daizong of the Tang put Xiangshan County under Mingzhou's jurisdiction, bringing the total number of counties to five. When Xianzong reigned, Wanghai Town was set up from eastern Mao County to Yong River seaport. In 821 A. D., Emperor Muzong had the prefectural seat of Mingzhou moved from Xiaoxi to Sanjiangkou (the Three-River Junction). During the Five Dynasties, Mingzhou was known as Mingzhou Wanghai Prefecture, with Yin County, Cixi, Fenghua, Wenshan and Wanghai under its jurisdiction. In 960 A. D., Emperor Taizu of the Song changed Mingzhou Wanghai Prefecture to Mingzhou Fengguo Prefecture with Yin County, Cixi, Fenghua, Dinghai, Xiangshan, Changguo under its jurisdiction. In 1194 A. D., Guangzong raised the status of Mingzhou Fengguo Prefecture to Qinyuan Prefecture. In 1276 A. D., the prefecture was upgraded into Qinyuan Province by Emperor Zhu Yuanzhang of the Yuan Dynasty.

How Ningbo Got Its Name

The origin of the name Ningbo could date back to 1381 A. D., when a scholar named Shan Zhongyou who lived to the west of the Wanshou Temple was summoned by the Emperor to Nanjing to produce poems as he was a very talented poet and was appreciated by Emperor Zhu Yuanzhang. Shan said to the emperor, "I believe it inappropriate to call it Mingzhou Prefecture because Ming is the name of our country. " Zhu responded by saying, "What you said makes sense. Since there is Dinghai (Peaceful Sea), why not change Mingzhou to Ningbo (Peaceful Waves)?" That was how the name Ningbo has been used to refer to the city for over 600 years.

In the Qing Dynasty, Ningbo Prefecture was used. In 1687 when Emperor Kangxi reigned, Dinghai was used to name a county on zhoushan Islands, and the Dinghai county of Ningbo Prefecture was renamed Zhenhai County.

In Republic of China period (1912—1949), Ningbo Prefecture was replaced in name by the Yin County.

When Ningbo was liberated on May 5th, 1949, Ningbo city was established as a provincially administered municipality. Ningbo, as the second governmental office in Zhejiang, had Yin County, Yuyao, Cixi, Zhenhai, Fenghua, Dinghai and Xiangshan under its jurisdiction. In 1952, Ninghai County, which was previously part of Taizhou, became part of Ningbo. In 1962, Dinghai County was separated from Ningbo to form the Zhoushan Prefecture. In 1958, Zhenhai and Yin were included in Ningbo Municipality. In July 1983, municipally-affiliated county system was introduced and the prefectural administrative office repealed. Yin County, Yuyao, Cixi, Fenghua, Xiangshan, Ninghai were put under the jurisdiction of Ningbo Municipality. In April, 1984, Ningbo Municipality was made one of the 14 port cities opened up to international economic operations by the State Council. The same year, Haishu District and Zhenmin District were integrated as Haishu District. Jiangdong and Jiangbei Districts were expanded. Zhenhai County was divided to form Zhenhai District and Beilun District. In July 1985, Yuyao became a municipality upon the approval of the State Council. In October 1988, Cixi and Fenghua counties were also made county-level municipalities. In 2002, Yinxian County was repealed and was incorporated into Ningbo as one of its municipal district.

1.2 Enceinte Construction

The construction of Ningbo's enceinte can date back to the East Jin Dynasty (317 A.D.—420 A.D.). In 400 A.D., Jin's general Liu Laozhi built the enceinte to deter Sun En rebels. At that time, only earth walls were built along Sanjiangkou (the Three-River Junction), defended by station troops on three sides of the river. This was the rudiment of Ningbo's enceinte. It is recorded in *Qian Dao Tu Jing* (a book of maps) that rampart foundation can be found outside the west city, on top of which grow some small bamboos. The walls are called Xiaoqiang (short bamboo walls), which is the site of the present Xiaoqiang Lane.

In 821 A.D. when Emperor Tang Muzong reigned, Han Cha, prefectural governor of Mingzhou, had Mingzhou capital site moved from Xiaoxi to Sanjiangkou, where an urban area was built as the governor office site encircled by a wall of about 1500 meters. The current Gulou(the Drum Tower), located by the Zhongshan Road, is the south gate of the wall.

In late Tang Dynasty, Huang Cheng, who was the prefectural governor of Mingzhou, found that citizens were constantly subject to thieves and burglars because there was no city wall in place in the precariously situated area of Mingzhou. For that reason, he called upon the general public to build a spectacular city wall of 9 kilometers. The grand landscape was recorded in the tomb tablet inscription of Governor Huang Sheng, that before he took office, there was no urban land layout and houses spread irregularly. Governor Sheng built the grand city, protecting people and fending off invaders.

The city wall was not demolished until in 1928.

1.3　The Trading Port

Ningbo is located by the coast of the East China Sea and at the southeastern corner of the Yangtze River Delta. As a city that faces the sea with soil fertility and flat landscape, Ningbo is a cradle of Chinese ship-building and shipping industry and also an important port for foreign trade in China.

Seafaring and port use of Ningbo can be traced back to Hemudu Neolithic Period (7,000 years ago). At Hemudu site, 6 wooden oars, a porcelain model boat and several fish osseous remains were unearthed, testifying to the fact that Ningbo was capable of building ships 7,000 years ago. It is recorded in the *Book of Zhou* that during the reign of Zhou Chengwang, or King Cheng of the Zhou Dynasty (1024 B.C.—1005 B.C.) Kingdom Yue presented boats as tribute to the King of Zhou. During the Warring States Period (312 B.C), according to *Zhu Shu Ji Nian (Bamboo Annals)* Kingdom Yue again had boats presented to the Kingdom Wei as gifts. According to historians, these ships must have been well-equipped big sea boats as they had to go through long sea journeys to arrive at the political centers of Kingdom Zhou and Kingdom Wei.

Ningbo was referred to as Mao (Trade) because local residents were often engaged in foreign trade. Later thriving business there prompted Mao to be upgraded to Mao County. As recorded in Annals of Yin County, "Mao was reputed for seafood. After seafood trade was expanded, hence the name of Mao County (the county of trade)." In 210 B.C., Qinshihuang, the First Emperor of the Qin Dynasty(259 B.C.—210 B.C.), came to Mao County and stayed here for over 30 days during his southern tour. He ascended the Mountain Kuaiji and engraved characters in a stone according to *A Collection of Lu Shilong*. Why did he come? Also according to a local document, he climbed atop Mountain Kuaiji to inscribe heroic acts on rocks as a way of remembering them. The legend has that Xu Fu, also named Xu Shi, a noted warlock at that time, submitted a letter to the king which said that at sea were Penglai and Yingzhou, where immortals lived. They required offerings of boys and girls. As a result, thousands of boys and girls were sacrificed for the sake of meeting the immortals. Xu Fu departed from Mountain Dapeng of Cixi, Ningbo, for Japan, there he stayed for many years and won great respect as he brought Chinese culture to Japan. This story shows that even at that time, Ningbo's shipping industry was quite developed. During the Three Kingdoms Dynasties, Ningbo served as an important military port, as recorded in the *Shih Chi (Records of the Grand Historian)*, which says that the Lord of Dongyue rebelled, and General Yang Pu was sent to bring him to justice. General Yang sent Han Shuo to go overseas to contact Yizhou and Tanzhou. The same story was told in *San Guo Zhi (The History of Three Kingdoms)*, which says in 230 B.C when Emperor Wu reigned, General Wei Wen was sent to Yizhou and Tanzhou with 10,000 army men.

In the Tang Dynasty, Ningbo enjoyed high-level international trade. "Foreign businessman and ships came one after another", recorded *Ningbo Annals*. Celadon wares and silk fabrics that were produced in Ningbo were sold far overseas covering over 20 countries including Japan, Korea, Southeast Asian countries and regions. The trade spike in Ningbo put the city on a par with Yangzhou and Guangzhou as the third largest foreign trade port nationwide.

In 990 A.D., the first year of Chunhua period (the Song Dynasty), Ningbo set up an agency called Shibosi administering foreign trade and tariff. There were only three such agencies in China at that time, with the other two at Guangzhou and Hangzhou respectively. In the meantime, Ningbo was among China's top three ports, together with Quanzhou and Guangzhou, particularly in the Southern Song Dynasty as Ningbo is close to the then capital Lin'an (today's Hangzhou), so foreign trade was taken all the more important then.

In the Yuan Dynasty, Ningbo remained a major shipping and foreign trade port. At that time, offices for foreign shipping were set up in Ningbo (then Qingyuan), Quanzhou, Shanghai and Ganpu.

By the mid-Ming Dynasty, Ningbo remained an important port for foreign trade, with complete set of agencies for foreign trade including taxation, warehouse management, promotion, and guesthouse. But in 1523, Ningbo was ransacked by Japanese samurais amid the so-called Zhenggong Incident, a row between two Japanese trade groups, during which two famous but rival Japanese samurai groups sent their trading boats to Ningbo, one of which received unfair treatment at the customs which was bribed by the other trading group. In revenge, it killed and pillaged and created great losses to Ningbo. This event together with the subsequent ting of Japanese pirates created tensions for Ningbo and destroyed the necessary social environment for trade in Ningbo. As a result, the Ming Dynasty government ordered the closure of the agencies and thus foreign trade came to a halt.

In 1685, at the beginning years of the Qing Dynasty and under the reign of Emperor Kangxi, customs was set up in Ningbo and hence foreign trade resumed. But in 1757 under the reign of Emperor Qianlong, the government followed the policy of self-seclusion, and foreign trade ban was imposed. On August 29, 1842, After the Opium War ended, the Qing Dynasty government was forced to sign up the *Treaty of Nanjing*, and Ningbo was listed among the five ports opened up to foreign trade, besides Guangzhou, Xiamen, Fuzhou and Shanghai. Then foreign countries came one after another to set up consulates and their agents gradually controlled Ningbo customs and monopolized foreign trade. This situation remained unchanged until the founding of the PRC in 1949.

2. Historical Sites

2.1 Cultural Relics Protection Units at State Level

Hemudu Culture Site

Hemudu Culture Site, a site under state-level protection, is situated on the bank of the Yao River (or Yuyao River), 25 kilometers west of Ningbo, 22 kilometers east of Yuyao and 4 kilometers away from the Xiaoshan-Ningbo Railway. Backed by the Mountains Siming and facing the Ningshao Plain, it dates back to the Neolithic Age. In the site a large number of rare historical objects have been unearthed, totaling 7,000 pieces of wares made of stones, bones, wood, pottery and jade, over 500 thousand of pottery shards, animal and plant remains, huts of wood stem-columns as well as 20 tombs, all in an area of 40,000 square kilometers. The site testifies that over 7,000 years ago, primitive people already made home at this place, doing business and establishing a splendid primeval culture. The fact that plenty of well-preserved golden rice remains of artificially cultivated indica rice, and many *Si* (a spade-shaped farm tool) made of bones have been unearthed from the site proves that primitive people started to plant rice as early as 7,000 years ago, belying the argument that "there was only round-grained rice but no long-shaped rice in the Neolithic Age" and establishing the unique status of Ningbo as one of the earliest places planting rice.

Tools such as bone knives, wood knives, stabs and arrows unearthed from the site demonstrate that hunting, fishing and breeding were prevalent. Actually, a kind of bone-whistle made from animal bones can still perform the complete musical scale even today.

Ceramic and stone spinning tools such as wood knife, bone needle and spinning wheel unearthed prove the then rather sophisticated spinning and weaving process.

Furthermore, a tenon-and-mortise wood structure was unearthed in the site. It is a

139

ganlan-type house built on wood columns, 23 meters in length and 7 meters in width. The columns, beams and purlines are jointed with tenons. The wooden components even have carved patterns on them as decorations.

People also found a large number of black potteries, painted wooden bowls, wooden slips, craft jewelries, ivory carvings and toys there. The discovery of Hemudu Culture Site renders the Yangtze Lake Basin a significant status similar to that of the Yellow River, a cradle of Chinese civilization.

Thousands of relics were unearthed after two excavations. Some of them are collected in the Natural Museum of Zhejiang Province and the rest are exhibited in Hemudu Culture Site Museum nearby, with the inscription written by Jiang Zemin, former General Secretary of the CPC.

Shanglin Lake Yue Kiln Sites

Shanglin Lake Yue Kiln Sites are located at the Mountain Kaolao, the highest peak among the mountains of Cixi, on the shore of a narrow lake. The sites have more than 90 ancient kilns left from the Han Dynasty to the Song Dynasty, which are scattered around the long and narrow lake. Porcelain chips and dilapidated kiln beds have been discovered in an area of 90,000 square meters. Archeological findings show that china production of Shanglin Lake Yue kilns started from the Eastern Han Dynasty and reached its prime in the Five Dynasties Period. As one of the first kilns to produce porcelains, Yue kilns thrived for thousands of years till the Song Dynasty, and produced more than 1,000 kinds of delicate porcelains, mostly daily utensils like tea sets and decoration crafts, with colorful designs like birds, beasts, flowers and plants.

Porcelain products were particularly rich in shapes and functions during the periods from the Tang Dynasty to the Five Dynasties, including ring-foot bowls, lotus-shaped bowls, lotus-mouth bowls, plates with lotus leaf patterns, as well as plates, dishes, oil boxes, trays, lamp holders and water jets of various shapes. For smooth and solid texture, crystal glaze and exquisite carving, Shanglin Lake Yue Kilns were ranked the first among all the major kilns around the then China. Thereafter the central government set the "Tribute Kiln" at the Shanglin Lake, to make "Mystic-Glaze Ware", a kind of porcelain with high artistic value for the court.

Royal musicians of the Tang Dynasty injected into porcelain containers different amount of water and played music on them with bamboo sticks, which produced varied tunes. People described this kind of priceless musical porcelain as "blue as the sky, bright as a mirror, thin as paper and loud as a chime". Poet Lu Guimeng, a Tang Dynasty poet eulogized it in this way:

The Yue Kilns Open in autumn when cool dew drops hang on leaves,

There you behold a world of porcelain wares with verdant colors and myriad shapes.

As the porcelain wares were exquisite and popular, they were exported to more than ten countries from Mingzhou (Ningbo) as the key commercial goods since late Tang Dynasty, thus forming the ancient "Porcelain Road" leading to countries along the Persian Gulf and the Mediterranean coast, and making significant contributions to cultural communications and trade exchanges.

Embraced by verdant mountains and the never-dried-up lake, Shanglin Lake Yue Kiln Sites are cultural relic sites under the state-level protection.

Baoguo Temple

Baoguo Temple, seated on Mountain Lingshan in Jiangbei District and 15 kilometers away from downtown Ningbo, is a thousand-year-old temple. The Grand Hall in the Temple is one of the oldest and best-preserved wooden structures in the

region south to Yangtze River, invaluable to the nation's architectural studies. The temple is surrounded with mountains, with Shiyan Peak on the right, Mount Maan on the left and backed up by Mount Mao. Therefore, it gives rise to a saying: Temple in mountains but where is the entrance? Yan Jing, head of the secretariat of the Ming Dynasty in the mid-16th century and a native of Ningbo, named it the First Mountain in the East. As historical records go, in the Guangwu reign of the Eastern Han Dynasty, Zhang Qifang, head of the secretariat, retired in this place after quitting officialdom. His hut was later turned into a temple and named Linshan Temple. It was later ruined, and then rebuilt, destroyed again in the Huichang Reign of the Tang Dynasty when Buddhism was denounced as heretic. In 880 A.D. of the Tang Dynasty when it was rebuilt, the temple was named Baoguo Temple by Xizong, the then Emperor of the Tang Dynasty. The existing Mahavira Hall was built in 1013, the 6th year of the Zhenzong Period of the Northern Song Dynasty. Numerous officials and personages and even emperors of different dynasties left their inscriptions in the temple when they visited it.

Baoguo Temple, being one of the national key cultural relics protection units, has its distinctive and unique architectural style. A few hundred steps up from the foot of Mountain Lingshan and following the Zigzag path after you pass the Diejin Platform, you can see the towering ridges and cornices of the Hall of Heavenly Kings. Behind the hall, there is a lotus pool with clear and crystal water. And then further behind you see the magnificent Main Hall. The roof is supported by using precision tenon technology and well-connected brackets, and no nails. On the ceiling of the hall are three well-like hollows cleverly connected with the whole frame. They somewhat conceal the skeleton-like beams from the visitors to the hall, that is why it is called "A Beamless Hall". The hall depth is bigger than the width, that is rare among all the Buddhist hall of the same time. The inside pillars are melon-shaped by piling up small wood blocks. It looks great and resounds when knocked. One more incredible thing about this hall: no bird nestles, no worm damage, no mouse holes. A popular explanation goes that this is because a kind of yellow cypress was used as the building material, which gives off an irritating smell can keep these creatures away, but no convincing evidence has been given, so this remains a mystery to be solved.

The temple is surrounded by a number of spectacular sights, such as the Duojiao Pavilion on the Shiyan Peak, the Wanghai Pavilion on the Xiangbi Peak, both boasting a panoramic view.

Tianyige Library (Tianyi Pavilion)

Tianyi Pavilion, or Tianyige Library, stands on the bank of the Moon Lake. It is the oldest private library extant in China and has been made one of the key national heritage sites. For centuries it has been known as the "city of books in the South" for its

143

enormous collection of rare ancient books and documents. It was built in 1561 in the Ming Dynasty (1368—1644). Fan Qin, the owner of Tianyi Pavilion Library, was born in Yinxian County and lived during the reign of Emperor Jiajing. In 1532 when he was 27, Fan passed the highest imperial examination and earned the title of jinshi, a successful candidate in the imperial examination. After that he served as an official in many places of China. Later, being weary of politics, Fan Qin resigned as senior minister of the Ministry of Military Affairs and returned to his hometown. Having a liking for books, Fan collected rare books of various dynasties and contemporary anthologies. When he was to pass away, he left a testament disallowing his descendents to distribute the books and prohibiting the books from being taken out. Quan Zuwang, a historian of the Qing Dynasty, praised this practice by saying: for two hundred years the books are kept intact, here you see a collector unparalleled in China.

Originally, the library had 70,000 volumes of books, mostly block prints and manuscripts from the Song Dynasty and the Ming Dynasty, including Confucian classics, history, philosophy and belles-letters, and some of them are rare or the only extant copies in the world. Unfortunately, only 13,000 volumes remained when the PRC was founded in 1949, because a great many of them were either expropriated by the bureaucracies, stolen or fell into decay. The government and recent generations were committed to the protection and expansion of the library. Premier Zhou Enlai urged the People's Liberation Army to protect Tianyi Pavilion in the wartime. In October, 1962, Guo Moruo, a famous literary master, paid a visit to the library. He wrote a poem giving high regards to the library, the collections and the beautiful environment. Thanks to the efforts of the administrative office, the collection has increased. At present the number of volumes has reached 300,000, including 80,000 rare books, mostly block-printed editions and manuscripts. These books are important historical documents for researchers of history, folk customers, astronomy, geography, hydrology, medicine, etc.

The library was originally called "Dongming Cottage" and the layout of the construction was elaborately designed by Fan Qin himself. Borrowing an idea from *The Book of Changes* suggested in "Heaven embodied in One gives birth to water, while Earth represented in Six makes it grow", Fan Qin named the new house "Tianyi Pavilion" (that is "Pavilion of Heaven and One"). Books are most vulnerable to fire, he said, but water can suppress fire. Thus the name "Tianyi" hints at the fact that water curbs fire. Fan Qin hoped his stock might forever be clear of the destructive might of flames. Yianyi Pavilion is not only famous for its book collection, but also for its unique library buildings and the beautiful garden designs.

The library is situated in the north of the yard and faces south so as to let in sunlight and prevent the books from getting molded and damp. He also wedged a magic idea into the structure of the library, where one large room constitutes the upper floor, implying "Heaven joined with one make water", as was told in the primeval classic Hetu. This place was called Treasure House, dry and bright, where rare ancient works are kept; downstairs there are six chambers in a row, alluding to the message of Hetu "Earth coupled with six makes it thrive". These rooms downstairs are of primitive simplicity. In front of the library lies the Tianyi pool which was intended to guard against fire disaster, and on the water is a pavilion surrounded by green woods and strange rocks. On the back is a park with flowers, grasses and tall bamboos, and the famous "Steles Forest of Mingzhou" which has over 80 inscription tablets, including 7 tablets of the Song Dynasty and 16 tablets of the Yuan Dynasty and many tablets from the Ming and Qing dynasties, valuable among them are three Tablets of the Song Dynasty: the anonymous Epitaph of Hermit Zhao, Poems on Cultivation and Weaving autographed by Lou Yue and Charity for the Hungry by Bingzi from Shaoxing. These tablets are treasured resources in historical study. Today the renovated Tianyi Pavilion presents itself to the public with elegant simplicity. The ancestral hall of the Qin Family standing behind the Tianyi Pavilion looks magnificent and resplendent, bringing out the best of each other with the pavilion.

Baiyun Manor

Located at the western corner of Ningbo and by the bank of Guanjiang River, the Baiyun Manor was an academy where Huang Zongxi (1610—1695) gave lectures. Huang, whose style name is Taichong, was a well-known thinker, writer and historian of the late Ming and early Qing periods. Together with Gu Yanwu and Wang Fuzhi Huang was known as one of the "Three Great Thinkers" of the late Ming and early Qing periods. Huang cultivated a great many outstanding scholars who formed the East Zhejiang School. Originally the Baiyun Manor was the property of the Ministry of Revenue officer Wan Tai, where later his son Wan Sixuan, who authored the *Baiyun Ji (Baiyun Collection)*, was buried, hence the name of Baiyun Manor. Baiyun Manor was the place where Huang Zongxi lectured. When the lectures were given, the manor was crowded with people coming for attendance.

The main building of the Baiyun Manor faces the East and has two rows of brick flat roofs. The west side was the former residence for the Wan family, where Wan Sitong, another figure of the East Zhejiang School, once lived. At the northwest side are the tombs of Wan Bangfu and Wan Sixuan. The former was the father of Wan Tai, and the latter was the fifth son of Wan Tai, an outstanding figure among his contemporaries, for whom Huang Zongxi autographed the epitaph.

Baiyun Manor, a symbol of the East Zhejiang School, enjoys high reputation both at home and abroad and it is now one of the heritage sites under provincial-level protection. Inside the manor there is a display of the objects of the Yongshang Zhengren Academy, which was set up by Huang Zongxi, and an introduction of the life of Huang Zongxi.

Qing'an Guild Hall

Qing'an Guild Hall, built during the reign of Daoguang (1850) of the Qing Dynasty, is located at the Muhang Road, on the east bank of Sanjiangkou (the Three-river Junction). It was founded by shipping merchants and the construction began in 1850. It was meant to be a gathering place for shipping merchants, featuring an opera stage to honor Matsu, a goddess who allegedly protects fishermen and sailors. There is still the stone inscription tablet carved by Dong Pei (1828—1895), a famous scholar in the Qing Dynasty. Qing'an Guild Hall is a landmark of Ningbo, a port city in China, which has witnessed the flourishing overseas transportation and cultural exchange with foreign countries in both ancient and modern times, thus making itself important remains of Maritime Silk Road Culture. Meanwhile, as a large hall of shipping industry, it has also witnessed the development of shipping industry in Eastern Zhejiang Province. In 1853, Zhejiang Tribute Grain was shipped by sea while Qing'an Guild Hall (including Anlan Guild Hall on its south) became the major management and service facility of Zhejiang Tribute Grain in the Qing Dynasty (1616—1912) and river-sea transportation for vertical trade, in which Nanbei ship business played a significant role. Therefore, Qing'an Guild Halls is the material proof of the unique river-sea transportation of The Grand Canal (Ningbo section) as well as the core heritage of its culture. In June, 2014, as one of the 27 cities related to the application of The Grand Canal for World Cultural Heritage, Ningbo was listed as a World Cultural Heritage Site while Qing'an Guild Hall, as a core constituent part of "two sections and one point" of The Grand Canal (Ningbo section), was honored as the first World Cultural Heritage site in Ningbo City.

With the traditional architectural ornaments of gold, wood, brick and stone carvings, the splendid and resplendent hall is deemed as a mini architectural museum.

The extant part of the building includes the gate, main hall and rear court room, covering an area of 3,900 square meters.

The Qing'an Guild Hall represents the highest accomplishment of stone carving. The main building is more than ten meters high. On the two green-stone-carved columns in the outer room are two dragons spiraling up, with bare fangs and brandishing claws. Their opposite phoenix columns in the side room also have exquisite hollow carving. Besides, most of the surrounding walls are embedded with shallow reliefs of the "Ten Scenes of the West Lake" and other important historical materials of the carving arts of the Qing Dynasty, standing as a reminder of Ningbo's port trade to the outside world.

Qianye Hall (Monetary Guild Hall)

Qianye Hall (Monetary Guild Hall), a provincial-level key cultural relics protection unit, is located at No. 10, Zhanchuan Street. In 1864, the third year of reign of Emperor Tongzhi (1856—1874), the office near the Binjiang Temple was set by the Monetary Guild, which was the predecessor of the Qianye Hall. Later, it was once destroyed by flames of war. The new Qianye Hall was completed in 1926. It covers more than 1,500 square meters, with two rows of houses, pavilions, parks, drama stages and a meeting hall, all of which are well preserved. As the place of decision making of the financial industry, it was designated as one of the provincial heritage sites after 1949. The hall has a nice environment inside and enjoys facile overland and water transportation conditions.

Facing the south, the Hall is a wood and brick structure that well combines Chinese and Western elements, the stone tablet of which bearing the best testimony of its brilliant days. Banks came into being in the early Qing Dynasty. According to *Annals of the Yin County*, there were 36 major banks with a capital of over 60,000 yuan, and 30 minor banks with a capital of over 10,000 yuan, and over 4,000 banking agencies offering money-bill exchange services. The strength of Ningbo's banking industry even dwarfed that of Shanghai. By 1931, the Hall had 160 member banks with the total capital asset of 38.66 million yuan. Ningbo was the place where the cash-free payment method was initiated, well testifying Ningbo's economic boom at that time.

Laowaitan (The Old Bund)

Seated on the north bank of the Sanjiangkou, Laowaitan (the Old Bund) of Ningbo became one of the five open ports in 1844 (even 20 years earlier than the Bund in Shanghai) and has long been one of the busiest trading ports since the Tang and Song Dynasty. After 1992 the Old Bund became a tourist attraction as one of the few extant bunds in China with a history of over 100 years.

Back in the Tang Dynasty, Ningbo was one of the four major ports in China. It was where Monk Jianzhen started his journey to Japan. During the Southern Song Dynasty, as one of the three major official ports it was governed by special foreign trade government agencies. Despite the close-door policy by the Qing government, Ningbo managed to keep commercial links with Japan and Southeast Asian nations. China imported copper and silver from Japan and exported silk, cotton and porcelain to Japan via Ningbo. When a rigorous close-door policy was practiced by the early Qing government, Ningbo was the only port to preserve the exporting rights in the following 40 years, from 1644 to 1684.

After the Opium War in 1842, the Qing government signed the *Treaty of Nanjing* with Western powers, in which Ningbo was designated as one of the five ports opened up to foreign trade. Businessmen from all over the world flocked into Ningbo. Britain, France and other countries turned it into a semi-colonial port as they grabbed the sovereignty, took over the administration power of the customs, controlled the see access, monopolized the navigation, and exercised foreignization. Later it became the concession area of the UK, France and the US. The thriving of Shanghai port weakened its status. In 1927 the Chinese government resumed the exercise of the administrative rights of the concession strips. Thereafter, the Old Bund became a symbol mirroring the port culture and modernization progress of the city. There were electric lights, chime clocks, bikes, western-style houses, churches, hospitals and banks. It is the only bund extant in Zhejiang that can well document and reflect the progresses of the port culture.

According to a recent survey of the cultural relics in Ningbo, at least 31 of all the 54 historical buildings of the Old Bund are associated with Ningbo Overseas Trade Group (Ningbobang). These buildings, with both western and Chinese elements of the late 19th and the early 20th centuries are places for work, religious services, trade and residence. Therefore the Old Bund was designated as a place for conservation in the Ningbo City Master Plan together with five other landmarks. At present the Police Station, Hong Yuanchang's, Zhu's Residence and the Mansion of the Yans are listed as the municipal heritage buildings. Extant buildings carrying strong western flavor stand in striking contrast with the traditional dwelling houses.

Foreign consulates, Catholic Church, banks and piers line up the river, recording the whole history of the port. There is Zhejiang Customs, Basilica of Bom Jesus, Ningbo Postal Services, Commercial Bank, etc. There are old residences and time-honoured stores, too. The constructions are of different styles, British, French,

German, Dutch and others, forming a sharp contrast with traditional Chinese residences.

Ancient County Town of Cicheng

Cicheng is listed among the well-known historical and cultural towns in China. It is taken as the No. 1 ancient county town and a town of ancient documents in South Yangtze Area. In 738 A. D., the Tang government set the county seat of Cixi in this place, hence the name of Cicheng. It is the most well-preserved millennial county in regions south of the Yangtze River. In the town there are abundant historic relics and the ancient architectural complex has been designated as the key cultural relics site under the state-level protection. The geographic and geomorphic conditions of Cicheng is distinctive and the environment beautiful. With a twin-chessboard layout, the town has been commended as " a representative of Chinese traditional county seats " by architectural experts.

Cicheng, situated on the coast of the South China Sea and the bank of Yao River, is entitled as "Town with the Most Beautiful Environment". Its history can be dated back to 473 B.C. Previously known as Gouyu and Gouzhang, it got the name of Cixi County in the 26th year of Kaiyuan Period of the Tang Dynasty. With a history of 2,400 years, Cicheng has developed a profound culture, represented by the ancient architectures including the ancient *yamen* (government office), Confucian temple, the examination hall in feudal China, Qing Taoist temple, Chenghuangmiao (the City God temple) and mansions of aristocratic families while there still remains an abundance of cultural relics

151

and historical sites such as ancestral temples, memorial archways, ancient schools and academies, white walls and windows engraved with exquisite patterns. There are as many as 33 key cultural relics sites under the state-level, provincial-level, city-level and district-level protection and the architectural complex was enlisted as the key cultural relics site under state-level protection in 2006. At the same time, Cicheng has fertile soil which has produced a long list of eminent scholars including 519 jinshi (successful candidates in the highest imperial examinations) from the Tang Dynasty to the Qing Dynasty, thus gained its reputation of "a blessed land producing a galaxy of talents" while a large pool of personages have been fostered on this land such as Zhou Xinfang (a famous artist of Peking Opera), Ying Changqi (a successful businessman), Feng Jicai (an excellent writer, painter and folk artist) in the modern times.

The cultural value of the ancient Cicheng county town lies not only in its long history, but also in its unique landscape. The waters and mountains contrast finely with each other with the mountains and hills such as the Mountains Wulei and the Mountains Taizong encircling the town and forming a festive shape called Nine Dragons playing with pearls, and lakes and rivers such as the Yao River and the Cheng River crisscrossing the town form another auspicious shape called Residential Complex Nurtured by Four Waters. The townscape features vaulted shapes and the streets are laid out in squares like turtle backs. Coupled with a beautiful and tranquil surrounding, the layout of the town embodies the wishes of the ancient people for a harmony between the nature and people.

Tuoshan Weir

Near Mountain Tuoshan, Tuoshan Weir is one of the most famous ancient water conservancy projects and a key site under the state-level protection of cultural relics. On 13th, October 13, 2015, it was listed as the first World Irrigation Engineering Heritage in Ningbo City.

Tuoshan Weir, which was so named because of its location in Mountain Tuoshan, has a history of more than 1,150 years. In 833 A.D., Wang Yuanwei, the administer of Mao (Ningbo), who was very much concerned about people's livelihood, decided to start an irrigation and drainage project after on-the-spot investigation when he saw people suffer from the casualties and destruction to crops by flood and drought, because the Yin River failed to conserve water from various streams while salt tide would pour in during rainy days.

Tuoshan Weir, 134.4 meters long, 4.8 meters wide and 10 meters high, was built up with stone slabs, with 36 stone steps on either side. The body of the weir was piled by thousands of huge trunks covered with flagstones. In order to prevent it from being washed away, a huge trunk of plum-wood called "Dameimu" (Umenoki) was placed under the weir, with both its south and north ends joining the rocks, withstanding endless surge while still remaining firm. Dameimu came from Dameishan (Mountain Damei) in the Yin County and legend has it that it was cut into three sections by Sun Quan (King of the Wu Kingdom) with one made into Dianjiangtai (Call-the-muster-roll Platform), another one into the crossbeam of the Yuwang Temple and the third one into the crossbeam of the Weir, firm as ever for over one-thousand of years.

Seated at the throat of the waterway, the Weir assumes the functions of water diversion, storage, flood relief and irrigation. In times of flood, 70% of the water was discharged through the river, with the remaining 30% going to the brook; in time of drought, 70% of the water was diverted to the brook, with the remaining 30% going to the river. Intercepted by the Yin River, the Weir diverted the water through the water gate in the south of Ningbo City before emptying into the Sun Lake (no longer existent now) and the Moon Lake. The two streams, with diversions by distribution networks, transverse the towns in Yinxi Plain, and irrigated thousands of hectares of farmlands in 7 towns (benefiting 16,000 hectares of farmland even today). Although Tuoshan Weir has weathered storms of hundreds of years, the Weir still played a major role in blocking seawater and retaining freshwater.

To commemorate Wang Yuanwei, locals in Ningbo built a temple and erected an inscription tablet near the Tuoshan Weir in honor of his feat in constructing the Weir.

Surrounded by verdant hills and clear waters, Tuoshan Weir presents the most splendid look to the world with its striking beauty. After rainfalls, it becomes a luxuriant and wonderful spectacle with clouds, mists and waterfalls on the meandering mountains far away.

Relics of Coastal Defense Works Zhenhaikou (Sea Access of Zhenhai)

Situated in the middle of China's coastline and the gateway of the Yongjiang River, Zhenhai is a transport pivot reaching Shandong in the north, Fujian and Guangdong in the south, and Suzhou and Hangzhou by going along the Yongjiang River. Zhenhai boasts a favourable geographical condition and has always been a busy port and a center for businesses. A couplet on the pillars of the Banshan Pavilion of the Zhaobao Hill reads: Numerous boats on the river carrying goods to and from foreign land, the mount called Zhaobao standing by as loyal guard is well known in China. The couplet well testifies the busy marine transport at the sea access of Zhenhai. For its unique location, Zhenhai has been an important strategic place for coastal defense. It has been known from ancient times as "Hai Tian Xiong Zhen" ("grand town facing the sea") and "Zhe

Dong Men Hu" ("gateway to east Zhejiang").

Zhenhai used to be a battlefield with numerous coast defense works which witnessed the heroic and soul-stirring struggles of the patriots in their resistance against the foreign pirates and invaders. Now the Site of Coastal Defense Works has become an important place for patriotic education.

According to historical records, Zhenhai has weathered 46 times of warfare since the Eastern Jin Dynasty. Fights against foreign forces since the mid-Ming Dynasty left touching stories of heroes and precious costal defense sites. In November of 1996, the State Council announced these over 30 costal defense sites scattering within 2 square kilometers around Zhenhaikou as National Cultural Heritage and National Socialist Education Base for the Youth.

In the north of Zhenhai Port, there are important heritage spots left by people's resistance against Japanese pirates in Zhejiang province in the Ming Dynasty, namely Weiyuan Town, the city of Moon, Anyuan Battery, Location of Martyrdom, the steles of the Ming and Qing Dynasties and the Houhaitang Relics. The Houhaitang Relics indicate the combination of seawall and city wall which can fend off the sea tides as well as marine invaders. The city wall was made up of bulk flagstones magnificently winding for thousands of meters. In the south of Zhenhai Port, there are such scenic spots as Tuwang Platform at the top of Mount Golden Rooster, Jingyuan Battery, Hongyuan

Battery, and Camps & Ramparts of Qi's. The relics of Coastal defense works of such intensity are very rare in the whole country. They are historic monuments built up with the flesh and blood of our forefathers, simultaneously recording the countless crimes committed by the foreign invaders. In addition to the above mentioned sites, there are also inscriptions made by military and political officials of different historical periods, the locations of martyrdom, the landing positions of foreign invading armies and cultural relics like weapons and other historical materials documents.

Xikou, Fenghua

Xikou, a town located 20 kilometers southwest of Ningbo, Zhejiang Province and under the administration of Fenghua City, is the birthplace of Chiang Kai-shek, former president of the Republic of China (1912—1949). It used to be the command center for Kuomintang (KMT), and is now one of the nationwide famous tourism towns accredited as National 5-A Scenic Area. There are scenic spots of Wuling, Shanxi and Mountain Xuedou. Occupying 140 square kilometers, Xikou also boasts of its former residence of Mr. Chiang, which is now listed as the state-level unit of cultural relics protection.

According to the *Fenghua Annals*, Fan Liangzhong, then supervisory censor gave up his post to get away from politics and settled down in Xikou. Statistics show that the population in the Baoqing reign of the Song Dynasty reached 8,000. And in 1184, Wei Qi, prime minister of the southern Song Dynasty was buried in the Mountain Feifeng, Xikou, which showed that Xikou had made a name even at that time.

Xikou Town is situated northwest to Fenghua City and 22 kilometers away in the southwest to downtown Ningbo. Xikou, or literally the Mouth of the River, derives its name from the Shanxi Creek, a river that originates in the Mountain Dahu of Shanjieling Range, from which it winds its way through Xinchang County to Fenghua, wherein it runs across Fenghua Town from west to east, flowing out of the mouth between Mountain Wuling and Mountain Xinan, hence the town got its name: a town at the mouth of the river. Xikou the town is also called Wuling, a name after the Mountain Wuling that stands south of the town. Xikou has picturesque scenery and landscape. It is surrounded by clusters of green mountains with Shanxi River flowing across. In the Qing Dynasty, scholars summarized Ten Attractions of Xikou, which are Towering Wenchang Pavilion, Fondling Waves of the Shanxi Creek, verdant riverside, fishes in green pools, moonlight over pine trees, night boating in the creeks, autumn moon and

156

murmuring creeks, sunset on the snow mountains, snow over Wuling mountains in the fine day, plum blossoms in the early spring on the south bank of the creek. Of special importance is the Xuedong Mountain Scenic Area of Xikou, which has a number of scenic spots and is ranked among the best tourist sites in the east Zhejiang Province.

Small as it is, Xikou was once the eye of Chinese political storm. It is the hometown of Mr. Chiang Kai-shek and his son Chiang Ching-kuo, two important historical figures in the modern history of China. They often came back when they had the supreme political power of China in grasp and plotted events here. Zhang Xueliang, the famous general who led a muting and captured Chiang Kai-shek in Xi'an Incident, was detained in Xikou after the incident was peacefully settled.

Chiang's birthplace, former villa and ancestral hall are scattered along the Wuling Street in Xikou Town, some of which have been listed as state-level cultural relics.

In the Song Dynasty Xuedou Temple was deemed as one of the most famous Buddhist temples in China, as the place where Maitreya Buddha practiced his Buddhist rites.

It is these unique cultural and historical heritages, natural sights and Buddhist culture that make Xikou attractive as a tourist site.

2.2 Cultural Relics

The Drum Tower

Located at Gongyuan Road, Ningbo, Gulou (the Drum Tower) is the only city tower of Ningbo. In the first year of the Changqing Period in the Tang Dynasty (821 A. D.), Han Cha, governor of Mingzhou (now Ningbo) relocated the prefectural government from Xiaoxi to Sanjiangkou, Ningbo. Centering on the area which nowadays is from Zhongshan Park to Gulou, government premises and city walls were built up and formed a region historically called "Zi Cheng"(an extension of the old city), of which Gulou is the south gate. Later the south gate was named as Wang Hai Jun Men (sea-gazing barrack gate), Feng Guo Jun Lou (barrack tower of national defenders) and Feng Guo Lou Shen Ci (shrine tower of national defenders), etc. Destroyed at the beginning of the Yuan Dynasty, it was named "Mingyuan Lou" after reconstruction. When Fang Guozhen led his rebellious army attacked and occupied Ningbo, Mingyuan Lou was destroyed again in fire, and was renamed as "Haishu Lou" and the two characters "Haishu" was taken from the poem "Yun Xia Chu Hai Shu, Mei Liu Du Jiang Chun (clouds are tainted with sunglow when the dawn comes upon sea, and the Yangtze River is tainted with spring when plums bloom and willows green)", when being rebuilt in the Wanli Period of the Ming Dynasty. In the Qing Dynasty, Haishu Lou was rebuilt for quite a few times. When being rebuilt in the fifth year of Xianfeng Period (1855), it started to become widely known as "Gulou" (the drum tower) because there is a watchman's drum on it. After the Qing Dynasty, a quadrate steel reinforced concrete observatory and an alarm bell stand were built in the three-story tower, along with an etalon clock being set on top, which can be seen from all directions, and this is just how Gulou looks like now.

Gulou was entitled Feng Guo Jun Lou Shen Ci (shrine of barrack tower of national defenders) by Emperor Gaozong in the Southern Song Dynasty. According to *Annals of the Yin County*, at that time, statues of Zhang Xun, Xu Yuan and three other generals, who sacrificed their lives fighting against the rebellious army of An Lushan in the defending Suiyang during the Tianbao Period of the Tang Dynasty, were enshrined in the tower. Zhao Gou, Emperor Gaozong of the Song Dynasty, made a narrow escape from Jin troops by hiding in the tower. He thought he was saved by the five generals, so he issued an edict to honour the five generals, and entitled the tower as Feng Guo Jun Lou Shen Ci.

Gulou is a three-floor timber frame building, appearing grand and unsophisticated. The wall is built with bricks, with a base of huge stone slabs. It is eight meters tall and six meters wide, and has a north-south doorway in the middle leading to the roof. When you ascend the Haishu Lou, you see everything in full view. It is a famous place of interest in Ningbo.

Old Chenghuang Temple (Old Town-God Temple)

The Old Chenghuang Temple, or the Old Town-God Temple, or County Temple, is located on the east of Xianxue Street, with the full name of Ningbo Fu Cheng Huang Miao (Chenghuang Temple of Ningbo Prefecture). It was built in 916 A.D., the second year of Zhenming Period of Later Liang in the Five Dynasties Period, and was later relocated to fifty steps southwest of Zicheng, the extension of the old city, where is nowadays southeast of Gulou. In 1216, Cheng Qin pled to the central government for permission to build a temple in supplicating for God's blessing. Because there were too many worshippers burning joss sticks and candles, the temple was destroyed by fire many times. In 1371, after it was once again burned up, the county governor Zhang Qi relocated the temple to "old site of Dishi Temple on Wolan Lane", which is nowadays the location of old Chenghuang Temple on Xianxue street. In the beginning it was not big until 1437 when the Zhang Luo, magistrate of the prefecture, rebuilt the halls, corridors and side rooms, as well as the pavilions and columns on the south of the main hall, adding much more grandeur to the temple. In 1884, the temple was rebuilt again in a much bigger scale than previous times, adding a first gate, a second gate, a stage and four rows of big halls and rear big halls. Between the second gate and the big hall which is the main construction, there are wings on the two sides, and the caissons of the

159

stage are all decorated with gilt carved brackets spiraling up on them which are unparallel in delicacy. In front of the temple gate there is the arch camber Moon Palace wall, and in between a screen wall is right ahead of the gate with a flagpole set up; the gate door consists of three clamshell doors, and there is a pair of stone lions on each side of the gate. The whole construction group looks magnificent and unsophisticated, full of overhanging eaves, shrug ridges and delicate carvings, splendid and sumptuous.

In old times there were statues of the Town God, devils of bull head and horse face and devils in hell with ferocious faces in the temple, and the couplets on the columns read: "the heaven knows, the earth knows, you know and I know, who says no one knows; reward for the good, repay for the bad, pay off late, pay off early, retribution always comes", all mysterious and scary. Every day the temple was immersed in coiling incense smokes, throngs of devout men and women came to worship. There were also fortune-telling poems, Fang Yan Kou (a ritual to feed the starving ghosts) and sales of office passports; and all sorts of people gathered in and out around the temple doing glyphomancy, physiognomy, fortune-telling on the paper, singing stories of the wit, telling stories of the valiant, teaching moral stories and so on. As for booths and stalls for drinks and snacks, they were everywhere in and out of the temple, and there was meat and vegetarian flour snacks, wonton and steamed stuffed buns, casual drinks, fruits and cakes, and anything one could think of. In the first month of the lunar year which was the time for Dengtou plays (plays played ahead of lanterns) or festivals when Choushen plays (plays to pay tribute to God) were to be put on stage, all kinds of good plays would be performed on the stage. At the meantime lanterns and streamers were put up, looking lively and boisterous. Apart from worshiping Bodhisattva, people came to the temple more to enjoy the lively atmosphere and buy some snacks, so the temple was always crowded with people, and the bustling never faded.

In June 1645, the second year of Shunzhi Period of the Qing Dynasty, when the Ming Dynasty was about to end and the Qing troops were launching a massive attack southward, national heroes Qian Sule, Zhang Cangshui, Dong Zhining and so on called on thousands of civilians to gather in the temple for uprising against the Qing troops. In 1927, the Bodhisattva statues in the temple were destroyed, so there was no Bodhisattva any more in the temple. After the War of Resistance against Japanese Aggression (1937—1945), Bodhisattva statues were restored.

In 1938, the temple underwent a big repair and took on a new look. In 1995, it had a large scale expansion. The newly-built shopping mall inherited the Ming and Qing dynasties' architectural style of the old temple, which is unsophisticated and elegant, grand and spectacular. The total area after expansion is 20 thousand square meters. Between the old and new buildings is a 108-meter long and 6-meter wide pedestrian street, along which there are 29 different kinds of stores, making Chenghuang Temple a famous tourist place with large shopping mall, special stores and restaurant complex.

The Moon Lake

The Moon Lake, or the Yuehu Lake, is located in the southwest corner of Ningbo city, which used to be called "West Lake" by locals. It is only a hundred steps away from Ningbo Railway Station. It is long and narrow with an area of 0.2 square kilometers. Its shape is randomly tortuous; the round places are like full moons while the curved places are like crescents. In the past there was a lake not far from east of the north lake called "Sun Lake (Rihu Lake)". The names Ri (sun) and Yue (moon) of the two lakes are the result of decomposition of the Chinese character "Ming" in Mingzhou. Now the Sun Lake is gone, only the Moon Lake survives. The Moon Lake was dug by magistrate of Mao county Wang Junzhao in 636 A. D. In 1093 A. D., the chief of Mingzhou Prefecture Liu Shu organized large force to dredge the lake, plant pine trees and willows around the lake, and fill in earth to separate the lake into ten islets. During

Shaoxing Period of the Southern Song Dynasty (1131—1162), prefecture chief Liu Cheng built pavilions, terraces and open halls, and planted flowers of all seasons on the islets, forming up excellent views of the ten islets: the east three islets are "Chrysanthemum Islet", "Moon Island" and "Bamboo Islet"; the west three are "Lotus Islet", "Snow Islet" and "Fume Islet"; the center four are "Fragrant Grass Islet", "Willow Islet", "Flower Islet" and "Bamboo Islet". Then three dikes and seven bridges were built in Jiaoyou Period of the Song Dynasty and Wanli Period of the Ming Dynasty: Yanyue (crescent moon) Dike on the north of the lake, Guangsheng Dike in the center and Taohua (peach blossom) Dike on the South; the seven bridges are Mid-lake West Bridge between Flower Islet and Fume Islet, Mid-lake East Bridge between Flower Islet and Moon Island, Chongchong West Bridge between Willow Islet and Fume Islet, Chongchong East Bridge between Willow Islet and Chrysanthemum Islet, Rainbow Bridge between Snow Islet and Lotus Islet, Gunxiu Bridge between Lotus Islet and the north bank of the lake, and Siming Bridge between Chrysanthemum Islet and the north bank, part of which now have been rebuilt and turned to be roads.

The Moon Lake was a gathering place for the literati in history. It's told that the famous poet of the Tang Dynasty He Zhizhang (659 A.D.—744 A.D.) once lived by the Moon Lake for some time after he resigned from office. He called himself "wild fellow of Siming". People respected him for his brilliant talent, and now there is still a "He Mi Jian Ci (Memorial Hall of He Zhizhang)". When Wang Anshi(imperially titled as Lord Jingguo) served as the county governor of Yin County in the Song Dynasty, he built "West Pavilion" on the west bank, which was called by the folks "the Reading Platform of Revered Lord Jingguo" (now collapsed). In the Southern Song Dynasty, Shi Hao, chancellor of two reign periods, once built a "Zhenyin Lodge" (Real Hermit Lodge) on the Bamboo Islet, and Emperor Xiaozong of the Song Dynasty presented him his own inscription "Si Ming Dong Tian" as gift. Many renowned scholars at that time lectured here. Later on, Quan Zuwang (1705—1755), the famous historian of the Qing Dynasty built up an "Academy of Three Mentors on Bamboo Islet". So the atmosphere of learning never waned for hundreds of years.

The Moon Lake to Ningbo is like the West Lake to Hangzhou. Since the Tang and Song Dynasties, it has been a flourishing place in the city. It is recorded in local annals that "the sceneries in different seasons are different, and the ladies come to visit mostly in spring and summer when their carriages form shades and the reflections of sightseeing boats ripple on the lake, the days are never whiled away."

Since the founding of the People's Republic of China in 1949, the Moon Lake has been dredged many times. Trees and flowers are planted around the lake, pavilions, terraces and halls have been built, making the lake even more charming. When strolling along the bank or boating in the lake, you will feel you are walking in a landscape painting.

Tianfeng Pagoda

Tianfeng Pagoda is situated on Dashani Street of Ningbo and is near the Chenghuang Temple. Because it was built during the time when Empress Wu Zetian of the Tang Dynasty was enthroned (695 A.D.—696 A.D.), so it was called "Tianfeng Pagoda" (Tian means the God, Feng means enthrone). Legend goes that as the then Ningbo city, shaped like a boat floating between the Fenghua River and the Yuyao River was often flooded. So the pagoda was built in the center of the city like a mast set on the boat, thus the boat was controlled and flood no longer came. The pagoda is as tall as 54.5 meters, and is shaped hexagon with seven lighted storeys, seven dark storeys and four storeys underground. A famous nursery rhyme tells the role the Pagoda plays in the life of the People: "Ningbo Tianfeng Pagoda, eighteen storeys in the sky." It is recorded that a great deal of silt was piled up to send bricks and stones up to the top when the pagoda was being built, and was sent away after the construction. The silt used in the construction of the Pagoda was so massive that two streets near the pagoda were named Dashani Street (Big Silt Street) and Xiaoshani Street (Small Silt Street), showing how difficult and enormous the construction project was. At that time, when climbing up to the top of the pagoda and looking far into the distance, one could see boundless clouds and all the surrounding countryside. Three rivers were like three flood dragons, converging on the east of the city and winding away through the Mount Zhaobao into the sea. One poem on this sight goes:

> *The immense sky and the land are joined with the ocean miles away,*
> *Thundering tides come with waves one after another upon the city,*
> *At the top of the Pagoda you partner with heaven,*
> *Downlooking, you find scudding clouds flowing as currents.*

As the symbol of Ningbo in ancient times, the Tianfeng Pagoda has long enjoyed a great reputation. It's told from generation to generation that another aim for the construction of the tower is that people used it as a beacon tower. Both Tianfeng Pagoda and Zhenmang Pagoda on Xiaobai Hill of Dongxiang were built in the Tang Dynasty. The two towers overlook each other across a long distance. If intruders approached or wars broke out, smoke signals would be sent on the towers to call up surrounding garrison troops. While in peace time bright lights were hung on top of the towers as beacons. As Tianfeng Pagoda played such a great role in protecting the people, it was regarded as a treasure. But also because of this it once suffered unexpected calamity. In December 1129 A.D., the southward Jin troops lost a battle in chasing Emperor Kang, so they gave an order to burn the city before evacuating and the Tianfeng Pagoda was almost burned to ashes. Later, the eminent monk Zhengjue of the Song Dynasty managed to raise money for the repair of the tower in 1144 A.D. The reconstructed Tianfeng Pagoda was even more spectacular than before.

As an old pagoda of more than 1,000 years, Tianfeng Pagoda has experienced all kinds of hard weathers and war fires, and has been destroyed and rebuilt for countless times. Since 1949, the people's government had taken many measures to protect the tower, but it still kept tilting, so the government decided to pull it down and rebuild it. When clearing the tower footing in 1982, people surprisingly found more than 150 cultural relics, among which there was a silver model of the underground vault of

Tianfeng Pagoda with an inscription written in the 14th year of the Southern Song Dynasty, silver censors, the ancient "Mahayana Lotus Sutra" paper money of the Yuan Dynasty, stone caskets, Buddha statues and so on, providing mock-ups for the rebuilding and the Xieshan Roof style hall architectures, a typical Jiang'nan style building (Jiang'nan: regions south of Yangtze River) in Shaoxing Period of the Southern Song Dynasty.

As the tallest building of the city in old times, Tianfeng Pagoda enjoyed a high reputation in earlier times. It was a must-visit place for celebrities and literati of all dynasties and there are many poetic inscriptions about it. Li Tang of the Ming Dynasty wrote a poem for the pagoda, which reads:

Up-pointing is a jade hairpin in the firmament,
I step my foot on the entrance and go up to the pointing tower head.
The sun is near and the light dazzling,
Mist waving, and under the eaves the green of trees creeps in.
The wind blows cool and rustling,
Flowers falling like sparse rain.
I laugh to say the clouds are around and the stars are my reach within

The rebuilt Tianfeng Pagoda is at the original location and resembles the pagoda style of the Song Dynasty. Tianfeng Pagoda now still adds up much grace and charm to Ningbo.

Xiantong Tower

Xiantong Tower, also called Tianningsi Tower (Tower of Tianning Temple), is seated on the entrance to Zhuangjiaxiang Alley on Zhongshan West Road, which is now under provincial-level protection.

Xiantong Tower is simple and solemn. But as it is quite undersized and looks like a tortoise, it is also called "Tortoise Tower". It is the oldest tower and the only Tang Dynasty tower in Zhejiang. It was originally called Guoning Temple and was built in the fifth year of Dazhong Period of the Tang Dynasty (851 A. D.). It was a large temple then. Later the name of the temple was changed many times and was changed to Tianning Temple in 1912, the first year of the Republic of China. There were formerly two towers in front of the Tianning Temple on both sides, but the left tower collapsed during Guangxu Period of the Qing Dynasty, and the right tower is Xiantong Tower, the name of which came from the epigraph written in regular script "The brick is made in the fourth year of Xiantong Period" on its right tower brick. In the first years after the Liberation, Tianning Temple was pulled down. Large amount of temple relics were gone and only the tower was left. The tower was built with bricks, the plane square, the base covering more than 10 square meters, each side 3. 2 meters long. Outside the tower there is no tower spire on its top anymore and the height of the tower is about 12 meters; inside the tower the room assumes square shape and the ceiling is arched and vaulted. The body of the tower is almost upright with no tendency to incline, but is eroded and weathered severely. The tower has five stories; the bottom storey is higher with a Hu Door on it and the upper stories are shorter and shorter. On each floor there are Buddha statues enshrined in each wall, and corbel eaves are built with bricks on each side with a projection density of about 0. 7 meters. The tower is old-styled and solemn without any columns, square-columns or crossbeams, and every storey is covered with waist eaves layer upon layer, showing distinctive features of thick-eave brick tower of the Tang Dynasty. It is the only wholly kept thick-eave square-shaped brick tower of the Tang Dynasty in the region to the south of the Yangtze River.

Xiantong tower is of great value in analyzing the environment coordinate of the ancient southern city of Mingzhou (i. e. Ningbo), technologies of brick architectures, brick making technology, history of religions and the sizes of the temples in Tang Dynasty. It also especially shows the solemn and implicit features of the Tang Dynasty towers in the region, which is a symbol for the spirit of reason and aesthetic pursuit of the Mingzhou people in the Tang Dynasty.

In December, 1981, it was included in the municipal key cultural relic protection units. On December 12, 1989, it was announced to be a provincial key cultural relics protection unit. After repairing and maintaining, it has restored the mien it once had in history.

Liang Shanbo Temple

Liang Shanbo Temple, also called Liang Shengjun Temple, is located near Gaoqiao in Xixiang, Yin County, about 10 kilometers from downtown Ningbo. There is a saying among locals: "if you wish to keep your marriage to the end, visit Liang Shanbo Temple and your wish will be fulfilled." On March 1 and August 17 in Chinese lunar calendar each year, many couples come visiting the temple.

The two folktale characters Liang Shanbo and Zhu Yingtai are household names in China. It is said that there are as many as seven tombs of Liang and Zhu across China, but there is only one Liang Shanbo Temple in China, which is based in Ningbo. Recorded in *Memoir on the Temple of King Yizhong*: "his sacred name is Churen, courtesy name Shanbo, surname Liang, and he is from Kuaiji, born on March 1 the year of Renzi in Yonghe Period of Emperor Mu of the Jin Dynasty..." Zhang Du of the Later Tang Dynasty said in his book *Xuan Shi Zhi (A Collection of Short Stories)*: "Yingtai, a young woman from Zhu family in Shangyu, disguised as a young man to go to school and studied together with Liang Shanbo from Kuaiji. Shanbo's courtesy name is Churen. Zhu returned home first and Shanbo visited her in the second year, till when he knew she is a woman and felt at loss. He asked her parents to marry her to him, but Zhu was already engaged to a man from a Ma family. Shanbo later became the governor of Mao County, and was buried in the west of the city after he died of illness. When Zhu was on the way to marry Ma, her boat passed the tomb where wind and wave became still. She was told there was the tomb of Shanbo. She landed on the tomb and burst into wild cry. Suddenly the earth opened and Zhu was also buried. Prime Minister Xie An of the Jin Dynasty pled to the emperor to name the tomb "Grave of Loyal Woman".

167

Shanbo was entitled as "King Yizhong" (King of Allegiance), because it was said that his ghost had helped to suppress insurgence. The above records show that Liang Shanbo and Zhu Yingtai, and the character Ma are not fictional.

In the last years of the Northern Song Dynasty, Li Maocheng, an official of Mingzhou, wrote an article recording in detail that Liang Shanbo was born on March 1; the given name of Zhu Yingtai was Zhen; Ma was from Langtou, Mao County; Zhu was married on August 16, 373 A.D., the first year of Ningkang Period of Emperor Xiaowu of Jin Dynasty, and the joint tomb is in Jiulongxu, Qingdaoyuan on the west of Mao County, etc. The prose written by Li Maocheng seven hundred years after the death of Liang and Zhu is more detailed than *"Xuan Shi Zhi"*, reflecting people's strong opposition to feudal ethics and wishes to pursue a free and happy life.

In Liang Shanbo Temple, the straight plaque hung on the main hall says "the Temple of King Yizhong", inside the hall there is a sitting statue of Liang Shanbo wearing official hat and broad girdles, on whose right side sits the statue of Zhu Yingtai wearing wedding dress, and boy and girl servants are carrying loads of books and hampers on each side. The back hall is the sleeping chamber of Liang and Zhu, with delicate carved wooden bed, silk curtain, brocade quilts and necessities. Behind the hall is the tomb of Liang and Zhu, with a stone tablet with the inscribed characters of "Tomb of Liang Shanbo".

Seventeen-House Complex of the Zheng's

Located on the south of Mountain Ze in Xiepu town, Zhenhai District, Zheng Shi Shi Qi Fang (Seventeen-House Complex of the Zheng's) is the biggest construction complex of the Ming and Qing Dynasties in China. There are two main versions with regard to the origin of the name. One is that "the Seventeen Houses", referring to seventeen prominent families in a clan. The other is that the Seventeen Houses were built by the sixth-generation descendents of the posterity of a man called Duke Seventeen of the Zheng family in Xiepu in the Ming Dynasty. Whatever origin it has, both the exquisite and ingenious structure and rich historical connotations of the buildings have taken on distinct characteristics of the Ming and Qing Dynasties.

The complex is not far from the sea. The castle on Mountain Ze is 30 meters in height with a perimeter of more than 200 meters. There are two gates on the west and east sides which are built with boulder strips. Stepping on the highest place, one can observe the sea. While walking down the mountain along the courier road one can get straight into the complex. Overlooked from the mountain, the whole complex takes the shape of chessboard squares. The buildings are surrounded by Hao River, and every household is connected with the water system and faces the river. Clear waterways run around the households through ditches. This pattern of "every household has a port and every family is near a bridge" designed hundreds of years ago by the Zheng folks for their posterities is convenient in transportation and has the functions of burglary prevention, fire prevention and temperature adjustment.

The extant construction complex covers an area of more than 40,000 square meters just for Dazu House, Xiaojiu House, Lu House, Front Court of the Third House, the New House, Li House, Heng House, Houxin House and Luyan Zheng House. Apparently the houses are connected as a whole, and corridors, hall gates and courtyards of every household are linked, but actually the distinctions are clear. Some gate towers are decorated with patterns of plants and flowers, while others are pictured with animals like insects and birds. Plants can be divided into grasses and flowers, and for animals they are different in strength. The low-rank households are decorated with grass patterns, while the high ranks are decorated with flowers patterns, higher ranks with insect and bird pictures, and beast pictures are for the highest ranks. Brick carvings on eaves, crossbeams, wall corners and buttress walls also follow the pattern standard and violation whatsoever is strictly forbidden.

Corbiestep is a distinctive feature of the architectures in the Ming and Qing Dynasties. Normally the corners of the gables are spread with plasters in other places of China. But in the "Seventeen Houses" the corners are decorated with all kinds of beast, insect and bird patterns, and have the division of three steps, four steps and five steps. It is said that the number of steps is the symbol of the official rank of the owner.

The architecture style can well represent the court-centered planning of the capital cities of feudal China: a 100-meter west-east long axis is the backbone of the whole complex and all the key buildings stand along it. Every house forms into a courtyard and all the courtyards are connected, showing an air of large-scale and imposing manner. Some of the buildings have decorations of crossbeams, winding corridors, painted beams and carved pillars. This palace and temple-imitating construction style shows the prominent social status of the owners of the houses. There are still many memorial gateways, horizontal inscribed boards, stone drums and flagpoles existing, and inscriptions like Both Father and Son Receive Official Positions and Both Father and Son

Pass the Imperial Examination still can be seen in some of the houses. Besides, hundreds of ginkgo-made window decorations, latticed doors and slab stones with the pattern of Eight Centigrams (Baguio) on them are seen everywhere.

Like a piece of unprocessed jade, the residential complex is giving off more and more dazzling brilliance.

Qinatong Ancient Town

Established in 1233 A.D. and located in the southwest of Ninghai County, Zhejiang Province, with an area of 68 square kilometers and a population of 26,000 people, Qiantong Town is a typical south China town with a long history, rich culture and unique geographical conditions. It has been successively entitled Famous Historic and Cultural Town of Zhejiang Province and Tourism Town of Zhejiang Province.

Qiantong Town is on the southwest of Ninghai, Zhejiang. The Streets of the town as well as base of the houses are all paved with cobblestones. The streets and alleys are narrow, buildings are quite dense, and the villages are laid out in 8 tri-grams and 9 halls diagram (Jiugong Bagua) patterns like a Chinese character "Hui". The ancestors of the Tongs learned from Bagua principles to draw water of Baixi Creek into the villages, so the clear creek water circulates around the households so that people can wash

171

vegetables and clothes in the water. Every household is connected by waterways, small bridges and cobblestone lanes. The green vines creeping on white walls, black tiles and the windows decorated with stone engraved designs, and carved beams, painted pillars and arched gateways, all reveal the prosperity of this place in the past.

Qiantong has rich tourist resources: complete ancient building complexes, splendid cultural landscapes and beautiful scenery. Conservation districts of historic sites and cultural heritage featuring ancient architecture and life style are established. Four main tourist spots, traditional residence district, Lianghuangshan scenic area, Shixie Longyin scenic area and Fuquanshan scenic area have been established, attracting flocks of tourists from home and abroad.

Qiantong is famous for its peculiar layout, well-kept building groups of the Ming and Qing Dynasties and numerous talented people in different historical periods. It was first built in the last years of the Song Dynasty and became prosperous in the Ming and Qing Dynasties. Till 2005, there are still more than 1,300 houses of different kinds well preserved. In Qiantong, "every household has carved beams and fresh water", the clear water of Baixi Creek flows into the villages through ditches and circulates around every household, forming a special view, typical of regions south of the Yangtze River. The Bagua-shaped waterways circulate through every household and the cool water flows humming and steadily, making Qiantong more like a riverside town than the real ones. The northwest and southeast sides of Qiantong are surrounded by mountains. The height of the highest peak in northwest Lianghuangshan Mountain is 768.2 meters. The central part of the town is plain with rivers. The main streams are Baixi Creek and Lianghuangxi Creek. Baixi Creek enters into the territory of Qiantong through Chalu Town on the west, then flows across the front of Qiantong Village and runs through Zhulin Village. Lianghuangxi Creek origins from the southeast foot of Lianghuang Mountain, then flows across the back of Qiantong Village and detours into the back of Zhulin Village where it converges into Baixi Creek. There is a Lianghuang Temple (Chongfu Temple) built during Wude Period of the Tang Dynasty (618 A.D.—626 A. D.) on the south foot of Mountain Lianghuangshan. The famous geographer and traveler of Ming Dynasty Xu Xiake once climbed the mountain. On the foot of Mountain Nanqiaoshan in Qiantong is a Shijing Lecture House built by Tong Boli, a Confucian scholar of early Ming Dynasty, where Fang Xiaoru once gave lectures. The beautiful Mountain Tashan and Mountain Lushan stand on the west and east side of Qiantong.

Historic sites like Xiaonyu Lake, Miaohu Lake, Zhisi Hall, Xueshi Bridge and Nangong Temple still exist. The ancestral hall of the Tong's family designed by Fang Xiaoru is well preserved. The ancestral halls built in Hongwu Period of the Ming Dynasty have caught special attention of experts. There are also graves and tablet pavilions for the revolutionary martyrs in the Mountain Lushan.

In the history of Qiantong, talented people came out in succession. In the age of Imperial Examination, more than 200 Qiantong people passed the exam and won scholar and official ranks. There were also great many talents in modern times, like Tong Baoxuan who became governor of Zhejiang at 25. The main features of the whole Qiantong Town are ancient villages, honest folks, marvelous springs and beautiful mountains. Ancient and rare trees like the King of Camphor Tree in Zhejiang in Zhulin Village and the cypress planted by Fang Xiaoru are all taken as treasures; the fantastic medicinal springs in Liantou have marvel curative effects; the exquisite handcrafts have been selected into the Forbidden City and the Great Hall of the People; Lianghuangshan Mountain is the first stop where the master travelogue writer Xu Xiake (1587 A. D. — 1641 A. D.) wrote his travelogue; and the beautiful Lushan Mountain, Tashan Mountain and Shijingshan Mountain are attracting tourists from all around. On the top of the Fuchuanshan Mountain in the northeast of Qiantong there is a Fuquan Temple, where there is a "Tie Liu" Memorial Hall in remembrance of the East-Zhejiang guerrilla

troops led by a communist leader named Wang Huaiqiu. The Fuquan Temple and the nearby Liantoushan Mountain are famous tourist attractions of the Ninghai County. In June 2007, Qiantong Town was granted the title National Renowned Historic and Cultural Town.

Shipu Ancient Town

Shipu is an ancient fishing port of more than 600 hundred years, long known as "key city on the middle maritime route of Zhejiang". It is located on the south part of Yangtze Delta Economic Zone, on the middle coast of Zhejiang, and in the south of Xiangshan County of Ningbo. Backed by hills and facing the sea, Shipu Harbor covers an area of 119.5 square kilometers, including 176 coastal islands. The ancient town is built along a mountain, nestled by the hills and facing the sea, so people depict it as "town on the harbor, hills in the town. One side of the town being the harbor, the other side is deep into the valley in the hills. The city wall is built along with the rises and falls of the hills, and the town gate is constructed according to the landform of its location, up high overlooking the harbor. Now Shipu is a national renowned historical and cultural town and one of the six central fishing ports in China.

Shipu has a long history. It is called Shipu because the ancestors live in the valley of Mountain Dajinshan, where it is surrounded by mountains on three sides, and "the mountain rocks stand approaching the sea where streams flow into". Shipu once belonged to Yin County before the Tang Dynasty. In "the Book of Han · Treatise on Geography", there is content referring to the ancestors living by and fishing on the sea. In 706 A.D., the second year of the Shenlong Period of the Tang Dynasty, Xiangshan County was established, and Shipu became one of its villages.

It was renamed as Dongmenzhai (East Gate Mountain Village) in the Song Dynasty, being part of the Houmen District of Guiren Town. In the Yuan Dynasty Dongmen Xunjiansi (an agency of patrol and inspection) was established, and in the Ming Dynasty it belonged to the third Du(the then name of a residential gathering) of Guiren Town. In 1396, Shipu Xunsi (then branch police station) was established, which was part of Dongmenzhai Xunjiansi(then police station). In the 20th year of Hongwu Period of the Ming Dynasty (1378), Changguo Wei (Changguo Fortress) was removed to Mountain Dongmenshan, and Shipu Xunsi was relocated to Mountain Qingtoushan. The front and back Suo of Changguo are relocated to Shipu and build a city which "the southeast is facing the sea, the northwest backs against the mountains, as high as 6.5 meters, as wide as 20 meters, and six hundred and 22 meters in circumference, with three gates on west, south and north sides". It was the right flank fortress in fighting Japanese pirates, thus called "key fortress on the coast of Zhejiang".

In the last years of the Ming Dynasty and the first years of the Qing Dynasty, General Zhang Mingzhen of Shipu established the supreme headquarter against Qing Dynasty in Shipu. Later Zhang Cangshui also was based here to fight against the Qing troops until he was arrested. In the 18th year of Shunzhi Period of the Qing Dynasty (1661), in order to eliminate the anti-Qing forces, the government forced the coastal residents to move inside, and Shipu fortress city was destroyed, leaving more than 700 meters of city gate still exist now. In the 23rd year of Kangxi Period (1684) it was repaired and it was under the charge of the twenty-first Du of Guiren Town.

In the thirty-third year of Kangxi Period (1694 A.D.), the city was rebuilt, and Changshi Battalion was established, guarded by Qian Zong (the lieutenant). During Yongzheng Period (1723—1735 A.D.), Changshi Navy Battalion was stationed here. In the fifth year of Daoguang Period (1826) the Tongzhi Agency for Coast Defense of Ningbo Prefecture was established. In the second year of Xuantong Period (1910) Shipu was under the charge of Changshi Town. In the first year of the Republic of China (1912), Changshi Town and Diannan Township were put under the jurisdiction of Nantian County, and the county government was moved to Shipu, but in the next autumn it was incorporated back to Xiangshan. In the 21st year of the Republic of China (1932), Shipu was divided into four sub-towns of Donglai, Nanxun, Xicheng and Beiping, which in the 23rd year were incorporated into two towns of Donglai and Jinshan, and later changed into Shipu Town the next year.

In April 1930, Japanese troops occupied Shipu and the occupation lasted for nearly five years. In July 1949, Shipu was liberated and became the location of the government of Shipu District. It later became a people's commune, and was a town again in 1961. In 1973 Shipu was nominated one of the four major fishing ports in China by the SPC (State Planning Commission). In 1984 Fantou Township was incorporated in. In 1991 it was entitled a Provincial Renowned Historic and Cultural Town. In 1992, Shipu District was abolished and Shipu Town was expanded by incorporating three townships: Jinxing, Dongmen and Tantoushan. In 1993 it was enlisted into the Class-2 open ports. And Changguo Town was incorporated in it in 2002.

In 2005 Shipu was entitled as a National Renowned Historic and Cultural Town. In the December of 2009, it was approved by Ningbo Municipal Party Committee and Municipal Government to become one of the pilot towns in constructing the first satellite towns in Ningbo. In the December 2010, it was approved to be one of the pilot towns for constructing the first group of satellite cities.

2.3 Famous Ancient Temples

Wulei Temple

Wulei Temple, formerly called Linshan Zen Temple, is located at south of Xiangwang Mount in Mijiadai of Cixi city and its construction was prepared by Master Lingyong in the Tang Dynasty. It was recorded by "Wuleisizhi" (the Record of Wulei Temple) that Na Luoyan, a renowned Indian Monk once settled here in the period of the Three Kingdoms Dynasty (238 A.D.—251 A.D.). Wulei Temple was endowed with the name of Wulei Puji Temple in the Northern Song Dynasty and denominated as Wulei Zen Temple in late Ming Dynasty while it was destroyed in a huge fire in 1853 of the Qing Dynasty and has experienced reconstruction and repairmen for many times since then.

Wulei Temple is of grand construction scale with its former Qiangxiang Pavilion, Fazang Pavilion, Jingxiang Pavilion, Bingxiang Pavilion and Guiguang Pavilion according to the record of the temple, surrounded by impressive peaks and a magnificent and changeful prospect.

Wulei Temple is full of scenic spots and historical sites. There is a pool called Zhenming Pool in front of the temple with the blue water gurgling from the Xiangyan Grave at the east side and flowing to the Moon Lake through the small ditch all year round. It was said that the pool was dug by Nryana, the legendary Indian giant, and many of his disciples day and night during which many people were killed and injured as a result of fighting with the demons in the mountain, thus gained the name of "Wangongchi" (Thousands of Workers Pool). The pool water is crystal and sweet and is said to help people cure diseases and drive out evil spirits. There are five Pinus densiflora near the pool planted by the descendants of the later generations as the incienso of Wulei Temple while there stand several grand and ageless trees on the hillside not far from the temple. The temple is mostly covered with flourishing and evergreen camphor trees, adding radiance and beauty to each other with the golden constructions in the temple. It was in 888 A. D. of the Tang Dynasty that Wulei Temple had a massive expansion and was developed into a full-fledged scale.

Wulei Temple once had a massive rebuilding under the support of government in 1995. The reconstructed Grand Hall covered an area of 490 square meters with seven-room width and six-room depth, costing a total amount of RMB ￥ 1.5 million, apart from donation, most of which came from the bit by bit savings of the temple. By October, 1995, the construction area of Wulei Temple was 7,800 square meters with 221 halls and guest rooms, around 28,667 square meters of foundations inside the wall and courtyard, 6,670 square meters of empty land, 20,010 square meters mountains covered with bamboos and 62,698 square meters mountains planted with firewood. There were 11 resident monks, more than 20 resting monks, 14 service staffs working in each department with 10 buildings and 17 bungalows, covering a construction area of 2,001 square meters while there is a total number of 230 rooms with the construction area reaching 8,000 square meters now, distributed on three axes, namely, the Gate, the "Wangongchi", the Grand Hall, the Hall of Buddhist Abbot on the central axis; Bell Tower and Garan Temple on the eastern axis; Drum Tower, Guanyin Hall and

Triple Saints' Hall on the western axis.

Wulei Temple is regarded as the Spiritual Mountain in the Buddhist world. In the period of the People's Republic of China, Master Hongyi once established a research institute of the Buddhist Law here, now partly restored and reopened to the public. It attracts a large number of tourists around the Tomb-sweeping Day every year.

Asoka Temple

Asoka Temple is situated at the foot of Mountain Taibai, 5 kilometers from Tiantong Temple in the southeast and 16 kilometers away from downtown of Ningbo. As a famous temple of Zen Sect of Buddhism in China, Asoka Temple has an important role in the history of Buddhism in China. It has high prestige less because of its beautiful scenery but more because of its Sarira pagoda. The legend goes that during the 3rd Century B. C., King Asaka of India, the first man who unified India, built 84,000 pagodas with the ash bones of Shakya Muni. He distributed and hid the pagodas all over the world at the places with 8 auspiciousness and six differences. In the year of 282 A. D. and during the Western Jin Dynasty, Monk Huida was instructed in his dream when he was ill to look for Sarira Pagoda. Once day when he came to the foot of Mountain Taibai, he heard bell rang underground. There he prayed wholeheartedly for three days before a pagoda sprung up from the underground with shining light. In 405 A. D. the first year of Emperor Yixi of the Eastern Jin Dynasty, to protect this Buddhist treasure, a pavilion and a Buddhist meditation hall were built. In 522 A.D. and during the Liang Dynasty, the Buddhist Temple was built and Emperor Wudi named it Asaka Temple.

The temple is large in size and symmetrical in layout. Along the central line there are the front gate of the temple, Free Life Pond, Devaraja Hall, Mahavira Hall, Sarira Hall, Preaching Hall, and Scripture Repository. Along the left lie the Yunshui Hall, Maofengcao Hall, Shicuilou, the Founder's Hall, Cheng'en Hall, Abbot Hall, Chenkui Building, and Monks' Cell. Along the right lie the Songguang Room, Bell Building, Sarira Room, Xianjue Hall, and Dabei Room. All together there are 660 rooms covering 11.7 square meters of floorage. The Sarira Hall, which houses the Sarira Pagodas for worshipers, is the most solemn place of the temple. It was built in 1909 modeling after the imperial palaces of Beijing. It is covered with yellow glazed tiles which make the hall magnificent. The Sarira Pagoda is unique in the county. It is about 48 cm in height, and 24 cm in width, with five layers and four corners, and with windows on four sides and Bodhisattva statues on each layer. A chime is hung on inside top of the pagoda, which contains the sarira. Worshipers have to be attentive to catch sight of the sarira. As people view the sarira from different angles, they can see different colors. It is said that red color means good luck and blue color is second, and black color comes the worst. Reverend Monk Dianzhen went to Japan six times to give Buddhist lectures. Before he went to Japan for the third time, he came and lived in the Asaka Temple and paid homage to the Sarira. Many important historical figures like emperors, high-level monks, literary masters left their scripts and inscriptions here. Notably among them are the board scripts by two emperors and the hundred minus stone tablet inscriptions, board scripts, couplets, epitaphs by literary masters including Zhang Jiucheng and Su Dongpo of the Song Dynasty and Dong Qichang, Mei Diaoding, Zhang Binglin of the Ming and Qing Dynasties.

Asaka Temple has good scenery. There is an Upper Tower on the east and a Lower Tower on the west. Nearby there is a group of scenic spots including Buddhist Footprint Pavilion, Fairybook Rock, Blessing Spring, and the Seven-Buddha Pool.

Asaka Temple has big influence in Japan and Southeast Asian countries. It was involved in many international cultural exchanges in the its long history. One ancient envoy from Japan visited the temple and wrote a poem for it:

Out of accidence I come to the Mao Mountains,
Walking on snow and plodding along the winding trails.
Wind piercing through forest and hungry tiger roars,
Monkeys sadly cry and clouds haunt the ageless trees.
Here I see the east pagoda and west pagoda,
Here I move on from the front to back terraces.
What a Buddhist realm this is before my eyes,
Like a wintersweet tree giving off fragrance in cold winter days.

Tiantong Temple

Tiantong Temple, a state-level cultural relics protection units and a renowned scenic resort, lies in the Mountains Taibai, more than 30 kilometers east of the city proper of Ningbo. The temple was built in the first year of Emperor Yuankang, West Jin Dynasty (or 300 A. D.). The legend goes that a traveling monk called Yixing came and settled down here. He opened land and build the first hut, prayed with piety, which moved the King of Heaven, who sent God Taibai incarnated as a boy servant for him to help him build a house for him and did not go back until it was finished. Thus the mountain was named Taibai and the temple Tiantong means "heavenly child". In 732 A. D. of the Tang Dynasty, monk Faxuan established the temple in the mountain side while in 757 A. D. the monk Zongbi chose another location to build a new temple, the present address of Tiantong Temple. The existing architecture was reconstructed in the Qing Dynasty and renovated in 1979.

Tiantong Temple, built down the hillside and ascending layer upon layer, consists of more than 20 ancient architectures including the Hall of Heavenly Kings, the Grand Hall, the Arhat hall, the Thousand-Buddha Pavilion, the Sutra Depository, the Imperial Library, the Hall of Light Recovery, the Hall of Enlightenment, the Bell Tower, the Hall of Abbot, and the Hall of Disciplining. The temple used to have 999 rooms, now 730 rooms remain, covering 58 thousand square meters, a size which is rare for Buddhist temples in China. Inside the hall stands a 7-meter-high statue of Buddha hakyamuni and four heavenly guardians. Inside the temple there are Cypresses of the Tang Dynasty, imperial pardons, edits, seals, inscriptions and many other ancient relics. The halls and palaces are magnificent, with towering ridges and cornices. In front of the temple, there is a Wangong pool, meaning 10,000 people attended the construction of the pool. Before the gate there is a Pipa Stone and to the west of the temple there is a rock with exquisite shape called Linglong Rock. To the east of the temple lies the site of the ancient temple and the Tomb of Monk Yihe. The Tiantong Temple is surrounded with mountains, ancient trees and the landscape is unique and splendid.

Tiantong Temple has over 1600 years of history. In its prime time, it was the home of thousands of Monks. It has "Thousand-Monk-Pot", a cooking utensil of the Years of Emperor Chongzhen, over 350 years ago. Tiantong temple is also the ancestral place for the Caodong School of Buddhists of Japan, which has over 8 million of believers. A renowned Japanese artist, Xuezhou, created a large number of works in Tiantong

Temple during the 15th century. In the autumn of 1980, the leader of Caodong School of Buddhism of Japan and Biqiuqinhuiyu, abbot of Yongping Temple on Mountain Dabeng, together with his followers, erected a monument in memory of Dogen, a Chan mater in Japan.

The temple, surrounded by the dense woods and covering an area of 533.5 hectares, was zoned as one of the Tiantong Forest Parks in 1981. It is regarded as a natural summer resort for its well-preserved vegetation, profuse varieties of trees and emerald green spreading around the mountain.

Xuedou Temple

Xuedou Temple, located in Mountain Xuedou , also known as Xuedou Zisheng Temple, is one of the ten best-known Zen Temples in China. It is the residence of Daci Maitreya as well as one of the five Chinese Buddhist mountains, others being Mountain Putuo, Mountain Wutai, Mountain Emei and Mountain Jiuhua. Situated 8 kilometers northwest of Xikou Town in Fenghua City, Mountain Xuedouis distinctive and famous for its nine closely connected mountain peaks, which are grand and magnificent with various shapes. The time-honored temple was once the residence of Buddhist nuns in the Jin Dynasty, named as Waterfall Temple while it was renamed as "Pubu Guanyin Temple" or literally "Bodhisattva Temple near Waterfalls" after being moved to the present site in the Tang Dynasty (841 A.D.) and then experienced a massive expansion in 892, with the total construction area of 6000 square meters and temple land of 90 hectares. The temple was the favorite of several generations of emperors of the Song Dynasty, who issued successively some 40 imperial edicts to the temple to its great honor. In 999 A.D. in the Northern Song Dynasty, Emperor Zhao Heng named it "Xuedou Holy Temple". Story has it that in 1037 A.D., Emperor Renzong of the Song Dynasty once had a dream in which he was touring Xuedou Temple and thanks to his dream, the temple was named "the Temple in the Dream". In the Ming Dynasty, the mountain was known as one of the ten famous Zen temples of China.

Since its establishment, Xuedou Temple has gone through several destructions and reconstructions while the last destruction happened in early 1960s. However, the jade signet, dragon robe, dragon bowl and 5,760 Buddhist scriptures presented by Emperor Lizong of Song Dynasty(reign: 1224 A.D. —1264 A.D.) remained well preserved. The latest reconstruction of Xuedou Temple was in 1985 with Guangde, then the abbot of

Xuedou Temple, in charge of making preparations for the rebuilding. The Grand Hall and Maitreya Hall were rebuilt successively while the whole construction was resplendent and magnificent with traditional upswept eaves.

In its long history, Xuedou Temple enjoyed a high status in the Buddhist world with a booming pilgrimage and a wealth of eminent monks from various Buddhist sects practicing Buddhism. Zen master Yongming Yanshou in the Song Dynasty spoke the Dharma and wrote 100 volumes of "Zong Jing Lu" (The Mirror of Orthodoxy) in Xuedou Temple, one of Buddhist classics enjoying a high reputation both home and abroad while Chongxian, also a Zen master in the Song Dynasty, once stayed at Xuedou Temple, named as Xuedou Zen master. In the early years of the Republic of China, Master Taixu, then Head of Buddhism Association of China, held the post of the abbot of Xuedou Temple at the invitation of Chiang Kai-shek and investigated Buddhism in many other countries with *Taixudashiquanshu (Master Taixu's Encyclopedia of Buddhist Culture)* as his master work. He passed away in Yufo Temple in Shanghai, with his ashes buried in Xuedou Temple.

Xuedou Temple, as the Bodhimanda, or place of awakening of Maitreya, has different scale and regime from other temples. In the Great Buddha's Hall sits up Maitreya, the Buddha of the future who is commonly known as Cloth Bag Monk with his alternative name as Changtingzi because he was from Changting in Fenghua. He always carried a cloth bag in which he put all his necessities of life on his shoulder with a cane and he was said to have a good sense of humor and always topless and smiling, explaining why people called him "Happy Monk" while his mysterious words and deeds were spread around the local area. It was not until several years after his death when people met him in Fujian Province and was reminded by him of the omnipresence of Buddha dharma did people begin to realize that he was the incarnation of Maitreya. Since then every temple began to model the Maitreya Statue according to the figure of him and placed it in the Hall of Heavenly Kings. A grand dedication ceremony of Maitreya was held in the Maitreya Hall in Xuedou Temple in the first half of 1994 with around 1000 Maitreya Statues being lifelike and having thriving incense.

Qita Temple (Seven-Pagoda Temple)

Qita Temple, or the Seven-Pagoda Temple, is located midway along Baizhang Road. The temple, plus Tiantong Temple, King Asoka Temple and Guanzong Temple, are four famous Buddhist monasteries in east Zhejiang Province. It was approved by the State Council as one of the first national key temples opened up to international visitors in the year of 1983. The temple is elegant-constructed with primitive simplicity and grandeur, with an architecture typical of the seven rooms of Buddhist Zen School. It is mainly composed of the Hall of Heavenly Kings, the Grand Hall, Three-Sage Hall, the Hall of the Abbot, the Library of Sutras, the Hall of Providence, the Hall of Jade Buddha, the Towers of Bell and Drum, the Praying Hall, and the East and West Wing-rooms. In the Hall of Jade Buddha, a Jade Buddha is placed. Before the hall are rockeries and beautiful bamboos. Usually Grand Halls are places to enshrine the statue of Sakyamuni, but here in Qita Temple, the Thousand-handed Guanyin is enshrined. Therefore it is called the Minor Putuo. The temple boasts of a collection of treasures including a sarira pagoda for the zen master Xinjing of the Qixin Temple during the Tang Dynasty, two bronze bells made during the South Song Dynasty, a wooden construction molding board (cha) of the Ming Dynasty, and a five-hundred arhat portrait carved on the Grand Hall.

The temple was built in 858 A.D., and has a history of 1,140 years. The temple record goes that it was initially named Dongjin Zen House. At that time, a man called Ren Jingqiu, who was once the county magistrate of Fenning County (today's Xiushui County) in Jiangxi Province and donated his former residence, to the local Buddhist society, who turned it into Dongjin Temple, the structure that later evolved to be Qita Temple. Ren Jingqiu also invited Master Xinjing (meaning the Mirror of the Heart), the abbot of Tiantong Temple, to serve as chief of the new temple. Known as Zanghuan before he became a monk, Master Xinjing was born and brought up in Huating. During the Huichang years of the Tang Dynasty, he served as abbot at Tiantong Temple and led his people to build Five-Buddha Pagoda at Xiaobailing. As the first abbot of Qita Temple starting from 858 A.D., Master Xinjing dedicated himself to the temple's renovations and the cultivation of Zen spirit. According to historical records, a gang of rebellious soldiers broke into the temple in the 3rd year of Xiantong period in the Tang Dynasty (861 A.D.). They were astounded by what they saw: Master Xinjing sat there in meditation, completely unmoved by the commotion. In great awe, the rabble hushed, did kowtow to the abbot and withdrew. To honour the virtuous abbot, the county gentry sent a report to the emperor in request of renaming the temple as Qixin Temple (meaning where the heart rests). In the year of 1008, the Song Dynasty emperor issued an edict board naming the temple the Chongshou Temple(Temple of Longevity). In the early Ming Dynasty, Japanese pirates often ganged up on coastal villages of China, leaving the residents no peace. To protect the civilians, in the 20th Hongwu year (1378 A.D.), Emperor Zhu Yuanzhang sent General Tanghe, the Duke of Xinguo, to evacuate the islanders of Zhoushan to Jiangdong, Ningbo. In addition, the Duke also moved the statue of Guanyin (or Avalokitesvara), which was enshrined in Zhoushan's Puji Temple to Qita Temple and renamed it as Butuo Temple. For this reason, Qita Temple has close contacts with Mount Putuo, for ever since pilgrims and visitors to

Mount Putuo would also come to worship the Thousand-handed Guanyin (or Avalokitesvara) in Qita Temple. Erected in the 21st year of Emperor Kangxi in the Qing Dynasty (1682 A. D.), the seven pagodas represent the seven Buddhas, Sakyamuni in our world and his six predecessors: Vipasyin, Sikhin, Visvabhu, Krakucchanda, Kanakamuni and Kasyapa. From these structures the temple got its present name. During the years of chaos caused by the Taiping rebellion, the temple was burned down to ashes. Then it was rebuilt, but during the Cultural revolution, it was ruined again. In 1980, the municipal government of Ningbo organized an agency for the reconstruction of the Qita Temple. The agency was headed by Monk Yuexi. With great endeavour and the support from all walks of society, the temple was rebuilt. It regained its grandeur and became the only large size Buddhist temple in the downtown of Ningbo.

3. Famous People

3.1 Historical Figures

Yu Shinan

Yu Shinan (558 A. D.—638 A. D.), of Han nationality, was born in Yuyao County, Yue Prefecture (currently Minghe Town in Cixi City of Zhejiang Province). With courtesy name as Boshi, Yu was a well-known calligrapher, litterateur, poet and statesman in the early Tang Dynasty, and was also one of the 24 meritorious officials of the Tang Dynasty enshrined in the Lingyan Pavilion. His father Yu Li and his elder brother Yu Shiji served as government officials in the Chen Dynasty and Sui Dynasty respectively

Quiet in nature, he spent much of his time on learning and acquired extensive knowledge. During the Chen Dynasty (part of Southern Dynasties), he once served as an adviser of the army; In the Sui Dynasty, he worked as an official in the Department of Palace Library and an Imperial Diarist in succession. After the fall of Sui, he was appointed the Vice Minister of the Chancellery by Dou Jiande. After Li Shimin eliminated the forces of Dou, he asked Yu to be the adviser of his office. After ascending the throne with the title of Emperor Taizong of Tang, Li appointed Yu as Scholar of the Institute for the Advancement of Literature where he and Fang Xuanling, one of the Eighteen Scholars in the Tang Dynasty, were together in charge of imperial writings. Later, Yu also assumed other official posts in succession. Delicate as he looked, Yu Shinan was a strong-minded minister in fulfilling a minster's obligation, brave in criticizing errors of the government and even the emperor, which won him great praise from Emperor Taizong. During the "Reign of Zhenguan", Yu Shinan was conferred Yongxing County Viscount and Yongxing County Duke. He passed away at the age of 81 in the 12th year of Zhenguan Period (638 A.D.). Upon his death, he was allowed to be buried in Zhao Mausoleum, the imperial mausoleum for royal families and meritorious ministers, with the title of minister of the Board of Rites and posthumous honorary title of Duke of Wenyi conferred on him. In the 17th year of Zhenguan Period (643 A.D.), his life-sized portrait was displayed in Lingyan Pavilion.

Emperor Taizong praised Yu Shinan as "a man of five absolute merits", which were virtue, loyalty and uprightness, erudition, writing skills and skillful calligraphy. He was regarded as one of the four greatest calligraphers in the early Tang Dynasty along with Ouyang Xun, Chu Suiliang and Xue Ji. He also edited *Beitang Shuchao* (*Documents in the Northern Hall*), boasting the reputation as one of the four encyclopedias and also one of the earliest extant now. Originally this book consisted of 30 volumes, but later many of them were lost. Zhang Shouyong, a prominent scholar in the Republic of China, edited four volumes of this book into *Yubijianji* (*Collection of Yu Mijian's Works*), which was later compiled into *Siming Congshu* (*Anthology of Works of Siming*).

Wang Yingling

Wang Yingling (1223 A.D.—1296 A.D.), courtesy name Bohou, styled himself Hermit Shenning Jushi or Houzhai. He was born in Yin County in Yingyuan Prefecture (currently Yinzhou District of Ningbo in Zhejiang Province) and his ancestral home was Kaifeng in Henan Province. Becoming a *jinshi* in the first year of Chunyou Period (1241 A.D.) and obtaining the title of erudite literatus in the 4th year of Baoyou Period (1256 A.D.), he successively assumed a number of official posts, including Imperial Secretariat, magistrate of Huizhou Prefecture, and minister of the Board of Rites. As an integral and straightforward person, Wang offended the

宋代王应麟书法

then powerful ministers several times, and then as a result of their revenge he was dismissed from his post. Therefore, Wang returned to his hometown where he began his

188

writing career. His writings included more than 20 categories, totaling 600 volumes. It is said that the famous *Sanzijing* (*Three Character Classic*) was composed by Wang.

He was committed to Academic studies and writings for 20 years. Especially during the years after the destruction of the Song Dynasty, he lived in seclusion. In his first years of academic study, he concentrated on regulations and laws, ancient classics, astronomy and geography. His compilation of *Yuhai* (*Sea of Jade*), a Song-period encyclopedia, served as a miniature of his erudition. It falls into 200 chapters with coverage of 21 categories such as astronomy, geography, official system, food and money. This encyclopedia includes abundant citations, particularly those for the history of the Song Dynasty. In addition, "Literature" part in this book fully recorded references to bibliography, ranging from treatise on literature and various catalogues compiled by the Song government, to books and treatise on literature in the Han, Sui and Tang and well-known bibliographies of private collections of Tang and Song. Due to such an extensive collection of references, this book plays a vital role in the research of culture and scholarship in the Song Dynasty. Apart from the detailed contents of *Yuhai*, its organization of catalogues by subjects also brought him accolades, regarded as a new trend toward thematic catalogue.

After the fall of the South Song, a shattering blow to Wang, he denied himself to visitors completely and dedicated himself to writing diverse books. As prolific writer, his works amounted to over 600 volumes covering more than 20 fields. His works included *Kun Xue Ji Wen(A Miscellaneous Collection of Academic Study)*, *Xiao Xue Gan Zhu* (*Book for Enlightenment Education*), *Tongjian Dili Kao Ji Tongshi* (*Geography*), *Yuhai(Sea of Jade,Chronicles of the Song Dynasty)*, *Shi Dili Kao(A Histographical Enquiry into the Poems)*, *Tong Jian Dawen* (*Q&A of Classical Works*), *Hanshu Yiwen Zhi Kaozheng(An Investigation into the Selected Classical Works Compiled by Ban Gu of East Han Dynasty)*, *Shen Ning Ji* (*Collected Works by Shenning School Scholars*), *Yutang Leigao(A Miscillaneous Collection of Works)*, *Shigao(Poems)*, etc. Among all his works, *Sanzijing(Three Character Primer)* enjoys the highest reputation.

Fang Xiaoru

Fang Xiaoru (1357 A. D. —1402 A. D.), courtesy name Xizhi or Xigu, styling himself Xunzhi, was born in Ninghai. As his hometown was also called Goucheng at that time, he was addressed Mr. Goucheng; He was also known as Mr. Zhengxue because his study was once granted the title of Zhengxue by Prince of Shu when he served as a professor in Hanzhong Prefecture. He was a minister in the Ming Dynasty, scholar, litterateur, essayist and thinker. In 1399, Zhu Di, Prince of Yan, usurped the throne by launching Jingnan Incident, he commanded Fang to write an inaugural address for him, but Fang refused. As a result, he was executed altogether with his 870 blood relatives, friends and students, the only case in Chinese history of an "extermination of ten of kinships". But he was conferred a posthumous title Wenzheng during the reign of King Fuwang .

Fang was proficient in writing political essays, historical essays, prose and poems and most of his writings were collected in *Xunzhi Zhai Ji* (*Collection of Works from Xunzhi's Study*). Besides, his literary works, such as *Wendui* (*Mosquitos Dialogues*), *Zhiyu* (*Finger Revelations*),

Yuewu (*A Wizard in Yue*), *Bidui* (*A Dialogue with Nose*), *Wushi* (*A Man in Wu Area*), *Yueche* (*Chariot of Yue*) have unique features. His literary works usually have distinctive themes and around this theme was his sharp remarks and full disclosure of the dark side of society. His *Yuewu* (*A Wizard in Yue*) was a good illustration of this style. This story, a wizard who bluffed and swindled others by proclaiming himself to be able to vanquish ghosts and monsters was frightened to death by other people's trick of disguise as ghosts, satirized the vile and brutal fact that many wizards in society fed themselves on duping others. Additionally, he was good at expressing his sense of justice with various images.

Take *Wushi* (*A Man in Wu Area*) as an example, the image of Zhang Shicheng was depicted to satire those partial high-rank officials who are imprudent in appointing their lower-rank officials. The portrait of a group of incompetent and cowardly men disclosed the social trend toward pomposity. The third feature of Fang's works was his deep delving into a subject. *Zhiyu(Revelations of Disease in Finger)* is such a representative work, which is an argumentative prose consisting of a story and argumentation which was naturally elicited from the former. Fourthly, the use of metonymy and the comparison in a fable played an important role in his works. His literary works evidently displaying this feature are *Bidui (A Dialogue with Nose)* and *Wendui (Mosquitos Dialogues)*. The latter is a prose of ethics, illustrating major philosophies of life eliciting from a trivial thing in daily life that is being bit by mosquitoes. His other works include *Zhou Li Kao Ci(An Enquiry into Zhou Rites)*, *Da Yi Zhi Ci(An Enquiry into the Book of Changes)*, *Wu Wang Jie Shu Zhu(Annotations to the Warning Book of King Wu)*, *Song Shi Yao Yan(Lessons from the Song Dynasty)*, *Di Wang Ji Ming Lu (Lessons from the Life of Emperors and Kings)*, *Wen Tong(Literary Traditions)*, etc., but most of them are lost.

Wang Yangming

Wang Yangming (1472 A.D.—1529 A.D.), also known as Wang Shouren, of Han nationality, was born in Yuyao County, Shaoxing Prefecture (currently a county of Ningbo). Named Yun in his childhood, he styled himself as Boan, alias Yangming. He once built a room in a cave of Mount Kuaiji, which is now known as Yangming Cave. Wang Shouren addressed himself as Yangmingzi, and thus was called Mr. Yangming, or Mr. Wang Yangming by scholars. Wang Shouren is a well-known thinker, writer, philosopher, militarist in the Ming Dynasty, and is considered a master of Lu Wang Mind Studies. He was exceptionally versatile, not only expert in Confucianism, Buddhism and Daoism, but in the art of wars. He was conferred the title of "A Sage of Confucianism" and was enshrined at the 58th place in the east chamber of Confucian Temple. In the 12th year of Hongzhi Period (1499), Wang became a *jinshi* in the imperial examination. Since then, he successively assumed a number of official posts, such as magistrate and governor in Guizhou, Luling, Guangdong and Guangxi and other places. In his later years, his ranking ascended to Nanjing Minister of the Board of War and president of the Court of Censors. Owing to his success in pacifying Chenhao Turmoil (1519), he was given the title of Earl Xinjian, and posthumously conferred Xinjian vassal in Longqing years. After his death, he was styled as Wencheng.

Therefore, later generations addressed him as the Revered Wang Wencheng.

Wang Shouren (master of Mind Studies) and Confucius (founder of Confucianism), Mencius (utmost master of Confucianism), Zhu Xi (or Chu Hsi) (founder of Neo-Confucianism) are known as Kong, Meng, Zhu and Wang. Their thoughts spread all over China and to Japan, Korea and Southeast Asia as well. With overwhelming success in his time, Wang was high in morality and productive in theoretical studies, with achievements dwarfing his counterparts in the Ming Dynasty. He had a great many followers and students, who formed into the Yaojiang School. His articles are vigorous and inspirational and his works are collected in the *Complete Works of Wang Wencheng*. He compared himself to Zhuge Liang and resolved to make a difference. He was not only good at academic learning, but also at horse riding, arrow shooting and military strategy and tactics.

In 1517, the 12th year of Zhengde Period, an uprising broke out in southern Jiangxi and mountainous areas in the border regions between Jiangxi, Fujian and Guangdong. The rebels organized themselves an army in an expanse of 500 kilometers. Not knowing what to do, local officials reported it to the emperor. The Ministry of War recommended Wang Shouren to assume the office of the governor to Jiangxi to suppress the turbulence. In the first lunar month of 1518, Wang beat the Chi Zhongrong's (Chi Dabin) troops and appealed to the central government to have a Heping County (Peace County) set up and run schools. In the third lunar month, shortly after taking office in Jiangxi, he assembled military forces from the three provinces of Jiangxi, Fujian and Guangdong and successfully suppressed uprisings in places like Xinfeng. In the seventh lunar month, considering the huge war-inflicted damage, Wang pleaded to the emperor to grant amnesty to the rebels. The Ming government thus appointed him the head of the local government to prepare for it. In the tenth month, Wang destroyed military camps headed by Lan Tianfeng, Xie Zhishan from Chongyi County, Jiangxi which were his strongest enemies, and joined his forces at Zuoxi. Wang offered amnesty to the enemy troops. In the eleventh month, Wang sent envoys to demand surrender, and cracked down the Lan Tianfeng army. The two years of successful warring experience show that he was not only a thinker and a scholar, but also a practitioner, a result of his philosophy: the unification of knowledge with action. Wang's most important military feat in his lifetime was pacifying Zhu Chenhao rebellion in Nanchang.

Wang Shouren advocated a clear-cut "rewards and punishments" system to raise the efficacy of governance and preventing crimes with ethics and virtues. In law enforcement, he valued the principle of "balance between sentiments and law" and opposed "ruthless killing" and the practice of making no discrimination between the good and the wicked, upholding "rules" and rigid management of law enforcers. He insisted on the prohibition of "killing beyond law", believing that "malpractice of the superiors causing failures of law enforcement". Wang Shouren was a great master of subjective idealism in the Song and the Ming Dynasties.

Wang Yangming's philosophy is so admirable that Togo Heihachiro, a noted militarist in modern Japanese history, deliberately wore a seal reading "Worshiping Yangming Forever". Until today, Mito, a city in Japan, still kept Zhu Shunshui's sculpture as it was he who introduced to Japan Yangming studies in the late Ming Dynasty. In Meiji Restoration, Yangming Studies became the basis of traditional thoughts fighting against indiscriminate westernization. This partly explains the fact that some traditions in Japan are much better preserved than in China.

Huang Zongxi

Huang Zongxi (1610 A. D.—1695 A. D.) was born in Yuyao County, Shaoxing Prefecture (currently Yuyao County of Ningbo City, Zhejiang Province). Courtesy name Taichong, Alias Nanlei and a series of other names, Huang Zongxi styled himself Taichong and Debing, and scholars usually call him Mr. Lizhou. Known as the Father of Chinese Enlightenment, Huang was a Confucian classics expert, prominent historian, thinker, geographer, almanac expert and educator during the latter part of the Ming Dynasty and the early part the Qing Dynasty. He was named as one of the Three Greatest Thinkers of the late Ming and early Qing Dynasty along with Gu Yanwu, Fang Yizhi and Wang Fuzhi, one of the Five Great Qing scholars and the "Three Great Masters", "Father of Enlightenment in China" and also one of "the Three Great Confucian Scholars in China" together with the other two being Li Yong in Shaanxi and Sun Qilong in Zhili (part of Beijing).

Huang Zongxi's learning covered a wide range of fields, such as classics, history, astronomy, arithmetic, music and Buddhism and Taoism, among which it was the history that he made particularly remarkable achievement. In the process of writing the Mingshi (History of Ming) by officials of the Qing Dynasty, they frequently sought advice from Huang Zongxi when they encountered disputes. Witnessing the replacement of the Ming Dynasty with the Qing, Huang stated that a dynasty could collapse but the recording of the nation's history couldn't be stopped. He emphasized that fidelity to facts should be the principle which history recording must adhere to. In terms of other fields, Huang also formed his own unique understanding. About philosophy, he regarded qi (material force) as the stuff of all phenomena and thought that li (principle or pattern), serving as a guide for qi, could not exist without it; he meanwhile held that xin (mind) was the same as qi and it was xin that filled the heaven and earth. In terms of politics, Huang Zongxi criticized the system of feudal autocratic monarchy, and declared that the world should belong to the people, proposing that an emperor should be deposed if he caused damage to his people. He proposed to replace the imperial laws with the people's laws. In addition, he proposed to take schools as the place for discussion of governmental affairs. Apart from his achievement in these aspects, Huang Zongxi also put forward his own insightful and valuable ideas for studying history, identifying the truth of historical events, and revising historical books by use of his great learning in ancient calendar, geography, mathematics and bibliography of book editions, which produced immense and far-reaching impact in the whole Qing Dynasty.

The writings by Huang Zongxi covered diverse subjects up to 50, including history, classics, geography, calendar, mathematics, and literature. Important among his 300 plus volumes of books are *Mingru Xue'an (Cases in Ming Confucianism)*, *Songyuan Xuean (Cases of Pedagogy in the Song and Yuan Dynasties)*, *Mengzi Shishuo (My Teacher's Teachings on the Mencius)*, *Zangzhi Huowen (Issues on Funeral System)*, *Poxie Lun (On Suppressing Evils)*, *Sijiu Lu (Records on Thinking of the Past)*, *Yixue Xiangshu Lun (On Yi-ology)*, *Ming Wen Hai(Collected Works of Ming)*, *Xing Chao Lu(A History of the South Ming Dynasty)*, *Jin Shui Jing(An Investigation of Watercourses)*, *Da Tong Li Tui Fa(Datong Calendar)*, *Simingshan Zhi(Chronicles of Mountains Siming)*, etc. Huang Zongxi also made collections of his works when he was alive. So many works were completed to voice his enlightenment ideas by his own thinking instead of learning from foreign ideas, an absolute miracle in Chinese history which earned him the title of the Father of Chinese Enlightenment.

Zhang Cangshui

Zhang Cangshui (1620 A. D. —1664 A. D.), also known as Zhang Huangyan, of

195

Han nationality, was born in Yin County (currently a district in Ningbo of Zhejiang Province). Courtesy name Xuanzhu, alias Cangshui. Living during the Southern Ming Dynasty, he became a juren (a successful candidate in the imperial examinations at the provincial level). After that, he assumed an official post and got promoted continuously, and was finally made the minister of the Board of War. As an outstanding general, he was known for his great deeds in the fights against Manchu troops. After the fall of Nanjing in 1645 which was the first year of Shunzhi Period of the Qing Dynasty as well as the first year of Hongguang of the Southern Ming, Zhang, along with Qian Sule, continued their fighting against Qing. Later, he followed Prince Lu and asked 13 farmer armies to join their actions. By cooperating with Zheng Chenggong, he led his army recapturing over 20 towns in Anhui Province. He kept his resistance to the Qing Dynasty for nearly 20 years.

In 1664 (the third year of Kangxi Period of the Qing Dynasty), Emperor Yongli, Prince Lu and Zheng Chenggong died successively. In light of the great fall in the resistance force, Zhang Huangyan disarmed his army on an island and began his secluded life. Also in this year, he was captured and then was killed. Twelve years after his death, he was granted a posthumous title Zhonglie. His biography was written into the *Ming Shi* (*History of the Ming*) by the Imperial Historiography Institute of the Qing Dynasty.

196

Not only an outstanding general, Zhang Huangyan is also a renowned poet. Despite his short life of only forty-five years, he left us abundant writing works. Those writings were collected and compiled into a book entitled *Zhang Cangshui Ji* (*Works of Zhang Cangshui*). However, as this book was listed as a banned one in the Qing Dynasty, only manuscripts was available. In 1901, Zhang Binglin, one of the most prominent Confucian scholars, printed this book with a supplement *Bei Zheng Lu* (*Records of Expeditions to the North*). Later in 1909 and 1959, this book was reprinted with more supplements of his life chronicle, biography, preface and postscript.

In fact, most of Zhang's writings were finished during his martial career. Tragic and solemn feelings pervaded those works. Zhang, along with Yue Fei and Yu Qian, was named as "Three Heroes of the West Lake". Among his various poems, *Wengzhou Xing* (*Journey to Wengzhou*), *Minnan Xing* (*Journey to Southern Fujian*) and others described his hard battling life. Especially *Jue Ming Shi* (*A Will of Death*) which was written prior to his death, telling of tears and blood, was considered as his greatest poem.

The National Archives of the Qing glorified him by writing his biography which was included in History of the Ming. In 1776, a temple was built to enshrine him. His name was included in the list of martyrs of the Ming Dynasty by the Qing government.

Zhu Shunshui

Zhu Shunshui, or Zhu Zhiyu (1600 A.D.—1682 A.D.), born in Yuyao (a city in Zhejiang, China), whose courtesy name was Chuyu or Luyu, was one of the greatest scholars and educationalists in the late Ming and the early Qing dynasties. He took part in the imperial test in the Ming Dynasty and was enlisted as a Gongsheng (an academic title lower than Jinshi). He declined two invitations to be government official from the Ming Dynasty and the South Ming Dynasty, hence the nickname "Zheng Jun" (a man wanted by the imperial governments).

As a scholar, Zhu advocates learning for practice. He said, "the essence of learning lies in practice and the theory of the sages are for application." His theories exerted influence in Japan. He is ranked with Zhu Zhiyu, Huang Zongxi, Wang Fuzhi, Gu Yanwu and Yan Yuan as the five great Chinese scholars in the late Ming and the early Qing dynasties. He is also placed among the four sages of Yuyao together with Wang Yangming, Huang Lizhou and Yan Ziling .

The Manchu army marched southward after they broke the Sanhaiguan Pass in 1644. In the fighting against Manchu invaders and for the revival of the Ming Dynasty, Zhu, as a young hermit, took active role regardless of his personal safety and assisted Wang Yi, the leader of an Anti-Manchu army with their base in Zhoushan Peninsular off the east coast of Zhejiang Province. Wang Yi died on Aug. 14, 1651 by the lunar calendar. To commemorate Wang Yi, Zhu held a ceremony of condolence for him the next day, and abolished for life the custom of appreciating the full moon on the 15th day of the eighth month by lunar calendar. After that, Zhu also participated in the northbound crusade led by Zheng Chenggong and Zhang Huangyan, fighting enemies bravely. In 1657, Zhu planned to return home and support the Anti-Manchu activity led by Zheng Chenggong when he was then in Vietnam. Coincidentally, the Vietnamese king was then recruiting literates to do the civil service, and someone recommended Zhu Shunshui. Zhu failed returning home and was brought into the palace of Vietnam. Confronted with a foreign king, Zhu would rather die than bow down, which irritated the Vietnamese king and the king threatened to kill him. Then Zhu said, "I'll be regretless if I die for abiding by the etiquette of the Ming Dynasty today. After my death, please write down"Tomb of Zhu-Envoy of the Ming Dynasty"on my tomb. The dauntless act of Zhu won the respect of the Vietnamese king, and finally the king sent him back home. In 1659, after the Manchu army conquered Zhoushan, Zhu saw the gloom over revival of the Ming Dynasty, and fled to Japan.

In Japan, Zhu often burst in tears when he was homesick and became indignant at the thought of Manchu's invasion. He named himself "Shun Shui", which was the name of a river in his hometown, implying that he would never forget his hometown. He thence began his teaching life in Japan for twenty years. Zhu, though in exile, was respected by the Japanese cultural circle. Known as "the Confucius of Japan", He lectured in Japan for more than twenty years and many of his students became the elites in Japan.

Zhu Shunshui not only spread Confucianism and thoughts on morality in Japan, but also introduced Chinese skills on apparel, architecture, food and others to Japan. Nowadays people in many different areas, while doing academic research, can still take for reference from Zhu's books. Zhu adhered to the traditional Chinese culture and required his descendants maintain their identities as descendants of the Emperor Yan and Emperor Huang, the two forefathers of the Chinese nationality. Zhu died on April 17, 1682 at the time of Edo Japan. Tokugawa Mitsukuni, prime minister of the day, gave Zhu an elaborate funeral and buried him in Tokugawa feudal family cemetery. Though Zhu was only an expatriate, his cemetery was located in the central position of the cemetery and his tombstone was inscribed characters in official script, an ancient style, "Tomb of Mr. Zhu-envoy of the Ming Dynasty" autographed by Tokugawa Mitsukuni. Zhu was granted a posthumous name — "Wengong", a word extracted and recomposed from a verse in ancient Chinese, indicating Zhu was a learned and determined man.

Quan Zuwang

Quan Zuwang (1705 A.D.—1755 A.D.) was born in Yinzhou County (currently a district of Ningbo in Zhejiang Province). Named Bu in childhood, Quan addressed himself as Jieqi Magistrate, courtesy name Shaoyi and alias Xieshan, and he is usually called as Mr. Xieshan by scholars. Known for his erudition, he is a famous bibliophile, historian, philologist, and also an important figure of the Eastern Zhejiang School in the Qing Dynasty.

Being a *gongsheng* in the 7th year of Yongzheng Period (1729), Quan Zuwang passed the provincial examination three years later. In the first year of Qianlong Period

(1736), he was granted the title of erudite literatus; also in this year he passed the imperial examination and became a *jinshi*(a successful candidate in the highest imperial examinations), then he was selected as one of the officials in Hanlin Academy. However, as Quan was not willing to play up to the powerful, he encountered much trouble in his political career. Therefore, he resigned just one year later, not striving for an official career any longer. Since then, he devoted himself to research and writing about history, and later began to lecture in various places, including Jishan Academy in Zhejiang. He made complete annotations to the 40 volumes of Commentary on the Waterways and spent most of his life collecting and organizing an ancient classics. He was a representative phinologist of that time.

In academic studies, he paid high esteem to Huang Zongxi, and claimed to be Guangzhou disciple. He was also an adherent of the practical philosophy of Wan Sitong. He focused on the study of the writings in the Southern Song and late Ming periods, collecting historical books of his own hometown, especially those classic writings and old rubbings which were compiled into *Tianyige Beimu*(*Monument List of Tianyige*). In fact, Quan spent most of his time on collecting and compiling important books and produced a lot of excellent works, including 38 volumes of *Collected Works of Magistrate Jieji*, 50 volumes of *A Miscellaneous Collection*, 10 volumes of *A collection of Poems*, 100 volumes of *Cases of Pedagogy in the Song and Yuan Dynasties*, *Chronology of General History*, *Classics Q & A*, *Dialects. Annotations to Commentary on the Waterways*, *Annotations to Kunxuejiwen* (*Kunxuejiwen*: a book by Wang Yinglin on Issues about Academic studies), *Poems by a Senior of Ningbo*, thus contributing greatly to the classic Chinese cultural treasure-house.

Quan Zuwang died at the age of 51 and was buried near his father. His tomb was in the shape of horizontal rectangle with "Tomb of Xieshan, Quan Taishi" inscribed in its stone.

With his pursuit of historical truths and superb writing skills, Quan Zuwang made remarkable achievement in historiography. He is taken as the most creative historiographic writer after Sima Qian. Due to his outstanding writing talents and his uprightness that was never changed by the hardships he experienced in his early political career, Quan became a sage admired by generations of people in the east Zhejiang.

Chiang Kai-shek

Chiang Kai-shek (1887—1975, pinyin: Jiang Jieshi) is a renowned modern Chinese political and military leader. Named Ruiyuan in his childhood, Zhoutai in the pedigree of his clan and Zhiqing as the formal name used in school, he is known as Chiang Chung-cheng (pinyin: Jiang Zhongzheng). With his ancestral home being in Yixing, Jiangsu Province, Chiang was born in Fenghua, Zhejiang. He held various political and governmental positions, including Commandant of Huangpu Military Academy, Commander-in-chief of the National Revolutionary Army, President of Nationalist Government, President of the Executive Yuan, Chairman of the Military Committee of the Nationalist Government, Super Admiral of the Republic of China, President of the Chinese Nationalist Party, Commander-in-chief of the China War Zone of the Allied Nations during the WWII, President of the Republic of China.

The rise of Chiang Kai-shek in the Chinese political arena in the early 20th century was much owed to Sun Yat-sen (pinyin: Sun Zhongshan). Chiang's telant was appreciated by Sun Yat-sen and he was taken as his successor. After the death of Sun Yat-sen, Chiang assumed the leadership of KMT for half a century and was always the central political and economic figure when KMT ruled China. He led China in the Anti-Japanese War, served as the president of the Nationalist China for 27 years. But he was also subject to severe criticism for his statesmanship and dictatorship. His political life spanned the Northern Expedition, Political Tutelage, Civil War, Anti-Japanese War, Constitution Enforcement, Retreat to Taiwan, and the Cold War. He assumed a very important position in the history of modern China.

Chiang Kai-shek went to Japan in 1908 and joined Tongmenghui (Chinese Revolutionary Alliance) there. In 1924, he was appointed by Sun Yat-sen as Commandant of the Huangpu Military Academy. In 1926, Chiang launched a series of events, such as Zhongshan Warship Incident, Finishing Party Case, and April 12 Incident, aiming to combat the Communist Party and the revolutionary forces. He later assumed the post of Chairman of the National Military Council of the Nationalist

Government of the Republic of China. In 1928 Chiang served as Chairman of Nanjing-based Nationalist Government of China, continuing his fights against warlords. After the Japanese invasion into Manchuria occurred in 1931, Chiang was then chairman of the military committee, and adopted the policy of "first internal pacification, then external resistance" and waged assaults on the Red Army's revolutionary bases. After the Xi'an Incident in 1936, Chiang was forced into making a "Second United Front" with the Communists against Japan. During the Anti-Japanese War, he served as the chairman of the Supreme National Defense Council, the Commander-in-chief of the China War Zone of the Allied Nations during the WWII. In 1941, he plotted the "Southern Anhui Incident" and later waged the third anti-communist campaign. Nevertheless, he persistently led the Nationalist Army in the fighting against the Japanese aggressors and deserves the name of a national leader despite the mistakes he made. In 1943, he attended Cairo Conference with Franklin Roosevelt, President of the United States, and Winston Churchill, Prime Minister of the United Kingdom, to outline the Allied position against Japan during World War II and made decisions about postwar Asia. After the victory of the Anti-Japanese War, he agreed to a temporary truce with CCP after peace talks with Communist leader Mao Zedong. However, in 1946 he broke The Truce Agreement and the Political Consultative Conference Resolution and ordered attacks on Communist-dominated areas. The next year, he wilfully convoked the national convention on constitution which promulgated a new Constitution. Then during 1948, he convened the first National Assembly without any authorization, where he was elected the first President of the Republic of China. After 1949 when Chiang Kai-shek retreated to Taiwan with his son, his government and his army, he stuck to determined opposition to any suggestion of Taiwanese Independence and declined the USA's request to hold in trust the sovereignty over Taiwan.

Chiang was an outstanding national leader. Without him, China would have been disintegrated by warlords. At that time, Taiwan and Northeastern areas were both occupied by Japanese armies; besides, China was also in the imminent danger of being divided into smaller countries by the then local warlords. The only figure who was able to control and command the party and the army of the National Government with millions of soldiers consisting of different fractions and organized them to resist Japan and eliminate local warlords was Chiang Kai-shek. Therefore, he played an extremely important role in safeguarding China's territorial integrity.

3.2   Overseas Ningbo Merchants (Ningbobang)

K.C. Wong

K.C. Wong (1907—1986, pinyin: Wang Kuancheng) was born in Yin County, Ningbo. In 1937, he went to Shanghai and set up the Weida Foreign Bank. After the War of Resistance against Japan, he set up subsidiary companies in London, New York and other places. In 1947, he moved to Hong Kong where he established Verder & Co. Hong Kong Ltd. and later Happiness Enterprise Co., Ltd and dozens of others engaged in finance, real estates, and domestic and foreign trade, etc. After the founding of the People's Republic of China, he served as a member of China National Democratic Construction Association, executive member of the fifth All-China Federation of Industry & Commerce, Chairman of China International Trust and Investment Corporation, honorary President of the Hongkong Chinese General Chamber of Commerce. He endorsed the policy of "one country, two systems", and served as the vice director of the Executive Committee of the Consultative Committee for the Basic Law of the Hong Kong Special Administration Region of the PRC, representative of the fourth and fifth sessions of the NPC, member of the second, third and fourth sessions of the CPPCC and member of the fifth CPPCC Standing Committee.

In the early 1950s, Wong donated a plane and other related materials to support the Chinese government fighting the Korean War.

K.C. Wong was deeply concerned about education and social welfare in Hong Kong and mainland China. For decades, he donated to support more than 20 schools and associations both in Hong Kong and mainland China, including the Hong Kong Pei Hua Education Foundation, China Foundation for Disabled Persons, China Soong Ching Ling Foundation, Cancer Foundation of China and other institutions.

Wong was the first man among the Ningbo barons in Hongkong and Taiwan to donate money for the social construction of Ningbo. In 1963, he donated one million yuan for the establishment of Dong'en Middle School and Dong'en Primary School in Ningbo. In 1980, Mr. Wong and Yu Zuochen jointly set up the Ningbo Hong Kong Fellowship Association, of which Wong was made the president and later the honorary president. In 1984, he donated to build the laboratory building in Dong'en Middle School and set up the Kuancheng Scholarship. He also donated one million yuan to help build Zhejiang Shuren University and subsidized Shanghai Institute of Business & Technology and Jinan University in Guangdong, etc. In 1985, he contributed 100 million USD to set up the K. C. Wong Education Foundation to help cultivate talents for China.

In August 1986, a few months before his death, K.C. Wong, in spite of old age, led a group of over 20 committee members from Hong Kong and Macao to visit Xinjiang, Shaanxi, Gansu and other provinces and put forward a number of insightful suggestions for the development of the Northwest region.

Throughout his life, K.C. Wong worked assiduously and conscientiously. To his friends and colleagues, he was always sincere, generous and helpful. However, he lived a frugal and simple life. All of these helped him win a great reputation both home and abroad. He made great contributions to the social and cultural constructions of his hometown. In 2000, Zhejiang Provincial Government awarded him the honorary title of "Model Compatriot Loving Hometown".

Dong Haoyun

Dong Haoyun (1912—1982), born in Zhoushan, Zhejiang Province, was the founder of the Orient Overseas Container Line with the reputation of "Modern Zheng He" and one of the World's Seven Shipping Magnates.

Dong Haoyun was born in 1911 and was admitted to Shipping Industry Training Class after graduation from middle school in October 1927. In 1928, he became a worker of Tianjin Shipping Company. Gradually, he was promoted to be managing director and started his life in shipping business. At the end of November 1931, Dong was sent to Tianjin from Nanjing with his friend, Gu Lianqing,

by train. From early December, he served as the secretary of Tianjin Shipping Company. Since then, his legendary life closely linked with oceans began. He worked for six years in the company and during the six years, he advocated the business principle of "self-owned ships, self-owned goods and self-owned transporting". In 1933, with the support of Yan Xishan, director of Pacification Headquarters in Taiyuan, Shanxi, Dong Haoyun broke through the heavy interference of British shipping companies and ended the long-term situation of foreign business ruling Chinese shipping. He transferred the material transportation right on Dating-Puzhou Road back to the Chinese. The Beiping-Nanjing Road authority followed suit. From then on, Chinese shipping began to take a bigger and bigger market share in the key part of North China, which laid a solid foundation for the development of China's ocean shipping.

On June 3, 1934, Dong was promoted as the director of Shipping Department of Tianjin Shipping Company. He served as the executive commissioner and then chief executive commissioner of Tianjin Ship Industry Association. From March to December of the same year, Manager Wang Gengsan of his company repeatedly went to Shanghai to perform official duties. During that time, Dong Haoyun drafted and reviewed all the business documents. He also took over the duties of the manager. His ingenuity and dedication to work helped him earn trust from the senior management of the company and widespread recognition from all his colleagues.

In 1935, he used diplomatic means to mediate between the British Municipal Council in Tianjin and the Port Authority. After a few months of debating, the No. 9 Port was finally reverted to Tianjin Shipping Company. On October 21, 1935, Tianjin Shipping Company moved to the No. 9 Port, ending the humiliating history of the Chinese people renting ports from the hand of foreigners on its own land in Tianjin.

From the end of 1935 to the beginning of 1936, an unprecedented ice damage fell upon the Dagu Port in Bohai Bay, trapping more than 140 Chinese and foreign ships for over 20 days with no water or food. People and goods on board were in great danger. At that time, Dong Haoyun rushed to the scene to inspect ice conditions for many times. He actively coordinated with the Haihe River Engineering Bureau, the Port Authority and Shipping Industry Associations to form a rescue plan. Meantime, he sent the company's "Sky" icebreaker to rescue the ships. Moreover, he personally took a plane to send food, water, coal and all the necessities to the trapped crews and passengers.

At the beginning of 1938, Dong Haoyun was transferred to Shanghai. He accumulated rich entrepreneurial experience during the six years in Tianjin, which laid a solid foundation for him to become a Ship Magnate of the World. With competitive spirit and entrepreneurship, Dong Haoyun strived to create a number of "first" in the history of the shipping industry in China, Asia and even the world. Thus he was given the reputation of "Modern Zheng He". He had 149 ships with the total tonnage of 11 million tons, almost twice of Onassis's, one of the World's Seven Shipping Magnates. Though his number of ships was less than Yue-Kong Pao's World-Wide Shipping Group, Dong's ships had more types, larger single ship tonnage and newer machinery equipment.

Yue-Kong Pao

Yue-Kong Pao (1918—1991, pinyin: Bao Yugang), also named Qiran, was born in Ningbo, Zhejiang Province. He was the founder of Hong Kong's World-Wide Shipping Group. Besides, he also served as Honorary Chairman of Ningbo Fellowship Association and Ningbo Hong Kong Fellowship Association and Vice-Chairman of the Hong Kong Basic Law Drafting Committee. He was one of the twelve Chinese magnates in the world with more than US $ 1 billion of assets and a universally acknowledged Chinese shipping magnate. In 1978, Pao's shipping empire reached its peak and became one of the top ten Hong Kong consortiums. He himself became the No. 1 shipping magnate of the world. Pao founded Hong Kong's World-Wide Shipping Group. Also, he was the first Chinese chairman of the British-owned Hong Kong and Shanghai Banking Corporation Limited. In 1976, he was knighted by Queen Elizabeth II. Pao had great passion for China. Apart from setting up Zhaolong School, Zhongxing Middle School and Ningbo University in his hometown, he also built the Beijing Zhaolong Hotel, Bao Zhaolong Library and Bao Yugang Library in Shanghai Jiao Tong University and set up Bao Zhaolong and Bao Yugang Scholarships for overseas students.

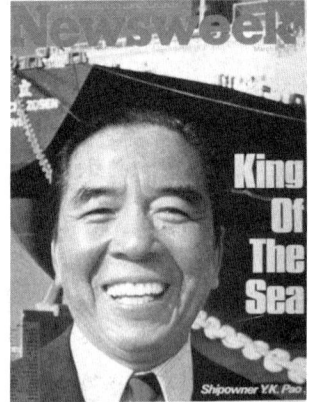

Different from other shipping magnates, Pao proceeded safely and steadily in his career. His diligence and strong sense of ambition and responsibility won him the reputation of Shipping Magnate of the World. In Hong Kong, Pao's merchant shipping fleets exceeded a tonnage of 4. 5 million, only second to the United States. Thus, Hong Kong became one of the world's shipping centers. These achievements were inseparable from Pao's contribution to the shipping industry. Due to his position in the international shipping industry, he received much attention and appreciation from heads of state and entrepreneurs. He was knighted by Queen Elizabeth II and received many high-level medals from the king of Belgium, president of Panama, president of Brazil and the emperor of Japanese. He was the only businessman in the world to receive such great honor. Former British Prime Minister Edward Heath once specially invited him to dinner in his villa and asked about his business methods in details. In 1981, Sir Yue-Kong Pao was invited as a guest to attend the inauguration of US President Ronald Reagan. What's more, he could make telephone calls directly to the White House and talk to the US president.

Nevertheless, he was a plain and modest person. He never allowed himself and his relatives to live an extravagant life. On September 23, 1991, Sir Yue-Kong Pao died of illness in his home at the age of 73. His death caused a huge stir in the world and marked the end of an era.

Run Run Shaw

Run Run Shaw (1907—2014, pinyin: Shao Yifu), former name Shao Renleng, was born in Zhenhai District of Ningbo, Zhejiang Province. He was the Honorary Chairman of the Hong Kong Television Broadcasts Limited, one of the founders of Shaw Brothers (HK) Ltd., permanent honorary president of Kiangsu Chekiang and Shanghai Residents (Hong Kong) Association and Ningbo Fellowship Association, and member of the Preparatory Committee for the Hong Kong Special Administrative Region of People's Republic of China.

Run Run Shaw established the Shaw Brothers (HK) Ltd. in 1958 in Hong Kong which shot more than one thousand Chinese films. His Hong Kong Television Broadcasts Limited (commonly known as TVB) dominates the television industry of Hong Kong.

In 1977, Run Run Shaw received a knighthood from Queen Elizabeth II and became the first "Sir" in Hong Kong's entertainment industry. In 1990, the Chinese government named Planet 2899 discovered by China "Planet Run Run Shaw". In 1991, San Francisco established that the 8th of September of each year would be "Run Run Shaw Day". In 2002, the Shaw Prize, often referred to as the Nobel Prize of Asia, was established. Each year, scientists who have achieved great accomplishments in the fields of mathematics, bioscience, medical science, and astronomy are awarded. Shaw officially retired in 2011. He was the world's oldest CEO of a listed company with the longest tenure. On January 7, 2014, Shaw died 107 years old.

Run Run Shaw was not the richest man in Hong Kong, but he was among the most generous philanthropists among Hong Kong's billionaires. His tremendous influence in Hong Kong came from his television empire. However, his reputation in the mainland was a result of his charitable donations. According to statistics, he has donated over 10 billion Hong Kong dollars for public welfare and charity affairs over the years. The educational and medical projects he sponsored reached more than 6,000. Shaw had special concern for education and science. His educational funds were used throughout China. Most colleges and universities across China have buildings named after him. In Hong Kong, many buildings in colleges and universities were donated by Shaw, for example, Run Run Shaw College in the Chinese University of Hong Kong, Run Run Shaw Building at the University of Hong Kong and Run Run Shaw Library in City University of Hong Kong.

Lu Xuzhang

Lu Xuzhang (1911—1995) was born in Yin County (currently Yinzhou District) in Zhejiang Province. He was a financier, a government official and former manager of China Import and Export Corporation. He was considered as one of the pioneers and founders of China's foreign trade industry. When he was only 14, he went to Shanghai and became a trainee in Shanghai Yuantong Shipping Company. In his spare time, he studied in the business night school of Shanghai General Chamber of Commerce and actively participated in social activities. After graduating from college in 1933, Lu co-founded Guangda Chinese Bank with others, mainly dealing with import and export business. In

1940, he took the position of general manager of Guangda Chinese Bank. In 1937, he joined the Chinese Communist Party. In 1940, he went to Chongqing and became a right-hand assistant of Zhou Enlai. In 1945, Lu Xuzhang returned to Shanghai.

In 1949, after the liberation of Shanghai, Lu worked for the Shanghai Military Control Commission. He also served as deputy director of the Trade Committee of Shanghai Municipal Office of Finance and Economics and vice minister of the Ministry of Trade of East China Military and Political Committee. Soon, he was sent to Tianjin as the manager of China Import and Export Corporation which moved to Beijing shortly after. In September 1952, Lu was transferred to work as director, assistant minister and vice minister of the Ministry of Foreign Trade. During the Cultural Revolution, Lu experienced horrible torment. After the breakdown of the "Gang of Four", Lu Xuzhang returned to Beijing, working as an adviser of the Ministry of Foreign Trade. In August 1977, he was transferred to work as a Party Member in Overseas Chinese Affairs Office of the State Council and the president of Overseas Travel Agency. In the following year, he was pointed as first director and party secretary of the newly founded China National Tourism Administration, becoming a pioneer in China's tourism industry. In February 1981, Lu Xuzhang was transferred to be the vice director of China Import and Export Committee and Foreign Investment Committee. In August, he was transferred back to the Ministry of Foreign Trade as vice minister and deputy party secretary. In March 1982, Lu resigned from the leading post and became an adviser of the Ministry of Foreign Trade and Economy. Lu Xuzhang was one of the pioneers and founders of China's foreign trade industry. He made significant contributions to the development of China's foreign trade.

Lu Xuzhang paid two visits to Hong Kong and met with people of Ningbo origin including Yue-kong Pao and Run Run Shaw, introducing Ningbo to them and inviting them to return home on a tour of investigation. Thanks to the efforts of Lu Xuzhang and promotion of some famous members of Ningbo Confraternity, more than 50,000 members of the confraternity have returned to Ningbo to visit their relatives and take a trip, contributing a share to development of Ningbo by donating a large sum of money to support welfare work including education and healthcare as well as making investment to set up business. In October, 1988, under the initiation of Lu Xuzhang and some other famous members of the confraternity, Association for the Advancement of Economy in Ningbo was established, with Lu as the first chairman.

3.3 Artists

Zhou Xinfang

Zhou Xinfang (1895—1975), was a descendant of an art Family in Cicheng of Ningbo. As a prestigious artist of Peking Opera, Zhou acquired the stage name "Qi Lin Tong" and founded a unique genre of Peking Opera-the Qi School.

Zhou had masterly basic skills. His voice was wide in range and sonorous and raucous in quality. In his later years, his voice turned mellow, showing fullness in high pitches and deepness in low pitches. Characterized by vigorous singing style, his sound was plain but profound. He paid special attention to the expression of figures' emotions and showed uniqueness in some specific singing styles. In the spoken parts of his performances, he performed with relatively strong Zhejiang accents. With special attention on rhythm, he showed great power and frequent use of modal particles in his performances, reflecting strong living atmosphere. All kinds of moods, be it humor, solemnity, anger or sadness, could be performed by him naturally and vividly. In addition, he was good at utilizing long sleeves, varied gestures and footwork and eye and facial expressions according to different plots and figures' thoughts, demonstrating his excellent ability in refining and reflecting daily lives. His application of some special skills with props involved, like Kaoqi, Rankou, Wig and Maochi, added colorful touches to his performances. His master works include *Xu Ce Pao Cheng*, *Wu Long Yuan*, *Xiao He Yue Xia Zhui Han Xin*, *Si Jinshi*, etc.

Zhou Xinfang was passionate in innovation. He made great revolution and innovations on the basis of traditions. Apart from amending and optimizing the traditional plays, he also made distinct designs on singing, chanting, gesturing, fighting, play list, libretto, costume, make-up etc., which well fit his own style. For example, he absorbed new acting methods from modern drama, which were to shape the characters with exaggerated appearance and movements, to form intensive artistic appealing.

Pan Tianshou

Pan Tianshou (1897—1971), a Chinese painter and art educator, is known by the names of Tianshou, Dayi, Ashou, and Leipotoufeng Shouzhe, Xinalanruozhuchi, and Shouzhe. Pan was born in Ninghai, Zhejiang. He specialized in bird-and-flower and landscape painting and he was also well-known for his calligraphy, poetry and carving. In 1915 he was accepted into the Zhejiang First Normal School in Hangzhou and taught by Jing Hengyi and Li Shutong. He firstly studied the birds and flowers painting from Wu Changshuo and later from Shitao, Bada, forming a style of unexpected painting arrangement and refined brushwork. He served as the president of Zhejiang Academy of Fine Arts and vice-president of Chinese Artists Association. Besides, he was also the delegate of the first, second, and third session of the National People's Congress, member of CFLAC and he was awarded Honorary Fellow of Russian Academy of Arts in 1958. Pan Tianshou wrote A *History of Chinese Painting* and *Ting Tian Ge Hua Tan Sui Bi (Essays on Tingtiange Pavilion Paintings).*

In 1924, Pan became a professor of the Shanghai Academy of Fine Arts. In the same year, he began to write *A History of Chinese Painting* which was published in 1927. Then Pan was appointed head of the Chinese painting department by National Art Academy, Hangzhou, and was offered a position of mentor for the Calligraphy and Painting Association. Pan since then lived in Hangzhou and taught in Shanghai Academy of Fine Arts and Xinhua Art College. In 1932 Pan published two selections of paintings entitled the Baishe Selected Paintings. He played an important role in Works Exhibition by Professors of Xinhua Art College. In 1933, he contributed works to the 1933 Paris Exhibition of Chinese Art organized by Xu Beihong and in the same year, Pan began writing *A History of Chinese Calligraphy*. In 1936, he published his revised edition of *A History of Chinese Painting*, which was listed among Recommended Books for College Students. In August of the same year, he finished his painting *Huangshan in Dreams*. On April 1st in 1937 Pan's works *Cat in Ink* and *Vertical Scrolls of Running*

Script were displayed on The Second National Exhibition of Arts held in Nanjing Art Museum. And his work *Jiangzhou Ye Bo* (*Mooring at Night at Jiangzhou*) was put on display in The Sixth Exhibition of Chinese Painting Association. In 1943, he published *A Research of the Chinese Academy of Fine Arts.* In the same year, he made a collection of his poems and published it under the title *of A Collection of Poems of Tingtiange Pavilion.* In addition, he created his painting *Autumn* and published *Reviews of Running Script and Paintings.*

After the founding of the new China, in 1950 he was appointed as head of the Research institute of Ethnic Fine Arts in the East China Branch of Central Academy of Fine Arts. He, together with Wufu Zhi, worked on purchasing and evaluating folk's paintings. They categorized and mounted those works, which turned out to be a huge treasury for painting pedagogy.

On April, 1962, Pan published *Views on Huang Binhong's Achievements in Landscape Painting* on a magazine *East Ocean.* Pan painted *After the Rain* in January 1963 for the Embassy of Myanmar in Beijing. Work Exhibition of Pan Tianshou, planned by Shanghai Artists Association and National Painting Academy of China, was held at Shanghai Art Museum. With the help of Ma Jinliang, his student, Pan established the School of Calligraphy and Carving.

Pan was a master in bird-flower painting and mountain-river painting, especially in the painting of eagles, mynah birds, vegetables, pines and plums. Pan's brushes are bold but details are refined, creating a style of power and vibrancy. Pan mostly painted eagles, lotus, pines, "Four Gentlemen (plum, orchid, bamboo and chrysanthemum)" mountains, rivers and figures. Each work has precarious but balanced frame arrangement and carries profound significances.

Sha Menghai

Sha Menghai (1900—1992) was formerly called Wen Ruo. His courtesy name was Menghai, also known as Shihuang, Shacun and Jueming. He was born in a famous doctors' family in Shacun, Yin County. He received good education and practiced seal cutting since his childhood. He studied in Cixi Jintang school and graduated from The Fourth Normal University of Zhedong. In 1922, Sha went to Shanghai and worked as a private teacher, during which he was fortunate to meet masters like Kang Youwei, Wu Changshuo, who exerted profound influences on Sha's calligraphy and seal cutting. In

1925, he taught in the Commercial Press, during which he learned palaeography from Feng Junmu and Chen Qihuai and made great progress. His inscriptions on ancient bronzes and stone tablets were published many times in *Huaguo Monthly* sponsored by Zhang Taiyan. Sha used to work as the standing committee member of Cultural Relics Management Committee of Zhejiang Province, the honorary curator of Zhejiang Province Museum, Vice-chairman of Chinese Calligraphers Association, Chairman of Zhejiang Province Calligraphers Association, and Proprietor of Xiling Society of Seal Arts, Dean of Xiling Painting and Calligraphy Institute, the honorary chairman of Society for Zhejiang Province Archaeology. He drew lessons from ancient masters, among them are calligraphers Zhong Yao, Wang Xizhi, Ouyang Xun, Yan Zhenqin, Su Shi and Huang Tingjian. While learning from calligraphers in both ancient and modern times, he developed a unique style of his own. He was also adept at seal character, official script, running script and regular script. The features of Sha's calligraphy were vigorous, robust and with great momentum. Sha was very knowledgeable and he did a lot of research on language, literature and history, archaeology, calligraphy and seal cutting.

Before the age of thirty, Sha's works copying inscription rubbing included *Collection of Wang Xizhi's Calligraphy Works*, *Stele of Zheng Wenlong and Zhang Menglong*, etc. This period could be called as a period of pursuing even and straight structures of characters. At his middle age, with his increasing knowledge and rich experience, Sha paid more attention to the pattern and style of characters and the momentum of layout of calligraphy works. Of course, he did not completely give up regular script, which he wrote meticulously and occasionally. He would occasionally write regular script. During this period, his works could be described as a period of "aware of the even and straight structures but pursuing the precariousness". This period lasted for nearly forty years. After 1980's, with the revival of "the new period" of literature and art, Mr. Sha ushered in the spring of his calligraphy works. Mr. Sha threw himself into the work of calligraphic creation with great passion and a high spirit. His works entered into a golden age which is featured by: "mostly pursuing evenness and straightforwardness but occasionally creating precariousness." Running script and big characters were dominant among his works during this period. It was through these two kinds of calligraphy works that people saw hope in the contemporary calligraphy circles.

The style of Sha's calligraphy works went through from elegance to boldness and vigorousness, and finally turned towards plainness and unadornedness. It is similar to the plants which are gorgeous and colorful in the spring and luxuriant in the summer; and was also similar to the humans who are magnanimous in the late autumn and eventually become vast and boundless in the winter. Mr. Sha's calligraphy works were combined with features of vigorousness and naturalness.

Shao Quanlin

Shao Quanlin (1906—1971) has his paternal origin in Cixi of Ningbo. Formerly known as Shao Yimin, he had several pseudonyms called Quan, Lifu and Qiruo. Shao was a theorist of Chinese literature and art, contemporary literary critic and writer. He used to work as Vice-chairman, Chairman and Secretary of Party Committee of the China Writers Association. In his early years, he enrolled in the department of Economics in Fudan University and participated in the students' patriotic movement. Shao joined the communist Youth League of China in 1926 and in the same year, he joined the Communist Party of China (CPC). He participated in the third Shanghai workers armed uprisings in 1927. And in 1934 he worked as Minister of Propaganda in Anti-imperialist and Anti-war Alliance. In the same year, he was arrested and imprisoned. In 1937, after he got out of jail with the help of the Communist Party of China, he was engaged in the work of revolutionary literary and artistic creation and translation. He published a collection of short stories titled *Heroes* and a collection of script called *Xi Jiu* (Wedding Feast). He has translated the novel *The Insulted and the Injured* written by the Russian writer *Dostoevsky*. His important paper published included *On Subjective Problems*, which revealed his unique insights in understanding the current situation of Chinese literature and art and theory.

Shao began writing and translating literary works in the year 1936 or so. His early works included *Sugar* and *In Front of the Station*. After the Anti-Japanese War broke out, he took part in the cultural leadership group of Zhejiang Province under the guidance of the CPC and was appointed as the Secretary of Cultural Council of Southeast Communist Party of China. He was the editor-in-chief of the *Southeast Front*. After the Southern Anhui Incident broke out in 1941, he went to Guilin, working as the group leader of cultural group of the CPC. He edited the *Cultural Magazines* and established the *Youth Literature and Art*, supporting actively the new works and giving a lot of tutoring to the young authors. His collection of short stories *Heroes* (written in 1942) and *Hotel* (written in 1946), and his one-act play *Xijiu*(Wedding Feast) were greatly valued in the literary circles. After the victory of Anti-Japanese War, he first went to Wuhan to recover the united front work in the cultural field, then he went to Hongkong via Shanghai and worked as the cultural council member of the CPC Hong Kong Working Committee and the Secretary of the Southern Bureau. During this period, he edited *The Public Literary Collection*. He wrote political comments and published papers on literature and art on *The Masses*(Hong Kong version), *Zheng Bao* and the *Huashang Daily*, promoted the CPC's literary and artistic principles and policies and introduced the literary achievements of the liberated area. His paper entitled *On Current Literary and Artistic Movement* and *On Subjective Problems* exerted a great influence on the development of literary and artistic movement in the KMT controlled area. During this period, he also translated works entitled the *Guerrilla Fan Sijia* (1941), *The Insulted and the Injured* (1943), *Unexpected Surprise* (1943) and *Shadow and Light* (1946, written by Eugene Ryss), etc.

After the founding of the People's Republic of China, Shao worked as Deputy Secretary General of the Cultural and Educational Committee of Government Administration Council, member of the party committee of the Cultural and Educational Committee and Deputy General Secretary of Propaganda Department of the CPC Central Committee. In 1953, he was appointed as Secretary of Party Committee of the China Writers Association (formerly called the Chinese Literature Workers Association). In the meantime, he was elected to be Vice-chairman of the Chinese Literature Workers Association and edited *People's Literature*. Shao was also elected as a member of the 1st, 2nd and 3rd National People's Congress. In July, 1962, he presided over the Short Story Writing on Rural Themes Forum in Dalian City. At the forum, he emphasized "deepening the development of realism", advocated diversified characters and paid more attention to depicting ordinary characters in addition to the positive and negative characters. His advice was helpful to overcoming the problem of dull phenomenon in creating novels on rural themes. However, he suffered public criticism due to this advice. He was persecuted in the Cultural Revolution and died uncleared of a false charge in jail on June 10, 1971.

On September 21, 1979, people held a memorial meeting for Shao, announced to get him rehabilitated for his reputation. In April, 1981, People's Literature Publishing House edited and published the *Collections of Shao's Comments*.

Ba Ren

Ba Ren (1901—1972), also known as Wang Renshu, was called Zhaolun in his childhood and Yuntang in genealogy name. His courtesy name was Renshu, self-titled Yu'an. His pen name was Ba Ren. He was born in Dayan village (now it is called Dayan town), Lianshan Township. His works included the novel *The Rebellion led by bold intellectuals*, essays *The Neighbors*, *Rensheng and His Fellows*, the monograph *On Literary Works*, Short Story collections *Prisons*, *In the Fall*, *Dilapidated House*, drama scripts *Miss Feina*, *The Man Yangda* and the novellas *Wanderings of Ah Gui* and *the Badge*.

In March, 1941, Wang Renshu was sent to Hong Kong. He then went to Singapore in July, teaching at Nanyang overseas Chinese Normal University, where he led the cultural circles to struggle against fascism with other famous writers like Hu Yuzhi and Yu Dafu, etc. In December, the Pacific War broke out, he was appointed as the Minister of Propaganda of Xinhua (Xin refers to Singapore) Wartime Corps. In February of the following year, he wandered to Sumatra, Indonesia with Lei Derong and others, going from places of Pematangsiantar and Medan. In 1943, as he was listed as wanted by the Japanese army who invaded Indonesia, he had to live a secluded life in the small village located in the primeval forest and made a living by the slash and burn method. After Japan surrendered in August, 1945, Wang Renshu joined Sumatera Island Overseas Chinese Democratic Alliance. He edited *Weekly Progress*, *Daily Democrat* written in Indonesian and wrote the drama *Wuzu Temples*. In July, 1947, he was arrested by the Dutch forces. After he was rescued by the CPC, he went to Hong Kong in October. In August, 1948, he was ordered to Pingshan County, Hebei Province and was appointed as the group leader of the third comprehensive research group of The United Front Work Department of CPC Central Committee. In the following year, he attended the First National Literature and Art Workers Congress and the first plenary session of Chinese People's Political Consultative Conference (CPPCC). In 1950, he was appointed to be the Chinese ambassador plenipotentiary to Indonesia. In January, 1952, he left office and returned to China, working as a party leadership group member of Ministry of Foreign Affairs and a member of the Council for Policy Studies. In 1954, his works *The Draft of Literary Theory* came out. In April of the same year, he was transferred to be deputy director and editor in chief of People's Literature Publishing House. In 1957, he was appointed as director of the publishing house and secretary of the party committee.

In 1959, Kang Sheng (1898—1975) openly criticized Ba Ren, pointing out that Ba Ren was a townsmate of Chiang Kai-shek and that he used to work for KMT. This incurred severe criticism of Ba Ren, the representative man in the literary circle, Shang Yue in the historian circle and Sun Yefang in the economic circle. They were also removed from party posts. After Ba Ren was deprived of his rights to write literary works, he turned to study science of history. He finished his first draft of the great work *The History of Indonesia* in 1966, which was about 1.6 million words in total. He was criticized and separated for censorship during the Great Cultural Revolution. And in 1966, his house was searched and he suffered unimaginable torture. From 1968, there were posters spreading the rumor that Ba Ren was the traitor who approached Japanese with information in the incident of killing Yu Dafu, which led to more severe persecution to Ba Ren. He was sent back to his hometown in March, 1970 and stayed in the two old huts in the west of the village. He almost broke down by these tortures. On July 25, 1972, he died of illness and was buried back in the hill in Dayan Village.

Chen Yifei

Chen Yifei (1946—2005) was born in Ningbo. He was a famous oil painter, cultural industrialist and director. After Chen Yifei graduated from Shanghai Art College (the current name is Fine Arts College, Shanghai University) in 1965, he went to the oil painting and sculpture studio of Shanghai Art Academy and worked as the head of oil painting group. During 1960s and 1970s, he produced excellent oil paintings of *Ode to the Yellow River*, *The Occupation of the Presidential Palace*, *Strolling* and *Zhouzhuang*, etc.

In 1980, Chen Yifei went to the United States for further study with only 38 dollars in his pocket. When he lived in the United States, he concentrated on the research and creation of Chinese oil paintings. He received Master of Fine Arts degree in 1984. After that, he was engaged in oil painting creation in New York and also held personal art exhibition in Washington, New York, Tokyo and other cities. His works were sent to Hong Kong and domestic oil painting auctions for many times, among which the painting Shandifeng received the highest auction price among the Chinese oil paintings. His works were collected by the National Art Museum of China, the Military Museum of the Chinese People's Revolution and collectors at home and abroad. The main themes of his painting included water villages, musicians, traditional Chinese beautiful women and Tibet. When the American oil baron Armand Hammer paid his visit to China in 1985, he presented Chen's painting work The Memories of Home—Shuangqiao to Deng Xiaoping as a gift.

Chen Yifei is no doubt an important figure in the hundred years' history of Chinese oil painting. To put it in an exaggerated way, the accomplishment and success of Chen is like a myth. In recent years, it was Chen and his painting works that set new high records one after another in art market that stirred and shocked the art societies in China and Asia. In 1991, his painting *Xunyang Yiyun* was sold in Hong Kong Christie's at HK $ 1. 375 million, setting a new record for the Chinese oil painting works. In 1994, his works *Shandifeng* on the theme of Tibet was auctioned to be sold at the high price of 2. 86 million RMB in China Guardian International Auctions.

Adhering to the pursuit of doing "bigger art", Chen Yifei made creative achievements in many fields including movie-making, fashion design and environment design and became a cultural celebrity, both at home and abroad.

On April 10th, 2005, he passed away due to gastrorrhagia in Shanghai Huashan Hospital.

3.4 Academicians

Tong Dizhou

Tong Dizhou, or Tung Tichou (1902—1979), was born in Tangxi Town, Yin County (now Yinzhou District), Ningbo, Zhejiang Province. As a CPC member, he enjoyed wide reputation at home and abroad as a prestigious biologist and educator and served as the vice president of Chinese Academy of Science and the director of the Institute of Zoology of the academy. He graduated from the Philosophy Department of Fudan University in 1927, worked as an assistant in the Biology Department of National Fourth Zhongshan University (the predecessor of Nanjing University) from 1927 to 1930. After that, he taught at Shandong University for a long time and was appointed as the vice president in 1951. He was a brilliant experimental embryologist, a main founder of Chinese experimental embryology and a pioneer in bioscience research in the 20th century. In 1978, he was awarded the title of "Advanced Worker of National Science and Technology" at the National Science Conference.

Human beings have experienced arduous scientific explorations for thousands of years with an attempt to discover the genetic myths of reproduction. In the 20th century, great breakthroughs were made in global life science research. In 2000, scientists from China, the U. S. and the U. K. announced the accomplishment of Human Genome Project simultaneously. In fact, Tong propelled the research on biological evolution and cell heredity and variation in the early 1960s and discovered the way of artificially cultivating new species according to needs, thus receiving the reputation as the father of cloning. In 1990s, he was listed among the top 100 Greatest Scientists in the world.

Bei Shizhang

Bei Shizhang (1903—2009), born in Zhenhai of Ningbo, was an experimental biologist, cytobiologist and educator and the founding member of China's cytology and embryology. As the father of China's biophysics, he served as head of biology department and dean of School of Science of Zhejiang University.

Bei took on the research on experimental embryology and cytology about invertebrate, particularly in the relation between eutely creatures and cytothesis. In 1930s, he discovered intermediate fairy shrimp and found the mutual transformation of male cell and female cell of the shrimp; in 1970s, he put forward cell reconstruction theory. He paid special attention to interdisciplinary studies and contributed to China's biophysics research. He led the establishment of many branches in this area and related technology, including radiation biology, cosmobiology, bionics, bio-engineering, biocybernetics, etc. and cultivated a group of talents in biophysics. Bei was among the first group of the academicians of the Chinese Academy of Sciences (CAS) and the Chinese Academy of Engineering (CAE) and the last living one among the group, and he served as honorary director of the Institute of Biology and Physics Research of the CAS.

For his scientific achievements, Bei was elected as the academician of Academia Sinica in 1948. Also in the same year, he was invited to act as the researcher of the Institute of International Embryology in Netherlands. He was elected as the member of the committee of the institute in 1949 and engaged as the member of the committee of biology department of the CAS in 1955. He visited, as a scientist or a scientific organizer, many countries, including the UK, Sweden, USSR, Canada, the US, France, Italy, Austria, Czech, Hungary, Nepal, Pakistan, Vietnam, etc. Particularly since 1972 when the 20-year Sino-US confrontation finished, he led a group of Chinese scientists to visit US as envoys of friendship.

Bei made great contribution to China's cause of science during his 70 years of scientific research and teaching.

Tan Jiazhen

Tan Jiazhen (1909—2008) was born in Ningbo, Zhejiang. He was a world-known geneticist, founding member of modern Chinese genetics as well as scientist and educator. He cultivated lots of talents in genetic research and served as the dean of the School of Sciences of Zhejiang University and the vice president of Fudan University. After the founding of new China, he established at Fudan University the first major of genetics, the first institute of genetics, the first school of life sciences, and served as the deputy editor of Da Ci Hai, an extra large-scale comprehensive dictionary.

In 1978, he launched the establishment of the Genetics Society of China, and successively served as the vice president, president and honorary president of the society. He also founded and headed *Journal of Genetics and Genomics*, Chinese Environmental Mutagen Society and China Society of Biological Engineering. With great reputation in the international society, he served as the former executive director of the 8th International Congress of Genetics, the vice president of the 15th, 16th, 17th International Congress of Genetics and the president of 18th International Genetics Congress in 1996. Since 1978, he has been elected as the honorary member of the Genetics Society in Japan and UK, engaged as the senior researcher by Eleanor Roosevelt Institute for Cancer Research and earned a series of titles and awards like the Eminent Alumni Award California Institute of Technology, the Merit Award of University of Constanz and honorary citizen of the California government. In addition, he was employed by UNIDO International Centre for Genetic Engineering and Biotechnology Center as scientific adviser and by the International Journal of Genetics, the International Journal of Biology and Philosophy and *American Scientist* as consulting editor. In 1984 and 1985, he was awarded honorary doctorate of science by York University of Canada and University of Maryland respectively. In 1995, he was given the Award of Distinguished Scientists by Truth-Seeking Science Foundation. In 1999, No. 3542 asteroid, which was discovered by Zijin Observatory of the CAS, was officially approved to be named as "Tan Jiazhen Star". Tan was elected academician of the Chinese Academy of Sciences (CAS) in 1980, the foreign academician of the US National Academy of Sciences in 1985 and the academician of the Third World Academy of Sciences. In 1987, he was elected the foreign academician of Italian National Academy of Sciences and in 1999 the honorary life-long academician of the New York Academy of Sciences.

Chen Zhongwei

Chen Zhongwei (1929—2004), born in Ningbo, Zhejiang, was an orthopedic specialist. In 1954, he graduated from the medical department of Shanghai Second Medical University. Later he worked in the Shanghai Sixth People's Hospital and served as the director of the orthopedic department and then the vice president of the hospital. His titles include: staff room director, professor in orthopedics and doctoral tutor of the department of surgery of Zhongshan Affiliated Hospital, School of Medicine, Fudan University, academician of the CAS, academician of the Third World Academy of Sciences, executive director of Chinese Medical Association, founding member of the International Society for Reconstructive Surgery Microscopy, member of the International Society of Surgery and guest professor to 12 internationally-renowned medical centers. He was an expert in orthopedics and microsurgery.

In 1963, he finished the world's first broken arm replantation operation successfully. In 1974, he made the initiator report on "amputated limb replantation" at North America Annual Meeting on Hand Surgery and received the international reputation as "the father of replantation". In 1978, he achieved another success in broken finger replantation. He invented six new techniques, including "broken hand replantation and broken finger replantation". In 1996, he cooperated with Shanghai Jiao Tong University in creating the first "finger-controlled electronic prosthetic hand." Because of his outstanding contribution in microsurgery and amputated limb replantation, he was recorded a special merit by the Central Ministry of Health in 1963. He was awarded the National Science Conference Prize by the State Council in 1981 and received the Distinguished Scientist Award issued by the Truth-Seeking Foundation and presented by Premier Li Peng in 1994. In 1999, he won the "Millennium Award" given by the World Society for Reconstructive Microsurgery. He produced 10 monographs, including *Microsurgery* and *Orthopedic Trauma and Amputated Limb Replantation*, invented a variety of microsurgery and published 130 papers, including 33 published in the medical journals abroad.

Li Qingkui

Born in Ningbo, Zhejiang Province, Li Qingkui (1912—2001) was a member of the Jiu San Society. He was a famous soil scientist, agricultural chemist, academician of the CAS and one of the founding members of China soil plant nutritional chemistry.

Li was mainly engaged in the nutrition, fertilization, basic properties, classification, utilization and research of soil-plants. In 1937 he published *Soil Analysis* which was reprinted many times after 1953 and plays an important role in the field of soil analysis. The early 1950s witnessed China's urgent demand for higher productivity. Shouldering national mission, he led a group of scientists to explore and study rubbers and presented the grounds for rubber plantation to the South of the Tropic of Cancer. Through the study of climate, soil conditions and effective fertilization favorable for the growing of rubber, he extended the cultivation line to latitude 18°N to 24°N, providing a model for rubber plantation in the northern margin of the tropical areas around the world. With the total amount of 125.000 tons in 1981, China's dry rubber output ranked 6th in the world, making Li win the first prize of National Invention Award. In the early 1970s, he put forward ammonium bicarbonate deep application technology, contributing to the rational utilization of nitrogen fertilizer and the improvement of nitrogen application. In 1978, he won the National Science and Technology Award.

He systematically studied phosphatic fertilizer and potassic fertilizer of the soil in China and the effects brought by the application of the two fertilizers. In addition, he presided over the making of the first map on the distribution of phosphorus in the soil in

China, which supports the development and application of chemical fertilizer in China. By exploiting effective conditions and rational fertilization technique, rock phosphate was produced on a large scale with the biggest achievement of more than 1,000 million tons in a year, scoring remarkable social and economic benefits. He was the editor of *China's Agricultural Use of Phosphate*, a monograph with great value in the rational utilization of phosphate rock resources in China and technical diversification and appropriate application of phosphatic fertilizer. He won the third prize in the National Science and Technology Progress Award in 1990. With years of researches on red soil, he edited *Chinese Red Soil*, a book discussing the formation, development, basic characteristics, development, utilization and improvement of Chinese red soil with full materials and playing an important role in agricultural production. In 1987, he was awarded the third prize of the National Natural Science Award.

Li was elected three times as the Model Worker of Jiangsu Province from 1959 to 1980. Also, he served as the member of the editorial committees of a series of national journals, including *Chinese Science*, *Chinese Science Bulletin*, *Acta Pedological Sinica*, *Progress in Soil Science*, *Research of Agricultural Modernization* and the an international journal *Fertilizer Research*. He trained and cultivated 12 postgraduates and doctors, edited monographs including *Chinese Red Earth*, *Chinese Soil*, *The Agricultural use of Chinese Phosphate* and *Chinese Paddy Soil*, and published over 90 papers. Due to his great contribution to China, he enjoyed special allowance provided by the State Council.

Li was always concerned about the cause of the patriotic united front. In 1953, he joined the Jiu San Society and actively participated in and contributed to the construction and development of the Jiu San Society for several decades. When he served as the deputy to the National People's Congress, he kept a close contact with the people. With a high sense of responsibility, he performed his duties according to law, actively participated in the formulation of local regulations, advocated democracy and the rule of law in China, made in-depth surveys and researches on China's national conditions, found people's demands, listened to people's opinions extensively and put forward many good ideas and suggestions. He made a lot of positive contributions to the development of the causes of education, science, culture and health in China.

Weng Wenbo

Weng Wenbo (1912—1994) was born in Xixiang Town, Yin County (now Yinzhou District), Ningbo. He graduated from Tsinghua University in 1934, and went to Imperial College London for geophysics study two years later. He received doctor degree in 1939 when China suffered under Japanese aggression. So he decided resolutely to return back through France and Vietnam for oil geophysical exploration and research. Thanks to his efforts, a group of talents were cultivated and a series of achievements were made. Especially in the late 1950s and early 1960s, he made major contributions to the discovery of the Daqing Oil Field and was entitled "Outstanding Scientist in oil Industry". In 1966 when Xingtai was stricken by an earthquake, he began studying prediction theory and devoting himself to earthquake prediction research. He made a breakthrough in this area, and increased the accuracy rate in earthquake and drought disaster prediction to 82.7%, making China a forerunner of the world in prediction science, and he was hailed as "contemporary guru in prediction". In 1980, he was elected as the academician of the CAS. He served as the former director of the National Committee of Natural Disaster Prediction, honorary chairman of the Chinese Geophysical Society, chief engineer of the Institute of Petroleum Exploration and Development of the Chinese National Petroleum Corporation and member of CPPCC National Committee. He is the writer of a series of monographs, including *Chinese Oil Resources* and *Prediction Theory Basis*.

After the founding of the People's Republic of China, Weng not only founded the country's geophysical, geochemical theory, but also actively participated in China's oil and gas exploration, and made outstanding contributions to the finding of Daqing oil field as well as the training of oil industry talents. His great contribution to Daqing Oilfield won him the National Natural Science Award which is of the highest level in China; and was titled "Outstanding Oil Industry Scientist" for his outstanding contributions to the oil industry. In 1966, after the earthquake in Xingtai, he was entrusted by Premier Zhou Enlai to begin the research on natural earthquake prediction,

225

and later extended the prediction into long-term predictions on floods, droughts and other disasters, making major breakthroughs on both prediction theory and practice, and established his original information prediction scientific basis. According to statistics, he made 252 predictions of natural calamities, among which 211 actually occurred, a forecast accuracy rate of 83.73%. Thus he was praised as "disaster forecasting guru".

Weng served as Deputy Director at the Exploration Department of the Central Ministry of Petroleum in Fuel Industry Bureau, Chief Engineer in the Exploration Division of the Ministry of Petroleum Industry, Deputy Director of the Science and Technology Commission of the Ministry of Petroleum Industry, Vice President of the Research Institute of Petroleum Science, Chief Engineer, Director of the Postgraduate Department and tutor of doctoral students in the Research Institute of Petroleum Exploration and Development Science, as well as chairman and honorary chairman of the Chinese Geophysical Society, vice chairman of China Petroleum Society, Honorary Member of the Seismological Society of China, member of China Association of Science and Technology, Director of the Professional Committee of Natural Disasters Forecasting of Chinese Geophysical Society, etc. He is also deputy of the 3rd National People's Congress, the 5th, 6th and 7th CPPCC National Committee.

4. Folkways

4.1 Ningbo Opera

Yong Ju (Ningbo Opera)

Ningbo Yong Opera, performed in Ningbo dialect, falls under Huagu Tanhuang tune. The local opera, known as Chuanke, was first sung in Ningbo and its neighborhood in late Qianlong Period (1790—1795). It was later known as Ningbo Tanhuang after Chuanke Troupe gave a performance in Shanghai in 1880. It was also known as Simingzhixi (opera of Ningbo) when Ningbo Tanhuang became a banned practice in Shanghai in 1924. Its name was later changed into Reformed Yongju in 1938 when fashionable dresses were in the vogue. It was not until 1950 that the opera was officially named as Yong Ju (Ningbo Opera).

Rich in tunes with over 90 types, Yong Ju includes, among others, Jibendiao (basic tunes) evolved from field folk songs and twin folk songs, Yuediao, Sanwuqi, Kuaierhuang, Manerhuang, Simingnanci and other local tunes. Basic tunes, also known as old tunes, reflect complex thoughts and expressions of characters in the opera. Xiaodiao, or minor, represents alternations between plots.

Many Yong Ju troupes emerged in Shanghai, Ningbo and other cities before the liberation of China in 1949, with performers best represented by He Xianmin, Xu Fengxian, Jin Cuixiang, Jin Yulan, Huang Junqing and some others. Jiongfeng Yong Ju Troupe was established in Shanghai and Ningbo City Yong Ju Troupe in Ningbo respectively after the PRC was founded. The troupe in Shanghai has focused on the adaptation of traditional theatrical pieces, including *Banba Jiandao (Half Scissors)*, *Tianyaoluoyu Niangyaojia (Widow to Marry Rain to Fall)*, *Shuangyuchan (A Couple of Jaded Cicadas)*, *Jie Qi (Borrowing Wife)*, etc. while the Yong Ju Troupe in Ningbo has focused on producing dramas themed with modern lives, such as

Liangxiongdi (Two Brothers), *Liangyange (Bright-eyed Brother)*, *Hongyan (Red Rock)*, and *Tianluo Guniang (Lady Tianluo)*, etc.

Yong Ju has earned broad recognition among the general public and governments at all levels as the opera is suitable for actors and actresses to wear clothing prevalent in the Qing Dynasty, suits and cheongsam in the 1930s, and it is well-placed for modern operas in particular. Most Yong Ju troupes could be found in Ningbo, Shanghai, Zhoushan, among others. After 1949, several Yong Ju Opera Troupes gave performances in Beijing, among which were Jingfeng Yong Ju Opera Troupe in 1962, and Ningbo Yong Ju Opera Troupe in 1990 and 1995, all of them received high remarks. As of now, Ningbo City Yong Ju Troupe is the only existing professional troupe for Yong Ju performances. In June of 2008, Yong Ju(Ningbo Opera) was included into the second batch of state level Representative List of the Intangible Cultural Heritage.

Ningbo Yong Ju Troupe became part of Ningbo Artistic Theatre in 2000. The new name for the troupe was Ningbo Yong Ju Troupe of Artistic Theatre led by Wang Jinwen, reputed Yong Ju actress. New creations, such as *Dianqi (Wife Selling)*, *Qiuhaitang (Autumn Crab Apples)*, *Guifuhuanxiang (Rich Lady Returned to Hometown)*, have made extraordinary differences in the opera community. Wang

Jinwen won the 7th Shanghai Michelia Alba Award and the 20th China Plum Blossom Prize.

Ninghai Pingdiao

Ninghai Pingdiao, one of the ancient local operas in China, has a history of more than 300—400 years starting from late Ming Dynasty and it became popular in the Qing Dynasty. The ancient opera was prevalent in Ninghai, Xiangshan and Sanmen. As a branch of High Tune System of Zhejiang, a kind of rhyme scheme of Chinese opera, Ninghai Pingdiao is sung with Ninghai dialect that produces gentle tunes, that's why it is called Pinghuan. What Shuaya and teeth play is to Pingdiao is just as what Bianlian, or face-changing, is to Sichuan Opera. Shuaya is rough yet delicate, producing a sense of smartness amid wildness. Of 100-odd traditional theatrical pieces, among them the best known are two collections of dramas called the previous 18 dramas and the subsequent 18 dramas.

Ninghai Pingdiao produces resounding yet graceful tunes with one main vocal and many singing along and drums beating hard. Its vocal accompaniment takes many forms, including mixed accompaniment, Qing (clear) accompaniment, Quanju(complete sentense) accompaniment, Pianduan (broken sentence) accompaniment and Yizi (one word) accompaniment. Apart from the clown role that sings in Suzhou dialect, the rest roles of Ninghai Pingdiao sing in Ninghai dialect and reciting tones. As such, the form of opera, also known as a local singing troupe, was once very popular in Ninghai, Xiangshan, Huangyan, Wenling, Linhai, Xianju, Tiantai, Fenghua, among other places. Later, it staged for a short-term performances in Ningbo, Zhoushan, Hangjia Lake and Shanghai.

Since the late Qing Dynasty, many artists have come from Yong Kun Troupe, one that focuses on Kunqu opera and aria. They were popular in east Zhejiang in early Qing Dynasty. After mid Qing Dynasty, the troupe became a unique school but was influenced by Qingqu opera. Pingdiao emerged as a result of a mixed influence of Diaoqiang tune, Kunqu opera and tune name, as well as of local geographical locations and individual elements.

Ninghai Pingdiao gained popularity after the Revolution of 1911 but started to decline in 1932 and was cast into oblivion before the founding of the PRC in 1949. In 1956, relevant departments of Sanmen County brought together a dozen Pingdiao performers or so in ways that formed a semi-professional troupe. It was credited with performances in Hangzhou in 1957 that included *Jinlianzhanjiao* (*Jinlian Kills a Dragon*, an adaptation of *Xiaojinqian* or *Little Money*). In early 1960, Ninghai Pingdiao Troupe was officially launched and the troupe started exploring and sorting out a batch of traditional pieces and modern operas. It was dismissed in 1966 and later restored in 1978. In 1982, Ninghai County officially set up a collection and study team dedicated to reviewing Pingdiao pieces and reforming them systemically. In October 1999, the team won 11 awards in a national opera performance contest, known as Yingshanhong (Azalea), held by the Ministry of Culture, Changsha City, Hunan Province. In July 2004, *Yinpingxianlu* (*Fairy Drops from a Silver Bottle*) performed by the team was well received in the 7th National Art Show held in Hangzhou. Guided by cultural advancement as a major trend in China, the time-honored Ninghai Pingdiao is set to flourish all the more down the road like a booming flower. As part of efforts to preserve intangible cultural heritage as a national priority, Ninghai Pingdiao was listed among the first group of items of State-level Non-Intangible Cultural Heritage.

Yao Opera

Yao Opera was originally called Yuyao Tanhuang, a local opera for Han ethnic groups popular in Yuyao, Cixi, and Shangyu. The opera was renamed Yao Opera after 1950. Yao Opera was developed on the basis of local folk art forms like shadow picture lanterns, land boat dance, and tea-picking basket dance. Therefore, in Yuyao, it is also called Lantern Operas or Lantern Opera Troupes.

Yao Opera is featured by rural voices, simple but beautiful and with rapid rhythms. It has a basic tune and a minor tune. The basic tune is either flat or tight, with rising, evolving, and descending in development. The flat tune is sung accompanied only with drums. Males and females sing the same tune with different voices, and with natural turns. The flat female voices are often lined with ai-ai-yo, clear and graceful, usually for lyrical sentiments. The rapid rhythms are used mostly for stories where the plot tension is high, and the air is hot. Another Yao Opera form is dittos, totaling more than 40, they are either folk songs typical in south Yangtze River, or local songs passed down from the Ming and Qing Dynasties. Representatives are Sight-seeing Every Night, Young Boatman, Purple Bamboo Tone, Flower Songs, Dawn Tone, and a few others. These songs are rhythmic and rich in local flavors.

Yao Opera performers are mostly farmers and handcrafters, including painters, mat makers, bricklayers, palm mattress makers, and idle season workers. It uses simple prop, a handkerchief, or a fan will do. This makes it easy to be performed in the countryside. But peopled to have prejudice against this opera and also because it contained much porn dialogue, it could only be performed in the fields, with a simple stage made with a few pieces of boards on a few rice barrels. It was not allowed to be performed in ancestral halls or temples,

After the founding of the P. R. China, reforms were made on the contents and forms of Yao Opera, such as performing modern dramas, co-staging of man and women. In 1954, official Yao Opera Troupes were formed. In Yuyao, the northwest area of Cixi and the east area of Shangyu, spare time Yao Opera Troupes came into being like bamboo shoots after rain, totaling over 150 in the fifties and the sixties, an evidence of the vitality and popularity of Yao Opera Troupes among the grassroots people. On June 14 of 2008, Yao Opera was listed on the second batch of the state-level non-material cultural heritage (under the category of traditional operas).

4.2 Ningbo Quyi Folk Shows

Siming Nanci

Once known as Ningbo Wenshu, or Siming Wenshu, Siming Nanci is a kind of folk performance shows in Ningbo dialect in place of Zhejiang Province where the ethnic Han prevails. Siming Nanci can date back to more than 300 years ago in eastern Zhejiang Province. The folk show, originally sung by amateurs, was later performed by professional artists. In early times, roles in Nanci fell into four main types of characters: sheng (the male character), dan (the female character), jing (the painted face) and mo (the clown). Later, they evolved into a string player, a dulcimer player, two or three pipa players, and Erhu players. The libretto carries 7 characters. Traditional books have 30 long pieces, including *Zhenzhu Ta (Pearl Tower)*, *Yu Qingting (Jade Dragonfly)* and *Shuang Jiefa (Double Hairdressing)*. Siming Nanci derived from Tao Zhen of the Song Dynasty and Tanci of the Ming Dynasty, was spread to Ningbo downtown and suburban areas. It hit the heyday between late Qing Dynasty and early days of the Republic of China, but declined in the 1940s. And it is in danger of being lost forever.

Generally speaking, Nanci can be summarized in a Chinese character Wen (Graceful). Its tunes are elegant and it was recreated by men of letters. Some lines have to do with love affairs, others are flashy yet implicit. As they were well received by scholar-officials, Nanci pieces were played on such occasions as birthday parties and other celebrations. They were very flexibly played in different forms, including double scales, three, five, seven, eleven and thirteen scales, and played with such instruments as Xiao, Sheng, dulcimer, pipa, Erhu and Xiaosanxian, among others. While playing them, performers can use free play while still focusing on its main tune in accordance to their respective features, thus producing elegant and touching melodies.

In 1958, former Ningbo Folk Art Troupe set up a Siming Nanci Troupe, which was later dismissed as a result of Cultural Revolution (1966—1976). In the 1980s, reputed old performers staged performances in exhibitions. In 2000, Ningbo Municipal People's Art Gallery organized reformed amateur performances in different singing forms. Siming Nanci was spoken and mainly sung in a Ningbo local dialect. Performers played and sang altogether with level and oblique tones. Tunes are composed of up, middle and down rhymes. Fudiao and Cidiao are basic tunes and vocal music has exerted influence on Yong Ju and Ningbo Zoushu.

In June 2008, Siming Nanci was (placed) among the second batch of items on the list of State-level Intangible Cultural Heritage.

Ningbo Pinghua (Popular Stories)

Ningbo Pinghua, also known as Wushu among the general public, is different from Siming Nanci. Pinghua is a singing and story-telling art form among the Hans of Ningbo. Pinghua is performed by professionals and amateurs that include Nanci performers and Zoushu performers known as Danpai. It is said that Ningbo Pinghua was prevalent in the Song and Yuan Dynasties when history-telling and story-telling were common practices mainly in teahouses and story-telling houses of downtown Ningbo, Yin County and Cixi County.

When telling a story and performing different roles, performers resort to no more than a piece of wood, a foldable fan and a mouth without any music or accompaniment. Their stories are so vivid and lively that the audience abandons itself in the little world. With only an attention-catching block and a fan in place, performers can talk volubly with what their supreme speaking skills have to offer. One story-teller can play several and even a dozen roles, producing no one but the very character they intend to play with accurate figure, personality and way of speaking. The fan in his hand is likened to either a sword or a pen, while the block serves both as a way of quieting the scene and producing intended effect in telling a story. Traditional plays include *Outlaws of the Marsh*, *the Romance of Three Kingdoms and the Legend of Yue Fei*, among others.

Ningbo Pinghua, mainly performed in teahouses and story-telling houses in downtown areas, is prevalent in coastal cities of east Zhejiang. During the reigning period of Emperor Dao Guang in the Qing Dynasty, Pinghua performers in Ningbo had tens of sites for performances. The practice showed no signs of abating in the Republic of China period, producing famous performers including Zhang Ailin, Chuang Caizhang, among others. In particular, *Outlaws of the Marsh* told by Zhang Ailin, Zhang Yice and Zhang Shaoce enjoyed enormous reputation with its diversified and distinctive content thanks to repeated adaptations and upgrading by several generations of these artists.

Ningbo Zoushu

Previously known as Lotus Wenshu, or Lihua Wenshu, Ningbo Zoushu art represents one of the local operas in Ningbo dialect favored by the Hans of Ningbo. Ningbo Zoushu was a name settled in 1956. First taking shape in a village of Yuyao in between 1875 and 1908, Zoushu was introduced into Ningbo city in the late Qing Dynasty, and later into Zhenhai District and Zhoushan. In the 1950s and 60s, the singing art went popular in broader regions to include Linhai, Tiantai, Huangyan, Hangzhou other than Ningbo and Zhoushan. The art form withered in the 1990s.

Mouth-to-mouth rumor has it that Ningbo Zoushu(walking singing art) came into being in Shangyu. At that time, laborers working in the field sought to shake off tiredness by entertaining themselves with singing. The singing shifted from small tunes to pieces with plots, accompanied by nothing but a pair of bamboo clappers and bamboo root tips with simple tunes. During the reign of Emperor Guangxu (1875—1908), the singing form was spread to villages in Yuyao. Later, farmers, vendors and manufactures dedicated to the folk art in their spare times established Hangyu Society, where they exchanged experience and studied the related books. Among them was Xu Shengchuan, a senior practitioner, who was very popular among the general public as he drew upon tunes of Lotus singing from Shaoxing and took the initiative to sing to the accompaniment of Yueqin, a four-stringed plucked instrument. He inspired many performers to play varied instruments for accompaniment and they upgraded their performances by learning from Siming Nanci, Ningbo Tanhuang and local tunes. Meanwhile, *Story of Four Wives*, *Jade Chain*, and other long pieces were added to their performances. The performances were extended into Ningbo, Zhoushan and Taiwan. At first, Ningbo Zoushu was performed by a single person, and later, simple accompaniment was added with the performer sitting behind the desk and the band sitting beside the desk. Performing behind the desk, singers were called Li Zoushu (Inner Zoushan) as they did their job behind the desk with limited space. On the other hand, some were called Wai Zoushu (Outer Zoushan) as they had a spacious area for performance. Some distinctive performers were pretty well-known at that time, such as the performance of Xie Baochu from west Yin County, vocal music of Duan Desheng from downtown Ningbo and Kungfu of Mao Quanfu from north Cixi.

Zoushu is so named because performers walk and sing while Nanci performers sit and sing. Zoushu performers can do their job alone on the stage, singing with simple languages that won't cause misunderstanding or comprehension failure. There is no limit to the number of accompaniment. Tunes are rich and diversified with emotion-focused and narrating features. Traditional pieces included *Bai He Tu (Hundreds of Cranes Picture)* and *Huang Jin Yin (Gold Stamp)*, among others. In June 2008, Ningbo Zoushu was among the second batch of items of State-level Intangible Cultural Heritage.

Jiaochuan Zoushu

Jiaochuan Zoushu represents a kind of folk art by the Han ethnic group with distinctive local features. Originated from the Qing Dynasty when Emperor Guangxu reigned (1875—1908), Jiaochuan Zoushu was prevalent in Zhenhai, Zhoushan, Yinzhou, among other regions.

According to senior performers of Jiaochuan Zoushu, during Guangxu period, Jiaochuan Zoushu got its name when a performer, Xie Ashu, or Xie Yuanhong, saw an arched wall with inscribed characters Jiaochuan on a south gate in Zhenhai where he lived and then so named the opera. The result is that Xie has been taken as the founder of Jiaochuan Zoushu. There is no record as to from whom Xie learned to sing the opera.

As is mentioned earlier, performers used a simple strategy in doing this with only two small wine bowls and chopsticks, beating with tempo and singing with self-abandonment. Prior to the War of Resistance against Japanese Aggression (1937—1945), the solo form changed into two-people performance. Performers started to use a block, a fan and a handkerchief while singing to the accompaniment of bamboo clappers and drums on a small platform set up in a temple, an ancestral hall or a bleacher. At the end of each tune, they produced a basic tune to the effect of Ei Ei Li A.

Erhu and Yangqin (dulcimer) among other instruments were played before the war broke out.

237

After the PRC was founded, other instruments such as Pipa, Sanxian, Xiao and whistle were added to the existing network of instruments.

Traditional pieces include *the Eastern Han Dynasty* and *the Western Han Dynasty*. In June 2006, Jiaochuan Zoushu was listed in the first batch of intangible cultural heritage list of Ningbo City.

Xiaorehun

Popular in Zhejiang, Jiangsu and Shanghai, Xiaorehun is a bantering form of the Wu dialect of the Han ethnic group. Also known as Xiaoluoshu or "He Who Sells Ligaotang"(Ligaotang is a kind of dissert of Shanghai), Xiaorehun is a talking-singing street art. It was performed in Wu Chinese and started from the street. The art form started in late Qing Dynasty and early Republic of China and was introduced to Pinghu in the 1920s. Xiaorehu literally means that a man speaks nonsense while suffering from fever. So Xiaorehun means a performer talking absurdity. Xiaorehun was well received by the general public as the art spoke for the common concern of the general public and unveiled social ills in a sarcastic manner with most of its contents coming from latest news. In an effort to escape from persecution of reactionary authorities, the singing art was disguised into the local language of Jiayucun, or absurd talks.

Performed in authentic Hangzhou dialect, Xiaorehun is accompanied by small gong or Sanqiaoban with ordinary melodies. Popular tunes included Luoxianfeng, Sanqiaofu, Dongxiangdiao, Wugeng, Siji, Shitan, among others.

There was no fixed time slot for the performance of Xiaorehun. The singing in the east side will probably continue if people were showing no signs of leaving, though it was performed for over, say, 1 or 2 hours. Performers would probably leave the east side for the west when few were showing up. By the same token, there was no fixed performing site. It could be a busy street, a wharf, a station or a marketplace, where singers circled a site with white powder and beat hard gong and drum to attract people. Performances wouldn't get started until there were enough people.

Xiaorehun was popular among the general public with its amusing language and it was easily understood. Among famous performers, there were Chen Zhangsheng, or Little Deli as his stage name, Chen Guoan, Xu Heqi, Yu Xiaofei. After the 1950s, Xiaorehun performers were seen as comedians, which bear on modern monodrama and farce, an easy art form prevalent in Shanghai Stage.

As part of strong national emphasis on the preservation of intangible cultural heritage, Hangzhou Xiaorehun was placed in the list of the state-level intangible cultural heritage in 2006, in addition to the protection list of Zhejiang Province Folk Art.

News Singing

News Singing, also known as News, is a folk art form of Han ethnic group popular in east Zhejiang. Evolved from Zhaobao local news (morning news), the singing art became prevalent in Beilun, Fenghua and Xiangshan districts. Singers were blind. The time-honored practice can date back to hundreds of years ago. In the Southern Song Dynasty, official news was sung and later social news.

In the 1950s, there were about 40-50 news singers in Zhenhai District, most of them were blind men. Among the most famous singers were Yan Meifang and Gu Ahuo. Most of the news focused on stories, both ancient and current, and popular tunes, performed with local accents and slangs. While singing the news, a singer held a pole and a wood piece with the right hand, a small gone with the left hand, a small drum on the knees, singing and beating the instruments at the same time. Performers often did their job on the street, near a barn, in a courtyard, in a wharf and on a steamer. They had over dozens of tunes, performed either solo or in duet.

Before the founding of PRC in 1949, the blind performers had to sing out the news by walking street by street, household by household. What they did was really a humble job. They sang news in three chief ways: first, at doorsteps for the sake of some money in return, second, in a courtyard or a hall for a few bucks; third, in a steamer of a popular waterway days and nights, fourth, in a temple fair or a market, fifth, in a particular site, say, a story-telling house by relatively more competent performers, though this particular group was small in number.

News is sung by either one performer or two, accompanied by drums, gongs and bamboo clappers. Scripts fall in to small scritps and big scripts. small scripts include *Guanggun Diao* (*Song of Bachelors*), *Dayangsheng* (*Health Keeping*), *Youmatou* (*Visiting Wharfs*) and news, among others; big scripts *Sanxianbingsheng* (*Interrogation by Three County magistrates*), *Chaiyuanyang* (*Separating a Couple*), and *Dingxieji* (*Nailing Shoes*), among others.

News Singing was included in the list of the Ningbo municipal intangible cultural heritage in 2006 and among the third batch of items listed in state-level intangible cultural heritage.

4.3　Festivals

Spring Festival

The Spring Festival, which falls on the 1st of January of Lunar Calendar, represents the most important traditional festival in China, the same in Ningbo. People typically get up early in the morning and wear new clothes and shoes, adults and kids alike, as a way of bidding farewell to the old and ushering in the new. Men in a family do the job of opening the door and setting off three firecrackers in the courtyard, an action known as Door Opening Firecrackers, with greater cracking sound presaging a more auspicious new year. Later, they put in place joss sticks and candles, fruits and pictures of their forefathers for the sake of honoring their ancestors, the heaven and earth as a whole. Sometimes the worshiping takes place in the ancestral hall, if there is one. Younger members of a family pay a new year call to senior members, a ritual known as Baisui, and they cup one hand in another while meeting relatives and friends as a token of a new year call, greeting them with Gongxi Gongxi or Xinnian Facai, auspicious greetings. Breakfast is traditionally served with stuffed lard and sesame dumplings. The dishes serve as a symbol of sweetness and family reunion. Red date soup and longan soup are also an option, signifying prosperity and family reunion. After the breakfast, juniors serve their parents and grandparents with Chinese olive and kumquat tea, or what is known as Yuanbao Tea. On the first day of Spring Festival, people refrain from paying visits, sweeping the floor, using knives or scissors or lighting lamps. Rather, they go to bed early after finishing dinner. On the second day, mutual visits and Bainian begin with liquor gifts, cakes, complements, among others. Each family treats guests with melon seeds, peanuts, sugar and fruits.

What is most interesting is to watch and engage in various cultural and recreational activities. Among other activities, there are gong and drum performances, dragon dance and lion dance, horse race lamp, fireworks, juggling in city streets and parks, pastry supply, goods and new theatrical pieces and movies in Heather, like *Tiaojiaguan (Masked Dancing Pray for Higher Rank)* and *Yingcaishen(Welcome God of Wealth)*. Some lantern theatrical troupes are organized on an ad hoc basis for lantern horse races from household to household in exchange for some items or cash. Some loafers, with

festoons on their heads, act like they are sweeping the floor with brooms covered by colored ribbons when they reach a household. Saying out loud or singing auspicious words while doing the sweeping, they can win favor from home owners, who, in turn, distribute cash and rice cakes.

Spring Festival is over after the 5th day of January in Lunar calendar when employees return to work and businesses are open.

Lantern Festival

The Lantern Festival, which falls on the 15th day of January in lunar calendar, is a traditional Chinese festival that dates back to the Qin Dynasty over 2,000 years ago. It is recorded that importance was assigned to the festival in as early as the Western Han Dynasty, when Emperor Wu started a campaign worshiping Taiyi, god governing the universe, at Ganquan Palace in the first month of Chinese lunar calendar. The move has been seen as the pioneering act of god worshiping on the very day of the Lantern Festival.

The Lantern Festival literally means the night of lanterns, later it focuses more on eating Tangyuan, round rice dumplings than on lantern appreciation. On the night of the Lantern Festival, people appreciate lanterns, guess lantern riddles and eat sweet dumplings, ushering in another round of festivity height after the Chinese year is over.

242

This, as a result, has turned into a convention. The very festival was dubbed 15th of January, Half Moon, Yuan Day or Yuan Night. At the beginning of Tang Dynasty, the festival was called Shang Yuan, a measure of Taoism and known as Yuanxiao, Yuanxiao in late Tang Dynasty, Dengxi in the Song Dynasty, and Dengjie in Qing Dynasty. What's more, the Lantern Festival is also well-known overseas.

Legend has it that the festival was in honor of the removal of the Lü Family by Emperor Wen of the Han Dynasty. Upon the death of Liu Bang (Han Gaozu), Liu Ying, the son of Queen Lü, ascended the throne as Emperor Huidi. The new emperor was so weak and indecisive that his power was stripped of by Queen Lü, who took over the imperial court after his death. Ministers were in such indignation and fear that they dared not speak out.

After Queen Lü died of illness, Lü's family plunged into fear of possible persecution and marginalization. To avoid that, Lü Lu, a general, held a secret meeting on a military coup, which, if staged successfully, could make Lü replace Liu as the royal family. The plot, which was overheard by Liu Xiang, a member of the royal clan, decided to wage a war against the Lü's together with Zhou Bo and Chen Ping, the two senior ministers. Finally, the coup ended up in failure and Liu Heng, Liubang's second son, ascended the throne, who was also known as Emperor Wen of Han. The new emperor celebrated the hard-won peace by designating the 15th of January when the suppression of coup took place, as a Day of Fun for All. At that time, every household in the capital of Chang'an (currently Xi'an) put up diversified decorations, hence the Lantern Festival.

The Lantern Festival has seen longer celebrations as history evolves. It was marked for one day only in the Han Dynasty, three days in the Tang and five days in the Song. While in the Ming Dynasty, the festival started in the 8th and ended on the night of 17th of January in Chinese Lunar Calendar. It was the longest traditional festival, which took place after the Spring Festival was over, when days were much of a din while nights were set aflame with spectacular firecrackers. Especially those colorful, exquisitely made lights scaled the festivity to a new height. In the Qing Dynasty, more activities, including dragon and lion dances, folk dances, stilt-walking and Yangge dance among other forms were added to the already fabulous network of celebrations, though festival time was reduced to 4 to 5 days only.

Qingming(Bright and Clear Day or Tomb-Sweeping Day)

The Tomb-Sweeping Day or Qingming Festival, which falls on early March of Chinese Lunar Calendar, sees every household prepare black glutinous rice and green rice balls as offerings for their beloved but diseased ones. When sweeping the tomb, people do a lot of work including incense burning, kowtow, firecracker discharges and earth spreading. Well-off families carried out their version of sacrifice offering with ceremonious drum music. Bereaved relatives living far away must go back to their hometown to engage in the process. The Tomb-Sweeping Day is also called the Bright and Clear Day, it is taken as a day for outing as it marks the beginning of spring. As such, an entire family will probably go on a picnic nearby on grassland after sweeping the tomb. An old saying goes: "anyone that wears willow branches will surely have close relatives in the next life circle." Children often put a willow branch on their head, and they also snap a few branches of wild azalea. Those who are not sweepers also enjoy a visit to scenic spots in downtown areas like the Yuehu Lake (or the Moon Lake) on the very day, a scene of hordes of people filling tourist attractions.

Originated from the Zhou Dynasty when the Han ethnic group started commemorating the day, Qingming Festival can be traced back to more than 2,500 years ago. Affected by Han culture, the custom is also prevalent among 24 ethnic groups including Manchu, Hezhe, Zhuang, Oroqen, Dong, Tujia, Miao, Yao, Li, Shui, Jing, and Qiang. The day is characterized by tomb sweeping, ancestral worshiping and excursions.

Tomb Sweeping Day was at first just one day used in the 24 divisions of the solar year in the traditional Chinese calendar. It became a festival for remembering the dead ancestors because of its close relations with the Cold Food Day. About 2,500 years ago, a Lord Jin Wengong, to commemorate a devoted friend who once saved his life when he was in exile, designated April 4 (on which day his friend died) to be the Cold Food Day and the day after the Cold Food Day to be the Tomb Sweeping Day to remember the diseased ancestors. The Cold Food Day is still observed in most part of Shanxi province. In Yushe County, the Cold Food Day last for two days before the Qingming Festeval, and in Yuanchu County, the day before the Tomb Sweeping Day is observed as the Major Cold Food Day, and the day before this day is observed as the Minor Cold Food Day.

Legend has it that in the ancient days, the Tomb-Sweeping Day was exclusively reserved for emperors, generals and ministers when they mourned for the death of important persons. Later, the practice was replicated to the wider public, and the result is that Qingming has survived and thrived as a much-cherished festival.

On the 20th May, 2006, the Tomb-Sweeping Day, declared by the Ministry of Culture, was included on the list of the National Intangible Cultural Heritage upon the approval of the State Council.

Lixia (Beginning of Summer)

Lixia, the beginning of summer, is the 7th of the 24 solar terms. Lixia arrives probably between May 5th and 6th when the sun reaches 45 degrees in longitude. Lixia doesn't fall on a fixed day in Chinese Lunar Calendar but arrives around 1st April in Chinese Lunar Calendar. An ancient saying goes: "the beginning of summer begins when the big dipper starts pointing to the southeast. At that time, everything on earth starts to grow."

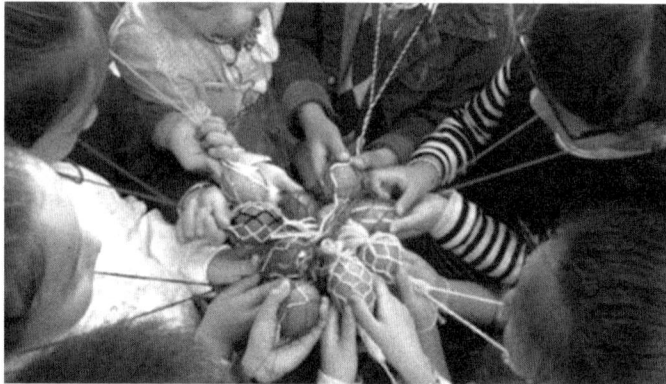

Astronomically, Lixia marks the end of spring and the beginning of summer. The day is regularly seen as signals of rising temperature and emerging thunderstorms, when crops are growing rapidly.

Lixia was established well in 239 A.D., presaging change of spring into summer. Lixia marks the beginning of summer. In fact, by climatology standard, summer begins when average daily temperature rises to over 22 degree centigrade. After Lixia, only Fuzhou and south of Nanling mountains see thriving trees and longer day time, while northeast and northwest of China have just entered into spring with most of China recording an average temperature of about 18-20 degrees. At that time, flowers are vying to be beautiful and fragrant. In May, sophora is in blossom in many places. Everything is flourishing after Lixia comes.

Ningbo households traditionally cook eggs with black tea leaves, known as tea eggs or Lixia eggs. The delicacy is eaten with broad bean, glutinous rice, black bamboo shoot, lichens, which are said to be beneficial to skin and body and the overall wellbeing. What made Lixia particularly interesting were two folk activities. The first one was called Zhudan, in which the parents, before Lixia came, knit an egg cover with colorful silk threads, then a tea egg was placed into the cover, and hung on the neck of the kids. The kids then squeezed their egg with each other to see whose egg could remain unbroken, and made fun in the game. The interesting game often attracted the grown-ups in participation. Another activity was to weigh people. People were placed in a big bamboo basket to get weighed. This custom is still kept in some rural areas; while in urban regions, the custom is no longer practised with the widespread use of electronic scales and platform scales.

Duanwu (Dragon Boat Festival)

On Duanwu, the Dragon Boat Festival, which falls on the 5th of May in Chinese Lunar Calendar, every household cooks glutinous rice Zongzi and cowpea Zongzi, a traditional Chinese rice-pudding rapped in reed leaves. The festival comes as summer begins when the weather is humid, prompting the infestation of many bugs and thus making people disease-prone. Quite a few Ningbo customs have to do with methods to diseases treatment by hanging calamus and moxa and by burning moxa leaves, rhizome atractylodis and radix angelicae at noon. It is a way of keeping away mosquitoes to exorcise evil spirits and dispel bugs. Another way of getting away from diseases is drinking realgar wine and applying realgar on the body. In addition, one can wear money-shaped accessories with May 5th in Chinese on the front of the coin and snake, scorpion, centipede, house lizard and spider on the back side. It is said those who wear the coin will be free from toxins of all kinds. Furthermore, it is most interesting to draw tigers and make perfume satchel. Tiger drawing is colored by children after a sketch of the tiger is either framed by an adult or bought from a store. After the completion, the tiger picture is hung on the bed or on the door for the sake of peace and security. Perfume satchel, made up of silks, satins and other materials, stuffed with cotton, perfume, among others, is hung on the bed, on a child's neck, or on a belt. It can be tailor made according to what one likes in the shape of a ball, diamond, star, hexagon, heart and twelve Chinese zodiac signs. It can be a colorful, cute and delicate handcraft, something that one can never resist if you send it to your relatives and friends as gift.

Duanwu Festival came into being as a way to commemorate Qu Yuan, a poet of the Chu Kingdom who committed suicide when Chu Kingdom was beaten and annexed by

the powerful Qin Kingdom in the Warring Period about 2,300 years ago. The tradition was that people on this day make a lot of Zongzi, threw them into the river, hoping the fish there would be attracted so that they would spare the body of the dead poet. Another traditional practice on this day was dragon-boat racing. The legend goes that when people heard the poet jumped into the river, people ran to the river, rowing the boat frantically, to rescue the poet. Boat-racing then became a tradition to commemorate the dead poet. In Ningbo, the racing used to be organized in Huxi Lake and rivers. The dragon boats, which take on the color of green, white and yellow, have dragon scales and shells drawn on both of its sides, a dragon head and a dragon tail at its prow and stern respectively. The boat crew in uniform of the same colour as the boat sit on both sides of the racing boat. During the race, a man stands in the front, shouting out commands while beating hard a drum. Rowers strive hard to race forward, accompanied by the drumbeat and waves of cheers from the bank, a spectacular scene one can never miss. The boat that reaches the destination first is declared winner, who will be awarded with jars of wine. The wine jar will be drunk on site as a way of celebrating the victory.

Qixi Festival

Qixi Festival, or Qiqiao Festival, the Birthday of the Seventh Sister in fairy tales, is a traditional festival of eastern Asian countries and Chinese communities, a day that draws much inspiration from Chinese culture. On the night of 7th or 6th of the seventh month by lunar calendar, women seek ingenuity in their courtyard from Vega, which was incarnated as a woman weaver, demonstrating how they worshipped nature and pursued better needlework. Later, the festival was given a Chinese version of Valentine's Day.

In China, Qixi Festival, also known as Qiqiao Festival or Daughters' Festival, falls on the night of 7th July, is a nice and temperate day when trees and flowers send out fragrant smells. This is the most romantic day in China and a day that was most cherished by girls. In the clear summer night, stars shine brightly overhead, with the white Milky Way crossing the immense sky, and Altair and Vega hanging high on two different sides of the Milky Way, seemingly looking out for each other. It is a custom to watch the stars, including the Vega on that night. Legend has it that Zhinü (the Weaving Maid) and Niulang(the Cowboy) date on the bridge of magpies. Zhinü was a beautiful, exquisite fairy girl, who was asked by mundane women for wisdom, weaving skills and bright marriage prospects. It is said that the scene of dating of Niulang and Zhinü is visible to the eye on the night of the festival and their sweet talks can also be heard under melon and fruits stands. Girls worship Zhinü for a satisfactory marriage on the romantic night. Marriage was a big event that decided a girl's happiness, so, many lovers would pray for a love while looking into the sky, praying to the starry sky for a happy marriage on the quiet night.

On May 20, 2006, the festival was included in the first list of national intangible cultural heritage by the State Council. It is considered the Chinese Valentine's Day.

Zhongyuan Festival

Zhongyuan Festival, also known as Ghost Festival or Obon Festival in Buddhism, is a traditional festival that falls on the 15th or 14th of the seventh month by Lunar Calendar. Each household worships their ancestors on that day, with some holding family banquets and performing acts of ceremony. After three rounds of wine offering when the banquet is over, the entire family start sitting down around for dinner. After night falls, people draw a circle with lime as a banned area close to a serene river bank. They put paper money offering the dead in the circle, light up candles and set off firecrackers as a way of commemorating the dead. This is also seen as an approach to

seeing off their ancestors. The civil society used to welcome the dead home starting from 7th to 15th of the seventh month in Lunar Calendar by offering tea and meals in the morning, in the afternoon and in the evening. At present, superstitious elements are gone, what is left is people's worshiping and commemoration for the dead.

The seventh month of the year is autumn days in Chinese Lunar Calendar. It is a custom to offer sacrifices and report grain output to ancestors when crops are ripe so that ancestors can have a first taste of the rice. Sacrifices for ancestors have become a norm during the period because July is the time when filial Chinese people start harvesting. In the Eastern Han Dynasty, Taoists established Sanyuan Festivals, Sanhui Festivals, and Wula Festivals. Sanyuan Festivals are made of three festivals for celebrating the birthdays of the Gods of Heaven, Earth and Water respectively; Sanhui

Festivals are three days for the Taoists to go to their temples to give report to the Gods and receive examinations, and Wula Festivals are five days for offering sacrifices to the Heaven, the Earth, the Taoist scriptures, and for life blessings, and higher social ranks. July 7th is Daodela Festival, it is also a day for celebrating the birthday of the God of Earth. So, gradually July 15th became a very important day of worship and sacrifices to ancestors.

Mid-autumn Festival

Mid-autumn Festival is also known as Yuexi, Autumn Day, Zhongqiu Festival, August Festival, Moon-chasing Day, Moon-playing Day, Moon-worshiping Day, Daughters' Day or Reunion Day. The festival, which falls on the 15th of the eighth month in Chinese Lunar Calendar, represents a popular cultural day among many nations and eastern Asian countries. Mid-autumn Festival got its name as the day falls on the middle autumn. In some places it is celebrated on the 16th of the month.

Starting from the Tang Dynasty and prevalent in the Song Dynasty, Mid-autumn Festival was put on a par with New Year's Day as a major traditional Chinese Festival in the Ming and Qing Dynasties. Influenced by Chinese culture, some eastern Asian and Southeast Asian nations also celebrate the day among the Chinese communities. The festival was made national statutory holiday in 2008. On May 20th, 2006, the festival was included in the first national intangible cultural heritage list by the State Council.

Mid-autumn Festival is among China's top three festivals when lanterns are used. Unlike the spectacular Lantern Festival, Mid-autumn Festival practises lantern viewing among children or family members.

The 15th of the eighth month in Lunar Calendar is considered the Mid-autumn Day, but Ningbo people celebrate it on the 16th day. This is explained in two ways in the Local records of Ningbo. One is that in the late Yuan Dynasty, Fang Guozhen, a rebel leader, made August 16th the Mid-Autumn Day as it was his birthday; another story goes that Shi Hao, Lord of Yue of Southern Song Dynasty, once celebrated the Mid-Autumn Day on August 16th as this day was the birthday of his mother. On that moon-lit day, Shi Hao hosted many guests as a way of celebrating his mother's birthday and staged a dragon-boat race on the Moon Lake with extraordinary jubilation and vitality, an event watched by tens of thousands of spectators. Since then, the 16th August has become the Mid-autumn Festival for Ningbo people, when there were celebrations, moon cake consumption, and moon appreciation with theatres staging dramas like the *Goddess Chang'e's Fly to the Moon.*

Chongyang Festival

Chongyang Festival, also known as Double Ninth Festival, Shaiqiu Festival, Taqiu Festival, is a traditional festival among the Hans. Celebrations include excursion, moon appreciation, ascending mountains for a bird-view look, viewing chrysanthemum, hanging cornel, eating Chongyang Cake, drinking Chrysanthemum wine, among others.

On the 9th of September in Chinese Lunar Calendar, Chongyang Festival is among China's top four sacrificing days. The festival came into being early in the Warring States Period, and it became an officially civil festival in the Tang Dynasty. Chongyang Festival has remained an important day since then. On Chongyong Festival, as on 3rd March in Chinese Lunar Calendar, every family member goes out for an excursion and climbs up high as a way of avoiding disasters.

With a history of over 2,000 years, Chongyong Festival made its mark back in Spring and Autumn Period. During the Warring States period, the festival was given high importance but was celebrated only within the Imperial Court. In the Han Dynasty, the festival caught on over time. At that time, Lady Qi, one of King Liu Bang's concupines, was murdered by Queen Lu, and one of Qi's maids, a Miss Jia, was expelled out of the court and later married to a poor guy. This maid told people what Chongyong Festival was all about. She told people on 9th of September, everyone was to wear cornet, ate millet cake, and drank Chrysanthemum wine for the sake of longevity. In Wei and Jin Dynasties, chrysanthemum appreciation and wine drinking became a norm. Later, Chongyang Festival was celebrated both in the imperial court and among the general public. In the Tang Dynasty, Chongyong Festival was officially taken as a festival. The festival was even more prevalent in the Song Dynasty. *Dongjing Menghua Lu*, a book recording the prosperity of Dongjing, the Capital of the North Song Dynasty, has passages recording the booming Chongyong Festival in the Northern Song Dynasty. *Wulin Old Days* also recorded the thriving festival within the imperial court of the Southern Song Dynasty. On the day, eunuchs and princesses of the Ming Dynasty ate cakes to celebrate the day, and the emperor visited Wansui Mountain as a way of marking the day. In the Qing and Ming Dynasties, the custom showed no signs of abating.

In the 1980s, the Double Ninth Day was made a day for respecting the seniors in an effort to foster a culture where the aged are respected, loved and helped. In 1989, the festival was officially named as Senior Citizens' Day. On December 28, 2012, the Standing Committee of the National People's Congress approved an amendment to the *Elderly Protection Law*. According the revised law, the 9th September in Lunar Calendar was designated as the Senior Citizens' Day.

The Winter Solstice

The Winter Solstice represents an important solar term in China's Lunar Calendar and a traditional Chinese Festival, also known as Dong Jie, Changzhi Jie, Yasui, among other names. Back in the Spring and Autumn Period about 2,500 years ago, the Chinese people were capable of observing the sun through earth sundial and finally found Winter Solstice, the first of all 24 solar terms that were discovered. Winter Solstice is around the 21st to the 23rd of December each year.

On this day, the sunlight reaches the southern end of the earth at the Tropic of Capricorn while the northern hemisphere embraces the least amount of sunlight, 50% less than that of the sunlight in the southern hemisphere. Days are shortest in the northern hemisphere and they are shorter if you move northward more. For example, China's southern end—Zengmu Ansha has 11 hours and 59 minutes, Haikou 10 hours and 55 minutes, Hangzhou 10 hours 12 minutes, Beijing 9 hours and 20 minutes. Mohe county, Heilongjiang province, the northern end of China, has 7 hours and 34 minutes in the day time. After the Winter Solstice, the sky is what it is supposed to look like in winter. At this time, the southern hemisphere is experiencing scorching hot days.

Dumpling eating has become the custom on the Winter Solstice. It is said that dumpling is a must for Winter Solstice. And Tangyuan, sticky balls, is popular in the south. There is an exception. In Tengzhou, Qufu and Zoucheng of Shandong Province, Winter Solstice is called Shujiu. On that day, people once ate lamb soup as a way of dispelling coldness. Dumpling eating is the most common food though different places

254

have different customs. People in Ningbo eat Jiangban Tangguo or Jiangban Yuanzi on that day. Yuanzi is made of glutinous rice flour, Jiangban(sweet wine) and sweet potatoes, which in Chinese means auspiciousness. Thick soup is also needed to worship ancestors. Those with an ancestral hall must visit it. Pictures of ancestors are hung above. Offerings will be put in place. Troupes will be invited for a performance, which lasts from the afternoon to the evening. Sesame cakes will be prepared for everyone as a sign of auspiciousness. On the Winter Solstice day, the night is the longest of a year. Ningbo people are used to sleeping early on the day in hope of having a nice dream and a peaceful year.

4.4　Folk Customs

Flying Kites in February

In February, spring comes back to earth, promising nice, warm days. It is said that people eat melon seed in January and fly kites in February. Kite-flying has become a much-loved outdoor activity among young people. Kites take on different shapes. They are made of bamboos and paper. They could have four long tails or be as simple as possible. Or they can be made in the shape of tiles tied by a rope. They are easy to be made, cost-effective, and produce good effects. In addition, colored kites can look like eagles, doves and centipedes. Some kites are tied with rubber bands and a small bell, which rings in the sky when the wind is too strong. The custom is here to stay. But few still make kites themselves. They buy kites from stores and it is less interesting.

Yuyao kites stand out for its exquisite workmanship and have won many golden prizes both at home and around the world. People use bamboo skin as the kite frame and bamboo sticks as the kite bone and they are tied together with symmetry. Then they use light paper of varied colors as the wings. Kites are shaped like eagles, butterflies, bees, swallows, cranes, phoenix, mandarin ducks, magpies, giant dragons and bats. Patterns on the kites can represent jubilance, good health, longevity, filiality, success and wealth. Some kites adopt silk or satin as they are elastic and easy to fold.

Newly made kites are like birds flying high in the sky. They are like real creatures crossing clouds, sometimes staying high and other times low. Viewers on the ground watch kites with joy while kite flyers enjoy the process enormously. Proverbs go that

children who fly kites high and far can go home enjoying rice cakes and sweet dumplings, while those who fly kites unskillfully go home crying.

With a ring tied to a kite, the sound it produces is pleasant to the ear. Proverbs go that as the kites resound in the day, the days are getting longer and longer. Meaning in March by the Chinese lunar calendar, the daytime is getting longer and longer day by day. In the night, people put lights on the kite. Streams of lights going up the sky make a spectacular scene. The kites with light is known as fairy lanterns.

In the past, people had the rope tied to their kite cut after it flew high in the sky. It is said that such a practice would bring good luck by repelling diseases.

Sand Beach Strolling on March 3rd

At Shipu and Changguo of Xiangshan County, there is a custom in which everyone goes for a walk along the beach outside of Changguo East Gate, or cook sea snails they picked up on March 3rd in Lunar Calendar. There is a story behind it.

Legend has it that in ancient times, a giant turtle lived in a village of Changguo, which often caused flood sweeping over houses, people and livestock, making people's life there destitute. At that time, nine dragons lived in that area, and they were so outrageous that they were determined to kill the turtle.

One day when the turtle once again stirred high waves to flood the village, these dragons flew to the beach after hearing crying from people in startled chaos. Knowing

that it was the turtle that caused so many disturbances, they blamed it by saying: "You evil spirit, scourge of people, we must bring you to Jade Emperor!" The turtle didn't subdue. Instead, their bickering evolved into a long-standing fight that lasted 81 days. At the end of the day, both sides were too exhausted to even make a move, but the smallest dragon still got some strength and it strangled the turtle. As a result, waves and tides faded away. The turtle sank deep down into the sand and the small dragon turned into a sand embankment.

As a way of honoring the dragons, on the 3rd March, when the nine dragons and the turtle picked up the fight, people went to the sand beach in threes and fours. And this has become a local custom.

Saihui (God Welcoming Gathering)

God Welcoming Gathering, or Saihui, is held in Ningbo, urban and rural areas alike, each year. It takes place in April, September, and October.

Five Gods Event, which takes place on 15th April, is the grandest of all because on this day five gods are received. Ningbo Five Gods Temple is located in Dashani Street and houses five gods in blue, yellow, red, white, and black respectively. From 11th to 13th April, people used to hold five gods' statues on the street. Funded by various

257

sectors and organizations, the activity is very luxurious. A variety of lanterns and exquisitely-made boats dot the street, where people play various characters and play many instruments including gongs, cymbals and bells, among others. A team composed of dozens of people played instruments, producing a lively scene, and they were lined up by passers-by. Incenses were burned to welcome the team. But accidents often took place. In 1869, Xinjiang Bridge was broken into two pieces as a result of overcrowded people and more than three hundred people were drowned. During the reign of Guangxu, a riot broke out between the military and the people. So the event was cancelled by the authorities.

On September 15, another god-welcoming event, also called Shehuo, took place on a simpler form of celebration.

In different localities, god welcoming events are held in varied forms and scales. What is most famous is Gaoqiao Event in Western Yinzhou, Libai Event in Jiangshan, Daohua Event in Dongnan Township, among others. Such events lasted 3 to 4 days, when streets were festooned with decorations and god-worshiping performances were staged. These events were also prevalent in counties and municipalities. The most spectacular event should be the Guanyin Welcoming Race along coastal areas in northern Yuyao, northern Cixi, northern Zhenhai on February 29, when 16 temples co-organized the celebrations. At that time, girls who rarely made public appearances also took part in the activity, old men and women danced, diligent women stopped cooking. Everyone was in high spirits. God-welcoming events in Yuyao and the southern part of Yuyao were as lively and exciting. Each time when the event comes, a boat racing will be held, which attracts about 40 boats. In the night, crowds of people gather along the river banks appreciating lanterns. Huangpu Fang, a poet in the Ming Dynasty, described it is this way:

Looking into the distance before the Three-Gods Temple you see the lanterns,
Spreading afar in endless bright dots they make the city sleepless.

Rice Flower Festival

Rice Flower Festival used to be a folk cultural event. The tradition has it that in every June, Yinjiangqiao in west Yinzhou, Zouxi in the east Yinzhou, Maoshan in south Yinzhou, Doumenqiao and Zhenhai held Rice Flower Festival, when farmers went to fields beating drums and gongs. The lively scene used to attract crowds of people. These celebration activities took place when rice began flowering, so it is called Rice Flower Festival. It is said that good luck comes after the festival celebrations.

Legend has it that farmers in places of Changshi in Zhenhai area used to live a wretched life as they had poor yields because of infertile soil with too much alkalization. When major disasters struck, they had to eat nothing but grass. But One day, a fleet

259

full of grain arrived, and its boss from Fujian wished to cash in on the grain insufficiency here. Captain He Xingjiu, a cashier, felt sorry for the people at the sight of the hunger-stricken people. As a result, he gave all the food for the vulnerable and distributed much grain seeds to every household so that it could grow grain next year. As a savior, he was greatly appreciated by the locals, but, on the other hand, he couldn't make his generous act known to his employer. So he stayed there and watched how farm work went about by visiting fields constantly. But later he killed himself at the thought of inability to tell his employer of what he had done. He left the world with a poem:

> Shiploads of grain given to people in necessity,
> But how can I report to boss who is dreaming of money.
> Nevertheless I am happy to see the rice flowering,
> I will rest in peace, even if I will die for this.

People couldn't help crying over the discovery of his body as the savior sacrificed himself for saving so many people. In an attempt to honor him, people buried him with a grand ceremony and later a temple was built in his honor. Rice Flower Festival was launched to commemorate him.

The custom didn't get repealed until a few years after 1949.

June 6 Festival

It is said that on 6th June, children who take a hot shower will not suffer from prickly heat, and cats and dogs that take a hot bath will not have fleas. Each and every

household will expose their clothes under the sun as a way of avoiding the risk of molding. On that day, colorful clothes, hats, shoes and quilts would be put out to air when the sunlight is sufficient. Some big households would take out their genealogy books as well. Buddhism believers will be asked by the temples to help with moving classics outdoors and praying to Buddha. Temple Fairs used to be held in Shipu, Xiangshan by parading statues including those of Town God, Qilaoye (Qi Jiguang) and Zhougonggong on the street, accompanied by music bands and colorful dragons. And every household lit incense to welcome these gods. Villagers nearby flooded in the street for this spectacular event. But the custom was repealed after New China was founded.

The day is highly recommended for exposing clothes to the sun as the rainy season is about to be over or has already passed. It is plausible to put clothes and other items under sun exposure as they have possibly gone mouldy through a long rainy period.

On the day, dogs and cats were showered in the river as people believed their pets would be free from fleas after the process. Domestic animals are subject to parasites when summer comes. It is therefore necessary to thoroughly clean the pets.

People used to give their children very humble names because they believed that kids with such names would be easy to bring up. On 6th June, people would have their children take a shower to avoid diseases and disasters, just as they did with dogs and cats.

On the same day, it is said that people put imperial robe out to the air. Rumor has it that Emperor Qianlong of the Qing Dynasty was soaking wet when it suddenly rained heavily during his visit to Yangzhou. The emperor refused to wear ordinary clothes so his servants had no way but to dry the wet robe up on a sunny day, which happened to be June 6th. Ordinary people would like to borrow this nobility and expose their own clothes on the same day.

Incense Lighting

On the night of July 30th, when Ksiti Garbha Ksitigarbha was born, Ningbo locals are used to lighting incense on the ground. Legend has it that the Buddha doesn't open his eyes until much incense is lit. According to a poem by Zhang Yanzhang (1887—1960), a famous poet from Ningbo, children scrambled to stick incense on the ground in Qinglian Temple, and tens of thousands of lanterns were flowing on the river on a windy autumn day in July.

Legend goes that incense lighting has to do with Ksitigarbha, who manages everything on the earth. At the sight of the spread of slash-and-burn cultivation and the hardships people endured, the god was very concerned and said to Bull Demon King, "Your all powerful strength is now laid idle, and why not go there to help people with farm work?" The bull refused by saying: "I don't refuse doing farm work, but I'm afraid that I will be killed as a dish when I get old." The god, however, dismissed his claim and said, "It is your duty to plow the field. If you are killed by people when you get old, you can take out my eye balls." Then Ksitigarbha pushed the king demon onto the earth in the shape of a bull, but all its upper teeth got broken. So it had to help people with the cultivation.

Ten years later, when the bull was too old to plow the field, he was killed indeed. The bull was so angry that it went to the Buddha, took out his eyes and threw them into the river. The eyes turned into escargots. The Jade Emperor was so infuriated that he broke into a torrent of abuse at the bull and punished it by making it a field plower forever without the possibility of returning to the heavenly palace.

Ksitigarbha was still preoccupied with human sufferings and he listened to what people were telling him because of sight loss. The Goddess of Mercy sent him a bottle of liquid which allowed him to regain his eyesight for one day in a year. To commemorate him, on the night of the 30th of the seventh month, folks would stick incense as offerings to him.

Temple Fair

Temple fair, also known as temple market or market, is a religious custom that is held during the Spring Festival and the Lantern Festival among the Han ethnic groups. As a form of village fair trades, temple fair has formed and developed under the influence of religious activities. It is held in temples or nearby across the country, with events including some offering sacrifices to gods, entertainment and shopping activities. Temple fair is a wide-spread traditional activity of folkways, with rich folkway flavor of of Han nationality. It is a cultural life created, enjoyed and passed on by the general public. Temple fair forms part of the cultural life. The way the fair was formed and evolved has a stake on people's life.

Famous temple fairs in Ningbo include Gaoqiao Fair of western Yinzhou, Zeshan Fair of Cixi, Rice Flower Fair of Fenghua, God-Welcoming Fair of northwestern Yuyao and Lord Hugong Birthday Party of Ninghai(Lord Hugong refers to Hu Ce, an upright official in the Northern Song Dynasty who loved and took good care of people). At that time, we can see many activities including dragon and lion dances, Yangge, stilts-walking, folk music and others, their parading stretching several kilometers. It happens when tens of thousands of people flock to streets to take part in the spectacular events. For example, Yinjiang Temple Fair is a traditional folk activity that integrates sacrifices offering, songs and dances, entertainment and business. It is on the list of Intangible Cultural Heritage under state-level protection. Temple fairs are held for three times on 3rd March, 6th June, 10th and October (Lunar Calendar), with the 10th October fair being the grandest.

After the founding of the PRC in 1949, temple fairs phased out and was replaced by massive cultural artistic festivals and commodity festival, among others.

Kitchen God worshiping

Kitchen God worshiping Day, which falls on the 23rd of December by Lunar Calendar, is also known as Songzao Day, Cizao Day, Small Spring Festival or Small New Year's Eve. Ningbo people traditionally get up early and offer sacrifices in front of the Kitchen God. In the night, they lit incense to honor the God. Sacrifice fruits are a priority. Sugar and fodders, coupled with ripe soybeans and a cup of water make up a good offering. People lit incense and offered shoe-shaped gold ingot and prayed to God. Kids shared the fruits.

The local folkway has it that men don't worship the moon and women don't worship the Kitchen God. In fact, men offer sacrifices, followed by women's worshiping. Offerings vary according to what individual households can afford. The rich could offer 24 dishes, including needle mushrooms, wood ear, tendon, pork skin, peanuts, melon seeds, malt sugar and cakes, tangerines, chufa, sugarcane, tofu, red dates, preserved fruits, among others. The poor could do with a section of sugarcane. On that day, when incense filled the kitchen, the Kitchen God would not see things clearly, so the owner would place new chopsticks on the desk so that the God could touch them and understand that the family should have a baby and deliver more wealth to its members.

After the ceremony, children started eating malt sugar and cakes. The custom stemmed from people's worship for fire and fire god. In ancient times, people used fire to warm themselves up, illuminate the night, and cook food. That is how they started worshiping fire as a God. With the advent of ovens, fire god turned into the Kitchen God.

A folk song in Ningbo entitled worshiping the Kitchen God goes as follows: "it is 23rd of December again, the Kitchen God is to rise to the heaven. Get the forage, mix the spice, and feed the horse, cover the avenue, cross the bridge, Kitchen God gets to the heaven in a few minutes. Do not forget the people who offer you sweets, before the Jade emperor say for them nice words. Always say good words and never evil, come back with grain of various kinds. Also bring fat boys to your subjects, you will be loved by all people and couples. Fruits and dishes will be offered to you on eve of the new year, from the countrymen you will get great receptions. Bring people favors and never troubles, you will be worshipped by the juniors and seniors."

Small New Year's Eve is still celebrated in Ningbo. It is a prelude to the New Year's Eve and the Spring Festival. The day has a rich festival atmosphere, marking the beginning of the New Year holiday.

Preparing New Year Rice Cake

Niangao, or rice cake, means making progress every year by its Chinese characters. That is why Ningbo people eat rice cake during the Spring Festival. Niangao in Ningbo, known as finely ground rice cake, differs from that in other places as it is deliciously chewy and delicate and no pasty tastes can be found. Many overseas Chinese from Ningbo miss the delicacy very much as Niangao elsewhere is not as good as that in Ningbo.

What is now called Shanghai White Rice Cake is Ningbo rice cake indeed. New rice is selected and ground into rice milk. It will be squeezed into pieces after it was steamed. It tastes soft, delicate and chewy after being squeezed into stripes. That is the way Niangao is commercially produced. In the past, Ningbo people saw Niangao making an important part of the Spring Festival. Children knew that rice had to be soaked in water for a couple of days before it could be ground into powder. On the 25th and 26th of January in the Lunar Calendar, men would wash clean rice and made rice cakes after they have been soaked in the water for some time. Then they put a big stone molar in the courtyard with a wooden hammer and a smasher made of stone and wood. Children would watch how their father struck the rice with gusto.

The more people strike, the more chewy the rice cake will come out. After half a day, women rub it into stripes with a red stamp on each one. Children couldn't wait but eat them in the middle of the cake making process. They rub and eat them at the same time, making much fun.

Shousui

Ningbo people are used to Shousui, staying up late on the New Year's Eve, when every household lights up and sets off firecrackers from time to time until daybreak comes.

An interesting legend has it that a long time ago, there was a demon living in

Mountain Taibai of Ningbo. The monster spewed so much water that it flooded houses and farmland, and it also made the sun unbearably hot and caused barrenness to the field. In an effort to avert the disasters, people had to cook delicious dishes to offer the monster in exchange for peaceful days.

Many years later, a wine master called Qingshui came to Ningbo for a visit. He detested the demon as it plunged the people into misery. In an attempt to help the locals, the master sought to make a special wine that could make the monster asleep a whole year. He referred to many types of wine books and as a result collected 11 kinds of rice and ciderage that weighed 16.5 kilograms. It took him three years before he finally managed to make a kind of strong liquor.

On the first day of the Spring Festival, Master Qingshui found himself, together with a couple of his students, drunken and soundly asleep on the ground after they merely smelt the fascinating wine he made. The demon couldn't resist the fragrance of the wine, so it went down the mountain and drank it immediately. But it fell asleep after going back to the mountain, murmuring "Good wine". The strong wine could only put the monster to sleep for 364 days and when the next New Year's Eve came, the demon woke up and came to cause mischief to the people. The master meant to make it drink again or offer sacrifices while preparing firecrackers to scare it off. Each household offered livestock, fruits and wines and cutting bamboos into pieces for burning fire. It turned out that the monster, tempted by the fragrant wine, came to the people but was hurt by firecrackers. As a result, it ran away out of fear, and never came back. The master, however, was so excited that he passed away the day the demon was scared off. As part of efforts to commemorate the savior, the general public offered sacrifices, including liquor, meat and fruits, and set off firecrackers. That is how the custom has persisted.

5. Crafts and Specialties

5.1 Famous Arts and Crafts

Ningbo Cinnabar and Gold Lacquer Woodcarving

Ningbo cinnabar and gold lacquer woodcarving is an ancient architectural decorative art featuring wood carvings. Excellent materials like camphor wood, bass wood, and Chinese gingko are selected for Ningbo cinnabar and gold lacquer woodcarving, which utilizes both carving and painting skills. The main techniques used are relief carving, openwork carving and circular carving. Making a piece involves a series of steps, including base carving, fine carving, polishing, paint rubbing and patching gold, to make it elegant, brilliant and resistant to erosion.

Ningbo cinnabar and gold lacquer woodcarving is mainly about joyous events and folklore. The tableau is carved in simple and unsophisticated style with extraordinary skills. The scenes, drawing materials from Beijing operas, are substantial and colorful, making the woodcarving both artistic and practical.

268

The craft has a long history, lasting from the Han Dynasty to the Tang and Song Dynasties. It is used extensively, from articles used in daily life such as wooden beds and bridal sedan chairs to buildings including temples and ancestral halls. The magnificent sedan chair in Ningbo Baoguo Temple is a prime example of the craft. From its crimson-lacquered floor upward, the elaborate ornamental engraving spread all over its richly gilded wooden body implanted with crystal glasses. On the whole, the sedan chair is composed symmetrically with delicate and intricate skills. Its top alone comprises 7 layers. On the sedan chair are carved nearly a thousand objects, including 24 phoenixes, 38 dragons, 54 cranes, 174 magpies, 92 lions, 22 eagles, 22 mantis, 12 angels, 124 pomegranates, 18 magpies on plum tree branches, 12 squirrels stealing grapes, and 250 ancient characters to reflect auspicious themes. From the complex patterns, one can see the immortals bestowing their blessing, the qilin sending a child, the god of literature selecting the best student, the top scholar taking an honorable position, the eight deities crossing the sea, the maid Wang Zhaojun Going beyond the Great Wall, the dutiful daughter Hua Mulan joining the army for her father, the great calligrapher Wang Whiz Pitying a crane and the poet Lin Heading herding cranes. Besides, the sedan chair is decorated with embroidered curtains, tassel, palace lanterns and bells, which produce pleasing sound when the chair is moved.

With the founding of PRC, Ningbo cinnabar and gold lacquer woodcarving met its prime time of development. It has been widely used in architects as decorations. Products with this art craft, like screens, cabinets, ancient figures, Buddhas, lions, and lanterns, are widely exported to countries around the world, and have received widespread welcome from all corners.

The woodcarving craft spread to Japan as early as the Tang Dynasty. During monk Jianzhen's second journey to Japan in 743, the crew and passengers encountered a storm in Zhengzhou(now Ningbo) and were placed by local officials in Asoka Temple, where he studied Ningbo handicrafts. Later he brought craftsmen of Ningbo cinnabar and gold lacquer woodcarving with him and successfully arrived in Japan in 753. He lived in Toyoda Temple in Cara and made a made a thousand-hand Bodhisattva more than 8. 3 meters in height with the craft there. Besides, Toshiba Temple, set up by Jian zhen and his followers, was decorated in Ningbo cinnabar and gold lacquer woodcarving as well as some figures dedicated to the Buddha. Ningbo cinnabar and gold lacquer woodcarving has become the testimony of the friendship between China and Japan.

269

Lacquer

Ningbo boasts a long history of lacquer making. In the 7000-year-old Hemmed Culture Site, a vermilion wooden bowl was unearthed, an evidence of this antique process of lacquer making in Ningbo.

China was the first country to use natural lacquer in the world, the use of lacquer is recorded in Han Feint (280 B. C. —233 B. C..), which says: "In ancient times, Lao abdicated the throne to Shun. People cut wood to make utensils. After cutting and polishing, apply acquire on it, and it is taken to the court as food utensil, ⋯ ⋯ King Au used it for worshiping, making it black outside and red inside ⋯ " Japan also has documents which says: "The use of Slackware originated in ancient China." According to extant historical records, Ningbo became a lacquer production site with its own styles in the Tang Dynasty, and since then has exerted big influence in Japan.

In the Tang Dynasty, jacquard production in Ningbo already achieved high level. In the Ming Dynasty, the production level became higher. According to *A General History of Shijiazhuang*: "During the Andean Years of the Ming Dynasty, Ningbo was famous for its illuminated painting and gold lacquer."

Ningbo lacquerware uses the Chinese raw acquire as its raw material, wood or bamboo as its base plate. It falls into three varieties: relief patterns, flat patterns, and sub-patterns. Relief patterns are art craft landscape miniatures heaped on acquire coating; when the heaped landscape miniatures get tough enough, gold color will be applied; flat patterns are paintings made on acquire coating; sub-patterns are decorative patterns made under the acquire coating. Poet Ba Juicy of the Tang Dynasty praised lacquerware in this way: "Jewels, diamonds, and micas get here for a meeting place, like a cornucopia of treasures vying for brilliance. "

Lacquerware from Ningbo was introduced to Japan in the Tang Dynasty, and the technology was developed there. Master Monk Jianzhen lived in Ningbo for some time before he departed for Japan. He gathered lacquer wares here and brought them to Japan. So the lacquerware technology was used in the making of Buddha statues for the Toshiba Temple. Later along with the increase of cultural exchanges, China and Japan learned from each other in lacqureware technology. The skills of material selection, process operation, and even designs and patterns used by Japanese in refined lacquer, green lacquer, liquid gold decoration, mother-of-pearl inlaying, and mica application are very similar with those used in Ningbo. The famous ancient warehouse Syosoin in Nara of Japan now still contains many lacquarewares of the Sui and Tang Dynasties from Ningbo. In addition, the Buddha statues and furniture made with ramie lacquer were also introduced to Japan, which influenced the craft skills used in Buddha and furniture making there and gradually evolved to be a unique Japanese craft skill-Maki.

Ningbo's lacquerware has experienced ups and downs during the thousands years of development. Since the founding of the PRC in 1949, the craft has been further developed, and today lacquerware has been an important export of the city. The products include screens, stools, tea tables, fruit trays, TV closets, cupboards, bookcases and writing tables, etc., all with carvings vivid, colorful and elegant.

Ningbo Inlay

Ningbo inlay is among the most outstanding Chinese ancient handicrafts. It had been well developed in the Sui and Tang dynasties (7th-9th centuries). When the time elapsed into the Qianlong period and the Daoguang Period of the Qing Dynasty, the bone and wooden inlay technique had been well known with its unique local flavor and exquisite craftsmanship. It was parallel to the mother-of-pearl inlay of Yangzhou and the ivory inlay of Guangzhou. The Ningbo inlay products were presented as tributes to the imperial courts, which are still displayed at the Summer Palace in Beijing.

Ningbo inlay falls into relief inlay and flat inlay. Relief inlays are bumped patterns and flat inlays are kept at the same level with the wooden base. In making inlay products, ivories, shells, wooden plates or copper plates are sawn into laces, which are inlaid into the wooden base and carved into decorative patterns. They are often used in architectures and furniture.

The bone and wood inlay craft, together with the gold and lacquer wood carving, was introduced to Japan by monk Jianzhen (688 A. D.—763A. D.) during the Tang Dynasty. Today's Toshodai Temple of Japan has kept inlaid crafts introduced from Mingzhou (Ningbo in the Tang Dynasty), and the monks are still using the inlaid chessboards introduced from Mingzhou. The inlaid patterns carry elegant classic beauty, and the carving has exquisite craftsmanship. According to historical records of Japan, Jianzhen brought to Japan embroidered images, paintings, carvings, sculptures, golden and bronze statues, inlaid bone and wood Buddhist utensils. The artcraft used in these objects, including image-making and carving, served as examples for the statue making and temple architectures for Japan.

Despite of long history, Ningbo inlay artcraftsmanship almost got lost before the founding of the PRC. Then after New China was founded, it was rejuvenated and a lot of new skills have been invented. Now, this traditional art has been extensively applied in the making of chairs, rocking chairs, tables, tea tables, screens, cupboards, cabinets and hanging screens, producing an effect similar to that of traditional Chinese painting, vivid and true to life.

Ningbo Embroidery

Ningbo embroidery is a traditional art boasting a long history. In the Ming and

Qing dynasties, the market of Ningbo embroidered fabric was greatly developed. It was seen in every household in Ningbo. Embroidery products were sold to the countries in Southeast Asia. From that time, Ningbo embroidery has been on a par with Suzhou embroidery, Hunan embroidery and Sichuan embroidery. According to Annals of Yin County, in 1932 there were as many as 15,000 embroidery products produced in Ningbo.

Ningbo embroidery has a unique local style with the general composition of pictures and beautiful colors including black, gray, cyan, strong brown, sienna, and celadon. There are many different stitches such as slanting needle, fibula, fat needle, silk reeling, silk clipping, drawnwork, and node needle. When the needlework has been finished, soutache embroidery will be used for its decoration with cannetille. The patterns are mostly based on traditional pictures such as dragon, phoenix, peony, and birds. With those beautiful patterns, the embroidery has the flavor of antiquity and elegance.

Different materials are used in Ningbo embroidery, such as authentic silk and rayon. Cannetilles are used to line up the patterns. The embroidery thus made take on a peculiar style of elegance.

For the past few years, Ningbo embroidery has been upgraded constantly. Now it is not only artwork, but also for daily use. Besides, it could serve as quality tourist souvenirs and gifts for friends. Zhao Puchu, the late vice president of Chinese People's

Political Consultative Conference and a well-noted Buddhist and social activist, highly credited the Ningbo embroidery when he visited Ningbo in 1978. He gave high remarks to Ningbo embroidery by saying that it is highly ingenuous, reflects of both ancient and current tastes, presents exotic flavors and wonderful stitch work.

Ningbo embroidery craftsman have tried to absorb foreign advanced methods while inheriting and developing the traditional aircrafts, promoting the art to a higher level. The large screen of Ningbo embroidery named "Hundreds of Cranes in Morning Sun" won a Hundred Flowers Awards for arts and crafts in 1989 and thus was collected by China Art Gallery.

Fanhuang Bamboo Carving

The Fanhuang bamboo carving is a traditional craft of Ningbo. In making carved bamboo ware, moso bamboos are first skin-removed and sliced, then molded and drawn with colors, and finally fine-carved and lacquered.

Bamboo carving enjoys a long history in China. Legend goes that back in the Wanli Period of the Ming Dynasty, Zhu Sulin's family in Jiading (a county in Zhejiang) cut drawings on bamboos, which became artwork most favored by the people. As East Zhejiang abounded in bamboo, the technique soon spread and there emerged many masterpieces.

Fenghua of Ningbo, a place with abundant moso bamboos, has a history of 100 years of bamboo carving. Before the New China was founded in 1949, there were quite a number of workshops of bamboo carving in Fenghua, such as Yi Su Zhai, Pauper Art Institute and Bamboo Product Company. The Ningbo Museum has a big collection of bamboo carving artcrafts produced by these workshops.

The moso bamboos used for carving must be fresh ones of large caliber and long bamboo joints. To make a bamboo carving, craftsmen need first to take out the yellowish inside of bamboo (around 2 mm thick), then boil it and fix it on a plate, a semi finished product, in a seamless way. After polishing, it will be carved, painted or decorated. The yellowish color will come out clear and pure, like ivory. After painting and waxing, it will look bright and pleasing to the eye, parallel to jade carving or lacquerware.

Fenghua of Ningbo produces about 100 varieties of carved bamboo ware, including mirror chests, baskets, vases, lamps, chessboards, caddy, animal toys and big screens, with patterns of figures, flowers, birds, landscapes, etc. The carved products are featured by a combination of the traditional Chinese line drawing with the primitive simplicity of the seal stone carving. They are highly populous both at home and abroad for their functionality and aesthetics.

Silk Weaving

Ningbo, one of the three biggest trading ports in ancient China and one of the five treaty ports opened to the world after the Opium War (1840—1842), was once famous for silk weaving. The silk weaving in Ningbo used to be better known than that in Hangzhou, Jiaxing and Huzhou areas.

Ningbo is a place suitable for growing mulberries as it is seated on an alluvial plain with mountains as the backdrop, sandy soil and humid climate. China has a long history of raising silkworms. Mulberry trees are called Nüsang in *Er Ya*, the first ancient Chinese Dictionary and a collection of ancient classics. Nüsang means comes from mourning of a girl. According to the *Sou Shen Ji* (Notes on Search for Mythic Gods) by Gan Bao, a historian of the Eastern Jin Dynasty, long long time ago, a man went far away for business, leaving his daughter and a horse at home. The daughter missed her father and one day, she said to the horse: "if you can find father and get him back, I will marry you." At her words, the horse broke away and found her father. Her father

came back with the horse, but the horse became manic upon sight of the girl. The father was curious and his daughter told him of her promise. The father killed the horse and basked the skin. His daughter kicked and skin and said: "You are a horse, how can you marry a human? You were courting death for yourself." Hardly had she finished her words before the horse skin leaped up and rolled the girl and flew away. Later the girl was found with the skin between twigs of a tree, but now she had become a silkworm within a cocoon. Mulberry can mean death or mourning when it is pronounced in Chinese.

Silkworm breeding in Ningbo dates back to 7,000 years ago, as is shown by an ivory carved with cocoons unearthed in the Hemudu Culture Site. Turning silk into silk fabrics has been evidenced in many historical records of China. The Hou Han Shu, or History of the Eastern Han Dynasty, recorded a story about a wife weaving silk on a loom, which was more than 2,000 years ago. In the Tang and Song Dynasties, there were about 1,000 households breeding silkworms, producing about 5,000 kilograms of silk. Poets in the Ming and Qing Dynasties also wrote about silk weaving in Ningbo. The tribute silk produced in Mingzhou is most suitable for making summer dresses. It is light, bright and felt cool. By the end of the Qianlong Period of the Qing Dynasty, Ningbo had got 850 silk looms, producing silk, damask silk, silk fabric, satin, and tough silk. At that time, silk weaving became such a trade that nine out of ten households engaged themselves in silkworm raising and mother-of-pearl breeding, especially in the villages of Zhangcun and Miyan. Later on, with advancement of technology, the production of silk was gradually shifted to mechanization from manual labor. Up to 1932, there were about 1,000 looms in Ningbo, producing thousands of kilograms of various silk products each year.

Ningbo's silk products and weaving technology have been well-known home and abroad since ancient times. The silk products of Ningbo have been important out-bound products. Back in the Tang Dynasty, they were exported to Japan, known as Silk from the Tang Dynasty. "People all like to wear the Tang Silk", as stated in the Record of the Clear Moon by a famous writer Fujiwara Sadaie. The technology of silk weaving was soon introduced to Hakata of Japan, the port that maintained transportation links with Ningbo. Hakata then became the center of silk trade in Japan and the weaving technique got the name of Hakata weaving. Ningbo's silk products not only went to Japan and Korea, but to Indonesia, Cambodia, Vietnam, Iran and other lands.

Later on, with the dumping of artificial silk from Japan and the decline of silkworm cocoon production in Ningbo, the silk business in Ningbo was on decline around 1949. Since the founding of the PRC, silk weaving factories have been established one after another and business is booming again. Above all, the quality is on the rise, too.

Porcelain

The history of porcelain of Ningbo is about 2,000 years, dating back to the celadon ware produced in the Yue Kiln in Yuyao.

Ningbo is the birthplace of the Yue celadon. Archeologists found that China already had pottery ware 8,000 years ago and that porcelain began to appear in the East Zhou Period and celadon began in the Eastern Han Dynasty. As Ningbo was part of the Yue Kingdom, the celadon kilns in Ningbo were called Yue Kilns. Yue Kilns were located near the Shanglin Lake of Cixi, scattering around Baze Lake, Du Lake, Shang'ao Lake and Yinding Lake, totaling about 120. The celadon baking began in the Eastern Han Dynasty and got prospered in the Tang and Song dynasties. The celadon works in the earlier periods were simple and rough, while in the later periods (Tang and Song dynasties) they appeared more delicate and smooth, similar to jade items. The celadon works produced in the Shanglin Lake area were soon taken as tribute to the Court. In addition to resplendent and crystal glaze, the decorative patterns were diversified:

dragons in water, phoenixes in sunshine, butterflies in pairs, peacock showing off features, mandarin ducks kissing each other, flying cranes in the air, birds amid flowers, tortoise with water lily, fish with water chestnut, parrot holding branch, fairies, monks and performers, to name just a few.

Celadon products from the Yue Kilns are most famous for its glittering and translucent glazing color and colorful patterns. According to the Classic of Tea by Lu Yu, "in terms of the quality of porcelain bowls, those from the Yue Kiln are the best, followed by those from Dingzhou, Maozhou, Yuezhou, Shouzhou and Hongzhou. Some people take the porcelain of Xingzhou as better than Yuezhou, But I think otherwise. First, porcelain from Xingzhou looks like silver, but those from Yuezhou look like jade; second, the porcelain from Xingzhou resembles snow, but those from Yuezhou resembles ice; third, porcelain from Xingzhou are white and looks pale, while the porcelain from Yuezhou looks blue and green".

More than 140,000 celadon items produced in Yue Kilns were presented as tributes to the Court and many more were exported abroad each year. Via the Mingzhou Port (Ningbo Port), the celadon exports went to Japan, Korea, Vietnam, Cambodia, Malaysia, the Philippines, India, East Africa and North Africa. A great many celadon relics have been discovered in India, Iran, Egypt and Japan, which well proved that Ningbo was the starting port of the Celadon Route by Boat.

Celadon items produced by Yue Kilns are as crystal as jades but not showy, like ice but not cheap. A poem by Shi Jianwu of the Tang Dynasty praises it in this way:

> Fresh Sichuan tea made in celadon from Yue Kiln,
> When stirred, from the green water arises smoke thin,
> When asked by the monk what the tea can be likened to,
> I want to say good wine, but hesitated, thinking that is a taboo.

Now porcelains produced in Yuyao have been fully developed along with the advancement of new technology and modern art and culture. Having inherited the traditional technology, researchers have worked out dozens of new recipes and successfully developed the fine china and the bone china. The fine china is clean as jade, smooth as mirror, and can produce voice as resonant as chime. The cooking utensils made of the fine china are white and pure, with crystal glaze, varied patterns, lively human and animal figures. They really provide a feast for the eyes and are considered comparable with the porcelain from Jingdezhen. The bone china is a new invention in Zhejiang Province, with various products most favored by consumers.

Grassmat

Grassmat is a specialty in Yinzhou District of Ningbo. Locals at Huanggulin Town started to make grassmats long ago as the natural conditions (climate and soil) were good for mat grass growing. The grass is light green, straight and even, thin and elastic. Mats made of the grass are soft and smooth and elastic. It is easy to roll up for storage when not in use. When to be used, it is generally cleaned with warm water. Then it is not only polished but gives off a delicate fragrance. The mat falls into white hemp mats and green hemp mats, with the former better in quality than the later.

Huanggulin enjoys a long history of grassmat making. Local annals say the grassmats from Mingzhou (Ningbo) were traded to all over China and other lands in the Tang, Song and Ming dynasties. The grassmat business of Ningbo went to its prime time in the Qing Dynasty when the mats were exported to Southeast Asia, Europe and Africa. Premier Zhou Enlai presented 40 Ningbo grassmats to foreign friends when he attended the Geneva Conference in 1954.

Ningbo grassmat is well known for its good quality, variety and exquisite craftsmanship. It even made a contribution in the war against the aggression of the troops of the Jin Dynasty. The story goes that about 800 years ago, Zhao Gou, or Emperor Gaozong of the Southern Song Dynasty, turned Lin'an (now Hangzhou) to be the new capital of the Song Dynasty after the previous capital was taken over by the troops of the Jin Dynasty. As his new dynasty was new and his military forces were weak, he could not repel the invaders of the Jin Troops. He gave up his new capital and came to Ningbo in 1129 A.D. As Ningbo was near the sea, he prepared ships and was ready to escape to the sea when the Jin troops came. In 1130 A.D., Jin Troops came. They crossed the Qiantang River, occupied Shaoxing and Yuyan, and came all the way to Mingzhou(Ningbo), Emperor Zhao Gou was shocked, he got on the ship with his subjects and concubines and departed for Dinghai on Zhoushan Island. But thanks to General Zhang Jun, who fought resolutely with his troops and repelled the enemies. The Jin troops retreated and stationed at Yuyao and asked for help from Jin Wuzhu, their Commander-In-Chief, who was infuriated and dispatched more soldiers to Mingzhou. General Zhang Jun came to the front at Gaoqiao, where he expected to fight against the enemies. He rode on a horse and inspected the positions, but suddenly horse slipped and rolled over with four legs in the air. General Zhang was overturned into slush and mat. He got up to find out that there are a few pieces of mats, and understood that the horse slipped because of the mat. He got an idea, and immediately convened the local civilians, asking them help fighting against the Jin invaders by laying mats on the roads. People were ready to help and followed his advice. The next day, Song Dynasty troops first hid themselves at Gaoqiao, and sent a small number of soldiers to seduce the enemy troops. The soldiers pretended to be defeated and led the enemy troops to the places where mats were laid. The Jin troops on horses got on the mats and many of the horses slipped and overturned. The soldiers in the back of the troops did not know what took place in the front and urged their horses on, and more got overturned and the troops got into confusion. At that time, the Song Dynasty troops came out from their shelters and pounced upon the enemies and killed many of the enemy soldiers. Jin Wuzhu and his soldiers ran away in stampede. In ancient times, Jin soldiers were called Dazi, after this fighting, people began to call mat Huazi(Hua means slippery). Huazi was used to refer to mats in honor of its contribution to the defeat of invaders.

Ningbo grassmats enjoy great popularity home and abroad, with yearly production of millions of pieces. They go to all parts of China, as well as Japan, Southeast Asia, Hong Kong and other countries and regions.

5.2 Famous Snacks and Dishes

Xikou Qianceng Cookies

Xikou Qianceng Cookie is a traditional snack of Xikou, Fenghua, the hometown of Chiang Kai-shek. It is square, with 27 layers, of golden color tinted with green. It is crisp, sweet, a bit salty and has been popular among consumers.

The history of Qianceng cookies is about 100 years. Legend has it that a local named Wang Maolong started to make the cookie in Xikou in 1882. Later on, his brother added some sea sedge powder to the recipe, which made it more delicious. Ever since, the recipe of sea sedge became widespread soon.

The cookies are made of choice materials: quality flour, refined and unboiled oil, sesame, sugar and sea sedge powder. In making it, 12 steps are needed, like mixing, steaming, filling, layer-making, baking and packing, etc. Each cookie, of 1.5 cm in thickness, has 27 layers, making the cookie crisp, sweet and delicious. The cookies have won some national and provincial awards for famous special local products.

As a famous local snack, the Qianceng cookie is most favored by tourists and the natives residing overseas. It is not only popular in east Zhejiang, but also in Japan, Southeast Asian countries, Hong Kong and other lands.

Dragon and Phoenix Golden Cake

Dragon and Phoenix Golden Cake is one of the top ten Ningbo local snacks, and particularly well-known in East Zhejiang. The most famous cake is prepared by Zhao Dayou Restaurant, a well-known restaurant in Ningbo for its Ningbo local snacks and cakes.

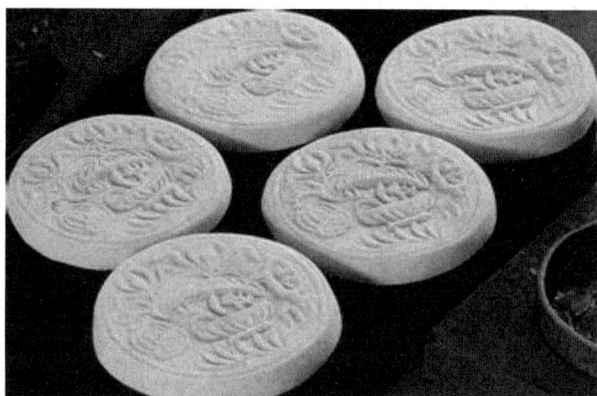

The history of the snack dates back to the South Song Dynasty (1127 A.D.—1279 A.D.). Legend goes that when the Jin invaders seized the capital of the South Song Lin'an (present Hangzhou), Zhao Gou the emperor fled to Mingzhou (present Ningbo) and there a village girl saved his life and served him food including a cake. When Zhao Gou recaptured the capital, he repaid his savior by naming the cake he ate in his refugee "Dragon and Phoenix Golden Cake" and from then on the cake has become a snack that must be served at weddings, symbolizing happiness of married life. Golden in color and with pattern of a dragon and phoenix, the cake is made of polished glutinous rice, with fillings of processed beans, sugar, orange peel, osmanthus flowers, and so on.

Shops of the gold cake were scattered here and there in the city. The most famous old brand was Zhaodayou. This brand was created by a Mr. Zhao from Shangyu. When the cake is made, 2 kilos of glutinous rice is mixed with3 kilos of stem rice, which is immersed in water for 10 — 14 hours depending on the temperature. Then the rice mixture is taken out from water, put into clear water again to rid the sour taste, then the rice is ground into powder. Asparagus bean or soybean is used as the filling, 0.75 kilos of the rice mixed with one kilo of sugar, other ingredient are orange cake, melon seeds, orange chips, red and green shreds. Then came the process of fry, sufficient but not to be scorched. When Mr. Zhao Dayou ran the business, he used the best materials, and was very careful in the making. He also charged reasonable price, and treated all customers well. Therefore, he became famous among the citizens. Thus Zhao Dayou became a brand, and many shops named themselves Zhao Dayou, thus we have a number of cake shops in Ningbo named Zha Dayou with a little variation.

The gold cake is an auspicious symbol, symbolizing happiness and reunion, mostly served in ceremonious occasions, such as weddings, birthday parties, etc.

Among different varieties of Zhao Dayou gold cakes, Dragon and Phoenix cakes are most popular. It is shaped like a moon, and yellow in color as gold, with reliefs of Dragon and Phoenix on the front, symbolizing reunion and auspiciousness. It has thin outer layer and rich filling, with fragrant and pleasant flavor, and appealing to whoever tries it.

Cicheng New Year Cake

The New Year Cake is a special food that the locals will prepare when the Spring Festival is coming each year. It uses selected raw materials and employs meticulous production process. It is made with high quality japonica rice, washed clean first, soaked for 3 — 4 days or one week, ground into pulp, pressed it and get it half dried and crushed, put it into steamer box and get it fully steamed. Then pound it, and finally cut it into different bar-shaped cakes.

Every year when the spring festival comes, the locals of Ningbo will be busy preparing for the holiday. One of the most important item of food to be prepared is the cake. This is partly because niangao, the Chinese pronunciation for the rice cake, is

similar to that of "Happy New Year". As Cicheng is the most famous production place of Niangao, therefore it is called Cicheng Niangao. As the rice cake is favored by the seniors and the juniors alike, the rich and the poor, therefore it is a very popular food. People use different plates to press various auspicious words on the cake, such as Happiness, Fortunes, Best Wishes, and also lovely animals are pressed on the cake, such as rabbits, goose, etc. In 1974, archaeologist unearthed remains of full grains of rice seeds at the Hemudu ancient cultural site, an evidence that our ancestors grew rice more than 7,000 years ago. And the cake-production history of Cicheng also lasted for more than 1,000 years. Legend goes that General Wu Zixu of the Wu state at the end of the Spring-Autumn Period once fought at Cicheng of Ningbo. Before he died here, he said to his subordinates: "If mishap befalls us and people starve, dig at the foot of the city wall for three Chis(one meter), you can get grain." Then soon after his death, the city was surrounded by the Yue troops, and many people starved to death. Then people remembered the words of General Wu, then they dug at the foot of the city wall, and got plenty of food shaped like city wall bricks. The troops got enough to eat and defeated the enemy. It turned out that General Wu, when he monitored the construction of the city walls, he prepared food for the arrival of hard times. After that, every year before spring festival comes, the locals of Cicheng made niangao to remember General Wu.

Ningbo Dumpling with Leaf Lard Filling (Zhuyou-Tangtuan)

In Ningbo, as in all China, sweet dumpling (Tangtuan) is a symbol of family reunion and happiness and in Ningbo it is a local custom for all family members to have dumplings on the morning of the first day of the lunar year.

Tangtuan is also named Yuanxiao, which originated from the Sui Dynasty. On the Lantern Festival of 610 A.D., Emperor Yang entertained his courtiers and concubines with Tangtuan soup. As it was on the Lantern Festival, the food was called Yuanxiao (Lantern Festival). When Tangtuan was introduced to Ningbo, locals used glutinous rice flour to make it and stuffed it with leaf fat, which tasted even more delicious.

Folklore has it that when Lu Tungpin, one of the Eight Taoist Immortals, turned into an old peddler, was selling Tangtuan by the West Lake, Xu Xian bought it. When he was eating it, one Tangtuan ball rolled into the lake and was swallowed by the White Snake, who turned into an immortal afterwards. Later, the White Snake and Xu Xian got married. A story also goes that when foreigners came into Ningbo after the Opium War, they were amazed at the delicious Tangtuan but had no idea how the filling got into the ball.

Ningbo has a history of 700 years in the production of tangtuan. It is made of glutinous rice, with a nickname — "suspended pulp tangtuan". When making, people first use 50 kilos of glutinous rice, ground into pulp, suspended in a cloth bag for dripping. When it is no longer sticky, it is used to make the dumplings. The dumplings thus made is thin-skinned, smooth, white and shiny, glutinous but not sticky. The filling is made with leaf lard and sesame powder, mixed with sugar. When being boiled, the dumplings float, a little cold water is added, that will end the process of making. In the old times, dumplings could be eaten only during spring festival. This made people long for this delicacy, especially the children.

However, to enjoy the most delicious Tangtuan, one has to go to Gang Ya Gou sweet food buffet, as saying goes: "Home-made dumplings are common things, but nothing is better than the dumplings in Gang Ya Gou," a time-honored brand in Ningbo.

"Gang Ya Gou" (water vat, sheldrake and dog), founded by Jiang Dingfa in 1926, is a hundred-year-old shop in Ningbo, famous for its snacks. Jiang Dingfa's childhood name was Agou (namely a dog), so he was called Jiang Agou. When he opened a snackbar on the Kaiming Street he had a water vat, a sheldrake and a dog painted on the billboard to attract clients. This logo worked and people flocked to his snackbar, and then his business expended and prospered. A popular ditty goes as follows: At three or four you are starving, go to Gang Ya Gou for leaf lard dumpling; All the money spent and you do not want to leave, take off your clothes as deposit you beg continuing.

Qingkuai and Mazi

Qingkuai and mazi are snacks popular during the Qingming Festival (around April 5).

Qingkuai, also called green dumpling, is made of glutinous rice flour and folium artemisiae argyi (FAA) leaves. As FAA is fragrant, the Qingkuai with that gives off a special fragrant flavor. When making, the steamed glutinous powder is rubbed repeatedly and made smooth and moderate in hardness and uniform in color, then it is turned into a long bar-shaped dough, and cut into small chunks, then bean paste or soybean paste in put into the chunks, which is rubbed into green balls and steamed for a few minutes. Before taken for food, it is applied with sesame oil. Qingkuai is fresh green, soft, glutinous and fragrant, It is a traditional food for the Qingming Festival.

A legend goes that in ancient times, people used to have tails of ten sections. When nine sections of the tail turned yellow, people knew they were to die. One man with nine yellow sections of tail went to the mountain, dug a whole, climbed into the whole and waited for death. Before death, he covered himself with a layer of mazi, on it spread pine flowers. When he was hungry, he bit a monthful of Mazi. But he did not die until he was over 100 years. People found that he lived longer because he ate something special, so people the Mazi left by him. Then when people went to visit tombs of their relatives, they ate Mazi. It gradually became a custom.

286

Crystal Sugar Turtle (Bingtang Jiayu)

Crystal Sugar Turtle, the number one of Ningbo top ten dishes. It takes on a yellow luster. It tastes glutinous and sleek, giving off the flavors of sweetness, tartness, fragrance, and saltiness. It retains heat as the turtle is cooked within the wrapping of the seed powder of Gorgon Euryale. Crystal Sugar Turtle is also known as "Number One Scholar Turtle". It was first cooked by the Zhuangyuan (Number One Scholar) Mansion Restaurant.

Legend goes that in the late the Qing Dynasty there was a small inn in the north bank of the Yongjiang River of Ningbo. The shopkeeper was well known for the dish of Crystal sugar turtle. This dish cooked by him has the flavor of faint scent, and its viscous, salty and sweet at the same time.

One day, two scholars came for drinking and enjoying the river scenery on their way to the capital for royal exams. When the servants asked what they wanted. The two scholars replied: Just bring all your specialties. "

The last dish was Crystal Sugar Turtle. It was shining brilliantly and had a delicate fragrance with the turtle head up. Impressed by its gluttonous and savory taste, the two scholars praised the dish highly and inquired about its name.

Seeing they were going for exams in the capital, the smart shop owner said that it was named "Number One Turtle". Thinking of it as a great name, the two scholars left with content.

When the exam results came out in the autumn, one of the scholars became zhuangyuan, the number one scorer. On his way back home, he came to the inn and ordered the "the Number One Dish" again. He said that the dish contributed to his success for its refreshing and nutritious efficacy. The owner made the dish with special efforts for the number one scholar and presented writing brush for the zhuangyuan to inscribe a name for the drinkery.

Being in a good mood, the zhuangyuan took the brush pen and wrote "Zhuangyuan Mansion" for the drinkery.

Afterwards, Zhuangyuan Mansion became a household name in the east of Zhejiang Province, and the dish became well-known domestically and overseas. Two other drinkeries "Yongjiang Zhuangyuan Mansion" and "Siming Zhuangyuan Mansion" were opened in Shanghai later on. Both of them are famous for good skills in cooking the dish.

Yellow Croaker with Rassica Juncea

Yellow croaker with rassica juncea is a famous local dish of Ningbo.

To make the dish, you need to take the following steps:

Cut a few openings on the back of the fish.

Cut salted brassica juncea leaves into little pieces and slice some winter bamboo shoots.

Fry the fish till the two sides turn yellow and then add some yellow wine.

Simmer the fish in a cover pot for a few minutes.

Add water, ginger, the brassica juncea, the bamboo shoots, salt, etc.

Boil it with big fire and then simmer it with low fire for a few minutes, till the soup turns milky. Then onion powder is added.

Yellow croaker with rassica juncea is crisp, fresh, nutritious and yummy. It is a most favorite dish among locals.

5.3   Local Specialties

Fenghua Ark Clam

Fenghua ark clams, boasting rich nourishment and fresh flavor, are one of the most well-known local specialties in Ningbo. Belonging to the family Arcidae under Bivalvia, the ark clam is also known as anadara granosa, Scapharca inflate and blood clam. This small-sized aquatic product with two white thin shells is cultured throughout the off-shore areas in Ningbo. Rich in nutrition, it is a kind of valuable food since ancient times, which can enrich the blood and promote digestion.

The mariculture of Fenghua ark clams boasts a long history. In 809 A. D. during the Tang Dynasty, Fenghua ark clams were among the list of "tributes for the imperial family". Every year, about 15 *dous* (150 litres) of ark clams were transported from Fenghua to the then capital Chang'an. The traverse covered several thousand kilometers and involved tens of thousands of labors. In 820 A. D. , Yuan Zhen, governor (Guanchashi) of East Zhejiang (headquartered in the current Shaoxing, Zhejiang), reported to Emperor Muzong upon seeing the labors' sufferings. Thanks to his efforts,

in 823 A.D., an imperial decree exempted people in Fenghua from the servitude brought by the transportation of ark clams, which greatly cheered the local people. This story was described in a poem in the Qing Dynasty:

> *Delicacies abound on the tidal-flat land of the sea to the east,*
> *Among them ark clam is the most prominent.*
> *A river there called Shanchuan yields the best clam,*
> *With good flavour, nutritious and wonderful taste.*
> *Yuanhe Emperors of the Tang gave it special preference,*
> *Decrees issued, demanding ark clams to the court transport.*
> *Thanks to governor with a heart that is compassionate,*
> *A petition to the throne, long distance of labor was exempt.*

Fenghua ark clams were mainly cultured in Jieqi and Chunhu. As was recorded in *Siming Xuzhi (Sequel Annuals of Siming)* in 1292, ark clams in Jieqi are fresh and crisp and can be naturally collected in winter or cultured in tidal flats. Located at the Shizikou in Xiangshan, Jieqi and Chunhu enjoy a favorable temperature and salinity, quality water and sediment rich in bait, providing a suitable environment for ark clams. The ark clams cultured there are large-sized, fat and fresh.

The mariculture of Fenghua ark clams can be dated back to the Yuan Dynasty and reached a substantial scale during the Ming Dynasty. As was recorded in *Feng Hua Xian Zhi(The Annals of Fenghua County)* in the Ming Dynasty, during the 24th year of the reign of Emperor Hongwu (1391), a piece of ark clam farm was 4.25 mu (about 0.283 hectares) and a piece of tidal flat for ark clams was 36 mu (2.4 hectares). Fed on diatoms, the ark clams is better to be farmed in ooze around estuaries or inner bays where there are restless tides, slight wind, small waves and constant fresh water. Ark clams usually become big enough after two years' mariculture. Building a dyke enclosing a part of the sea is the usual way of the mariculture of ark clams. The larval ark clams are mostly from Wendeng, Rongcheng and Rushan in Shandong Province and a few from Yueqing and Yuhuan. Ark clams are bred in winter and it is the best time to catch them from Slight Cold to Great Cold.

Ninghai Mud Crab

The mud crab, also named Scylla serrata or mangrove crab, belongs to the family Portunus trituberculatus under Crustacea. It prefers soft muddy bottoms as habitat and dig deep burrows where there is constant flow of fresh water. Mud crabs of Ningbo, featuring big size, fresh flavor and dark brown shell color, is a well-known quality sea product of Ningbo.

The mud crab has an oval shell and a flat body without hair. It has well-developed head and chest and is armed with a single pair of claws as well as legs resembling oars. Mud crabs can be caught and farmed throughout the year but those caught from the 3rd day to the 23rd day of the eighth lunar month are regarded as the best. Su Shi, a well-known poet, once wrote in his *You Mo* (*Mud Crabs*):

> *Yellow crab overy in the halfed shell calls for more wine,*
> *Snowy meat in the broken pincers is an augment to apetite.*

291

Mud crabs are fierce and aggressive, as has been recorded in many legends and poems. There is a legendary crab shrine in Jiangbin Park, Ningbo, which was built to memorize a fisherman who caught an enormous mud crab but in the end was killed by the crab's powerful claws. Another legend says that mud crabs are able to fight against tigers. As a saying goes, crabs in august are as fierce as tigers. An ancient poem *Zhu Xie (Boiling Crabs)* goes as follows:

> *In the kettle to and fro the crabs are crawling,*
> *Under it more and more firewood is added for burning.*
> *Remember old days how rampant you were walking?*
> *Tonight for you is the time of suffering.*

People in the offshore areas of Ningbo have long been engaged in the fishery of mud crabs. It is recorded in *Xiang Shan Xian Zhi (The Annals of Fenghua County)* that twenty fishermen from Hujiazhi Village sailed three local ships to catch mud crabs and sell them in Shanghai and Ningbo. Mud crabs will release the newly hatched larvae in shallow water in summer and bury themselves in holes during the winter. Taking advantage of these habits of mud crabs, people have developed many methods to catch them, for example, trawling, searching for holes where crabs hidden and digging holes to induce crabs. As wild mud crabs have a limited number, the offshore areas in Ningbo have started farming mud crabs in recent years, the scale of which has involved thousands of Chinese mu.

Mud crab meat boasts fresh and delicious taste and rich nutrition. One mud crab can be as heavy as 1 kilogram. It is a best dish to eat together with wine and to entertain guests. It is also an excellent tonic for woman in confinement and an effective "medicine" for children with enuresis.

Xidian Oyster

The oyster, also named ostrea gigas thunberg, is a member of the family Ostreoidea. There are mainly two kinds of oysters, that is, ostrea cucullata and southern oyster. The cultured oysters are mostly Ostrea cucullata, which is triangle with thin and fragile small shells. The oyster is a kind of shellfish seafood, which is regarded as one of the delicacies from the sea. Oysters usually cling to rocks in cluster. Whenever the tides come, they open their shells together, and feed on small living things when they get into their shells.

There are wild and cultured oysters. The wild ones are as big as thumbs and the meat is rather small. The culture of oysters is to place the larva on rocks in spring, choose some quality ones in summer and transplant them in autumn. After two years, the oysters can be collected.

Xidian is now the biggest production site of oysters in Zhejiang Province. The history of oyster culture in Xidian town, Ninghai County, can be dated back to 700 years ago. As is recorded in *Ning Hai Xian Zhi* (*The Annals of Ninghai County*), "on the Tiejiang River there are two small islands, which are 19 km away from Ninghai County. The one with flat land where an ancient temple stands is the then Xidian town. Feng Tangying, Jinshi (former third degree candidate in the imperial examination) in the Song Dynasty, retreated there to avoid social upheaval. Seeing the prosperous growth of oysters on rocks, he taught locals there to culture oysters on rocks. Oysters cultured there are deemed as the best." Tiejiang River mentioned in the annals is located at the Shizikou in Xiangshan port. It is a favorable place to culture oysters as it boasts clear and clam water, slight wind, broad tidal flats, fertile soil and constant inflow of fresh water from over 20 small rivers.

The oyster meat is a kind of nice sea food with high nutrition and is praised as "sea milk". The oyster meat can be eaten both cooked and uncooked and it can be cooked with eggs and boiled with noodles. Fried eggs with oysters are a specialty in Ningbo. Spring and winter are the seasons to eat oysters, especially during the Spring Festival when oysters are a nice dish to entertain guests.

The oyster can also be used as medicine. As is recorded in *Ben Cao Gang Mu* (*Compendium of Materia Medica*), oyster meat can help strengthen and detoxify the body and relieve thirst while the shells, after calcination for several hours, have astringent functions.

Changjie Razor Clam

Razor clam is a species of large marine bivalve mollusc in the family solenidae. It has an elongated oblong narrow shell inside which a groove extends from the upper part of the shell to the shell edge. The coastal areas of Ningbo abound with mud flats, which gives the city the superiority in cultivating razor clams, Ningbo's major seafood. Next to Sanmenwan Bay, Ninghai county and Changjie town have constant inflows of fresh water, sea water with proper salinity and silt-based sediment. Consequently, razor clams there grow quickly and feature big size, tender meat, white color and fresh flavor. The razor clam is very popular among both urban and rural residents.

The razor clam is better to be farmed in ooze around estuaries or inner bays where there are restless tides, slight wind, small waves and constant fresh water. Around the Qingming Festival it is time to sow the larval razor clams into farms. Usually after the fifth month in the next year when it can weigh about 5 gram each, it is time for trawling. According to the time of farming, the razor clam can be classified as yearly, biennial and triennial ones.

The razor clam boasts fresh flavor and rich nutrition. The razor clam can also be used as a medicine: its meat can help with postpartum deficiency and hot diarrhea while its shells can help with gastrosis and swelling and pain in throat.

The cooking of razor clams is quite simple. The first step is to place the clean razor clams in water with low salinity. Then cut open the connecting part between the two shells and put them in boiled water for several minutes. Add some scallions and here is a highly desirable dish of razor clams. The razor clam boasts fresh meat and a unique flavor and it is a good choice while drinking.

Mud Snail

Mud snail is also named Bullacta exarata. According to *Ci Yuan* (*A Dictionary of Chinese Etymology*): "the mud snail, also named "Tutie" in Chinese (which indicate the habit of mud snail to spit out soil), is a kind of sea food resembling the shape of beans in Ningbo; Tutie, also named mud snail, is a kind of mollusk with s spiral thin shell. It will spit out black sediment and it has the nicest taste during the peach blossom season." The mud snail is a well-known local specialty in Ningbo. Quan Zuwang (1705—1755), a prestigious scholar in Ningbo, once wrote: "Every year after the mould rains, tens of thousands of urns containing mud snails are transported to Suzhou."

Mud snails are cultured in all the offshore areas in Ningbo. During the peach blossom season, mud snails, having spitted out all the sediment inside, enjoy fresh and clean meat. The mud snails during this season, called Taohua mud snails, are considered as the best, especially those cultured in Longshan, Cixi, which are called "Longshan mud snails".

The earliest record of Longshan mud snails as food goes back to the Song Dynasty. As was recorded, mud snails in the peach blossom season enjoy the best quality. During this time, mud snails grow to a proper size without any sediment or bacteria. Guihua (osmanthus) mud snails collected around the Mid-autumn Festival, though not as good as Taohua(peach flower) mud snails, are big-sized and fresh. Mud snails collected in Longshan are especially nice because there are batches of fertile low tidal flats in the offshore areas in Cixi, which are formed by the sediment from the Qiantang River and Cao'e River as well as tides containing sediment from the Yangtze River. People like it as it is nice, with beautiful black color, and goes well with both rice and wine.

It is said that Yu Qiaqing, who made significant contribution to initiating the Chinese shipping industry, lived at the foot of Longshan Mountain in his childhood. Standing alone by the sea, his house looked like a huge mud snail crawling on the tidal flat. When he was a child, Yu Qiaqing also collected mud snails. When his family became illustrious, the local people gave him a nickname "Da Ni Luo" (big mud snail) and composed a local ditty about him:

> *Longshan has a brother called A'de,*
> *With a nickname of big snail in mud,*
> *His telephone reaches Ningbo,*
> *with trains coming to his hometown Cao'e*

Mud snails are usually edible after being processed with salt-water. Wash the newly collected mud snails with sea water and put them in a container and then add some salt. Keep the container undisturbed until the mud snails die, drain the container, add more salt and some wine and seal the container. After one week, the mud snails will be very nice to eat. You can also reserve it as long as you keep the container sealed.

Fresh mud snails can be used to make soup. Place them in clean water until they spit out all the sediment inside and then boil them. Add some soy sauce and chopped green onions and you can enjoy a nice soup.

There is a kind of toxin in the body mucus and guts of mud snails which can be eliminated through pickling and boiling. Some people may have the symptom of face puffiness and stiff toes after having mud snails not sufficiently pickled, which is called "mud snail fat disease". After several days, the symptoms will disappear. Consequently, the mud snail is suggested to go with vinegar, which not only is capable of sterilization but can add to the taste of the mud snail.

Mud snails are rich in nutrition and have certain medical effect. As was recorded in *Ben Cao Gang Mu Shi Yi* (*Supplement to Compendium of Materia Medica*), mud snails can nourish liver and kidney, moisten the lung, improve eyesight and promote the secretion of saliva. There is also a folk recipe: to soak mud snails in liquor, which can prevent and cure sore throat and tuberculosis.

Xiangshan Swimming Crab

Xiangshan swimming crab is a specialty in Ningbo.

The swimming crab is also named "Suozi crab" in Chinese as its carapace resembles a shuttle ("Suozi" in Chinese). Swimming Crabs show marked sexual dimorphism: male crabs have narrow and triangular pleon, long and large claws and their exoskeleton is black blue; female crabs have broader and rounded pleon with hairs and their exoskeleton is ochre. The crab has high economic and nutritious values, and can be cultured with sea water for fat growth. The swimming crab is an important commercial species in the offshore areas in China as it grows quickly and can engender huge profits. Fresh swimming crabs are best eaten boiled and can also be made into salty crabs and crab pastes. The crab eggs can also be made into a nice sea food after rinsing and drying in the sun.

Swimming crabs achieve the maximum size during migration in winter, which is usually 250 grams and can even exceed 500 grams. Its white and tender meat is rich in protein. Swimming crabs are prepared and eaten as a dish in several different ways, for example, steaming and frying. Swimming crabs stewed with bean paste or tofu, crabs fried with rice cakes or pickles are common dishes on the tables of the local people in offshore areas. Another way of processing the crabs is pickling, which is to steep fresh crabs into bittern for several days. In the past, there was a kind of "crab overy cake", which was very delicious. It was made when the production volume of swimming crabs was huge, and the fishermen selected fat crabs to extract crab overy. It was dried by airing, and was turned into overy cake. But it had quite low production volume and thus was beyond the reach of common people.

Fenghua Honey Peach

As an offshore city near mountains, Ningbo abounds in local products. And the honey peach in Fenghua tops all the nice fruits in Ningbo and enjoys fame around the country. Unlike those in other places, the honey peach in Fenghua boasts big size, thin rind, bright color, rich juice and pleasant smell.

More than 2,000 years ago, people in Fenghua started to grow honey peaches. As was recorded in *You Ming Lu* (*Record of the Nether World*), in the fifth year during the reign of Emperor Yongping in the Han Dynasty, Liu Cheng and Ruan Zhao from the Yan County went to the Mountain Tiantai to collect silverskin but lost their way back.

After 13 days when they were about to die as they ran out of food, they discovered peach trees and were saved by peaches. The Mountain Tiantai mentioned in the book refers to the now Mountain Tiantai and Mountain Siming, which are near Fenghua County.

Actually, back to the Ming and Qing dynasties, people in Fenghua mainly grew red and white peaches. Then during the reign of Emperor Guangxu in the Qing Dynasty, Zhang Chongyin, a gardener, was stranded in the Sanshiliu Village in Fenghua. Taking advantage of the particular geographical conditions there, he introduced from Shanghai a fine variety called "Shanghai Longhua Honey Peach" as the female parent and chose good local peach trees as the male parent. Through graft and long-term selection, he succeeded in cultivating the Fenghua Yulu honey peach, which was later popularized in the whole county. The single variety of Fenghua honey peach later was developed into more than 40 varieties, including Yulu peach, Yulu flat peach, yellow peach and Zhouyehuanglu.

There are particular steps in the cultivation and picking of Fenghua honey peaches. The first step is to grow seedlings, select seeds and graft. In the first year, the peach blossoms growing on the grafted trees should be removed to avoid congenitally deficient peaches. In the second year, remove most of the blossoms and select a few according to the taste of peaches growing. In the third year, special care should be paid to the fruit. Every peach should be wrapped in paper to prevent pest and exposure to the sun. The mature peach is cyan in color and without any red spot. It is tasty and refreshing and those that reach maturity on the tree are the best. The Yulu peach is considered as the best in terms of fragrance, flavor and sweetness. At its maturity, it has semi-transparent rind, attracting fragrance and sweet taste. There are three kinds of Yulu peaches, according to the time they appear in the market. The peaches first appear in the market in June each year, and continue to be marketed till the beginning of autumn. The honey peach is rich in nutrition. According to *Ben Cao Gang Mu* (*Compendium of Materia Medica*), peaches can boost human bile secretion and gastrointestinal motility and relieve constipation.

Fenghua Taro

"I have been to numerous passes and wharfs. I have also tasted Fenghua taro." People in Zhejiang Province would often brag in this way to show that they have rich life experiences, have tried delicacies of every kind and above all take pride in trying the tasty Fenghua taro.

Taro, also named "Min Zi", is an Araceae perennial plant which originated from Southeast Asia and was introduced to China during Qin and Han Dynasties (221B.C..— 220 A. D.). Taro is cultivated mainly in South China. Taro is one of traditional specialties in Fenghua, which enjoys a high reputation at home and abroad while taro from Xiaowangmiao Town is the most famous.

Fenghua enjoys a long history of taro cultivation. According to historical records, Fenghua has a 700-year history of planting taros. Chen Zhu, a Fenghua poet in Song Dynasty (420 A. D.—479 A. D.) once mentioned taro in his poem. According to the *Annals of Fenghua County* compiled in 1773, Fenghua taro was introduced from Japan. Cooked taros can be made into bricks for houses and kept for dozens of years without turning rotten. Here is a story about the taro bricks:

A rich man in Fenghua had only one son who did nothing but gambling, drinking and frequenting brothels. The rich man feared that his son might end up in death from starvation after he passed away. So he had an idea that he would build a house of cooked taro bricks. Ten years later, he told his son that the house was edible and he could sell everything but never the house! The father's words turned out to be true. The "house" finally saved his life in a year of crop failure and also the lives of all villagers.

There are many types of taros, including Xiangguang taro, black feet chicken, yellow pink dustpan, big taro and red taro. Among them, red taro is the most famous which is also called Fenghua taro. Those growing in dry fields are called dry taros and those growing in water fields are called water taros.

Taro is very adaptable to soil. Xiaowangmiao Town features moderate climate as well as fertile and sandy soil, which lead to big, smooth, bronzing, powdery and aromatic taros with thin skin. A taro can weigh 1-3 kilos. They are generally in season in early August and can be reserved for long when dried. There are many cooking methods in Fenghua, like steaming, roasting, frying, slicing, etc. It can also be made into taro paste or soup. It is fragrant and tastes like Chinese chestnut when steamed and like tremella when made into taro soup. Duck cooked with taro is a famous dish, often eaten and regarded as a delicacy at the Mid-Autumn Festival for Fenghua people.

Fenghua taro has a good name widely. It was very popular in Shanghai in the 1930s and cherished as a treasure. People from other corners of China buy taros from Fenghua. Ningbo people living in Hong Kong, Macao, Taiwan and Southeast Asia will often eat and take some taros back when they visit their hometown.

Xiangshan White Goose

Big white goose in Xiangshan is a famous specialty in Ningbo.

Xiangshan white goose, one of the best goose breeds in China, is not only good-looking, but also famous for its big size and delicious meat and shiny feathers. Frozen geese enjoy a good reputation in Hong Kong and Macao. It is said that Xiangshan white goose was firstly raised by Wang Xizhi (303 A. D.—361 A. D.), a well-known calligrapher during the Jin Dynasty (265 A.D.—420 A.D.).

Wang Xizhi used to be a general and a high-ranking official. He left a lot of stories. At the age of 35, he resigned and went back home, writing and raising geese. Retreating besides a beautiful river, he selected white geese of good breeds in the local and raised them carefully. So geese were big, white, tender, tasty and unique.

In his seclusion, Wang Xizhi loved raising geese and enjoyed imitating various postures of geese in calligraphy. The stone tablet with Chinese character "E" (goose) written by Wang Xizhi is kept in Guoqing Temple at Mountain Tiantai; the other stone tablet with Chinese characters "鹅池" written by Wang Xizhi and his son is at the Orchid Pavilion in Shaoxing. Wang Xizhi's calligraphy can be "flowing like a cloud and nimble like a dragon". However, he liked to tear what he wrote, so his calligraphy was rare to see. It is said that the Buddhist abbot of Guoqing Temple wanted to ask Wang Xizhi to

write for a stone tablet. Thus, he racked his brains and figured out a way. He selected a flock of big and shiny geese, raised them carefully and herded them to the Shanxi River (in Zhejiang Province) to wait for a chance. One day, Wang Xizhi walked besides the river after writing and he suddenly saw a flock of beautiful geese. Wang was so happy that he asked the old man wearing a bamboo hat besides to sell him the geese. Actually, the old man was the Buddhist abbot in disguise. He deliberately refused until Wang begged for several times. So he told Wang, "I can give you these geese for free as long as you write a character for me". Wang Xizhi happily agreed and wrote a Chinese character "E" (goose). The Buddhist abbot finally got the calligraphy, so he had it engraved on a stone tablet, which has been known for ages. Wang Xizhi continued to look after these geese which became the beginning of Xiangshan white goose. Later on, this goose breed was introduced in Xiangshan and Fenghua, and became famous gradually.

Xiangshan white geese have good adaptability and grow fast. Grown male geese are big and aggressive with sonorous sound, weighing 7.5 to 8 kilos; while grown female geese are gentle with low sound and wide belly, weighing 6.5 to 7 kilos. Owing to its tasty meat, Xiangshan white geese are always given as gifts for relatives and friends during festivals or happy events. Since Ningbo became one of five-port trading cities after the First Opium War in 1842, Xiangshan white geese have been sold overseas.

The number of white geese raised in Xiangshan is about one million, which feature big size, tender meat and shiny feathers. Frozen geese enjoy a good reputation in Hong Kong and Macao.

Cixi Waxberry

Located at the south bank of Hangzhou Bay by the Sea-Crossing Bridge and faces Jiaxing to the north, famous as "the hometown of Chinese waxberry", Cixi as the place of origin of waxberry has been officially certified. Cixi waxberry features big size, small core, beautiful color, tender and juicy taste. Owing to its high quality, Cixi waxberry can be eaten when fresh or processed. Now, Cixi waxberry has been sold to Hong Kong, Singapore, France and Japan, becoming a precious fruit in overseas market.

Waxberry is a famous specialty in Cixi. In March 2000, Cixi was named by the National Forestation Commission as "the Hometown of the Chinese Famous and Special Fruit: Waxberry". The two best breeds of waxberry are Biqi and Zaoda, which account for 95% of the total planting area, and feature big fruit, small core, beautiful color, tender and juicy taste. Owing to its high quality, Cixi waxberry can be eaten when fresh or processed. Now, Cixi waxberry has been sold to Hong Kong, Singapore, France and Japan, becoming precious fruits for overseas Ningbonese. Su Dongpo (1037 A. D. — 1101 A. D.), the famous literary master in the Song Dynasty (960 A. D. —1279 A. D.), used to say that "waxberries in Zhejiang and Jiangsu belittle litchis in Fujian and Guangdong as well as grapes in Xinjiang".

303

Waxberry from Meiyuan Village is the most famous. Meiyuan Village has several waxberry tourist attractions. In June, mountains in Meiyuan Village are decorated with dark red, lilac or white waxberries. Farmers pick waxberries happily with knives and bamboo baskets.

Youyuan waxberry has won many golden prizes in waxberry competitions. As a certified waxberry planting base and one of the waxberry tourist reception centers, Youyuan is a place whose soil is rich in selenium which makes the selenium content of waxberries here quadruple others.

There are green mountains, white clouds, green bamboo, tea gardens and red waxberries in the village. It is a good place to embrace the nature. In Mid-June each year, a waxberry festival is held in Cixi which selects a beautiful woman to be the waxberry fairy.

Qiuga Pickle

Owing to its fertile soil and plentiful rainfall, Ningbo enjoys a long history of cultivating potherb mustard in fall and winter. The fertile rice land leads to high yield of potherb mustard which can also increase their income. According to *Guangqunfangpu* (an agricultural book), "there is a kind of vegetable called Xuelihong (potherb mustard) at Siming, Ningbo. In winter, all plants are damaged except Xuelihong which literally means thriving in snow. Xuelihong is spicy and tastes good when preserved." It is a traditional specialty in Ningbo to preserve potherb mustard in winter and spring.

Potherb mustard pickle is also called "Xianji" (preserved vegetable). Qiuga pickle is the most famous one. Qiuga has nearly 100 years of history of planting and making potherb mustard pickle. Farmers there plant potherb mustard in the waste land after reaping late rice. Fresh potherb mustard in winter or spring is chosen for making pickles. After it is reaped, it will be spread out and dried for 2 to 4 hours. When leaves of potherb mustard turn yellow, cut the root and preserve it in a vat, a layer of potherb mustard with a layer of salt. Press the pickles next day, cover bamboo chips and put big rocks. Pickles are edible after one month. At first, farmers just make potherb mustard pickle for their own families. Nowadays, it has become a major moneymaking channel to cultivate potherb mustard which covers 133 hectares and over 10,000 vats of pickles. Local farmers not only directly sell potherb mustard pickle, they have also built a pickle factory to make pickles pouch packs for other places of China, even Southeast Asia.

Potherb mustard pickle is yellow, bright, tender, crispy, tasty, aromatic, sour and appetizing. Some old sayings in Ningbo area which say "no pickle soup for three days makes you listless within your bones." or "no bland meals at home with pickles". Li Yesi (1622—1680), a poet in the Qing Dynasty (1644—1912), praised potherb mustard pickle in his poem:

> Fresh and green mustard turns red at vinegar,
> Aromatic is the smell and the chewing crispy.
> Vegetables in the world are many and tastes vary,
> But the best is still potherb mustard grown at my county.

Potherb mustard pickle can be eaten when it is raw or cooked. It can serve as seasoning to make several dishes such as large yellow croaker with pickles or sliced pork soup with pickles.

Preserved Szechuan Pickle in Yuyao

Preserved szechuan pickle is a new specialty in Ningbo, particularly in Yuyao and Cixi. Owing to its superior soil condition and climate, preserved szechuan pickle in Yuyao is big, round, tender, crispy, bright, solid, aromatic, tasty and nutritious. Preserved szechuan pickle is also called stem leaf mustard, cruciferae. Its big succulent stem is preserved to make pickles. Currently, preserved szechuan pickle from Yuyao and Cixi has a wide range, which is cold-resistant, solid, and grows fast with high yield.

The cultivation of preserved szechuan pickle in Yuyao and Cixi started from 1960s. The successful introduction of preserved szechuan pickle in Xiaoshan leads to expansive cultivated area year by year. The annual yield now tops in China. Preserved szechuan pickle is sold to every corner in China, and is exported to Japan and Southeast Asia.

It takes 18 processes to make preserved szechuan pickle including 10 key processes, among them are removal of leaves, roots, aged veins, speckles, pool placement, salt layering, pickle pressing, bamboo chips placement and then pressured with rocks for dozens of hours. Then the pickles are preserved for several months to form its unique flavor due to the reaction of microorganism enzyme. Then the pickles are taken out, selected, washed, pressed and poured seasonings, put into vats and finally the vats are sealed with cement.

Preserved szechuan pickle made in Ningbo contains multiple nutritional ingredients such as vitamin C, Fe, P, protein, amino acid etc. It is aromatic, salty and spicy moderately, tender and crispy.

White Loquat in Ninghai

White loquats are planted at Yishi Town, Sanmen Bay, on the southeast Ninghai County. Yishi Town enjoys a superior location, surrounded by mountains while facing Sanmen Bay to the South; unique climate and edaphic condition. With mountains as the backdrop and a bay in front, Yishi Town features inviting scene. This white loquat is a new type, mellow and full, juicy, fragrant with light yellow skin and milky white pulp. This white loquat has thin skin but much juice, stress-resistant, fertile, which tops similar products at home and abroad in terms of the aggregative indicator. Experts remarked the loquat as "One Treasure of Ninghai", a breed representing the best loquat in South China. This white loquat is cultivated according to pollution-free standard. Since 1997 when the white loquat was produced at the first time, it has been awarded frequently at provincial, municipal or county expositions of agricultural products.

Shangtian Strawberry

Shangtian strawberry is a specialty at Shangtian Town, Fenghua, Ningbo. As the hometown of Chinese strawberry, Shangtian Town boasts a planting base of over 6,667 hectares with big, sweet, red and nutritious strawberries which are very popular among tourists.

Famous as "the first town of Chinese strawberry" and "the hometown of Chinese strawberry in Zhejiang Province", Shangtian Town is rich in rice, strawberry, watermelon and other industrial crops in its southeastern area. The best strawberry is produced at Lengxi Village which has 333 hectares of greenhouse strawberry production base. Recently, strawberry sales center, farmers' strawberry association and strawberry research institutions are established in succession. In addition, 16 major enterprises specialize in strawberry processing, which stimulates the modernized

agricultural mode combing cultivation, processing and sales together.

Owing to its great geographical conditions, Shangtian strawberry has been certified as standardized green cultivation and management. According to the Food Quality Supervision and Testing Center of Agriculture Ministry, the Fengxiang strawberry produced at Shangtian meets the national demands for green food in terms of product quality and pesticide residue analysis. As a fruit with high popularity, Shangtian strawberry is conducive to people's beauty, health and longevity.

Sanbei Crisp Bean Candy

Ningbo crisp bean candy, also called Sanbei crisp bean candy, is a traditional specialty and typical sweetmeat in Cixi, Ningbo, which is as famous as Sanbei lotus fiber candy and popular at home and abroad. As a traditional delicacy in Ningbo, it is crispy, dissolvable and smooth with an aroma of soybeans.

Ningbo crisp bean candy is nutritious, containing protein, carbohydrate, Ca, P, Fe, carotene and other nutrient content. It can remain fragrant, sweet, crispy and crumbly for long.

Sanbei crisp bean candy boasts a long history. It is said that 100 years ago, there was a tea shop called "Qianfeng" at Lubu Town where crisp bean candy was made. Due to the choice ingredients and excellent processing, the crisp bean candy was fragrant, sweet, crispy, crumbly and dissolvable. Thus, it even attracted a lot of customers from

faraway places and became famous in East Zhejiang.

The key to great crisp bean candy production is the strict choice of materials. After several steps of processing, crisp bean candy is made into square in paper wrapper without using any paste for seal in order to prevent the candy from being damp. Therefore, crisp bean candy can remain fragrant, sweet, crispy and crumbly for long, suitable for both young and elderly people. At the end of every year, rice cake is prepared in rural areas in Ningbo. Crisp bean candy made by hot rice cake is fragrant and glutinous, so it is popular among customers at all ages. After the establishment of New China, Sanbei crisp bean candy has been brought into a new high in making and consumption based on its traditional characteristics.

5.4　Time-honored Shops in Ningbo

"Gang Ya Gou" Desserts

Founded by Mr. Jiang Dingfa in 1926, "Gang Ya Gou" (a water vat, a sheldrake and a dog) is a hundred-year-old shop in Ningbo, famous for its snacks. Jiang Dingfa's childhood name was Agou (namely a dog), so he was called Jiang Agou. At first, he just had a booth selling sweet dumplings in sweet rice wine and red jujube soup at Town God's Temple (Chenghuang Temple). Then, he opened a shop on Kaiming Street.

309

Trying to be different, he adopted a design of "a water vat, a sheldrake and a dog" as his shop mark, which attracted plenty of customers. "Gang Ya Gou" specialized in sweet dumplings with lard oil, sweet dumplings with eggs in sweet rice wine, Chinese rice pudding and sweet dumplings with various fruits, whose desserts were glutinous, light, good-looking and sweet.

At the beginning of the 20th century, young Jiang Dingfa went to sea to help his financially challenged family. In order to be healthy and strong, he had "Agou" as his childhood name. At the age of 18, he was sent to learn business in a shop by his parents. Jiang was smart and smart, so he won the trust from the shop owner. Even when he was only 20 years old, he decided to go back home and looked after his mother. Believing in the traditional Chinese thinking, "a man should get married first and then have his career", Jiang married He Fengxiu later. One day, Jiang asked his wife He Fengxiu in private, "Why did you marry me? My father is dead and I have no possession at all." He Fengxiu's answer surprised Jiang a lot, "I ate the sweet dumplings your mother gave me. They are big and sweet, so I bet I won't starve by marrying you."

Jiang was inspired. The sweet dumplings made by Jiang's mother are greatly recognized by neighbors. Why not set up a booth selling sweet dumplings? Jiang's idea was supported by his mother a lot, so Jiang and his family left the house with some money and had a booth at Town God's Temple, Ningbo.

Jiang only sold sweet dumplings at first. He was so kind that he met all demands for more ingredients like sugar or sweet-scented osmanthus. Later on, he realized that it was not enough to just sell sweet dumplings, which would bore customers soon. Thus, he started selling sweet dumplings in sweet rice wine and sweet dumplings with red bean paste or other fillings, which drew more and more customers successfully.

Jiang Agou's booth became very famous for just four years. Then, Jiang rented a shop near Taihe Bridge at Kaiming Street. But he needed a brand name for his shop, which upset Jiang Agou who was illiterate.

Many regular customers shared their ideas, but not special enough. At last, Jiang decided to use his own childhood name "Jiang Agou" which was easy to remember. He even invited Mr. Wang Yunbiao, a famous choreographer at the Yue-Opera Troupe in Ningbo to draw a picture of "a water vat, a sheldrake and a dog" with two Chinese characters "Tangtuan" (sweet dumplings) in the middle.

One day, an old scholar (who passed the imperial examination at the county level) ate several bowls of sweet dumplings and didn't pay at the end. However, Jiang was not angry or upset. The old scholar said, "Your brand name is a picture, which is not easy to promote. I would like to create a shop name for you in return." After discussion, they agreed to use "Gang Ya Gou" which was homophonic with "Jiang Agou" in Ningbonese, understandable and easy to remember, which was corresponding to the current picture also.

There is an old saying in Ningbo about Gang Ya Gou: At three or four you are starving, Go to Gang Ya Gou for leaf lard dumpling; one bowl to you is not sufficing, two or three bowls you have more interest of staying. All the money spent and you do not want to leave, take off your clothes as deposit you beg continuing. Starting from an outdoor humble booth at Town God's Temple, "Gang Ya Gou" gradually became a popular and historic brand name in Ningbo.

Zhuangyuanlou Hotel

Ningbo Zhuangyuanlou (Number One Scholar) Hotel, called Ningbo Zhuangyuanlou and located at Sanjiangkou previously, is now at Dongmenkou, Ningbo. Founded in 1785, Ningbo Zhuangyuanlou Hotel is famous for authentic Ningbo cuisine.

It is said that two scholars (a successful candidate in the imperial examinations at the provincial level) drank at this hotel on their way to the imperial examination. Then, a steamed turtle in crystal sugar soup was sent to them. The dish was bluish yellow, glutinous, aromatic, sweet, sour and salty at the same time. The two scholars marveled at this dish, asking "what is this?" The waiter was clever enough to tell they were scholars, so he trimmed the sails and said, "it is called 'Coming out top'." The two

scholars were very happy. And it was very lucky for one scholar to get the Number One Scholar at last. When he returned home after getting fame and money, he went to the hotel again and wrote down "Zhuangyuanlou (Number One Scholar) Hotel" as the shop sign. Later on, the hotel became well-known for its cuisine and booming business, attracting a lot of officials and scholars. Thus, Ningbo Zhuangyuanlou Hotel was crowned with "Number One Hotel at East Zhejiang".

In 1936, Ningbo Zhuangyuanlou Hotel was moved to No. 16 on Rixin Street with three floors and five shops, which was run by 28 shareholders. Ningbo Zhuangyuanlou Hotel attracted the customers from industrial, commercial, financial, military and political circles. In 1945, Chiang Ching-kuo (1910—1988) along with his wife dined at this hotel for twice. Ningbo Zhuangyuanlou Hotel was moved to No. 4 on Jiangxia Street, Xinjiang Bridge. On September, 1949, the hotel was bombarded by the bombers of the Nationalist Party. Later on, it was reopened by 10 shareholders near Xinjiang Bridge and named "Yong River Zhuangyuanlou". However, the business was gloomy at that time. In 1956, the hotel became public-private partnership in a smaller scale, which stimulated the business. On October 1, 1959, on the 10th anniversary of the establishment of China, the hotel collapsed because all diners swarmed to the window to see the parade. The hotel was closed. For the later 20 years, a lot of people in Ningbo or overseas were expecting the rebirth of Ningbo Zhuangyuanlou Hotel.

In October 1985, supported by Ningbo Municipal Government and Ningbo Hong Kong Fellowship Association, Ningbo Catering Service Company was jointly founded and located on Heyi Junction, East Zhongshan Road, named "Ningbo Zhuangyuanlou Incorporated Company". it covered 1,100 square meters, with classical court arch, spacious lobby, elegant rooms and central air-conditioning. The revitalization of Ningbo Zhuangyuanlou attracted a lot of countrymen residing abroad, including the world's ship king Sir Pao Yue-kong (1918—1991) who once treated his countrymen here.

Thus, Ningbo Zhuangyuanlou is entitled with "Number One Hotel at East Zhejiang", famous for its Ningbo cuisine. In 1995, it was given the golden banner of "China time-honored brand".

Shengyangtai (Shop for delicacies from South China)

Founded by Magistrate Hua Shaohu in Ningbo during 1862 to 1874, Shengyangtai has enjoyed over 100 years of history. The name "Shengyangtai" symbolizes prosperity and safety. Shengyangtai specializes in making and selling delicacies from North and South China as well as Ningbo pastries on the spot including special ones such as crisp bean candy, sea weed biscuit, evergreen cake, scented cake, bean pudding, walnut and *Fuling* cake, salt peach cookie etc. Shengyangtai along with Datong, Dayou, Dongshengyang was called "Four Major Shops" for delicacies from North and South China.

Equipped with vending counters and kitchen, Shengyangtai is famous for making and selling the pastries on spot. Famous for fruit food from North and South China as well as Ningbo pastries, Shengyangtai's oil bread, scented cake, smoked bean curb, bean pudding, walnut and tuckahoe cake are the most special and local ones. As one of the "Four Major Shops" for delicacies from north and south China in Ningbo, Shengyangtai classifies and prices the fruit food based on different quality levels, well-known for its excellent service, honest operation and chosen packaging. Shengyangtai enjoys a great reputation in Jiangsu, Zhejiang, Beijing, Tianjin, Shanghai and among the Ningbonese in Hong Kong, Macao and overseas. Before the establishment of China, Shengyangtai was in the charge of by Wang Ruixiang and closed down in 1949.

In 1950, Shengyangtai was reopened by Ge Laichao in 1950 at the same place with the same brand name. In 1956, it was turned into an entity of public ownership. It was

313

renamed "Drum-tower Food Shop" in 1958. In 1987, "Ningbo Shengyangtai Mall" with 6 floors was built, covering 3,500 square meters with over 200 employees. The new mall continued its traditional business, while actively adopted modern facilities such as computerized collection system, and became the first supermarket in Ningbo.

Ningbo Shengyangtai Mall was reconstructed in 1992, covering 7,000 square meters with central air-conditioning and two-way escalators. It sold not only candies, cigarettes, wine, dairy products, cured meat products, preserved fruits and cereal products, but also frozen foods, general merchandise, household appliances, clothes, horologes, children products, leather wares etc. It also opened Shengyangtai Cake Shop, offering pastries, traditional and western desserts in all kinds every day. It was booming day by day with remarkable economic and social benefits.

It was renamed "Shengyangtai Ningbo Delicacy Mall" in September 2001, providing local food and souvenirs. It was listed as "tourist host organization" at the same year. In order to maintain its traditional management style, Shengyangtai invested to establish Shengyangtai Tourist Food Factory to regain its style of making and selling the products on spot. At present, Shengyangtai boasts nearly 200 products in different categories such as traditional Ningbo pastries, cakes with the Chinese character *tai*, green series, dried seafood, Ningbo moon cakes and other cakes. Among them, Ningbo crisp bean candy and lovesick cake are "recommended tourist food in Ningbo". Shengyangtai Tourist Food Factory was renamed "Designated Enterprise for Producing Tourist Goods in Ningbo". Meanwhile, Shengyangtai is revitalized by capitalizing on traditional culture. It draws the attention from old Ningbonese by offering new pastries with blessing words such as Zhuangyuan (Number One Scholar) Cake, Safety Cake, The God of Wealth Cake, Propitious Cake, etc.

Loumaoji Sauce Shop

Founded in 1743, Loumaoji was named "Lou Heng Sheng Mao Ji Sauce Shop", a famous time-honored shop in Ningbo with the history of more than 264 years. It specializes in soy sauce, rice vinegar, smoked bean curd, dried bean curd, rice wine etc. It is said that the shop was owned by a couple surnamed Lou. It was at first a beancurd workshop located at Baizhang Street and then named "Loumaoji".

Loumaoji provides a wide variety of delicacies typical of south Yangtze River Area, including pickles, sauce, vinegar, smoked bean curd, dried bean curd, and rice wine. Among them, smoked bean curd, superb in the color, and amorous in taste, is a most famous product in Ningbo, glutinous and refreshing. It is said during Kangxi Period (1662—1722), a couple surnamed Lou came to Ningbo and sold bean sprouts around Baizhang Street and Hui Street. They were kind and run the business very well. In order to expand the business scope, they opened a bean curd factory to produce and sell bean curd, bean sprout, soy chicken, smoked bean curd, dried bean curd and so on.

After years of operation, the scale of Loumaoji became bigger and bigger.

In 1743, the couple got the license of selling salt through an official relative in Beijing and began selling salt and making sauce. "Lou Heng Sheng Mao Ji Sauce Shop" was opened. It even had a branch in Fenghua, Ningbo during the years when Emperor Daoguang of the Qing Dynasty reigned.

In 1956 it was turned into an entity with public ownership and with a new name called "Loumaoji Sauce Shop". It was taken over by Ningbo Jiangdong Vegetable & Food Co., Ltd. in 1988 and was made into Ningbo Loumaoji Food Co., Ltd. 10 years later. Currently, Loumaoji food is not only sold in Ningbo and neighbor regions, but also Hong Kong, Taiwan, Europe, USA and Southeast Asia for products like sauce, vinegar, fermented bean curd, etc.

An old saying in Ningbo goes: if you do not have the smoked beancurd of Loumaoji, life will be meaningless no matter what you do and who you will be.

Dayou Shop

Established in 1853, Dayou Shop was owned by Zhu and located near Yaohang Street and Lingqiao Bridge, specializing in fruit products from north and south China, cakes and self-made pastries. Dayou Shop boasts chosen materials, exquisite production and products good at the color, aroma and taste. Among them, soy melon seeds, scented puddings and cakes are Ningbo delicacies. In the past, the façade of Dayou Shop was inlayed with a couplet which read "well-known in universe and best in southeast", showing the owner's ambition. Dayou Shop is one of the famous time-honored shops in Ningbo. At the beginning of the establishment of Dayou Shop, there were Datong, Fangyihe, Dongshengyang and Shengyangtai in the same industry in Ningbo. Owing to the sound management of Dayou Shop, Datong Shop across the street was acquired by Dayou Shop. Thus, there was an old saying like "Dayou prospers while Datong falls".

Different from competitors, the success of Dayou Shop results from its unique management. When Zhu Rongqing took over the shop, he reformed the management and marketing. He supervised the procurement in person and insisted on the principle of honesty and fairness. For example, different levels of dried fruits were classified in the shop; the number of dried longans should not exceed 192 per kilo; shoddy walnuts should be replaced at once. In terms of service attitude, Dayou Shop treated all customers the same, no matter rich people or fishermen. It used to give a lantern to

316

every farmer from the countryside with two Chinese characters "Da You" on it as the commercial. Some customers living in rural areas would ask a boatman to help them buy goods. Dayou Shop often treated these boatmen with tea, pastries, wine or dishes. Zhu Rongqing died in 1923. His son Zhu Yuansheng took over the shop, inheriting the tradition while innovating management. For instance, he carefully chose the directors of each department, shop assistants and order pickers. In addition, he gave higher salary with annual bonus attached, which made employees loyal. It is worth mentioning that Zhu Yuansheng reformed the packaging of "triangle cakes" and "axe cakes" by adopting paper box, printed with a colorful pattern and the brandname "Da You" and its address, beautiful, portable and influential.

In 1938, a warehouse of Dayou Shop was bombarded by Japanese bombers. Later on, when Ningbo was occupied, Dayou Shop was burnt in a fire and plunged into slump. After the Anti-Japannese War, inflation inflicted Dayou Shop greatly. In September 1949, it was damaged seriously by the Kuomintang bombers. In 1956 it was turned into an entity with public ownership. In 1970, a big fire almost paralyzed the shop. In 1980, Chinese government reinvested in the shop and reopened it at the same place, allowing Dayou Shop to inherit and develop traditional management, and encouraged Dayou to innovate its services. These efforts reinvigorated Dayou and its business prospered for some years before it disappeared due to urban reconstructions in recent years.

Zhaodayou Cake Shop

Established during 1862 to 1874, Zhaodayou has nearly 140 years of history. In 1911, directed by a mentor, a Ningbonese called Zhao Peide established "Zhaodayou Cake Shop" at Baizhang Street in Jiangdong District, offering joyous, seasonal and annual cakes including dragon and phoenix pudding, crystal oil cake, sweet-scented osmanthus cake, green pudding, snow pudding, preserved duck egg, rice cake made from finely ground flour, pepper mint patty, etc. Among them, dragon and phoenix pudding as well as crystal oil cake were the most famous.

Zhao the founder was from an old family which had made cakes for long at Shangyu, Ningbo. At that time, Shangyu was poor, so few people could make a living by selling cakes. In pursuit for a better life, Zhao and his families came to Ningbo with a boat of rice. They rented a shop in Jiangdong District, providing seasonal cakes with the brand name "Zhaodayou". They started business in November (the lunar calendar) and had a trial sale for two months. As they used much more glutinous rice, Zhaodayou was popular among customers. Additionally, its excellent operation and superior stone mills made rice cake more refined, smooth and chewy. And Zhaodayou Shop never sold products with sour powder, leaking filling, obscured pattern or fallen skin.

At that time, there were two other cakes shops in Ningbo. Zhaodayou Shop was aware of the competition, so it kept the production day and night from July 1 of that year (by the lunar calendar), which led the other two cake shops doing the same. Three

318

cake shops kept making cakes at night, illuminating the whole Baizhang Street. Zhaodayou was more popular as it offered best cakes in the eyes of customers. In about 3 or 5 years, only Zhaodayou survived on Baizhang Street.

The success of Zhaodayou Shop encouraged a lot of people of the Zhaos to open cake shops in Ningbo. Therefore, Zhaodayou Shop expanded from Jiangdong District to the downtown. People would buy the cakes from Zhaodayou Shop for every kind of events, such as travelling, visiting relatives, worshiping ancestors, celebrating birthdays, weddings and so on. Even Generalissimo of the national government Chiang Kai-shek (1887—1975) would buy the cakes from Zhaodayou Shop for relatives and friends every time he passed by Ningbo.

From 2003 to 2008, the shop won a series of honorary titles including "recommended products by customers", "honoring contracts and integrity". In 2008, it won "the most favorite time-honored brand in China" in Chinese Time-honored Product Expo. Currently, Zhaodayou Shop has 160 kinds of products featuring soft cake and flaky pastries made from sticky rice sold at over 300 supermarkets in Hong Kong, Macao, Taiwan and other places inside or outside Zhejiang.

Shouquanzhai TCM Drugstore

Established in 1760, Shouquanzhai TCM Drugstore, called "Shouquanzhai Traditional Chinese Medicine" at first, was founded by Wang Liao and Sun Jiangke (since Sun quit later, Shouquanzhai was taken over by Wang's family for several generations. It was firstly located at No. 56, East Zhongshan Road. The name "Shouquanzhai" symbolizes "long life and various medicines". Shouquanzhai offers genuine goods at fair prices and abides by traditional infusion tragacanth. Shouquanzhai specializes in ointment, pill, pellet, medicinal slice, ginseng and young pilose antler tonic wine, medicinal liquor, high-level ginseng tonic and authentic medicinal herbs. Shouquanzhai Drugstore was awarded "China time-honored brand" in 1995.

Owing to its completeness in the variety of herbal medicines, excellent processing and effects in prolonging people's life, it was named "Shouquanzhai". The name of the store was written by Yang Hengtai (a member of the Imperial Academy) and inscribed on a gild board. Shouquanzhai has a history of over 230 years and has been awarded "China time-honored brand" by the Ministry of Internal Trade.

Shouquanzhai sticks to genuine goods at fair prices and abides by traditional

infusion tragacanth, adopting ancient tools such as purple copper pot, iron ship, tin plate, porcelain cup, etc in making a variety of ointment, pill, pellet, medicinal slice, tonic wine and medicinal liquor such as the tonic ointment, water eye drops, goose quill eye drops, children antipyretic. Its unique infusion tragacanth and rigorous management can be attributed to four words: "trustworthy, guaranteed, careful and authentic". That is Shouquanzhai attaches great importance to the procurement of raw materials, guarantees quality during delivery, makes endeavors to process carefully in order to give out the authentic taste of medicines. Shouquanzhai has enjoyed a high reputation in Ningbo for more than 200 years. In spite of ups and downs, Shouquanzhai Drugstore is still a famous drugstore in the eyes of Ningbo people.

Now, Shouquanzhai Drugstore has moved to Yaohang Street, which is well received by Ningbo citizens. The Cream Formula Festival before Dongzhi Day (Winter Solstice) is one of the specialties for Shouquanzhai TCM Drugstore.

Since the establishment of Shouquanzhai TCM Drugstore, it has won support and trust from all customers. As a 100-year-old store, Shouquanzhai has received numerous awards including "China time-honored brand" by Ministry of Internal Trade and "famous shop in Zhejiang" by Zhejiang Provincial Government;

Yuankang Cloth Store

Established in 1904, Yuankang Cloth Store was founded by Tu Jingshan from Yinzhou District, Ningbo with a total investment of 30,000 yuan (US $4838.71) at that time. Located at Rixin Street previously, Yuankang Cloth Store had booming business and then moved to Dongmen Street. Yuankang Cloth Store specialized in black and white blue denim, wool, silk, hemp products etc. It featured low price, high quality, various patterns, top dye and excellent technique. Besides, it had a dyehouse. At that time, people admired Tu Jingshan a lot, a gingle went that "the boss Tu Jingshan, with 33,000 yuan, on Mar. 3rd cloth-selling business began".

Yuankang Cloth Store has major ups and downs during the 100 years of history. Yuankang adopted public-private partnership in 1955; doubled its space in 1973; regained the brand name "Yuankang Cloth Store" and had a sales department at the second floor to sell clothes in 1980; changed the name into "Yuankang Textile Mall" in 1987, including 8 sales departments to sell cotton, silk, wool, chemical fiber, textiles and clothing. Owing to its various, famous, high-quality and latest products, Yuankang tops other stores in the industry in Ningbo. Yuankang was awarded "Advanced Provincial Enterprise" in 1989 and "Time-honored Brand in Zhejiang" in 2010.

Offering famous, unique and top-flight fabrics, Yuankang topped other stores in the industry and prospered in Ningbo. Traditional and new high-quality fabrics were popular among existing and new customers.

Yuankang features a wide variety of patterns. Besides well-known black and white blue it also offers denim, wool, silk, hemp products and all cotton cloth. In Yuankang Cloth Store, salesmen doesn't stand behind one counter, but accompanies the clients through different counters buying all textiles or accessories like cotton cloth, wool fabric, silk fabrics, welt or waistband. and the processes of reception, payment collection and goods delivery are done by one salesman.

After the demolition at East Zhongshan Road in 1999, Yuankang first moved to Dongdu Road (No. 55, Cuiya Street), then to No. 207, Shizi Street in 2004, and then moved to No. 172, Shizi Street 3 years later due to demolition. Owing to its time-honored reputation and adaptable management, Yuankang still survives and thrives.

图书在版编目（CIP）数据

宁波地方文化读本 / 屠国元主编. —杭州：浙江
大学出版社，2016.10
ISBN 978-7-308-16206-7

Ⅰ. ①宁… Ⅱ. ①屠… Ⅲ. ①地方文化－介绍－宁波
Ⅳ. ①G127.553

中国版本图书馆 CIP 数据核字（2016）第 214741 号

宁波地方文化读本

主编　屠国元

责任编辑	余健波
责任校对	何　瑜
封面设计	张作梅
出版发行	浙江大学出版社
	（杭州市天目山路 148 号　邮政编码 310007）
	（网址：http://www.zjupress.com）
排　　版	杭州好友排版工作室
印　　刷	杭州日报报业集团盛元印务有限公司
开　　本	787mm×960mm　1/16
印　　张	20.5
字　　数	455 千
版 印 次	2016 年 10 月第 1 版　2016 年 10 月第 1 次印刷
书　　号	ISBN 978-7-308-16206-7
定　　价	58.00 元